MINERS, MARINERS
& MASONS

MINERS, MARINERS & MASONS

The Global Network of Victorian Freemasonry

ROGER BURT

Emeritus Professor of History
University of Exeter

UNIVERSITY
of
EXETER
PRESS

First published in 2020 by
University of Exeter Press
Reed Hall, Streatham Drive
Exeter EX4 4QR
UK
www.exeterpress.co.uk

Paperback edition 2023

British Library Cataloguing in Publication Data
A catalogue record for this book is available from the British Library.

ISBN 978-1-905816-16-3 Hardback
ISBN 978-1-905816-24-8 Paperback
ISBN 978-1-905816-18-7 ePub
ISBN 978-1-905816-19-4 pdf

*To **PACH***
WITH LOVE

CONTENTS

APPENDICES

ILLUSTRATIONS

FIGURES

TABLES

PREFACE

This book might look like an exercise in gender studies and in one sense it is. It is exclusively about mature men endeavouring to improve themselves and create some level of security for their wives and families in an insecure Victorian world. But it was not intended to be that. This was an old-fashioned research project that gradually unfolded as it went along and ended in a place which was far from where it started. Parts of the story were published along the way, but this is the story of the journey as a whole. It is an economic historian's attempt to make sense of a complex social issue: it started with only one vague question relating to information flows in a small, out-of-the way part of England and gradually moved on to a wider international and global stage. It had no initial understanding of the unexpectedly wide range of primary and secondary sources available, and it had no preconceived idea of an audience for the final outcomes of the research or how it might be promulgated. It is therefore very much the work of a late-stage and retired academic historian rather than one of the new school of closely focused and tightly constrained members of that profession. Whatever the strength of its final conclusions it has certainly turned up a wide range of important and previously little noticed issues.

The initial question was conceived in the author's familiar terrain of British mining history. In particular, how did Cornish miners, mine managers and investors network so well in finding jobs and making profitable investments, at home and abroad, in a notoriously high-risk industry? Religion was known to be a powerful connecting force but created few social contexts to promote business activity. Friendly societies and fraternal organisations, however, were well established in the region and brought together men, and sometimes women, from across a wide social spectrum. Of those organisations, the one that was most likely to be used as a vehicle for economic networking was Freemasonry, since it traditionally has been regarded as particularly middle-class and business-friendly. Fortunately, and perhaps surprisingly for a reputed 'secret' society, it was found to have more complete, detailed and available membership records than any of the others. It became the focus of the research and data was extracted on the membership of Masonic lodges in the mining-dominated western part of the county. This demonstrated that the lodges encompassed the full range of professional, mercantile, trade and public occupations that were conducted locally, and created regular opportunities for the exchange of views and ideas through regular dining and other social interactions. Random comparisons with other lodges elsewhere in the UK demonstrated that the Cornish experience was not uncommon.

Understanding of the scope of Masonic activity led to a second set of questions about why men joined the Order, what it offered them, and how it differed from other benefit and fraternal societies. The answers were many and various but one stood out as being particularly important—the support and facility that membership offered to those with mobile occupations. Once a member of one lodge, a Mason could look for help and support from all lodges and Masons everywhere. At a time of economic crisis in Cornwall, Masonic membership was particularly attractive to migrating miners, and the coastal port lodges were popular for large numbers of mariners, either locally based or simply sailing by. To explore what was on offer in more detail, attention was turned to the scale, nature and scope of Masonic charitable assurance and what form of welcome arriving Masons might receive in distant and foreign lodges.

These questions were first directed to the help and support that Freemasonry offered to mariners, but the main focus returned to miners and managers. The research was initially directed to the structure of lodge membership in frontier mining districts of the United States, which was one of the primary destinations for Cornish labour and managerial expertise. California, Nevada and Montana featured in this enquiry with their lodges demonstrating important support and networking opportunities for new arrivals, and significant advantages for integration into the local host community. The Masonic lodges and their members were also shown to have played leading roles in early community development and the construction of social capital as well as becoming highly influential across a wide range of regional and national affairs. To ensure that this was not simply an American phenomenon, similar analysis was conducted for lodges in the new mining districts of South Africa and Australia, which produced comparable results.

From this wide-ranging international investigation it is clear that Freemasonry had a great deal to offer its members—economically, socially, educationally and spiritually. It certainly provides an answer to the question that initiated the project, in that it clearly did provide useful networking opportunities for those connected with the mining industry in Cornwall, both at home and abroad. But it also goes much further than that. It demonstrates that by increasing information flows, powerfully reinforcing trust relationships, and creating safety nets for those that suffered misadventure, it probably also greatly facilitated the operation of the entire free-market capitalist system.

Of course there were constraints and offsets to these advantages. They were socially sectional—favouring the upper, middle, and artisan classes—possibly to the detriment of the interests of the mass of the working class. Women and the female-dominated trades were unable to enjoy the same benefits. Similarly, secrecy and preference could, and no doubt did, sometimes promote corruption and unfair advantage. All of this is well known and has been documented for centuries. For the first time, however, this investigation creates the evidence to view another side of that debate and to ask whether, overall, Freemasonry was a good or a bad thing?

ACKNOWLEDGEMENTS

Much of the research for this volume was conducted with the aid of a Leverhulme Emeritus Research Fellowship, held at the University of Sheffield Centre for Research into Freemasonry between 2005 and 2007.

I would like to thank Dianne Clements, Martin Cherry and Susan Snell of the Library and Museum of the United Grand Lodge of England for the guidance that they provided in tracing and interpreting the extensive archival material contained in their collection. Also Professor Andrew Prescott of the University of Glasgow and Emeritus Professor Aubrey Newman of the University of Leicester for their expert help and advice on matters relating to Freemasonry and the wider background of friendly societies and benevolence in the nineteenth century. Lastly to David Peabody who has always offered excellent advice on the evolution of Freemasonry and how it operates today.

Source of Illustrations

Front cover illustration, and illustrations 6, 7, 8 and 9: courtesy of the Library and Museum of the United Grand Lodge of England

Illustration 1: maps kindly supplied by Tim Absalom, GeoMapping Unit, Plymouth University. Sources for the maps: John Lane, *Masonic Records 1717–1894* (London, 1895); *A List of the Lodges of the Independent Order of Oddfellows (Manchester Unity) Friendly Society for 1892–3* (Manchester, 1892); Audrey Fisk, *The Ancient Order of Foresters in Cornwall* (n.p., n.d.); *The Independent Order of Rechabites. Directory and General Reference Book for 1887–8* (Manchester, 1887)

Illustration 2: author's photograph from *Mining World* 22 April 1911 p. 454

Illustrations 3 and 4: courtesy of Druids Lodge of Love and Liberality No. 589, Redruth, Cornwall

Illustration 5: courtesy of Mount Edgcumbe Lodge No. 1544, Camborne, Cornwall

Illustrations 10 and 13: author's photographs from a private collection

Illustrations 11, 12 and 14: author's photographs

ABBREVIATIONS

AQC	*Ars Quatuor Coronatorum. The Transactions of the Quatuor Coronati Lodge No. 2076*
EcHR	*Economic History Review*
FMC	*The Freemasons' Chronicle*
FM	*The Freemason*
FMM	*The Freemasons' Magazine*
FMMM	*Freemasons Magazine and Masonic Mirror*
FMQR	*Freemasons Quarterly Review*
JEcH	*Journal of Economic History*
JRFF	*Journal for Research into Freemasonry and Fraternalism*
MI	*Masonic Illustrated*
MM	*Masonic Magazine*
MP	Member of Parliament
PGL	Provincial Grand Lodge
PGM	Provincial Grand Master
PUGLE	*Proceedings of the United Grand Lodge of England*
RMBI	Royal Masonic Benevolent Institution
RMIB	Royal Masonic Institute for Boys
RMIG	Royal Masonic Institute for Girls
TLRL	*Transactions of the Lodge of Research No. 2429, Leicester*
TMAMR	*Transactions of the Manchester Association for Masonic Research*
UGLE	United Grand Lodge of England

CHAPTER 1

INTRODUCTION
FREEMASONRY:
A GLOBAL INSTITUTION

In Britain at the end of the seventeenth century the old world of continuity and tradition was drawing to a close. Most people still lived their lives and died in the communities where they were born. Everyone knew everyone and they enjoyed the support of their extended families, their churches, and much of their wider community. The work they did and the tools that they used stayed very much the same. Most regions were largely self-sufficient, producing most of the food that they ate and the commodities they consumed. Of course there was a strong commercial economy, based on specialisation and exchange, but the degree and rate of change and development was small compared with what was soon to come. The beginnings of industrialisation were about to change everything, in some areas more slowly than others, but great new national and international opportunities were about to be created. A commercial revolution in international trade expanded markets for materials and manufactures. Britain began to turn away from European to long-distance Atlantic and Eastern markets, and saw a major expansion of commercial shipping. At home, new technology and methods of organising production began to transform many established industries and create new ones. Some industries and localities saw a sudden boost to their fortunes only to be undercut by the next, increasingly frequent, wave of change. Old certainties disappeared as communities were fractured and families were forced to face an insecure future with few reliable indicators for success. The times were very redolent of those being experienced today.

With their old support structures disintegrating beneath them, all members of society needed to find new ones, not just to survive but also to try to take advantage of the opportunities that were opening up. Often forced to move away from existing family and community and establish new lives in the rapidly expanding chaotic and anonymous industrial towns, they desperately need to join together with others in similar circumstance to find some means of mutual support. Of course, none of this happened overnight. It took almost a century for the full effects of industrialisation to begin to be felt in all parts of the country, but from the outset new forms of popular association began to appear. They emerged not from the 'bottom up' but from the 'top down'. Middle- and upper-class men in expanding urban areas, particularly London, began to discover new forms of association in clubs, coffee houses and taverns, where they could enjoy jovial and intellectual entertainment.[1] A few began to find a home within traditional craft guilds, such as the stonemasons. In some of these multifarious groups, those involved began to swear oaths of mutual trust and support for each other, claim to have identified ancient origins, develop complex customary practices and rituals, and award themselves with grand titles and flamboyant regalia. As they became more firmly established, many began to attract craftsmen, tradesmen and additional working-class members, who were more interested in their potential for mutual support than entertainment. Growth remained slow but gradually different local groups with similar interests and aspirations began to draw together in regional, national and even interna- tional organisations

Slow but steady growth in the eighteenth century became an explosion in the nineteenth century, when industrialisation sharply gathered pace. Groups offering mutual assistance to their working- and lower-middle-class members proliferated: from trade unions, to co-operative societies and a host of benevolent, or friendly, societies. As Durr explained, they all derived from:

> an ideology of interdependence, its practical manifestations being giving and receiving, relieving and being relieved, supporting and being supported, either singularly or collectively, in money or in kind; that which social theorists call reciprocity.[2]

They differed considerably in the emphasis that they placed on these various activities but they all shared a common acknowledgement of the weakness of the individual and the strength of the group to which they bound themselves. It was an observation that came to be shared by families everywhere and, by the end of the nineteenth century, mutual societies of one form or another counted millions of members across the Western world and were the principal means of providing elementary social insurance and entertainment for those that could afford them—principally the upper working class and middle class—everywhere.

The economic, social and political conditions that had called forth mutuality began to change again from the early twentieth century. The evolution of the welfare state, the expansion of commercial personal insurance, alternative forms of entertainment, improved systems of communication and a host of other factors gradually eliminated the need for them. Their membership went into decline and most have either closed, diversified to other commercial activities, or continue only as a rump of their former selves.

This story has attracted considerable attention from historians over time and the general outline is well known. The literature covers most aspects of mutuality, from clubs and co-operatives to trade unions and friendly societies[3], and has clearly outlined their development and organisation. However, much remains to be done, particularly in terms of the details of their membership and activities, the reasons for joining, comparative costs and benefits, and general social and economic impact. More particularly, one large and undoubtedly important mutual organisation has been mostly left out of the general discussion, notably the Ancient and Accepted Order of Freemasons and its kindred internal associated orders. The reasons for this are unclear, particularly given the important influence that the Order is commonly accepted to have had, both past and present. In most respects, Freemasonry was little different from most of the other large friendly societies that prospered in the nineteenth century. It offered its members very similar systems of moral improvement, financial assurance as well as effective reciprocity in aid, assistance and advice. Its omission from the debate becomes even more inexplicable when viewed from the vast Masonic archival base, which is more complete, well maintained and more accessible than that for any friendly society. Similarly it has a large, though not very visible literature, published principally in the transactions of several lodges of Masonic research.[4] It was an organisation which, more than any other, embraced the most influential members of the Victorian and Edwardian world, at home and across the Empire—'the men that mattered' in industry, commerce, politics, culture and society—and to ignore it is to avoid one of the most important forces shaping that world.

Freemasonry was organised much like the other great mutual societies, such as the Independent Order of Oddfellows or the Ancient Order of Foresters, although it is more accurate to say that they were organised on a pattern similar to Freemasonry, since it was the older of the orders and possibly the inspiration for them. Members belonged to separate 'lodges', where each lodge provided entertainment through the practice of ritual and the wearing of regalia, and gave its members a sense of security in times of life crisis, such as illness, misfortune or death.[5] However, Freemasonry distinguished itself from friendly societies in terms of what it promised its members. Whereas the latter collected actuarially calculated subscriptions to provide *insurance* for specific risks such as illness, unemployment and death, Freemasonry provided open-ended charitable *assurance* in the event of any of the exigencies of life, but only on the condition of the tested needs of the brother and his family. This decision to maintain charity by assessment rather than guarantee may have cost Freemasons some members, but it enabled the Order as a whole to avoid the costly medical tests and complex actuarial calculations which became essential to ensure the financial viability of friendly societies. The comparative costs and advantages of Masonic and friendly society membership will be discussed in more detail below.[6]

The origins of modern 'speculative' Freemasonry are now commonly seen as evolving from the lodges of operative stonemasons in the late seventeenth century.[7] By the early eighteenth century a number of entirely speculative lodges had emerged in various parts of the country and moves were undertaken to bring them together under a London-based Grand Lodge around the beginning of the 1720s. Notwithstanding internal conflicts and a later split between two Grand Lodges—known as the Ancients and Moderns—the number of local lodges increased rapidly and by the end of the eighteenth century could be counted in their many hundreds in most parts of England and Wales. Those in Ireland were similarly organised under the Grand Lodge of Ireland in 1725 and those in Scotland, under the Grand Lodge of that name, in 1736. Freemasonry spread to a number of European nations from the 1730s and they, in their turn, warranted many other lodges. The rift in English Freemasonry was healed by the formation of the United Grand Lodge of England in December 1813 and the number of lodges warranted, both at home and in colonial possessions and other countries overseas, increased at an accelerating rate to around three thousand by the end of nineteenth century.

This institutional history of Freemasonry has been discussed at some length elsewhere,[8] however, and will not be considered in any detail here. Instead the focus will be on the much less researched issue of the activities of members in lodges and of Freemasonry as a whole in society. It will address four main questions: Who were the men that became Freemasons? What were their motivations in seeking membership? What did Masonic membership do for its members? What did Freemasonry do for the communities in which they lived? Those questions are posed not simply for the United Kingdom but for many other lodges and communities globally. If they are to be considered in some detail, however, there must be significant constraints on the selection of the communities to be studied. It is clearly not feasible to attempt the enquiry for millions of Masons, spread over seven continents, for more than half a century. To find preliminary answers, this investigation has focused on the functioning of one small but containable number of occupationally specialised communities, principally in Britain, but also the United States, Australia and South Africa, during the second half of the nineteenth century. They are the maritime and metal mining communities of West Cornwall and their counterparts in ports and mining districts overseas.

The study area was further refined by taking account only of those lodges operating with warrants from the United Grand Lodge of England and their daughter Grand Lodges overseas. This encompasses all of the lodges operating in Cornwall, but does not include those warranted by the Grand Lodges of Scotland and Ireland that were also common in many overseas mining areas.[9] Every Masonic lodge under the United Grand Lodge of England (hereafter the UGLE), across England and Wales and throughout the Empire, made an annual return of their membership, giving the names and addresses as well as age and occupation on initiation or joining. A complete set of these returns is held in the Library and Museum of the UGLE in London and, in principle, it is possible to identify every man who became a Mason under this constitution since the early eighteenth century.

The choice of this particular study group resulted from previous work which had suggested that Cornish metal miners, managers and investors appeared to have enjoyed efficient informal networking opportunities, locally and internationally, that seemed to have produced positive returns for business and job finding.[10] Similar opportunities also appeared to be available to mariners and those involved in the maritime trades. Of course, other fraternities and societies—of which there were many in Cornwall and elsewhere—might have played a similar role, but familiarity with mining and maritime communities suggested that Freemasonry may have had particular significance. Mining and coastal towns everywhere had seen the construction of Masonic halls and they were commonly among the largest and most impressive buildings erected by the communities. Size and quality matter as a physical expression of strength and influence, and only the church appeared as a rival of equal status. Similarly, the graves of the 'great and the good' of communities everywhere commonly and boldly claimed a Masonic identity as one of the few and most treasured pieces of iconography on headstones.

The study starts, in Chapter 2, with a broad outline of the economic development of Cornwall during the eighteenth and nineteenth centuries. It considers the long-term profile of the development of Freemasonry in the county, particularly during the years of rapid expansion from the 1840s to the end of the century. It looks at both the basic 'craft' lodges (in America, 'blue' lodges) to which all Masons must belong and goes on to explore the growth of various internal 'side' orders and the role of the Cornish Provincial Grand Lodge, which co-ordinated local matters. It then goes on to explore the demographic structure of those lodges.

Chapter 3 begins a detailed exploration of the demographic structure of the lodges' membership. Using data on age, occupation and residence from lodge returns, it investigates the social structure of lodges and the interrelationships of their membership. This section concludes that men from a very wide range of occupational and social classes were attracted to the lodges, and that many appear to have joined for the specific purpose of protecting or improving their economic circumstances, both at home and abroad. Limited comparisons with lodges in other parts of England suggested that the experience of the Cornish lodges was not unusual and was broadly similar to that in many other parts of the country.

Chapters 4 and 5 consider the numerous offerings of Freemasonry and why men became and remained members. These motivations were no doubt intimately connected in different combinations for different men but it has been convenient here to classify them under separate headings and divide them into two broad groups. Chapter 4 looks at those aspects of Freemasonry that both improved the quality of life of its members as well as providing reassurance in times of adversity. Thus, membership was perceived to improve reputation and respectability; to widen the range of influential friendships within the community; to provide morally improving entertainment and education through the learning and practice of ritual; and, for the many men enthused by the contemporary nostalgia for a mystic past, an offer to reveal the 'lost secrets' of ancient societies. Similarly, when life had its pitfalls, Masonic assistance—from other brethren, lodge funds, regional and national charities—provided an invaluable safety net. In dealing with these latter issues, lengthy consideration is given not just to Masonic benevolence but to how it compared with the offerings made by some of the major friendly societies. Chapter 5 continues the study of the 'usefulness' of Masonic membership by looking in detail at how it advantaged those engaged in particularly vulnerable mobile and hazardous occupations. Here, a discussion of miners is joined by an in-depth look at the advantages of Masonic membership for mariners, many of whom have also been identified in Cornish lodges. Like miners, mariners worked in close-knit, all-male groups, in a dangerous occupation and they enjoyed strong communal bonds. These chapters conclude that for large numbers of men Freemasonry was seen to provide significant protection against the consequences of misadventure during travel, and important opportunities for reliable information and job finding at the point of arrival.

Having established a significant role for Freemasonry in facilitating labour mobility, Chapters 6 and 7 investigate what migrant Masons might encounter when they visited or joined overseas lodges. Chapter 6 uses the same method that was used for investigating the structure of lodges in Cornwall to explore the composition of lodges in mining communities in California, Nevada and Montana in the USA. It finds high levels of socio-economic similarity and highly advantageous networking opportunities. Chapter 7 makes further investigation and comparisons with mining lodges in Australia and South Africa, and arrives at similar conclusions. Everywhere Masonic membership had much to offer itinerant miners and any other migrant who wished to become part of a mining community.

Discussion to this point is concerned primarily with what Masonic membership could offer to the individual. Chapter 8 moves on to consider what Freemasons and Freemasonry offered to the wider communities that hosted them. Examples are given of major Masonic acts of charity; their civic engagement and assistance in the creation of social capital; their effect on social cohesion; the general benefit to society of the moral improvement of their members; and increased economic efficiency resulting from improved information flows and stronger trust relationships in business. The latter issues are particularly difficult to assess and must be offset by the increased opportunities for conspiracy, narrow sectional advantage, exploitation and other forms of rent-seeking behaviour. These have been much discussed in anti-Masonic literature, however, and have not been explored in any depth here.

Chapter 9 concludes with an overview of the role of Freemasonry in helping to shape the lives of miners, mariners and other involved mobile occupations. It then moves on to take a broader view of fraternities, friendly and benevolent societies as a whole in facilitating the process of industrialisation and globalisation from the late eighteenth century. The rise and fall of mutuality almost exactly paralleled the trajectory of western industrialisation and its interconnections call for much closer study than has so far been appreciated. What directions might most profitably be studied in the future?

CHAPTER 2

CORNWALL AND CORNISH FREEMASONRY IN THE NINETEENTH CENTURY

The Background

Cornwall is a peninsular arranged on a roughly east-west axis protruding into the Atlantic. Even its eastern border is mainly a watery one, delineated by the Tamar River and its steep valley. Until the mid-nineteenth century the county was effectively an island, with communications to the rest of the country faster and more efficient by sea than by land. It developed an identity and culture to match, as much outward-looking to other parts of the world as to the rest of the nation. Some saw it as a kind of 'West Barbary'.

In the eighteenth and nineteenth centuries the county divided economically roughly into two halves, separating around Truro. The eastern district was principally agricultural and unchanging until the development of some mining activity near St Austell and in the Tamar Valley from the early nineteenth century. The western district was very different, being focused on commercial mining and shipping activities from an early period, and probably becoming the nation's most fully industrialised area by the end of the eighteenth century. With tin-mining traditions stretching back more than two thousand years and a great boost from copper mining starting from around 1710, it had produced a population far beyond the supporting capacity of local agriculture and one which was mainly wage-dependent—'proletarianised'—by the end of the eighteenth century. Those not directly employed in mining were heavily involved in servicing the mines and their owners, investors, managers and workers. Local industries smelted and refined most of the tin and lead produced: they supplied mining machinery and materials, from explosives to ore crushers, and they were among the world leaders in the development of, and application of, steam engineering.

The only exception to this internal focus was the significance of the maritime trades. Ports all around the coast supported important fishing activities and the coasting trade. A few, such as Falmouth and Penzance, acted as strategic first and/or last points of call, and also delivered repair and provisioning for shipping involved in the long-distance deep-water trades to the Americas, Far East and Mediterranean. With none of the western industrial areas more than ten miles from the sea—and many far less—the two economies became closely intertwined, with a particularly close symbiotic relationship developing through the exchange of Cornish copper for South Wales coal during the mid-nineteenth century. Everywhere the mining and maritime economies interwove with each other, from the mining communities' periodic involvement in fishing as an essential supplement to diet, to its adoption of maritime terminologies in the day-to-day conduct of its affairs: investors known as 'adventurers', mine managers as 'captains', financial officers as 'pursers', the depths of shafts measured in fathoms.

As British industrialisation progressed, so too did the demand for Cornish minerals and by c. 1850 the mining industry stood at a near all-time peak. There were at least 150 deep mines at work in the county, probably employing around 40,000 men, women and children. The numbers dependent on the industry—from supplying industries, professional services, food production, retail, transport, etc.—was at least twice that size. However, storm clouds were already beginning to gather. Lead and silver output was already in sustained decline with the exhaustion of some of the previously most productive deposits, and copper—the most important staple—was seeing increasing competition from cheap imported foreign ores. Imports of copper ore, principally from Chile but increasingly from Cuba and Australia, had started in the 1830s and grown rapidly by the mid-century to more than half as much as domestic production. Similar problems were also developing for tin, with rising imports from the East Indies.

For the moment all seemed fair and the industry remained buoyant until the end of the decade, but then things began to deteriorate rapidly in the face of what had now become a rising torrent of imports. Cornwall looked to the Government for protection but the growing influence of metal manufacturers and the steadfast pursuit of free trade policies put this beyond reach. Between the late 1850s and 1890 imports of copper ore and part wrought metal—particularly the latter—increased almost three times and copper prices, not yet buoyed by the demands of the forthcoming electrical age, fell by half. Between 1860 and 1870 copper production in the county shrank to just a third of its previous level and by the late 1880s it had stopped almost entirely.[1] Lead mining, a much smaller sector, held on into the late 1870s but then also fell sharply in the face of increasing foreign competition. Only tin managed to hold up. Imports also rose sharply, but so too did demand from the rapidly expanding tinplate industry and prices were little different in the 1880s than they had been in the 1850s. However, working costs were steadily rising with the increasing depth of

Table 1   Copper, Tin, Lead and Iron Miners Employed in Cornwall, 1851–1901

Date	Total Number of Miners
1851	30,454
1861	31,847
1871	21,282
1881	13,005
1891	9,986
1901	7,366

Source: Census data

operations and the number of mines in production gradually dwindled. By the end of the 1890s there were less than thirty tin mines operating in the county and less than ten were operating on any significant scale.

With this sharp contraction of the industry in little more than thirty years, employment fell dramatically (see Table 1). The mining contraction and job losses were spread across all of the mining areas within the county but were, of course, most serious in the western district. They also impacted badly on the support and ancillary industries as well as the urban infrastructure. Hayle took a particularly heavy blow with the closure of large and long-established copper-smelting and engineering works. In all coastal towns, the maritime trades suffered badly from the contraction of mining activity, with a decline in associated import and export activity. They also felt the detrimental effects of a shift from the coasting trades to internal rail transport as well as the increasing marginalisation of Cornwall as the first and/or last port of call in the long-distance trades, as shipping moved from sail to steam.

For those left without work there was little to do other than relocate. Local agriculture and china clay production, both of which increased significantly in their output, could soak up only a small part of the displaced labour, while the declining traditional industries of neighbouring Devonshire, such as woollen cloth production, created few nearby opportunities. The entire south-western region that had once led the nation into industrialisation was now leading it into de-industrialisation. Movement would have to be long-distance and long-term— either within Britain, to the rapidly expanding industrial areas of the North, Midlands, South Wales and London, or overseas.

This was not a new challenge for the Cornish. Miners work a finite resource and depletion of known deposits requires a constant search for new ones. Men, women and older children, working both underground and on the surface, were constantly on the move and limits to how far they could travel in a day to-and-from work meant that population centres were constantly moving and changing. It has been suggested that one of the reasons for the rapid expansion of Methodism and other dissenting sects in the county was that the Church of England had failed to keep up with these movements, stuck to its old parish structures and left many 'new' communities unprovided with spiritual care.

These long-established patterns were supercharged from the early nineteenth century. The mining industry was revolutionised by a new generation of mining entrepreneurs, using capital mainly derived in London, to break out of regionally confined activities to establish national and international operations. John Taylor, for example, took Cornish miners and mine captains to his lead and copper mines in Wales and the Midlands, and by the 1820s was employing large numbers in his Mexican operations.[2] Around the same time, many other British investors took advantage of the collapse of Spanish and Portuguese colonial rule in South America to reinvigorate mining in Mexico, Chile and Brazil, again staffing them largely with Cornish mining and managerial expertise.[3] In the 1840s and 1850s the Cornish joined in the rush of people from all nations to the newly discovered gold fields of California and Australia.[4] Long before domestic events began to oblige the Cornish to migrate, a tradition of continuous short- and long-term movement was heavily ingrained in the culture.[5]

However, what had been a steady trickle turned into a flood after the 1850s. Emigration to existing destinations continued to increase and attractive new destinations were found in Southern Africa and India.[6] Cornwall saw outward migration—domestic and international—on a scale unparalleled in any other part of England and Wales. While the rest of the country experienced steady population growth—nearly doubling between 1851 and 1900—the numbers in Cornwall declined by around 10%. It is possible that around 200,000 men, women and children left the county during those years, with the great majority being young males (see Table 2). Most of those that left were probably young males, twenty to thirty-nine years of age. The outflow of this group slowed down during the last years of the century but it left its impact in the form of a falling birth rate and rapidly rising average age of the population. The average age of males over twenty years within the population of the county increased by ten years over the period 1851 to 1911, from just over forty-nine to fifty-nine.

The only other part of the British Isles to see a similar, but much larger, decline in numbers was Ireland. Here outward migration reduced the population by half between the mid-1840s and the end of the century. In both cases the causes were similar in terms of the collapse of a regional resource base, but the consequences for their populations was much different. While the Irish fell into

Table 2   The Population of Cornwall, 1851–1911

Date	Cornwall Males	Cornwall Females	Cornwall Total	Eng. & Wales Total
1851	172,193	184,448	356,641	17.9m
1861	174,148	190,700	364,848	20.1m
1871	167,839	190,517	358,356	22.7m
1881	153,015	173,360	326,375	26.0m
1891	147,460	171,123	318,583	29.0m
1901	149,937	172,397	322,334	32.5m

Source: Census data

abject poverty and were forced to flee by conditions at home and to endure penury abroad, the Cornish exodus took more of a form that would be described today as economic migration. The same foreign mines that were producing the flood of cheap imports that undermined their domestic industry also created an insatiable demand for their skills and experience abroad. Opportunities for high earnings appeared as the result of a succession of discoveries of major new mining fields in Australia and the Americas, Africa and the Far East. Similarly, at home, the expansion of coal and metal mines in other parts of the country offered new opportunities.[7] This meant that for many, if not most, of the Cornish miners thrown out of work, leaving the county became not so much an issue of permanent emigration as periodic short-term migration or even 'commuting' to a constantly changing range of employers. With such wide exposure to an international job market it is not surprising that the remaining mine owners often complained about shortages of labour in Cornwall and an inability to reduce wages as part of cost-cutting measures. Overall, notwithstanding its very significant problems, Cornwall remained fairly buoyant during the difficult years at the end of the century, as attested by the vibrant intellectual communities of the major towns with their Royal Institution, Royal Polytechnic Society and Royal Geological Society, as well as the building of an entirely new cathedral in Truro in the 1880s.

With such insecurity and uncertainty, but still some cash surplus beyond daily needs, the emerging fraternal and benevolent societies of the late eighteenth century offered an attractive means of providing some future security and maybe movement and job-finding assistance. State welfare provision was parsimonious and degrading, commercial insurance developing only slowly and mutuality offered the only immediate and effective solution. Those in the most hazardous and threatened occupations were most likely to join but all could benefit, either

Table 3   Mutual Society Participation Levels in Two Mining Communities in the Late 1880s

Camborne		Redruth	
Oddfellows	275	Oddfellows	316
Foresters	106	Foresters	244
Rechabites	54	Rechabites	240
Freemasons	56	Freemasons	83
Total	491	Total	883
All Males 20+	3201		2300
Participation Rate	1 in 6.5		1 in 2.6

economically or socially. Thus, tradesmen, those involved in retail and hospitality, merchants and even professionals, providing legal, financial and medical services, could all see benefits. The balance of motivations no doubt differed between them but the overall outcome was the same.

Across Cornwall, large and small towns began to see the establishment of 'lodges' of one description or another, often in multiple numbers (see Illustration 1). Looking more closely at particular communities, Table 3 shows the major societies and orders operating in the central mining towns of Camborne and Redruth in the last two decades of the century, with an indication of the number of their members in the late 1880s. Although the figures should be taken only as approximations[8]—differing slightly between years and including some other variables—they do suggest a very high participation rate among all adult males and that a very general search for increased security and support in facing the vicissitudes of life was high on the agenda of all of those families that could afford it.

The general role and distribution of mutual societies across Cornwall will be returned to below, in Chapter 4, but this discussion will focus attention on the particular contribution of Freemasonry. Although one of the smallest of the orders it was arguably the most influential in urban communities and many saw it as the keystone of the whole structure of mutuality. It was the earliest, most exclusive, and probably the most inspirational for the structure and organisation of other societies and orders. It was also not invisible or insignificant in numbers, since at least one in ten of those fraternal members in Redruth, for example, was a Mason.

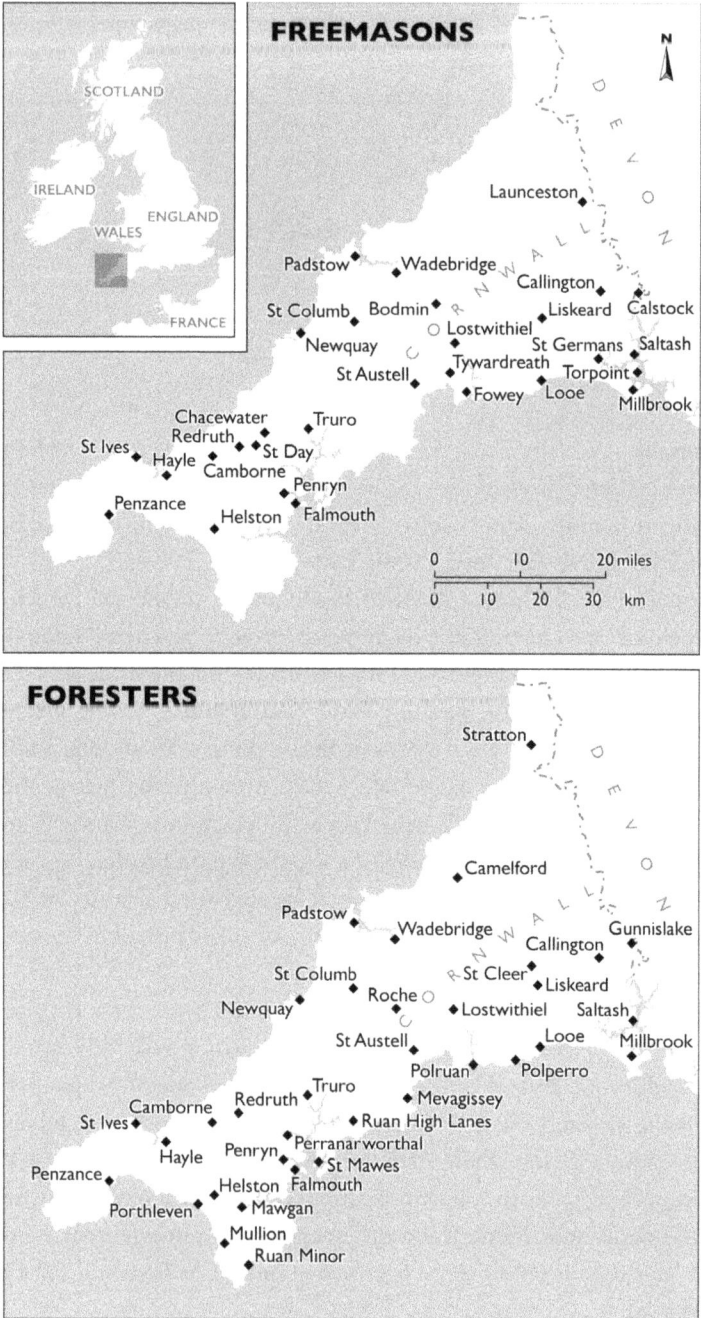

Illustration 1   Maps Showing the Distribution of
Fraternal Organisations in Cornwall, *c.*1890

The Freemasons, Oddfellows (Manchester Unity), the Foresters and the Rechabites were the
only major societies operating in Cornwall during the nineteenth century. Several had many

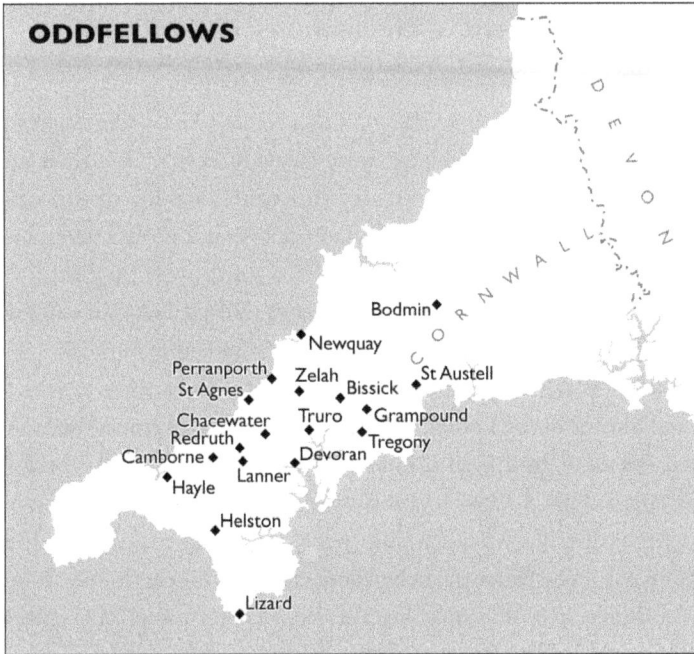

ODDFELLOWS

Bodmin
Newquay
Perranporth Zelah St Austell
St Agnes Bissick
Chacewater Truro Grampound
Redruth Tregony
Camborne Devoran
Lanner
Hayle
Helston

Lizard

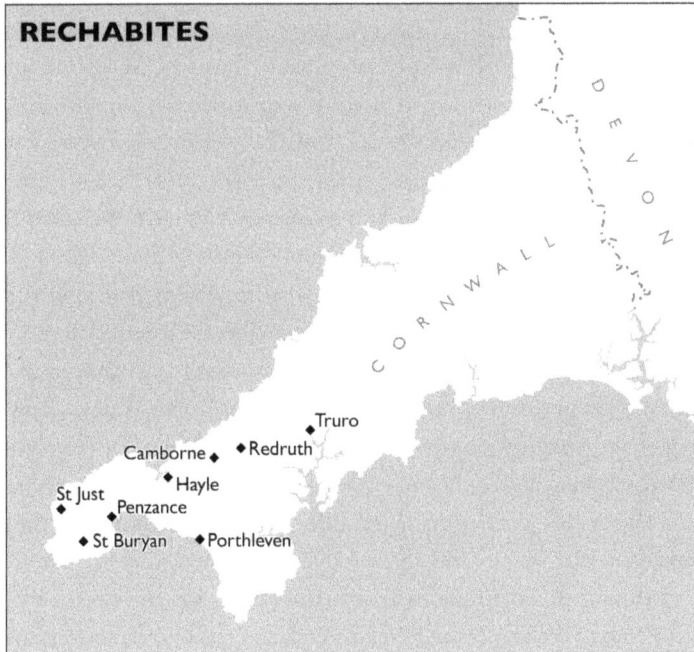

RECHABITES

Truro
Camborne Redruth
St Just Hayle
Penzance
St Buryan Porthleven

members in common and some used the same meeting place (e.g. both the Oddfellows and the Foresters met in the Redruth Masonic Hall in the 1880s). While the numbers joining Masonry steadily increased during the late nineteenth century, difficult economic conditions caused the number in the friendly societies to shrink.

The Early Development of Freemasonry in Cornwall

The origins of modern Freemasonry in England are usually taken from around the formation of the Grand Lodge of England in 1717.[9] The earliest lodges warranted by the new Grand Lodge were based in London but their members often travelled widely around the country for business and social purposes, taking their Masonry with them. With poor land communications, they commonly used sea routes to reach distant localities like south-west England.[10] It is not surprising, therefore, that the first regularly organised lodge in Cornwall was established in Falmouth, in 1751. The Lodge of Love and Honour, No. 75 on the earliest roll of Grand Lodge, met in private rooms in the Kings' Arms, Market Strand. The Master of the Lodge, William Pye, also the Mayor of Falmouth, was appointed the first Provincial Grand Master (hereafter PGM) the following year and supervised a rapid expansion of the Order.[11] Other lodges soon began to be established in other busy port towns, such as Truro (1752) and Penzance (1755), and from there business connections carried them inland to regional commercial and mining centres, such as Helston (1752) and Redruth (1754).[12] Coastal trading linkages gradually widened the geographical cover to St Ives (1765), Marazion (1777) and Penryn (1782). By the third quarter of the eighteenth century Cornwall was probably one of the most 'Masonic counties' in England in terms of the incidence of membership within the population. Activity, however, remained heavily concentrated in the western districts, with their strong industrial and external trading links. Launceston was the only town in the inland agricultural east of the county to see an early lodge (1767) and that was not followed by another until the formation of One and All in Bodmin (1810).[13]

Much of the early expansion of activity had probably been buoyed up by the new prosperity that copper mining brought to the county after 1710 but that went into reverse from the 1760s when the county experienced increasing competition from new mines opened in Anglesea in North Wales. Growth now became decline. New lodges were formed but by 1790 nine of the earlier ones had stopped working and had been erased from the Grand Lodge register. The situation became still worse during the difficult political climate of the French and Napoleonic War years. Only three lodges continued working, viz. Love and Honour in Falmouth, Fortitude in Truro, and Peace, Joy and Brotherly Love in Penryn. The end of the war brought no immediate respite and recovery was slow. Just five more lodges were established in the county during the next twenty-five years and three of those were short-lived.

By the second quarter of the nineteenth century Masonry had only a slender hold in the county, with activity confined to the four large towns of Falmouth,

Truro, Penzance and Bodmin. The Provincial Grand Lodge (hereafter PGL) of Cornwall had almost ceased to function and no permanent Grand Master could be found. Dramatic action was taken to resolve the problem when Sir Charles Lemon, a leading political figure in the county but not a Mason, was quickly initiated into Love and Honour in 1840, elected Master of the Lodge in 1843, and appointed PGM in 1844.[14] Such arrangements were not entirely unusual at the time and whether by design or good fortune, he was able to help generate a powerful revival of the Order during the next twenty years. That revival was considerably assisted by the beginning of an era of economic prosperity in the county, generated by another expansion of mining, quarrying and maritime activity. This time, Masonic activity was recorded across the county and particularly at its western and eastern ends. Four new enduring lodges were constituted in the 1840s, three in the 1850s and eleven in the 1860s. Thereafter, with representation in nearly all towns of consequence, new foundations declined to four in the 1870s, two in the 1880s and just one in the 1890s (see Table 4).

The increasing number and distribution of lodges in the county created the opportunity for a major expansion in the total number of members. In Cornwall, as in many other parts of the country,[15] lodge membership had languished during the first half of the nineteenth century and in 1840 the four active lodges in the county had less than a hundred members between them. By the early 1860s, however, a rapid expansion of mining, which achieved all-time peaks of production, underpinned a surge in economic prosperity which more than quadrupled this number to over 460. Ten years later it had doubled to 900 and by the late 1870s it stood at more than 1500. Expansion turned into a slight decline in the 1880s, as non-paying members were removed from the roll, but was resumed in the 1890s. At the turn of the century the number of Masons in Cornwall was almost exactly 2000 (see Figure 1). This pattern of development was probably not greatly dissimilar from that seen elsewhere in the country at the time. There are no available annual figures for national Masonic membership, but the chronology of the establishment of new lodges under the English constitution shows a sharp rise in numbers in the 1860s and 1870s, with a gradual tailing-off in the rate of growth in the 1880s and 1890s.[16]

Until the late 1860s, the expansion in the total membership simply reflected the widening geographical spread of Masonry within the county, but thereafter it was produced by a deepening of recruitment within existing communities. Average lodge membership increased sharply, from around thirty-five at the end of the 1860s to more than fifty by the mid-1870s. In the older lodges—those established before 1860—the average number of members reached an even higher sixty-six by 1880. The second surge in membership in the 1890s

Table 4   Cornish Masonic Lodges Working Through the Nineteenth Century

Name and Number of the Lodge	Location	Date of Warrant
Love and Honour, 75	Falmouth	1751*
Mount Sinai, 121	Penzance	1813*
Fortitude, 131	Truro (from 1814)	1772*
True & Faithful, 318	Helston	1800*
One and All, 330	Bodmin	1810
Phoenix Honour & Prudence, 331	Truro	1810*
Cornubian, 450	Hayle	1848*
Peace & Harmony, 496	St Austell	1844
St Martin's, 510	Liskeard	1845
Loyal Victoria, 557	Callington	1848
Druids Love & Liberty, 589	Redruth	1851*
Boscawen, 699	Chacewater	1857*
Dunheved, 789	Launceston	1859
St Matthew's / Restormel, 856	Lostwithiel	1861
Meridian, 893	Millbrook	1861
Three Grand Principles, 967	Penryn	1863*
St Anne's, 970	East Looe	1863
Fowey, 977	Fowey	1864
Tregullow, 1006	St Day	1865*
Zetland, 1071	Saltash	1865
Carew, 1136	Torpoint	1866
St Andrew's, 1151	Tywardreath	1867
Eliot, 1164	St Germans	1867
Tregenna, 1272	St Ives	1869*
Fort, 1528	Newquay	1875
Duke of Cornwall, 1529	St Columb	1875
Mount Edgcumbe, 1544	Camborne	1875*
St Petroc, 1785	Padstow	1878
Molesworth, 1954	Wadebridge	1882
Cotehele, 2166	Calstock	1886
St Michael's, 2747	Newquay	1899

* Lodges discussed in detail below.
Renumbering of the lodges after 1863 meant that they do
not always follow in chronological sequence.
Source: Lane, *Masonic Records 1717–1894*

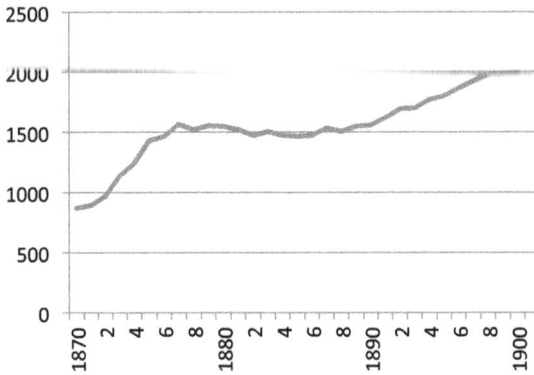

Figure 1   The Numbers of Freemasons in Cornish Lodges, 1869–1900

carried the overall average lodge membership to more than sixty and eight lodges counted over eighty members by 1900.

Throughout the period from the mid-century, the largest and most successful lodges in terms of sustained recruitment were located in the industrial and commercial centres in the west of the county, with a few eastern outliers in Bodmin, Calstock, and the suburbs of Plymouth (see Appendix 1). This pattern of development was reflected in many other parts of the country, including the neighbouring county of Devon. There, for example, the average size of lodges stood at an identical fifty-five in 1889[17] and the geographical spread of activity was focused around large towns, such as Exeter, Devonport, Stonehouse and Plymouth.

It is remarkable that the long years of Masonic expansion in Cornwall were presided over by just three PGMs. The first, Sir Charles Lemon MP, already mentioned above, resigned in 1863 and was succeeded by another influential political figure, Augustus Smith, MP for Tresco in the Scillies. He died in office in 1872 and was succeeded in 1873 by the 4th Earl Mount Edgcumbe, who held office for forty-four years, finally resigning in 1917. The latter also became the Deputy English Grand Master 1891–96. Together these three PGMs gave Cornish Freemasonry direct access to the seats of political and Masonic influence in London, and ensured its representation in the highest social circles.

Data on the causes of changes in Cornish Masonic membership are scarce before the early 1860s but thereafter W.J. Hughan's *Directory of the Provincial Grand Lodge of Cornwall*, published annually from 1870 into the early twentieth century, provided a wealth of information, by lodge, on the numbers of initiations, joining members, resignations, deaths and exclusions. That is a level of detail not commonly paralleled for many other parts of the country. There are, however, problems in using some of this data. It is not clear, for example, whether 'joining members'—i.e. those men who were already Masons, joining from another lodge—account only for those coming into Cornwall from elsewhere or whether it also includes those moving around within the county. Similarly, the returns of those leaving Masonry are not 'year sensitive' in that they are blurred by those who simply failed to pay their dues and were subject to periodic 'purges' from membership. For example, at a meeting of the PGL of Cornwall in 1883 the PGM inquired if the Secretary could explain the sudden reduction in the number of members of Cornish lodges—from 1,522 in 1881 to 1,471 in 1882. He replied that only those who had paid their dues for 1882 were returned this year and explained that:

> There were many brethren absent from some of the lodges, particu-
> larly in the lodges in the eastern part of the province. The numbers
> in one lodge had declined by more than 50, and this had arisen from
> many brethren engaged in mining, mining engineers and others,
> having gone abroad. Other brethren were at sea. The names of
> those were returned but they were not reckoned now as subscribing
> members.[18]

Similarly, the following year it was observed that:

> After the rapid strides of the last few years, the Masonic Craft in the
> West of England, as elsewhere, has enough to do to 'hold its own',
> and consequent upon a more rigid application of the payment of the
> annual subscriptions the number of members has been considerably
> reduced in many of the lodges.[19]

With such reservations, the best and most time-sensitive guide to the expansion of the Order is found in the annual numbers of initiations (see Figure 2).

As can be seen, the total number of initiates each year grew very little over the period, notwithstanding the increased number of lodges. In relative terms, this meant that the number of initiates to existing members was much higher in the 1860s and 1870s, compared with the 1880s and 1890s. For example, in the early 1870s there was one initiate annually to every seven established members, while in the 1890s this was down to one in every thirteen. As the Order matured so it also became more stable. Overall, there were more than four thousand initiates into Cornish lodges between 1869 and 1900, which had the effect of raising their membership by just over a thousand by the end of the period. Allowing for deaths, retirement through incapacity and migration/emigration, this suggests a

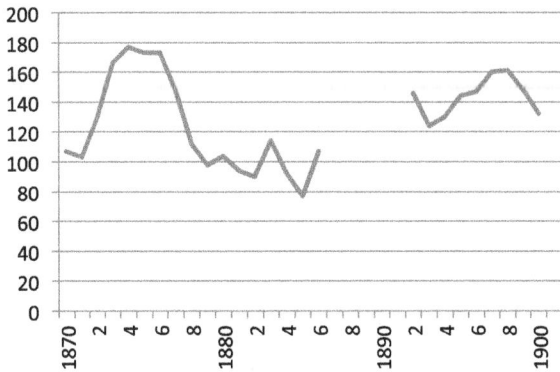

Figure 2   Annual Initiations into Cornish Masonic Lodges, 1869–1900

high level of retention of local members and some incoming 'joiners', and that most members derived significant spiritual, social and/or economic satisfaction from their Masonry, and made a strong and enduring commitment to it.

It is notable that the highest number of initiations took place not during periods of prosperity, as might have been expected, but when the mining industry was in serious recession and emigration was at its peak—viz. in the 1870s, following the collapse of copper mining, and in the 1890s, following a major downturn in tin mining.[20] As will be demonstrated below, many used what slim resources they retained to gain the support of Masonic membership before they left home. When coupled with the difficulties that many lodges faced in terms of maintaining subscriptions and general financial viability, this tended to create a free-for-all in propositions for initiation. Many established Masons became increasingly concerned about the 'quality' of the new members and their motivations for joining. In this sense it revived some long-standing concerns. As early as 1814 the Master of Love and Honour in Falmouth had observed that 'some lodges, much in debt and shackled by a barrenness of funds, consider the fact of five guineas entrance fee too powerful a temptation to be even prudently careful as to the character and position of candidates' and suggested that 'an increasing care should be exercised in the admission of members'.[21] Similarly, in 1875, at the height of the wave of emigration, the PGM admonished the Masters of all Cornish lodges to 'be especially careful not to sanction admission of candidates of whom they cannot personally approve' and cautioned them that 'we do not want a man to join because he thinks having a square and compasses over his door will help him in his business'.[22] Again in 1896, the PGM voiced 'a fear lest some of the lodges were too anxious to add to their numbers and through that anxiety accept everyone who came forward'.[23] A few years later, however, when initiations fell off, he was happy to conclude that 'the lodges were beginning to appreciate the fact the Freemasonry should be regarded as a luxury and not as a benefit society'.[24]

The Development of Side Orders

So far discussion has been focused on the development of what are commonly known as 'craft' lodges. All entry into Masonic membership is via initiation into a craft lodge—sometimes known as a 'blue' lodge in the United States. However, once all three stages of initiation have been completed, a 'Master Mason' may also join 'side orders', set up in association with craft lodges. Not every lodge established side orders and not every lodge that did so established them all. Accordingly, many members of one lodge often became members of a side lodge in another. This established a system of contacts and interactions between some Masons and lodges that extend beyond the bounds of the narrow localities in which most craft lodges operated. To understand fully the pattern of Masonic activity in Cornwall, or any other county, it is therefore important also to investigate the formation of side orders and to estimate the numbers of their members. As will be shown later, membership of the side orders also provides an insight into some of the reasons why men became, and remained, Masons, as well as the personal resources, both in money and time, that they were prepared to commit to it.

Unfortunately, this is less well documented than for the craft lodges. There were four main side orders operating in Cornwall during the second half of the nineteenth century: Royal Arch, Knights Templar, Mark and Rose Croix. Royal Arch was conducted within the same administrative structure as Craft Masonry, while Mark Masonry and Rose Croix were ruled and co-ordinated by entirely independent administrative organisations. All later came to accommodate further side orders within their own structures.[25] The central records of the Royal Arch, organised as 'Chapters' rather than 'Lodges', are located alongside Craft Lodge returns in the Library and Museum of UGLE. Like the Craft, they include details of all Chapters, both at home and abroad. Details of Mark Masons' lodges, and other associated orders, of which the Knights Templar is one, can be found in the archives of the Grand Lodge of Mark Masons, St James's Street, London. Rose Croix is centrally located in nearby Duke Street.

Royal Arch
Royal Arch Chapters were occasionally worked in Cornwall from 1754 but they were not formalised until 1791 when a dispensation was received from the Grand Chapter in London to establish Druids Chapter of Love and Liberality

in Redruth. The following year a warrant was received also to open a Knights Templar 'Encampment' in Redruth, effectively in association with the Chapter. Within a few years it had expanded to 120 members, making it one of the largest in the country.[26] However, further progress was slow. Penryn and Falmouth had active chapters by the early nineteenth century but it was not until the 1830s that a fourth was established in Penzance. It was only the general expansion of Masonry in the county from the mid-century that rekindled enthusiasm and this finally produced a flurry of activity in the 1860s and 1870s. With nine working chapters in Cornwall by 1877, the county was granted its own Provincial Grand Chapter, which in turn encouraged a further expansion of activity, although no further chapters were added between 1879 and the end of the century. While the origins of the Royal Arch were firmly in the west of the county, much of this later stage of development took place in association with the new lodges being formed in the east. Unfortunately there are no available figures of the membership of the lodges during the 1860s and 1870s, but Appendix 2 shows their continued expansion during the last two decades of the century, from a total of around 260 to almost 400.

Mark Masonry

Mark Masonry came much later to Cornwall than the Royal Arch but it expanded rapidly and had a very similar total membership by 1900. It was only in the 1860s that it was formally 'imported' into the county from a prosperous base in Plymouth. Then, in 1864, Meridian Lodge was established in Millbrook and was quickly followed by three lodges in the western Masonic heartland of the county—viz. Fortitude in Truro, Cornubian in Hayle and Love and Honour in Falmouth. In 1867, Meridian Lodge also migrated west, to Redruth, and the county was granted a charter for its own Provincial Mark Grand Lodge. Nine more lodges followed by the end of the 1880s, but then there were no new developments before the end of the century (see Appendix 3). The sizes of Mark lodges were very similar to Royal Arch Chapters, with the largest again being associated with the older and more successful craft lodges in the major urban centres. Mark Masonry itself also had side, or sub orders, which only Mark Masons could join. One of the most successful of these was the Degree of *Royal Ark Mariner*. Cornwall had just one of these, attached to the Boscawen Mark Lodge. However, it was not established until 1895 and although it later attracted many of the leading figures in local Mark Masonry, its impact during this period was limited.

Both Royal Arch and Mark Masonry expanded roughly in line with the growth of Craft Masonry in Cornwall, following similar chronological and geographical

Table 5   Members of Ancient and Accepted Rite, Rose Croix,
Cornwall Chapter No. 61, 1875–1900

1875	1880	1885	1890	1895	1900
27	47	41	46	40	34

patterns of development. In general terms they were all at their strongest in the industrial west of the county with relatively weak development in the agricultural east, though some of the eastern towns such as Liskeard, Launceston and Callington, as well as the districts adjacent to Plymouth, also had their successes.

Knights Templar

Knights Templar was among the very earliest side orders to be introduced into Cornwall, but the Order did not prosper and it had probably disappeared from the county by the late 1820s. It was resuscitated in 1863, first in Redruth and later in Truro, and further 'encampments' followed in Tywardreath, Liskeard and St Austell.[27] Again, however, it did not prove popular and by the early 1890s only one encampment appears to have been operating and its membership generally counted less than twenty.

Rose Croix

Rose Croix fared little better in terms of the number of its 'chapters' and members, but like Knights Templar, it established an influential role on Cornish freemasonry. There was only one lodge in the county during the nineteenth century—Rose Croix, Cornwall Chapter, No. 61, meeting in the Masonic Hall, Truro—which was not warranted until 1874 and never had more than fifty members (see Table 5). However, from the outset its membership included many of the county's social and Masonic elite, and it appears to have become even more exclusive as time went on. Certainly by the mid-1890s, all but two of its members had been Provincial Grand Officers and it gives every impression of having become the preserve of the local rulers of the Craft. These issues, however, will be explored in more detail below.

Freemasonry in the Community

The great expansion of Freemasonry in Cornwall took place against the background of a major decline in the population as discussed above. The consequence was that Masonry became far more visible in the county and it significantly deepened its routes in local society. As already seen above, the overall

Table 6   The Number of Masons Relative to the Number
of Adult Males in Cornwall 1861–1901

Date	Number of Masons	Number of Males Over 20	Ratio of Masons to Males Over 20
1861	c.450	85,745	1:190
1871	894	81,964	1:92
1881	1522	77,309	1:50
1891	1621	77,348	1:48
1901	c.2000	82,753	1:41

'Mutual participation rate' among the population increased with expanding numbers and a declining population in the last decades of the century and the specific 'Masonic participation rate' went with it. The number of Masons relative to the number of males over the age of twenty-one[28] increased nearly five times from the early 1860s, with a particularly rapid advance during the third quarter of the century to around one in fifty (see Table 6).

In some particularly fraternal towns, such as Redruth, it may have been as high as one in nineteen in the early 1880s. Of course some of the lodge members may have been drawn from beyond the census boundaries of the town, inflating the relative numbers slightly, but equally, if the calculation is confined to the age groups most like to be active Masons—say twenty-five to sixty—the percentage of Masons among the community becomes higher again. Similarly, if it was confined to the upper-working- and middle-class groups that comprised most lodge membership, the frequency of membership may have approached one in twelve or less. It certainly seems very likely that in Redruth and similar towns a very large percentage of middle-income family units counted at least one Craft member among their number.

Freemasonry clearly became popular in Cornwall during the second half of the nineteenth century, but was it unrepresentative of other counties? Data presented below suggests that it may have been more 'Masonic' than many other counties in proportion to population but a broad comparison with its larger and more economically diverse neighbour, Devonshire, suggests that it was not markedly out of line with other parts of the South West. In Devon in 1891, for example, the male population (299,676) was around twice that of Cornwall (147,460). Similarly, the total number of Masons in Devonshire in that year (3,253)[29] was almost exactly twice that in Cornwall (1,621). No doubt there were major variations between particular communities—the Devon Masons being mainly located in the coastal cities with relatively few in the interior of the county—but the overall pattern was similar. It might also be noticed that in the very broadest of terms, Cornwall emulated the larger economic geography of Britain as a whole. Almost an island, it was surrounded on three sides by the sea, with large and vibrant coastal cities and a heavily industrialised interior. It enjoyed rapidly improving road and rail communications, and experienced an increasingly close relationship with London for capital and enterprise. It was not the increasingly isolated social and cultural cul-de-sac that it became in the twentieth century, but very much exposed to national and international inter-actions and experiences. There was no reason—other than the unusually rapid rate of industrial decline—why its experience should have differed significantly from other areas.

So far, attention has been given to looking at how Freemasonry in Cornwall attracted increasing numbers of members at a time of significant regional economic decline and emigration. During the second half of the nineteenth century it greatly widened its geographical footprint and, notwithstanding concerns about 'dilution' of the quality of members, deepened its involvement in many of the major urban centres, largely in the west of the county. More men than ever were prepared to commit their time and money to active involvement in a widening range of lodges, chapters, encampments and fraternal groups which were being generated and promoted from outside of the region. Consideration will now be given to who those men were and why they may have been motivated to join the Order and stay within it.

CHAPTER 3

THE ECONOMIC AND SOCIAL STRUCTURE OF CORNISH CRAFT LODGES AND SIDE ORDERS

This chapter will examine the kinds of men that became members of Cornish Masonic lodges. It will start by looking at Craft lodges, the basic building blocks of the Order, and then move on to look at the main side orders, Cornish Lodge in London and the PGL of Cornwall. It will consider the age, occupational and social structure of the membership, while also considering its incidence within local communities. Aggregate estimates will be made as well as indications of differences between lodges. Consideration of the principal side orders will focus on the degree to which they differed from Craft lodges and how they may have complemented the overall operation and impact of Masonry in the county. Cornish Lodge No. 2369, meeting in Mark Masons' Hall in London, provided a venue for Cornish Masons visiting or resident in London, and its members included an elite group that played a central role in directing the affairs of the PGL. This chapter will look at those who joined Masonry in Cornwall and those who played the central role in directing its affairs and development.

Craft Lodges

The analysis of lodge membership conducted here is based on the thirteen craft lodges in West Cornwall and has been based primarily on their Grand Lodge returns,[1] supported by access to some of the lodges' own records. A database of their membership has been constructed for a period approximating to the second half of the nineteenth century. Some lodges were not warranted until later in the century, and for some others, slightly earlier data also has been included. The database includes over 4,200 names, but there is a considerable amount of double counting as men joined multiple lodges or moved between them. Unfortunately, thorough editing of multiple returns is complicated by slight differences in the names given, similar names for different people, repeated names for different generations, etc., and the data has been left largely unchanged.

Age Structure

Twenty-one was usually considered the minimum age for initiation as a Mason but exceptions were sometimes made for 'lewises', or the sons of Masons. It was, however, rare. Because of the expense of receiving the three degrees, most men did not seek membership until their late twenties and early thirties, when they would have been approaching their peak earning capacity. The information available in the lodge returns relates only to the age at initiation. It has, unfortunately, not been possible to track the average number of years that initiates remained as members. It has therefore also not been possible to calculate the average age of all members across the lodges and how it may have changed over time. However, as Table 7 shows, most men applied to become Masons in their late twenties and early thirties, though large cohorts also joined in their early twenties and late thirties. Although many—perhaps most—of those that joined also remained Masons for many years and the average age cohort was well over forty, very few sought, or were accepted, for membership after age forty-five.

Occupational Structure

Occupational data also relates to profession given at time of initiation and there might well have been career progression during periods of membership. From those giving details of their occupations in the thirteen lodges, the membership was drawn mainly from the ranks of the professions (accountants, architects, barristers and solicitors, doctors, dentists and surgeons, clergymen, engineers and surveyors: 707) and senior managers (mine and other agents, bank managers, various superintendents and master mariners: 651), supported by those in trade (auctioneers, chemists and druggists, dealers and drapers,

Table 7   Age Distribution of Craft Lodge Members on Initiation or Joining

Age Group	No. of Members
Under 21	12
21–24	423
25–29	713
30–34	606
35–39	412
40–44	215
45–49	145
50–54	65
55–59	32
60 and over	12

chandlers and merchants of every description: 511), and food and hospitality (keepers of hotels, inns and restaurants, brewers, confectioners and victuallers: 177). Taken together these groups accounted for over half of the recorded membership: 2,046 of the 3,991 providing occupations. Most of the others were drawn from among skilled artisans (assayers, blacksmiths, butchers, carpenters, cabinet makers, coopers, founders, mariners and pilots, painters, shipwrights, stonemasons, and tailors: 338), miners (miners, dressers, smelters: 344), white-collar workers (agents, clerks and secretaries, commercial travellers, journalists, railway staff, teachers, and telegraphists: 302) and public sector workers and the military (local and central government employees, and officers and NCOs: 148). These eight occupational groups accounted for more than three-quarters of the total recorded membership (see Appendix 4).

Breaking the numbers down by location, the coastal lodges were dominated by mariners and associated maritime trades, while most of the members of the inland lodges were miners, mine managers, and associated craft and service professions. Thus in Boscawen Lodge No. 699, half of the 315 members that gave their profession between 1863 and 1899 were directly employed in mining as mine managers and miners, while in Fowey Lodge No. 977 the same proportion of the 229 members gave their occupation as mariner, ship builder, ships carpenter or sailmaker.

The Incidence of Masonic Membership Within Occupations and Communities
Although the thirteen lodges drew members from most sectors of their local economies they were far from representing all of those sectors. Women were not permitted to become Masons and all of the activities in which they predominated, such as dressmaking and millinery, were excluded.[2] Of the many thousands of men that would have been employed in domestic or other service sector activities, only one butler, one coachman, one bailiff, and three waiters ever became lodge members. The very numerous unskilled manufacturing and extractive labour force was equally invisible, with just three 'labourers' and two 'carriers'. Fishermen are almost entirely absent as were fishmongers. There were no lodging housekeepers and very few grocers and shopkeepers, compared with the large numbers that were appearing in all towns by the last decades of the century. Even when a significant number from a particular occupation do appear, they often represent only a minute fraction of the total employed in the region. Thus, miners and master mariners appear in large numbers in several lodges but they were only a small portion of the men that pursued those occupations in the locality. Similarly, nearly a hundred members listed themselves as farmers or yeomen but that was hardly representative of their overall total.

Other agricultural activities, such as milling and dairying, hardly appear at all among the members of these essentially urban institutions. Even the substantial quantity of keepers of inns and hotels diminish in importance compared with the very large numbers offering those services in every town and village across Cornwall.

By contrast, members of the professions appear to have been far more interested in membership. A rough quantitative measure of the 'incidence of Masonry' among these groups can be derived by comparing lodge members with those listed in local directories. The directories were not totally inclusive of all trades in the towns but they give a general guide. Kelly's *Directory of Cornwall* of 1883 provides a useful midway view of the county during the period under discussion and has been used to estimate Masonic involvement among various groups. In that year, just less than half of the solicitors listed in Truro (six out of thirteen) were members of local Masonic lodges and seven of the twenty-one accountants noticed in all of the major towns of West Cornwall had also joined. Three of the four surgeons in Helston were Masons and six of the eleven physicians and surgeons practicing in Falmouth and Fowey belonged to local lodges, two of them in partnership with the few non-Masons. In the coastal towns, locally based maritime professionals, such as port and channel pilots, joined in large numbers, while inland, mining engineers and mine managers found lodge membership attractive. Thus, eight of the twenty-eight pilots working out of Falmouth in the early 1880s became members of the Lodge of Love and Honour while almost a third of the assayers working across Cornwall were members of West Cornwall lodges. Mine agents appear to have been particularly keen to join Masonic lodges and thirteen of the twenty-four mine agents listed in Redruth became members of Druids Lodge. Taking Kelly's list of the 157 mining companies operating across Cornwall, more than a third had one or more Masons as part of their managerial team (see Appendix 5). These included some of the largest mining operations in Cornwall and together they accounted for almost half of the country's total tin output in 1883[3], equivalent to just less than a tenth of world production in that year. Mostly the lodge members took the position of agent or purser. The latter were the chief financial officers and those that took such posts also listed themselves as accountants. Overall, it would appear that men involved in positions of trust and seeking financial networks were those that were most likely to seek membership.

In the same way that the 'incidence' of Masonic membership varied between different occupations and professions, it also differed between communities. Membership of a lodge was most common among the commercial classes of small towns and less so in larger communities, though their influence may have been equally strong. For example, eighteen of the fifty-three male 'commercial' entries for Chacewater in 1883 were members of Boscawen Lodge and twelve of the fifty-six entries for St Day. They included the keepers of some of the main hotels in both towns, as well as a range of different tradesmen, craftsmen and professions. By comparison, the members of lodges in larger towns, such as Penzance, Falmouth and Truro, were only a tiny part of a very much larger commercial population. However, they often filled important and influential roles within the town. In Penzance, for example, four members of the Mount Sinai Lodge—Frederick Jasper, William Mitchell, Thomas Reynolds and James Runnalls—were councillors of the City Corporation in 1883 and one, Francis Boase, a retiring Alderman.

Religion
No details of religious affiliation were given at initiation or in annual returns, but in principle it would seem likely that Freemasons reflected the general pattern of church membership in Cornwall. Some impression of this was given in the religious census of England and Wales, conducted in March 1851.[4] In that year, the county was one of the most religious in the country, with over 78% of the population attending a service on the census Sunday. Since membership of Freemasonry was dependent on professing a belief in God, it was likely that the great majority of Masons were among those worshippers. Although there were many different denominations active locally, over 70% were Anglican or Wesleyan Methodists, with the latter being in a substantial majority. In the very broadest terms, roughly one out of every three worshippers was Anglican and two out of three were Dissenters of one description or another.[5] It would seem logical to conclude that this balance may have been reflected in the allegiances of Masons, though possibly a considerably greater proportion leant towards Anglicanism overall. Given the propensity of the middle class to tend towards Anglicanism and the working class towards Methodism, it would also seem likely that this distribution was reflected within Masonry, with those lodges heavily dominated by middle-class members having a greater share of Anglicans and those with proportionately higher numbers of working-class members, including more Methodists and those of other dissenting sects, such as the Baptists.

However, it is important to observe that a large number of the dissenting churches held strong views against Masonry and this may have minimised their membership. For example, in 1869 the East Gennesser Methodist Episcopal Church Conference passed a resolution disapproving of Masonry on several grounds. Firstly, it created disaffection and division in charges and churches.

Secondly, it did not aid 'religiosity' and was derogatory to a holy ministry. Thirdly, it held out preference, position or gain as an incentive to become a Mason, either directly or indirectly. Fourthly, it 'ejected' the name of Christ. Fifthly, it brought Christians into juxtaposition instead of affinity with all classes of men, whatever their business, religion or nation. Sixthly, Masonic love and sympathy took precedence over the love of Christ. Seventhly, Masonic oaths were not reconcilable with laws of morality, Christianity, or the Lord.[6] Although not binding on all, such attitudes among the Wesleyans, New Connexion, Primitive Methodists, Bible Christians, Wesleyan Methodist Association, Teetotal Wesleyans and some other smaller sects thriving in Cornwall during the period[7] is likely have shifted the balance very considerably in favour of Anglicans. Similarly, many Anglicans took a poor view of dissenters and would not easily have welcomed them to their lodges. Certainly there was little ecumenical brotherhood when the Provincial Grand Lodge met in St Mary's Church, Truro, in July 1870. The vicar of the church read the prayers, the vicar of Par read the first lesson, the vicar of St Day the second lesson and the vicar of St Blaizey preached.[8] Nevertheless, dissenters were certainly not entirely absent. Cornubian Lodge counted two Wesleyan clergymen among its members in the 1870s and 1880s, and one of them—the Rev. Richard Kennedy—was installed as Master in 1880.[9] Several lodges had difficulties from dissenters and other teetotallers over the inclusion of the costs of drink in lodge dining fees and there was some quite widespread ill-feeling over the raising of funds for the building of Truro Cathedral.[10] An inspection of the names of lodge members reveals a few, but not many, Jews. Men such as Moses, Samuel, and Levi Jacobs (jeweller, watchmaker and mineralogist respectively), Israel Oppenheim (merchant), Abraham Jacobwich (gentleman) and Israel Levin (jeweller), became members of lodges in the larger more cosmopolitan towns such as Falmouth and Penzance. Overall, Freemasonry did not fairly represent the general distribution of religious affiliation in Cornwall but it equally was not simply an Anglican Order.

Residence
Information in lodge returns on the residence of lodge members is usually restricted simply to the name of the town or nearest hamlet. Street addresses were occasionally given but not sufficiently frequently or comprehensively to analyse the distribution of members within towns. As the list of professions indicates, the great majority were urban dwellers with relatively very few farmers or rural members. Most Masons belonged to the lodge in the town where they lived and, when there was more than one, divided themselves by occupation or by other interest or social group. Even when railways and improved road

transport facilitated movement between towns, few ventured far from their home base. Similarly, the advent of street lighting may have made it easier and safer to move about during the hours of darkness, but most lodges continued to meet on the night of the full moon.

Although this was the generality, every lodge had at least a few members living at some distance from West Cornwall, either nationally or internationally. Lodges with a large number of mariners, such as Love and Honour in Falmouth, counted the most out-of-district members. Love and Honour had members giving their primary residence in a number of major ports in eastern England— such as Harwich, Hull, Shields and Kings Lynn—as well as numerous overseas maritime centres, largely in the Baltic, Scandinavia and the Netherlands. Lodges with a large number of mining members, such as Boscawen, Mount Edgcumbe, Druids and Tregenna had members giving a home base in North America, Mexico, New Zealand or South Africa. Commercial travellers and railway staff gave every lodge a connection with London and shorter distance itinerants linked many with Plymouth, south coast ports such as Poole and cities in South Wales. A constant progression of visitors from other parts of the country and beyond also saved local members from becoming too parochial. Whereas today West Cornwall is a communications cul-de-sac, during the age of sail it was a vibrant point of transit as the first and last point of Europe, with much of the transatlantic trade in people touching or passing through it.

Social Structure

It is usual to take indications of social class from occupations. This, however, is a highly hazardous process. Firstly, the occupational markers were those given at the beginning of a Masonic career and not what they became later in life. Secondly, generic occupational names often disguise a wide range of income and status positions and, when dealing with a long time period, the status of some occupations might change significantly. For example, 'builder' or 'contractor' could mean an unskilled labourer or the owner of a large construction firm; 'brewer' or 'iron founder' could equally be applied to the owner of the establishment or simply a skilled worker; a 'master mariner' could be the captain of a small coastal vessel with a crew of two or three, or a large blue-water merchantman; 'merchant' could mean almost anything. In a similar way the economic and social status of several professions changed significantly between the middle and end of the century. Many 'surgeons' were little more than sawbones early in the century but most developed more advanced skills following the introduction of chloroform anaesthetics from the 1850s. Similarly, the increasingly complex affairs of expanding banks, public utilities and large manufacturing and natural resource enterprises elevated 'accountants' from little more than overblown bookkeepers early in the nineteenth century to essential consultants and senior managers by its end. 'Engineers' needed to master a rapidly growing and increasingly specialised body of knowledge, elevating many from little more than engine minders to become a technological elite that provided the backbone of Britain's industrial and imperial supremacy by the death of Victoria.

The problems are further compounded by regional variations in class relationship. In many respects, Cornwall was in the forefront of the changes of the industrial revolution, helping to pioneer steam engineering and large-scale industrial organisations, but it also remained an isolated and in some respects a more homogeneous and socially integrated community than those found in the Midlands and north of England. In particular, the dominant mining sector provided opportunities for career progression and social elevation rarely seen elsewhere. Until the very end of the century, when graduates of new mining schools began to appear in the industry, all mine captains and most mining engineers were 'apprentice trained', rising from the ranks of able working miners.[11] The potential for such earnings and class mobility also suggests that lodges may have seen significant upward social drift from the status indicated by the occupation of members on initiation.

Given this range of difficulties, it has not been thought appropriate strictly to adopt any of the occupational and social stratification systems used by other authors.[12] Instead a loose system has been devised based on impressions of property ownership, managerial responsibility, the nature of work conducted and the level of skill employed. It will have been noticed that the list of occupations given in Appendix 4 have been divided into five groups:

- *Category I* is the highest social group, consisting of gentlemen and the owners of land and the owners of property. Senior clergy and commissioned officers are also included.
- *Category II* is principally professional, managerial, retail and services.
- *Category III (N)* is skilled non-manual employees.
- *Category III (M)* is skilled manual employees.
- *Category IV* is semi-skilled employees.

No unskilled lodge members were identified, except possibly some of those placed in the semi-skilled category. Clearly many occupations can be moved between these groups but, as will be seen,[13] it does not significantly affect the overall conclusion about the social complexion of the lodges.

The immediate impression suggested by this range of occupations and class markers is that the Masonic lodges of West Cornwall recruited their members

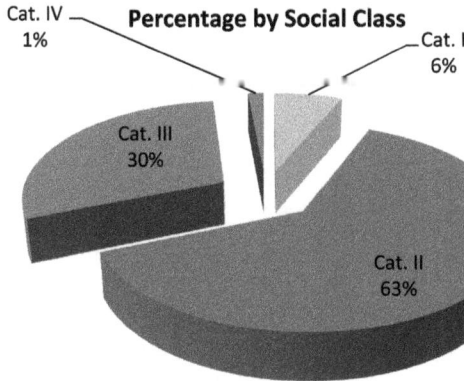

Percentage by Social Class

Cat. IV 1%

Cat. I 6%

Cat. III 30%

Cat. II 63%

Figure 3   The Membership of Thirteen West Cornwall Lodges by Social Class: Upper, Middle, Skilled Working and Semi-Skilled Working (see Appendix 4)

from across a very wide range of the community, from the gentry to the semi-skilled working class. Only the very poorest unskilled occupational groups appear to have been excluded, and then only probably because they could not afford membership rather than clear rules of social exclusivity. The lodges accordingly provided a platform for a cross-class dialogue in an increasingly segregated Victorian society,[14] and perhaps helped to ameliorate the increasing class conflict that afflicted many other parts of the country.[15] However, while there was a high degree of social mixing, the lodges as a whole were dominated by middle-class groups of professionals, managers, and men with small businesses in trade and retail services; the number of wealthier, property-owning upper-class members was relatively small (see Figure 3). This probably reflects the nature of the West Cornwall economy, with its pattern of relatively small-scale landownership, poor agriculture and absentee ownership of most of the larger and more profitable mines.

The picture was not uniform everywhere, however, and there were significant differences between individual lodges in the incidence of upper- and lower-working-class groups. While the lodges in major urban service and retail centres, such as Truro and Penzance, included a particularly large proportion of middle- and upper-class men, those in smaller mining and engineering towns, such as Chacewater and St Day, saw an equal and sometimes larger number of craftsmen, miners and other blue-collar workers. It is notable, however, that some of the most 'middle-class' lodges, such as Love and Honour, also had numerically large numbers of working-class members (see Table 8 and Figure 4). This suggests that, notwithstanding the difficult economic conditions in Cornwall at the end

Table 8   Lodge Membership Sub-divided by Social Class

Lodge	I	II	III	IV
Boscawen	6	138	176	4
Cornubian	22	250	52	4
Druids	6	244	122	5
Fortitude	20	253	102	5
Fowey	17	165	46	2
Love & Hon.	48	372	150	5
Mt Sinai	47	201	89	11
Mt Edgcumbe	7	159	66	7
Phoenix	46	190	39	4
Three G.P.	6	127	45	1
Tregenna	6	114	83	1
Tregullow	7	125	128	3
True & F.	17	135	56	2

of the century, many working men were able to acquire the surplus capital and income necessary to become, and remain, Masons.

There were two probable reasons for this. Firstly, although economic conditions in the county were difficult with the sharp contraction of mining, the high level of migration enabled wage rates to be sustained. Secondly, for miners, the largest section of the working-class cohort, the 'Cornish system of employment', which operated in all mines until the early twentieth century,[16] frequently enabled skilled and hardworking miners to share in fortunate changes in the structure and richness of lodes and to accumulate a small amount of savings. This might also explain significant fluctuations in the numbers of working-class men joining Masonry over time. During good economic conditions they were able to accumulate capital which could be drawn on to seek and subsidise Masonic membership when conditions deteriorated and they decided that they needed greater support and improved advantages. For example, during the period of moderate prosperity in West Cornwall 1860–64 just seventy-two working-class men were initiated while in the very difficult years 1872–76 that number tripled to 210 initiates. Similarly, during the mild prosperity of the period 1883 to 1887 initiations fell to eighty-two but picked up to 222 during the crisis years of 1895 to 1899. These issues will be discussed further below.

It is notable that these conclusions from the analysis of the membership of thirteen lodges in no way diverge from those suggested in earlier work, using a slightly different occupational class classification for just six lodges.

Fortitude, Truro   Mt. Sinai, Penzance

Boscawen, Chacewater   Tregullow, St. Day

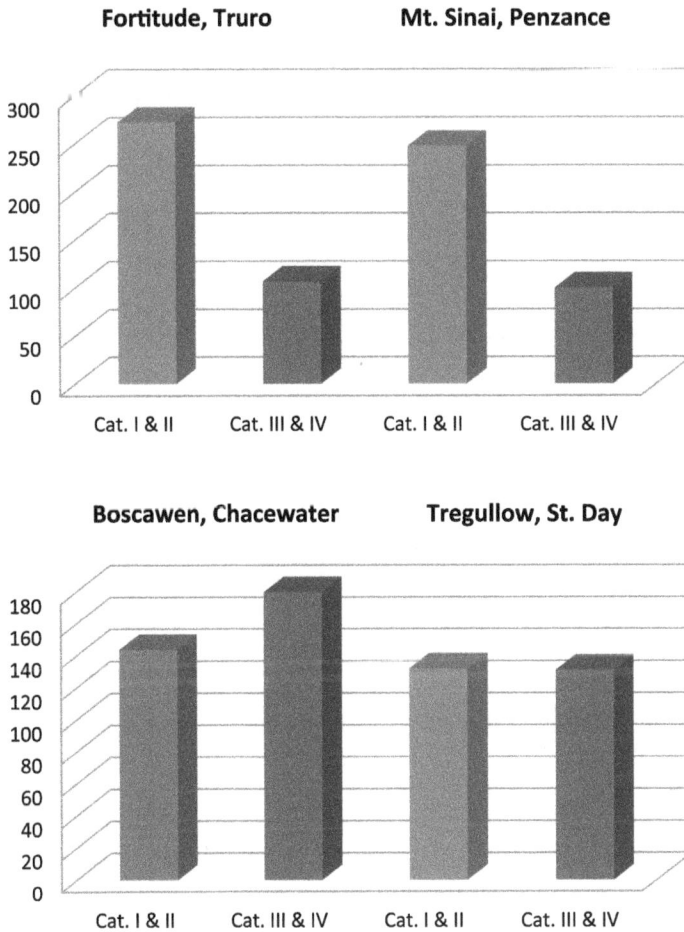

Figure 4   Differences in the Class Structure of Two Cornish Lodges

They re-emphasise the middle-class domination of Freemasonry but clearly indicate that it also had a large—sometimes very large—upper-working-class membership.[17] As previously observed, this picture differs from that commonly painted by historians. It does not, for example, match with Gorsky's view of Freemasonry being generally based on horizontal social ties, or with Tosh's description of the fraternity as socially exclusive. Indeed, it begins to look more like a part of the wider, socially inclusive fraternal and benevolent movement than an exception to it.

However, the question clearly arises, was the experience in West Cornwall significantly different from that of the rest of the country? It has not been possible to conduct the same depths of research as for Cornwall, but a good impression can be gained from an examination of membership lists published in lodge histories for various parts of the country as well as reference to lodge records. The picture that emerges is very similar to that in Cornwall with some lodges almost exclusively middle- and upper-class but equally some others with a very mixed social group. Again, like Cornwall, the latter seem to be more common in the newer and smaller industrial towns of the north of England than in the larger and more established regional service centres. For example, for most of the second half of the nineteenth century Union Lodge No. 52 in Norwich and the Lodge of Probity No. 61 in Halifax, Yorkshire, were almost exclusively middle- or upper-class, while Lodge of Peace No. 149 in Meltham, Yorkshire, recruited almost a third of its new members from the upper working class. They included tradesmen such as carpenters, painters, joiners, plasterers, slaters, plumbers and mechanics, as well as factory workers such as spinners and warehousemen, and clerks, bookkeepers and schoolteachers.[18] In the 1850s and 1860s, Lodge of Friendship No. 277, in Oldham, East Lancashire, recruited plumbers, joiners, mechanics and clerks as well as large numbers of cotton spinners.[19] In the 1880s Blackwater Lodge No. 1997 in Maldon, Essex, had a principally middle-class membership but also recruited two decorators, a stonemason, a bootmaker, two clerks, a mariner, three butchers, three musicians, three stewards, two customs officers and several army sergeants.[20] The situation was again the same in Bedford Lodge No. 282 in Tavistock, Devon, where they recruited the likes of clerks, miners, commercial travellers, stonemasons and silversmiths, messengers and gardeners, stokers, fitters and bricklayers throughout the second half of the century.[21] From the complaints often heard in PGLs about 'unsuitable' men being introduced into Masonry[22] and the Masters of lodges being instructed to raise their standards, it might be assumed that the numbers of working-class members were increasing everywhere. In other places, however, there appears to have been a reverse process of lodge membership drifting upwards from a less to a more socially exclusive group. Weinbren has shown, for example, how the membership of Philanthropic Lodge No. 107 meeting in King's Lynn, Norfolk, gradually changed from having numerous artisans and mariners in the first part of the century to an increasing number of gentlemen, bank managers and merchants during its latter decades.[23]

The only clear conclusion about the social structure of Masonic lodge membership is that it was—as it still is—extremely variable between lodges, reflecting the social composition of its host community. It was never generally socially exclusive except for the very lowest social classes whose occupations generally did not produce the surplus family funds to enable them to become Masons. When they occasionally did have the financial resources, the gardeners, stewards, waiters, labourers, servants, etc., could often find a home somewhere. It is important to note, however, that at its higher institutional levels, Masonry was run by a social elite of upper- and upper-middle-class members.

Side Orders

As might be expected for non-essential 'add-ons' for craft Masonry which could only be accessed at additional expense after becoming a fully initiated Master Mason, the numbers joining the side orders were much lower than those in Craft lodges; the men were older and were drawn from the better off. From Royal Arch Chapter returns and Mark registers it has been possible to identify 561 members of the fourteen Royal Arch Chapters in West Cornwall between 1846 and 1900 and 688 members of the thirteen Mark lodges. There is again a certain amount of double counting in these numbers because many men became members of both orders.

The average age of those joining the Royal Arch Chapters was thirty-seven years,[24] compared with an average of thirty-two years for those joining Craft lodges.[25] No ages were given in the Mark returns but it might be expected that they would be similar to Royal Arch. The membership of both Royal Arch and Mark was more upper- and middle-class than that of Craft lodges. In Mark, their share of the total membership was 75% compared with 69% in Craft and in Royal Arch it was higher again at 80% (see Figure 5). The upper- and middle-class groups were dominated by gentlemen, military officers and property owners, together with professionals such as accountants, solicitors, surgeons and merchants. There were numerous mine agents, managers, engineers, etc., but their number was probably relatively small compared with their membership of some Craft lodges. Clergymen appear to have joined the side orders in comparatively large numbers. There were some groups, however, that were singularly under-represented, most notably the Master Mariners. There were just eight in Royal Arch and six in Mark, with one out of each being the same man (see Figure 5).

While the side orders were dominated by middle-class members, it is notable they all continued to include significant numbers of working-class men, both white- and blue-collar. There were the usual cashiers and clerks together with butchers, smiths, plumbers and painters, as well as a few waiters, stewards, gardeners and railway guards. However, by comparison with Craft lodges there were remarkably few miners: there were just six in Royal Arch and twenty-one in Mark. Seven of these described themselves as 'gold miners', suggesting a return from a profitable episode overseas. Like the Craft lodges, the working-class

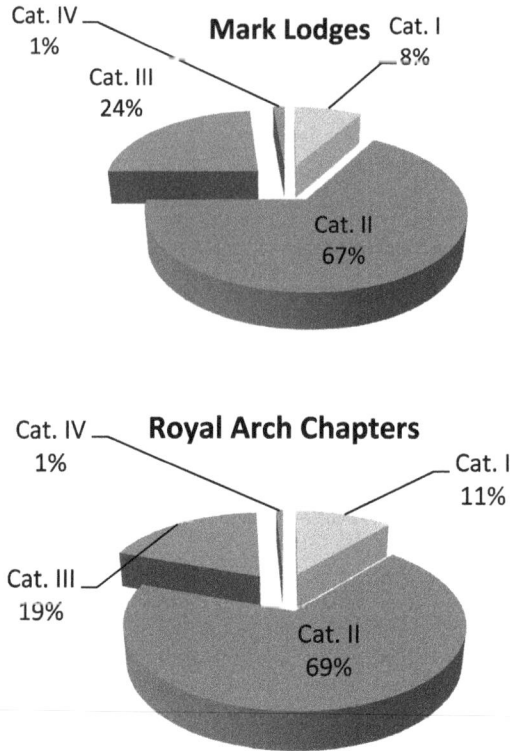

Figure 5   Social Categories of the Membership of Mark Lodges
and Royal Arch Chapters in Cornwall

membership of the side orders reflected differences in the middle-class/working-class balance of their host communities, with the larger city chapters and lodges being proportionately more middle-class and the smaller industrial towns more working-class. Thus only 16% of the members of Royal Cornubian Chapter in Truro declared working-class occupations (mainly white-collar), while 25% of Rose of Sharon Chapter, meeting in St Day and later Redruth, had such a background. This was largely because they drew around three-quarters of their members from the predominantly working-class mining lodges of Boscawen in Chacewater and Tregullow in St Day.[26] Similarly in Mark, Fortitude Lodge, meeting in Truro, had only a 18% working-class membership, compared with Boscawen Lodge, meeting in St Day, where it stood at 36%. When looking at the working-class membership of the side orders, it is important to emphasise that membership of the side orders brought few practical benefits beyond what had already been gained by joining Craft lodges. This suggests that while costs may certainly have been an issue for many, large numbers of working men not only had the resources to devote to Masonry but also a strong commitment to its ritual and spiritual offerings. Nevertheless, the slightly higher percentage of working-class members in Mark probably reflect a level of price sensibility since it was generally regarded as less expensive than Royal Arch.

While the two largest side orders created an inner circle of more socially exclusive chapters and lodges, the two smallest—Rose Croix and the Knights Templar—were entirely dominated by upper- and middle-class leaders of Masonry in the Province. Cornwall Chapter No. 61 Rose Croix had a particularly select membership of just sixty-five over that period. The declared identity of fifty-eight of these shows that eight were gentlemen, including two senior military officers; twelve were professionals (surgeons, accountants and solicitors); nine were merchants; and five were clergymen. The others included a plantation owner, a ship owner, two grocers, an ironmonger, a hotel owner, a Master of a Workhouse and the local MP. William Hughan, giving his profession as a 'cloth merchant', but much better known as an eminent Masonic historian and commentator, was also a member. The majority of Cornwall Chapter members were recruited from the more middle-class lodges in Truro and Falmouth (twenty-five members), supported by a smaller number from Redruth and Hayle. It has not been possible to trace the membership of the Knights Templar but, as suggested above, it appears to have been less successful in attracting members and by the 1890s did not have the same elite status as Rose Croix.

The main contribution of the side orders to the institutional strength and efficiency of Freemasonry was that they brought together members of many different lodges and broke down local lodge insularity. They created a structure and an opportunity for wider regional dialogue in a county that was otherwise known for narrow parochialism.[27] As has just been seen, Cornwall Chapter Rose Croix recruited from a number of different Craft lodges. Royal Arch chapters threw their net even wider. Hayle Royal Arch Chapter, for example, drew numerous members from lodges in Chacewater, Camborne, Helston and Redruth, as well as occasional men from Penzance and St Ives. Royal Cornwall Chapter in Truro was more locally self-sufficient in its recruitment, taking the great majority of its members from Fortitude and Phoenix lodges, but it also saw incomers from Love and Honour and Three Grand Principles in nearby Falmouth and Penryn, as well as some from as far away as Helston, Redruth, St Day and Chacewater. Mark was less diverse, with the lodges in Redruth, Camborne and Penzance finding nearly all of their members locally, but Boscawen Mark Lodge in St Day pulled in members from a number of surrounding villages and towns, and Cornubian Mark Lodge in Hayle recruited from points as far apart as Penzance, St Ives and Camborne. Duplicate memberships of both Royal Arch chapters and Mark lodges prevented the two orders from drifting apart and consolidated their networking potential. No detailed estimate has been made of the overall level of joint membership but the Masonic career of the Reverend William Henry Bloxsome, Rector of Mawgan, provides a good example. During the 1870s and 1880 he was a member of various Craft lodges as well as the Rose of Sharon and Hayle Royal Arch chapters, and Cornubian Mark Lodge. Similarly Sir Frederick Martin Williams, the MP for Truro between 1865 and 1878, no doubt found it politically useful to be a member of Rose of Sharon Royal Arch chapter and Meridian Mark Lodge as well as Boscawen, Tregullow, Three Grand Principles, Phoenix, Fortitude and Druids craft lodges. Both Bloxsome and Williams were also members of Cornwall Rose Croix Chapter.

Cornish Lodge No. 2369

When it comes to the drawing together of disparate parts of Cornish Masonry and the emergence of platforms for broader county-wide discussions, Cornish Lodge, warranted in 1890 and meeting at Mark Masons' Hall in London, played a strategic role. It occasionally initiated new members but most were established Master Masons, either resident or regularly visiting London, drawn from lodges across the county. Most came from the larger West Cornwall lodges, with Love and Honour, Mount Sinai and Mount Edgcumbe being particularly well represented, though many others came from Newquay, Liskeard, Padstow and particularly Bodmin and St Austell. Of its hundred or so members during the 1890s the great majority were upper- and middle-class, though it did include a few students, teachers, commercial travellers, clerks, etc. The membership included many of the county's elite, such as Earl Mount Edgcumbe, Sir Walter Molesworth St Aubyn (the MP for Helston 1880–85), Edward Carus-Wilson (a banker), and Sir Charles Graves-Sawle (the MP for Bodmin 1852–57). The most well known, however, was John Passmore Edwards, sometime MP for Salisbury, but also owner and editor of the *Echo* newspaper and eminent philanthropist, founding more than seventy public libraries, reading rooms, hospitals, homes, etc.

London Masonry also gave access to other London lodges with their myriad of national and international business connections. For example, Peter Watson, a major source of capital and financial expertise for Cornish and Devonian mining throughout the second half of the nineteenth century, was a member of Fitzroy Lodge No. 569, meeting at the headquarters of the Honourable Artillery Company in the City (see Illustration 2). Similarly, Charles Algernon

Illustration 2   Peter Watson, Mine Investor

23 July 1839 to 16 April 1911. One of the most important British metal mining investors of the late nineteenth and early twentieth centuries. He was reputed to have held shares in over 250 mines across Britain and was a director of many of the largest, including Grenville and Condurrow tin mines in Cornwall, Devon Great Consols copper mine, Roman Gravels and Tankerville lead mines in Shropshire, Van lead mine in Wales, Great Laxey Silver/lead mines in the Isle of Man, and Leadhills lead mine in Scotland. Watson was a long-time member and Past Master of Fitzroy Lodge No. 569, which met in the headquarters of the fashionable Honourable Artillery Company in the City of London and he devoted considerable energy to municipal affairs including local boards, district and county councils. He was a Justice of the Peace for Middlesex and presided weekly on the Brentford bench.

Moreing, a partner in the great Bewick, Moreing international mining consultancy, was a member of Westminster and Keystone Lodge No. 10[28] from the 1880s as well as the Royal Colonial Institute Lodge No. 3556 with its numerous links throughout the Empire. In the difficult years of the slump following the Great War, Moreing was to become the saviour of Cornish mining through his re-organisation and skilled management of the important East Pool mine. C. Algernon Moreing's son, Algernon H. Moreing, also became a member of the Royal Colonial Institute Lodge. He gradually took over from his father in the Bewick, Moreing partnership and the management of their Cornish businesses and became widely known and well connected in Cornwall. He was elected as the MP for the mid-Cornwall mining district in the early 1920s.

Whatever their personal or political activities in London, the members of Cornish Lodge played a strategic role in facilitating an increasing movement of capital from London to the South West. Although Cornwall, like other parts of the country, was largely self-sufficient in the supply of its capital requirements, the mining sector had become increasingly reliant on inflows of funds for both fixed investment and working capital in deep copper and tin mines from the earliest years of the century. Carus-Wilson's Miners Bank, with its interests in dozens of mines across Cornwall, helped to bring investors and borrowers together while the experience and personal connections of others opened Cornwall to London and the world. A short autobiography of Arthur Hodge, who joined the Lodge in the late 1890s, illustrates those contacts well. Having joined lodges in Redruth and St Austell early in his career, he had recently reported on and managed mines in several parts of South Africa and India, working for German investors and various 'Pittsburgh magnates' among others.[29] Levels of interpersonal trust, heightened by widespread investor Masonic membership, could have a similar influence to effective legal protection in favouring investment decisions.[30] Flying an influential flag for Cornwall in the capital was not merely useful for the county's Freemasonry.

Very few of Cornish Lodge's members held membership of Royal Arch or Mark in Cornwall but at least nine were members of Cornwall Chapter Rose Croix. The links between the two, and the stature of many of these members, gave this lodge and chapter great influence within the PGL of Cornwall and even the UGLE. All but two of the members of Cornish Lodge at some point held major active rank in the PGL of Cornwall and at least two were promoted to the UGLE. For example, when Earl Mount Edgcumbe was PGM of Cornwall as well as Deputy Grand Master of the Grand Lodge of England, the meetings of the PGL in the 1890s were usually conducted in Mount Edgcumbe's absence by Sir Charles Graves-Sawle as his Deputy, assisted by Edward Anderton, the

Provincial Grand Secretary. For their services those two were then also appointed to offices in the UGLE.[31] Those that were involved in other side orders often also held Grand Rank in them. Thus, Major S.H. Clerke served as a Sub-Prior within the Knights Templar Grand Priory of England.

Provincial Grand Lodge of Cornwall

The harmonious working and regulation of the numerous lodges and chapters within Cornwall was regulated by the PGL, the Provincial Grand Chapter and the Provincial Mark Grand Lodge. They had been delegated the authority to do so by the UGLE, the Supreme Grand Chapter of Royal Arch Masons of England, Grand Lodge of Mark Master Masons, all of which were based in London. The central bodies had the sole authority to issue warrants to lodges and chapters, without which they were considered 'irregular' organisations and would be excluded from all communications with regular Freemasonry. The metropolitan Grand Lodges/Chapter and their county-based provincial subsidiaries regulated the conduct of the thousands of lodges and chapters across the country, ensuring that they maintained standard forms of organisation, procedures, ritual, etc. Unlike local lodges, Provincial Grand Lodges/Chapters did not conduct the usual business of admitting and initiating new Masons, and the workings of the lodge through the practice of ritual. They rarely had a home lodge room of their own, preferring to be peripatetic and rotate their meetings around the various constituent members. Meetings were essentially ceremonial events, often involving public processions, church services and other public displays (see Illustration 3). They took the form of large assemblages that mainly agreed decisions taken by Grand Officers and various subcommittees. Attention was cast broadly on the overall progress of Masonry within their jurisdiction, the resolution of disputes, the maintenance of proper procedures, the raising of levies on lodges and their members, and the implementation of new directives from the Grand Lodge in London. PGMs constantly called upon the Masters of lodges to maintain the 'quality' of the men they admitted as an essential prerequisite for all other issues and they usually received, and congratulated themselves upon, the details of charity given and how it was dispersed.

Unlike ordinary lodges and chapters that ran on a very democratic basis— voting on the introduction of new members and the progress of Master Masons through the various offices of the lodges/chapters—the PGLs, like the UGLE, were self-appointing and autocratic. While the most lowly artisan or clerical worker might join and progress through to the Master's chair of his own lodge—often assuming offices that gave them lodge status and powers

Illustration 3   Church Parade in Redruth, Cornwall

Members of Druids Lodge of Love and Librality, escorted by a military band and watched by their wives and the general public, prepare to take their banner into St Matthew's parish church in Redruth, probably in the autumn of 1912. This was one of the oldest lodges in Cornwall and had seen periods when membership fell to low levels but at that time it was going through a major resurgence with active recruitment and a large number of members. This photograph was used in a display of the history of the Lodge in Redruth Masonic Hall.

well above ordinary upper-class members—the affairs of Grand Lodges were retained firmly in the hands of the middle- and upper-class elite. Lodges and Chapters might recommend members to be elevated to Grand Lodge/Chapter membership, but they needed to be the 'right kind of man' to be selected by those that were already in position. The evidence for this can be found in the choice, and manner of appointing, the PGM and his active officers in the PGL.[32]

The Cornish PGM at the beginning of the period considered here was Sir Charles Lemon, Bt, the fifth appointment to the position, who held it from 1844 to 1863. The previous occupant of the Chair had been Sir John St Aubyn, who had held it from 1785 but who died in 1839 with no clear successor. A quick search was made for a suitably eminent person and an offer was made to Sir Charles who was not at that time a Mason. Four temporary annual appointments were made while he was prepared for the position. He was duly initiated in Love and Honour No. 75 in 1840, became a Warden in 1842, and Master of that Lodge in 1843. Later that same year he was appointed to the Provincial Chair and was installed in April 1844. Sir Charles was the son of a local family of minor gentry and followed his predecessor as the MP for Penryn early in the century. Following the Reform Bill of 1832, he became the independent MP for the West Cornwall constituency from 1832 until 1857. Also like his predecessor, he had a distinguished intellectual record as a Fellow of the Royal Society and he built on this at the national level as a founder of the Royal Statistical Society, as well as becoming an active President of the Royal Cornwall Polytechnic Society and the Royal Cornwall Geological Society. He gave Cornish Freemasonry what they wanted and needed in terms of access to the political and intellectual life of the country at the highest level.

On Sir Charles's retirement, Augustus Smith, took office as the Sixth PGM of Cornwall from 1862 until 1872. On this occasion, provision had been made for the succession. Smith had been initiated in Phoenix Lodge of Honour and Prudence in 1852, passed through the Provincial Senior Grand Warden's chair in 1854 and was installed as the Deputy Grand Master in 1856. During ensuing years he also became a member of various other lodges, including Fortitude and Love and Honour. By comparison with his predecessors, his reputation was far less distinguished when he took office. A successful London banker, he had only acquired his claim to local hierarchical status by purchasing a thirty-year lease of the Isles of Scilly from the Duchy of Cornwall for £20,000 in 1832. Setting himself up in Tresco Abbey, he cleared the population from many of the smaller islands and adopted the quasi-aristocratic title of 'Lord Proprietor'. He became President of the two local learned societies but failed to make any mark that would see his elevation to national fellowships. He did, however, briefly become the Liberal MP for Truro between 1857 and 1865, and he played an important part in the expansion of Masonry in Cornwall during these years, particularly in the development of the Masonic charities. He was a keen Mason but did little personally to exemplify its aspirations towards education and regular improvement in the arts and sciences.

Whereas St Aubyn, Lemon and Smith had been fortunate enough to preside over the development of Masonry during Cornwall's golden age of mining and engineering, the Seventh PGM, the Earl of Mount Edgcumbe, was to preside over a long period of economic decline and contraction from 1873 to 1917. Unlike his predecessor he played little direct part in Cornish freemasonry, never joining any of its lodges but also, unlike Smith, he was very successful in embedding himself into the London Masonic establishment and the Royal Court, becoming Deputy Grand Master of UGLE between 1891 and 1898, and a close companion of the Prince of Wales (the Grand Master) from an early age. In terms of his connections with, and access to, the seats of power in Britain, he was without doubt the most influential of the Cornish Grand Masters. Remarkably, he was almost another 'import' into the county. Although the family's seat, at Mount Edgcumbe, was marginally within Cornwall, his early Masonry was in London and Devon. He was initiated in the prestigious Westminster and Keystone Lodge No. 10 in London in 1856 and joined Sincerity Lodge in East Stonehouse, Plymouth, the following year. Just one year later he was appointed Provincial Grand Warden of Devonshire. Outside of Masonry he became the Deputy Lord Lieutenant of Devonshire and the Hon. Colonel of the 5th Battalion Devonshire Regiment. However, he always tried to ride two horses, both sides of the Tamar, and took office in a number of prestigious Cornish societies including the Presidency of Royal Cornwall Polytechnic Society and the Royal Cornwall Institution. However, no matter how much he was admired by the Cornish Masons and honoured through his appointment as Provincial Grand Master, he played very little part in the day-to-day Masonic affairs of the county. He never joined a craft lodge in Cornwall[33] and it was not until 1873 that he became a Royal Arch member in the county, joining Royal Cornwall Chapter in Truro.

Earl Mount Edgcumbe was regularly substituted at meetings of the PGL of Cornwall by his Deputy, Sir Charles Graves-Sawle. Unfortunately, Graves-Sawle was also not resident in the county, being a member of Cornish Lodge and residing in London, and had only a tenuous connection to Masonry in the county through his membership of Cornish Chapter Rose Croix. It was thus up to Mount Edgcumbe to carry the main burden of representing Cornwall which he did at some considerable distance. He maintained some public role there by becoming a standard-bearer for various Cornish scientific and intellectual societies but was little more than a glittering ornament for the Province's Freemasons. Perhaps it was this that enabled him to serve so long, and to so late in life, as PGM.

While Cornish Freemasonry effectively engaged semi-detached metropolitan-based figure heads to bring status, reputation and influence to their Order, its local administration was largely conducted by a relatively small group of middle-class men recruited primarily from middle-class lodges. It has not been possible to test this proposition for the whole of Cornwall, but again the thirteen lodges of West Cornwall provide good evidence (see Appendix 6). Of the fifty-six of their members that were given active rank in the PGL between 1890 and 1895 only nine gave a profession on their initiation that suggested they might have been of working-class status.

Close inspection suggests that the number may have been even smaller. For example, William Colenzo, who joined Mount Sinai in 1877, giving his occupation as painter, was in fact a prominent missionary, one-time MP in New Zealand and a leading botanist, elected as a Fellow of the Royal Society. Frederick Rodda and James Wearne were not employed operatives but owned their own significant printing and stationery businesses in the High Street, St Ives and Market Place, Penzance. Similarly, Edward Edwards, the hairdresser, appears to have operated his own business in George Street, Truro[34] and Charles Bryant, who declared as a bank cashier when he joined Phoenix Lodge in 1877, had almost certainly made career progress to be appointed Provincial Grand Treasurer in 1893. Schoolmasters stood on the cusp of the divide between working and middle class in the late nineteenth century, and only John Langdon, the gardener,[35] who took the most junior post of Provincial Grand Assistant Pursuivant, appears as an anomaly.

Clearly such observations do much to undermine the basis of the class divisions used so far in this discussion, but it should be noted that the majority of this small group were located in the particularly blurred area between social groups. What is most relevant is that there were no representatives of the many hundreds of miners, blacksmiths, carpenters, clerks, minor officials and the numerous other more clearly defined groups that had flocked to some lodges. Indeed, even many of the less commercial industrial middle class—such as mine agents, captains and engineers, as well as master mariners and maritime service trades—are conspicuous by their absence. This skewed focus from the PGL was also reflected in the relative representation of the various lodges. Thus while Fortitude and Phoenix lodges in Truro saw twelve of their members given active rank, Tregullow and Boscawen in St Ives and St Day saw only five members similarly honoured. Cornish Lodge in London produced more members than Mount Edgcumbe in Camborne (see Appendix 6).

Conclusion

The Lodge Secretaries' notices to Grand Lodge on new members provide a great deal of information of those *joining* Freemasonry, but there is little to indicate their progress, economically and socially, thereafter. The annual returns of all paid-up members of the lodge usually omitted such details, simply giving names arranged in order of seniority in the lodge. Occasionally notes were included on deaths, resignations and departures but this does not appear to have been done systematically. Only through the laborious process of comparing one annual return with another is it possible to trace the length of member's time in any given lodge and this has not been undertaken. It may be possible to glean further details of lodge members' changing occupations from the returns made by each lodge to the justices of the Quarter Sessions under the terms of the 1799 Unlawful Societies Act, but these unfortunately are not available for Cornwall.

It is very disappointing, therefore, that one of the key questions about the long-term effects of membership on Masons' careers cannot be answered. For some groups, such as craftsmen and professionals with limited occupational mobility, information on joining may be adequate, but for many others it may disguise major changes—changes that may have been facilitated by their Masonic identity. For example, progression from miner to mine captain; from innkeeper to hotel owner; from coastguard to chief officer. Notwithstanding these difficulties and the many potential errors in drawing any line between what might be described as the upper working class and the lower middle class, a very general attempt has been made to categorise lodge members socially in order to derive an impression of the role that Masonic lodges may have played in shaping local communities and influencing Victorian social development as a whole.

The first and most obvious observation is that the membership of Freemasonry was dominated by the upper and middle classes but also included large numbers of working-class members. Only the lowest labouring classes were excluded, and this because of their financial limitations rather than any class-based selective policy. Clearly, different lodges had different ideas about which groups they preferred, but nearly all contained a social spectrum with varying degrees of balance. When taking account of the role of side orders in bringing together members from many different lodges in different towns or parts of the same town, Masonry was bridging the class divisions of society and creating provision for progression both within and without the lodge. In other words it helped to undermine an old 'triadic' view of society inherited from the pre-industrial age, with clearly defined upper, middle and lower classes, and to blur divisions by acknowledging multiple gradations of rank and status.[36] In West Cornwall at least, it joined with other institutional 'webs of affiliation' such as Wesleyan Methodism and ritual-based benevolent societies like the Oddfellows, Foresters and Rechabites, to resist the divisive lures of Chartism and radical unionism.[37] In this new graduated society, the increasingly important division was that between the 'respectable' and the 'unrespectable'.[38] By definition, membership of a Masonic lodge was taken to convey respectability. Membership was only by invitation; only the most respectable might be proposed; the slightest question mark against their character would result in them being 'blackballed' by any two members of the lodge; anyone who transgressed against the law or Masonic regulations was thrown out; PGL kept constant watch to identify any slide in standards and called culprits to account. Freemasonry was acting as a tribune in an evolving world

However, things were not all as they might seem. The new age was not entirely open for meritocratic advancement. Contemporaries still spoke of 'two nations' and, like society as a whole, the Masonic pyramidal structure had its glass ceiling. Working- and lower-middle-class Masons might progress to the top of their lodge, but the side orders and small lodges for the elite created a system for the upper classes to retain control at both the regional and national levels. PGMs were neither elected by, nor nominated by, the common body of their membership but were appointed by the Grand Master of UGLE. This gave him and the senior officers of Grand Lodge important central governing powers and enabled them to cement close relationships with the landed gentry, aristocracy and royalty.[39] Equally, the Grand Master himself and other Grand Officers were appointed by Grand Lodge without reference to the wider membership. Still today a small socially elite group continues to self-select appointments to senior positions in UGLE and Royal Arch Chapter of England. In that respect they continue to reflect the way that the political process is also conducted in Britain.

REASONS FOR JOINING, PART 1 LIFE-ENHANCING AND REASSURANCE: SOCIAL, INTELLECTUAL, SPIRITUAL, CHARITABLE

Introduction

Demonstrating the profile of the development of Freemasonry and Masonic lodges in the nineteenth century is reasonably straightforward. Understanding why men wanted to become Masons is much more complicated. At one level the answer is simple: men, perhaps more than women, like to bond and spend their time in medium- to large-sized groups—in pubs and clubs, sports teams and supporters clubs, churches, mosques and synagogues, regiments and street gangs—and they are usually much the happier and content for it.[1] As John Timbs saw it in the 1870s, men had an 'habitual gregarious and social inclination', and he drew attention to the universality of clubs founded on eating and drinking, 'where most men agree, and in which the learned and illiterate, the dull and the airy, the philosopher and the buffoon, can all of them bear a part'.[2] This may be true in general, but it provides little guide to why so many men chose to become Masons rather than other forms of sociability. Clearly there were very considerable differences between men—differences between individuals and groups—depending on their aspirations, activities, and internal dynamics. Similarly not all men were the same but had different backgrounds, resources, abilities, interests and motivations. Crucially, men rarely confined themselves to just one group but had a series of allegiances, which in themselves conditioned the range of their activities as one group lead to, or perhaps excluded another. As background to the whole, men did not act as free agents. Most had family commitments and responsibilities that had to be accommodated as well as economic and social aspirations that needed to be facilitated. Sometimes this caused them to invite women and young people into their groups but commonly they preferred to exclude them.

One obvious approach to unravelling the multiple factors that motivated Victorian men to become Masons would be to look at those that join the Order today. Scott Kenny has recently taken this route in a theoretical sociological analysis of lodge membership in today's Maritime provinces of Canada and has produced a useful schematic framework. He stresses the importance of social background and previous encounters with Masonry; access to information and awareness of what was required; the social and economic needs of potential members; curiosity about its rituals and secrets; and an ability to surmount the obstacles to becoming involved.[3] However, it is very difficult, and not entirely helpful, to apply it in a British Victorian context. The day-to-day life of men and their families has changed, the world in which they lived has changed and Freemasonry itself has changed. The broad issue may be the same but their relative importance has altered and factors which once were highly significant no longer have resonance.

Instead of theory-driven analysis, this discussion will take a simple historical approach, identifying the range of issues that seem to have attracted men to Masonry in the late nineteenth century, and noting that they generally operated in differing combinations for different men in different places and at different times. In so doing it will demonstrate that there were major features of Masonry a hundred years ago that are no longer present or relevant today and that the general social context of the late Victorian world was far more conducive to fraternal membership. In brief, it will be argued that while the 'life enhancing' aspects of Freemasonry were much the same then as they are now, there were previously important functional or 'practical reasons' for seeking membership. The late nineteenth century was a far more insecure and less 'connected' world than today and this encouraged men to take a far greater interest in the supportive and charitable aspects of Freemasonry as well as its ability to link them to others within the Order. In this sense, Masonry acted like many other, often larger, friendly and benevolent societies and orders, but a stronger middle- and upper-class membership suggested more successful outcomes for the 'investment' in the costs of membership. Widespread familiarity with fraternity, ritual and benevolence also advantaged Masonry by making it appear modern, fashionable and purposeful, rather than the out-of-date, old-fashioned, and irrelevant image that it has acquired today.

Discussion of these issues will focus firstly on the 'life-enhancing' aspects of Freemasonry, together with those that assisted social and economic progression. These might conveniently be labelled as the six Rs: ritual, rank, revelation, recreation, respectability, reputation. It will then go on to consider a seventh R: reassurance, viz. the assistance that Masons could expect from their brethren, institutional charities and networking mechanisms. A final section will look at the competition for Freemasonry. What other organisations might men have joined, such as associated friendly societies, that offered similar facilities, and how they compared, particularly in term of financial reassurance. The discussion will then move on in the next chapter to focus on how Masonic membership particularly advantaged mobile and vulnerable occupational groups during travel and migration.

Life-Enhancing Attractions

These were the aspects of Masonry that were most attractive to the great majority of Masons who might be described as sedentary, i.e. remaining in the same or nearby area for most of their lives. They were relatively successful and economically secure, joined a lodge near to where they lived and worked, and moved or travelled only occasionally. A future need for assistance or charity from fellow lodge members, or the extended brotherhood of Freemasons nationally or internationally, was remote and best not contemplated. They hoped only to be in a position to give, not receive. Certainly they might also have been attracted by the networking potential of the Order, locally and regionally, but their main focus was likely to have been on the possible ways of demonstrating their status within the community, exhibiting their upstanding honesty and reliability, and enjoying the numerous opportunities for local recreation and entertainment. All were well known and understood in the wider community and membership would be perceived as a seal of 'having arrived'. Together, they offered not only greater life satisfaction but also potential for further social and economic improvement. These three Rs—respectability, reputation and recreation—were the public face of Freemasonry, but once within the Masonic family, new members discovered other unexpected, and perhaps unimagined, issues which help to retain their long-term loyalty. These might be summarised as three more Rs: revelation, ritual and rank.

Respectability and Reputation

Being respectable, and being seen to be respectable, was the key to social and economic success in the Victorian world. It was what Best has described as 'the great Victorian shibboleth'.[4] Strict conformance with rules of dress, deportment, values and behaviour was critical for status in society and business. It helped to be born to it and it was difficult to achieve if you were not. All close family members—husbands and wives, children and grandparents—must constantly strive to maintain it and a lapse by one could besmirch all. Once lost, it was almost impossible to regain it. All classes aspired to it, particularly the middle and lower classes. It became the principal division in the lower classes, with the 'respectable working class' having the only real hope of progression. A 'respectable reputation' became their passport for crossing weakening class boundaries and progressing to middle-class status. There have been important debates about how the working class might obtain respectable status, and the particular role of membership of friendly societies,[5] but there can be little doubt that close association with the middle class through membership of Masonic lodges conveyed unimpeachable credentials.

It also worked at the other end of the social spectrum. Once Royalty became firmly ensconced in the senior echelon of Masonry in the eighteenth century, it became desirable for the aristocracy to emulate them and achieve proximity. By the nineteenth century, such familiarity had become irresistible. William IV was the Patron of the Order; the Duke of Sussex and later Albert, Prince of Wales were Grand Masters. The Dukes of Connaught, Albany and Clarence were PGMs of Sussex, Oxfordshire and Berkshire respectively. With the aristocracy keeping pace, so too the gentry and the upper middle class did their very best to keep up. Men like William Hughan and Frederick Binckes could rise from modest lower-middle-class backgrounds to associate as equals with the greatest of the good.[6] Frequent processions provided splendid opportunities to demonstrate that new-found status publicly.[7] According to Simon Gunn, 'In the later Victorian city, authority was conventionally demonstrated by the regulat, formalised and often ceremonial appearance of the rich and the powerful in the city centre.' These were 'the occasions on which wealth and authority were made visible, displayed to a large urban audience'.[8] An account of a meeting of the Provincial Grand Lodge in Truro in July 1870 provides a good example:

> The streets through the town were crowded with holiday folks to witness the public proceedings of the festival and at various point [sic] along the principal thoroughfares long lines of flags and banners proclaimed a general gala day to the towns-people.

After the meeting the Lodge adjourned in procession with regalia and banners, accompanied by two bands, through the streets to St Mary's Church. A procession was then led back to the Public Rooms where the first meeting had been held and over 250 subsequently dined.[9] These regular displays, rotated around the county as they were hosted by different lodges, were overshadowed by the spectacular public celebrations for the laying of the foundation stone for Truro Cathedral in 1880. The Prince of Wales proceeded through the city to lay two stones, one as the Crown's representative and one as the Grand Master, with the latter being observed by hundreds of Masons in full regalia.[10] It became the social and cultural fashion to be a Mason: membership was essential and irresistible. Only those subject to sanctions against membership—such as Catholics, orthodox Protestant dissenters and those with strong adverse personal principles—could resist its lure.

In many ways the rules or attributes of respectability were those necessary to survive in an insecure world, devoid of the safety net of state-provided welfare. Cleanliness and care—for home and person—encouraged good health; avoidance of debt and self-reliance assured economic security; honesty and trustworthiness provided the bedrock for economic success in business or employment. An industrialised society required men and women with self-discipline, regular work habits, loyalty and conformity, rather than the diverse, challenging and creative labour force required by today's service-based economy. With a limited state apparatus, social and economic order necessarily relied on internal self-discipline rather than our externally imposed systems of rules, regulations and inspection.

A man could not become a Freemason without being regarded as respectable. He could only become a Mason by being invited by the respectable leaders of his communities and obtaining membership bestowed the imprimatur of respectability. In the Victorian world there was a clear perception that Masonry was the most exclusive of social organisations, patronised by the religious, political and economic elite. Equally, the principles of Freemasonry, and their constant rehearsal in Masonic rituals, encouraged men to sustain the attributes of character necessary to defend their respectability. Crimes against respectability were crimes against Freemasonry and could lead to a member being admonished and, if they were serious enough, being ejected from the Order.

Respectability and a reputation for honesty and reliability gave Masons an advantage in a business world where most transactions were based entirely on trust and the necessary assumption that a gentleman's 'word is his bond'. This was the essential catalyst for business of all kinds. It also created a demand for Masons in positions of civic, charitable or commercial trust. A good example of this was the people that many of the benevolent societies chose to have in charge of their financial affairs. These societies were always very concerned about the possibilities of theft and embezzlement of their hard-pressed funds and looked for the most trustworthy among their number to appoint as Treasurer. More often than not they chose those who were Masons and even when such people were not already Masons they frequently were given admittance at a later date (see Appendix 7). One indicator of the specific importance of Masonic status can be found in the numbers of men that *became* Masons but did not regularly *take part* as Masons. Lodge minutes show that, in numerous lodges, many members

Illustration 4   Parade of Freemasons in Helston, Cornwall

This photograph was probably taken in the early twentieth century. Masonic parades, either on their own or in association with other civic events, were frequent until the 1930s. Concerns about the persecution of Masons by fascist and anti-Semitic regimes elsewhere in Europe then encouraged Masons in the UK to obscure their identities and parading stopped. Greater secrecy led to concerns about Masonic cabals in public service in the later 1990s in the UK and the Blair government attempted to require all Masons to declare their membership before or during employment. Limited parading has now resumed in some parts of the country while Masonic parading in the US has continued throughout.

seldom attended after they had passed the three degrees of initiation. They were apparently happy to pay their regular subscriptions for their Masonic 'status' rather than the pleasures of lodge activities.

Not only did they have the 'stamp of approval' for their honesty and integrity but they were able to display and celebrate it in parades at public events when all could witness the splendour of the community's great and good (see Illustration 4). Certainly not all Masons were respectable and many suffered major blows to their reputation, but most appeared sincerely to have aspired to fulfil their obligations and were successful in doing so, providing much of the 'glue' that held Victorian society together. It is unfortunately not within the capacity of this book to investigate why it all appears to have changed in the twentieth century and Masonic membership became instead almost a social crime, an indication of business conspiracy, an identity of opprobrium that needed to be hidden and perhaps denied. It is, however, research that badly needs to be done, since only through an understanding of that change might it be reversed and a more positive view of the role of Freemasonry in society be re-established.

Recreation

Whatever the attractions of the formal side of Masonry and the usefulness of the social status it bestowed, it was the 'recreational' opportunities offered by membership that may have figured most immediately in the minds of those that sought membership. In this sense recreation means not simply the practice of ritual, the eating of dinners and taking part in processions, etc., but the simple opportunity to share male fellowship, in and beyond the lodge. For whatever reason, men have long demonstrated a great proclivity to 'bond' and share the company of other men in social spaces outside of the home—the pub, club, sports field, ship, regiment—and the lodge might have been seen simply as an exclusive extension of those opportunities. Clark refers to Freemasonry as offering a 'nexus of contact and solidarity between people of different backgrounds', providing an important 'integrative function' in bringing strangers and outsiders into the sociable community and 'enlarging social contacts within and between communities'.[11] For the otherwise isolated professionals and businessmen, working alone or in small groups, lodge life offered the same kinds of close, friendly, mutually supportive 'camaraderie' that was enjoyed by working-class men in their places of work.

Stevenson and Jacobs have shown how the origins of modern Freemasonry in the late seventeenth and early eighteenth centuries must be seen in the wider context of the contemporary growth of coffee houses, taverns, clubs and societies for all interests—an expansion of the public space in which men of all social ranks might mix, interact, expand their minds and have fun.[12] This social revolution, which started in the metropolis and large provincial towns, was now extending to the suburbs and smaller towns. Members of the respectable middle and upper working classes, who often had few opportunities for social interaction in those smaller communities outside of the church, chapel and tavern, were now looking for much more. Their problem was compounded by the social tainting of much tavern society, as increased working-class incomes led to more drinking and raucous behaviour. New social spaces needed to be found and the building of dedicated Masonic, Oddfellows, Foresters and other fraternal halls became a feature of urban development from the mid-nineteenth century (see Illustration 5). They provided dedicated spaces where the theatricality of

Illustration 5   Laying the Foundation Stone of Camborne Masonic Hall

The Deputy Provincial Grand Master and the Provincial Grand Secretary are seen laying the foundation stones of Camborne Masonic Hall in 1898. They were watched by the members of Mount Edgcumbe Lodge, a relatively recent foundation, together with their families and some onlookers. The first meeting of the Lodge in the newly completed building was in October 1899. The decline of the tin-mining industry in the late 1890s suggested that it might have been an inauspicious time for such an expensive venture. However, the high levels of unemployment locally had the effect of swelling the numbers seeking initiation before emigration and the lodge had the largest membership in the Province.

fraternity could be safely practised behind closed doors, and lodge property could be securely stored. For lodges dominated by abstemious Anglicans and Methodists, dedicated halls created a haven free of the demon drink; for the less abstemious, an opportunity to indulge out of the public eye.

Revelation

During the long nineteenth century, from the end of the Napoleonic Wars through to the First World War, British society saw the emergence of a number of new threads in fashion and spirituality. They have been described by historians as a revival of superstition and mysticism, an abandonment of reason, escapism, even as an occult revival.[13] Society was being bombarded with a range of new knowledge and experience created by the global transport revolution; closer contact with exotic Eastern religion; archaeological revelations about ancient societies; and the evolution of new studies of anthropology and philology. At a time when science was already producing a new secularism and challenging the authority of established religion, and the excesses of industrialisation were generating a revulsion against modernism, all sectors of society increasingly looked backwards to an ancient or medieval golden age for inspiration Literature and poetry was transformed by the Romantics, architecture by the Gothic revival, painting by the Pre-Raphaelites, decorative arts by the Arts and Crafts movement. Many, if not most, of the fraternal benevolent societies that prospered during the period adopted regalia and rituals inspired by a supposed distant past and even some of the craft trade unions adopted similar ritual initiations.

With its long-established claims to ancient origins and secrets, Freemasonry found itself in perfect harmony with this evolving cultural environment and was happy to take advantage of a swift growth in membership.[14] New members were welcomed, not just in established Craft lodges, but to a rapidly increasing number of side orders, each with its own rituals and secrets, reimagining ancient events.[15] Of these, the Knights Templar, revived from 1845, and the Societas Rosicruciana in Anglia (S.R.I.A.), founded in 1865, were probably the most esoteric and influential.[16] Both found their origins outside Masonry and were incorporated into the Order to give them continuity and structure. The S.R.I.A. was the more spiritual of the two, claiming origins in the Fraternity of the Rose Cross (sometimes C.R.C.), founded on the ancient secrets revealed by Christian Rosenkreutz in the fifteenth century. It committed its members to an eternal search for knowledge and truth, and was particularly active in researching ancient esoterica.[17] By the last years of the nineteenth century it is

likely that the great majority of those with interests in the occult—or the men
at least—were Freemasons and many of them were members of the S.R.I.A. In
a way that scarcely seems possible now, to be a Freemason in the late nineteenth
century was to be in the forefront of intellectual fashion.

For those that still remained unsatisfied—and the women that could not
access the Masonic orders—a number of 'additional', 'higher' or 'side' degrees
began to emerge towards the end of the century, having varying degrees of
accommodation with Masonry. Some were accepted and others kept at arm's
length. They included the Rite of Memphis, the Rite of Mizraim, the Rite of
Swedenborg, the Order of Ishmael, the Holy Order of Knights Beneficent of
the Holy City and the August Order of Light—several imported from France
and America.[18] The Rite of Memphis was particularly successful in recruiting
working-class men and established lodges alongside regular Masonic lodges in
Canada, Australia, New Zealand and the United States.[19] The most celebrated
of these new groups, however, was the Hermetic Order of the Golden Dawn,
founded in 1888.[20] The Golden Dawn diversified its membership away from
Freemasonry, but recruitment was slow and they probably never had more than
a few hundred members during their most active, and fractious, years around the
turn of the new century.[21] Nevertheless, their influence was far more pervasive,
keeping alive and promoting wider public perceptions of the possibilities of
magic and occult activity.

It is clearly difficult to estimate the overall importance of the public interest
in esotericism to Masonic recruitment and membership, and there may have
been very few that joined specifically in pursuit of those subjects. However, it
was a significant part of a mix of attractions in an age that made a fashion of such
topics and the guarding of its 'secrets' remains a key part of a Masons' commitments to this day. Similarly, much of the public suspicion of Freemasonry rests
on its supposed heretical traditions and threats to established religious order.

Ritual
The main means of revealing the secrets and hidden knowledge of Freemasonry
and its various side orders was through the medium of ritual.[22] The performance
of ritual took up most of the time in a lodge meeting, being focused around
the opening and closing of the lodge, and the process of taking new members
through the three degrees of initiation. The rituals were based on the supposed
relationship between the master and workmen involved in the building of the
Temple of Solomon and the professional advancement of new workers from
apprentice, through journeyman or fellow craft status, to master craftsmen.
They employed allegories of the working tools of stonemasons to improve and

perfect the education and morals of men.[23] Instead of taking rough stone and carefully shaping it to be a true and regular part of a great physical structure, Freemasons were to work on their moral and spiritual development to achieve the same sound regularity as a member of society. Thus, organisationally, they adopted the same 'lodge' structure as the stonemasons that notionally built the biblical Temple of King Solomon and stonemasons' tools were displayed in the lodge to assist with its working. Masonic initiation ceremonies explained that the twenty-four-inch ruler was allegorically used to measure the passage of time during a day to ensure that appropriate periods are spent in prayer, work and leisure; the mallet became the force of conscience, to regulate thought and behaviour; the points of compasses, the advantages of education; the square, morality; the level, equality; and the plumb rule, uprightness of life and action. When the lodge opened, the 'Master', assisted by six officers, presided over what might be described as 'participatory theatre', with one of a number of various ceremonies being played out as the officers moved about the lodge and interacted with initiates and each other, employing fixed and carefully learned speaking parts.

These rituals stated—and constantly repeated and reinforced—the moral characteristics required of a fully-fledged Master Mason. His life to be firmly based on religion (not necessarily Christian) and the observance of moral law. His actions to be those of a gentleman, treating others as he would wish to be treated himself and living in harmony with those around him. He should be patient, meek, self-denying, prudent, dignified, affectionate and charitable to those in distress. He should be a loyal, peaceful and law-abiding citizen, shunning all plots and conspiracies, and he should studiously avoid bigotry, intemperance, rudeness, malice, and slander. 'Brotherly love, relief and truth' were acclaimed as the guiding principles of the Order, to which should be added temperance, fortitude, prudence and justice. As Moore put it, Masons should be 'good men and true, men of honour and honesty'.[24] Performance of these rituals was challenging, enlightening and improving, not only for those taking part but also for those observing, as they constantly rehearsed and reminded themselves of the obligations to which they were committed.

In today's world, such rituals are unusual and might be considered archaic. Ritualistic behaviour among men remains influential but is primarily informal and unstructured, being practiced by the supporters of sports teams, political parties, gang members and social groups of all sizes and descriptions. In the late nineteenth century, however, organised participatory rituals were commonplace. Most families attended church periodically, with varying levels and types of ritual, and most friendly and benevolent societies practiced ritual on a regular basis. As the numbers of separate orders boomed from tens to hundreds by the end of the century, every one of them demanded new rituals. The writing of rituals for new orders and side orders became a significant activity for some, generating income by the sale of degrees and promises of revealed secrets, as well as the merchandising of related regalia.[25] Orders competed with each other for members through the attractions of their rituals and regalia.[26]

In this context, the performance of ritual might be seen as little more than amateur dramatics, satisfying a simple need for entertainment.[27] However, historians and sociologists also have suggested deeper motivations and meaning. Lynn Dumenil, for example, has described it as the essential mechanism for separating men from the common world and creating for them an allegorical 'born-again' security among brothers in the lodge. They became 'insiders' separated from 'outsiders'. In this sense the lodge became a spiritual oasis, providing asylum in a changing and insecure world.[28] For Kaufman, 'Rites and rituals were not only amusing and fun but also provided an organisational structure that certified members' loyalty and bonded individuals to the organi- sation in such a way as to solidify their financial commitment to the groups.'[29] Carnes even suggests that there might be something special about certain rituals that 'attracted', 'charmed' or 'lured' members, and that many men may be predisposed to crave them. He also suggests a gender explanation, arguing that 'fraternal ritual provided solace and psychological guidance during young men's troubled passage to manhood'.[30] The fact that Masonic craft rituals were so widely copied, and that they are still practiced virtually unchanged by hundreds of thousands of Masons internationally, suggests that they might have such powers. What is clear is that in any period, there are some men—perhaps most men—who are attracted by ritualistic behaviour in one form or another and that ritual serves as a powerful means of binding them together as an exclusive group, promoting solidarity, trust and confidence. It was a tool extensively used in the nineteenth century to secure group well-being in a hostile world—by craft trade unions as much as friendly societies—and it is still used today by military forces everywhere to promote effectiveness in combat.

In a world where ritual was widely understood and appreciated, Freemasonry offered the most ancient, complex and revered forms. Most of the other orders readily acknowledged the influence of Masonic ritual in shaping their own proceedings. The author of the *Manual of Oddfellowship*, for example, was unequivocal in his view that 'the Oddfellows, Romans, Britons, Druids, Ivorites, Foresters, Shepherds, Alfreds, Knights of the Golden Fleece, Free Gardeners, Noble Mechanics, the Order of the Ark, Knights of Burgundy' had all consciously modelled themselves after Masonic ritual.[31] In this context, it would seem reasonable to assume that the 'other' orders supplied potential 'seed corn' for Freemasonry—that many of their members might aspired to 'upgrade' to Masonry for 'ritual-plus'. This would have had a particularly strong effect on the recruitment for Masonic lodges with a strong working-class membership. For example, by the 1840s, the Oddfellows counted thousands of craftsmen and tradesmen among their membership and many of the better-off blacksmiths, carpenters, butchers, bakers and miners might have been among those that became Freemasons.[32] Every town of any size counted at least one or two friendly and benevolent societies alongside Masonic lodges and it is known that many men held joint memberships.[33] Similarly, Durr has shown that nearly all craft unions adopted Masonic-like rituals of association from the late eighteenth century and actively practiced them through to the twentieth century.[34] Throughout the industrial period, these 'seedbeds' multiplied rapidly. By the mid-1870s the combined membership of just the four main ritual/regalia-using friendly societies—the Oddfellows, Foresters, Rechabites and Shepherds—exceeded one million and by the First World War it was approaching two million.[35]

Clearly the incidence of joint or progressive membership from the 'other' orders to Freemasonry needs to be investigated in greater detail but research so far has failed to reveal more than a small handful of comparable membership records for Cornwall.[36] Similarly, it would be highly desirable to investigate the degree to which there was a continuing ritual interaction between Freemasonry and the other orders. This might go beyond the simple issue of the Masonic inspiration for other orders to look at the 'return effect', focusing on the degree to which Masonic ritual was itself changed and evolved as a result of 'imports' from various developing orders. Such interactions have been considered in the context of American fraternity[37] but they have received no sustained attention in the UK, and the entire subject of ritual and its role in the formation of Victorian culture and society has been much neglected.

While it is difficult to assess accurately the role of ritual in the initial attraction and recruitment of men to Masonry, it is possible to gain a fairly clear view once they became members. Indeed, it can almost be valued, or 'priced', financially. The Cornish experience discussed above provides an example. By the late 1890s, for example, side orders such as Royal Arch and Mark counted almost eight hundred members, or 40% of all craft Masons in the county. Each Order required additional initiation and membership fees, multiple sets of increasingly complex and expensive regalia, often a considerable distance to travel to the nearest Chapter, and even more expenditure on post-lodge dining and conviviality. Many hours were taken up in learning, performing and attending meetings that might otherwise have been spent in business. A man's total expenditure on Masonry could easily be doubled or even trebled without any observable additional economic benefits above and beyond those offered by basic Craft membership. It is unsurprising that most of those that were able to exercise these preferences were well-off brethren from professional, managerial and commercial backgrounds.[38]

Rank

Just as men seem to have an enduring need for ritual and regalia, they also seem to be motivated by a desire for rank which elevates them above others in whatever world, real or institutional, that they inhabit and value. The practice of ritual within lodges created the opportunity to achieve that. The working of lodges required several officers and they usually held varying levels of seniority under the ultimate authority of the Master. Each office was signified by increasingly flamboyant clothing and accoutrements. Ranks continued beyond the initial craft lodge level to Provincial and Grand Lodges, and those that acquired offices there commanded high status within the Order. This was common, to one degree or another, in most of the various orders but particularly so in Freemasonry. Although never entirely open and democratic, this created opportunities for even those from the lowest social groups to become important and influential officers in the lodge and province, associating within the craft as equals with the gentry and aristocracy.

Membership of side orders offered further opportunities for the acquisition of even more elaborate regalia and election into offices with high-sounding names. Dedicated and capable men could achieve status within Masonry that they could never hope for outside.[39] Thus John Pearce Smith, a cooper in Cornubian Lodge No. 450 of Hayle, became Master in 1860 and Provincial Grand Deacon in 1865, and George Timmins, an innkeeper from Tregullow Lodge No. 1006 St Day, became Master in 1881 and Provincial Grand Assistant Director of Ceremonies in 1895.[40] This 'role play'[41] both confirmed and denied the fundamental principle of equality within Masonry. On the one hand it provided the chance for the most humble to rise to the most senior positions, while on the other it finely divided the membership by 'active' and 'past' status. Of course much of this would have been disguised from the general public outside of the orders and would probably not have figured as a major factor in attracting new members. However, the prospect of obtaining an ever higher and more prestigious rank was, and still is, a major factor in retaining membership.

A good indication of the role of rank in retaining, if not recruiting, men for Freemasonry can be found in the growing popularity of 'Past Grand Rank'. As has been seen, Masons commonly aspired to 'progress' in their lodge, seeking promotion through the various offices until they became Master of the Lodge. A few might go further, being appointed to offices in the PGL, and a tiny fraction might become officers in the Grand Lodge. However, the number of offices, and the slow rate of turnover of those that filled them, meant that even the most eminent Masons might never have an opportunity to be so rewarded. With a growing demand for titles within Masonry and the increasingly flamboyant regalia that they carried with them, something needed to be done. A solution was found around the mid-century by inventing the concept of 'Past Rank'. Under this arrangement, a worthy Mason could be afforded the title and regalia of an officer of Provincial or Grand Lodge without ever having actually held that position. At first closely restricted to 'Past Grand Rank', the numbers appointed remained very small until the 1880s, being mainly confined to the social elite. However, in 1887 UGLE made thirty-one appointments to Past Grand Rank from London lodges, forty-nine from PGLs and thirty-five from overseas lodges. They continued to be drawn from the political, social and economic elites but the precedent had been firmly established for an increasing number of annual appointments. From the 1890s, PGLs were also granted the authority to make 'Past Provincial' appointments and the numbers honoured increased very rapidly, creating a clear promotional path for those so motivated. Today there are over 6,500 holders of Past Grand Rank alone and many more that hold Provincial Grand Rank. Since such appointments are within the gift of the active officers of Provincial and Grand Lodges, they provide a mechanism for maintaining control of the direction of development of Craft Masonry. Past Provincial and Past Grand Rank appointees—as well as those that receive 'Past' promotions—pay for the privileges of their new positions and the income generated provides the various Grand Lodges with a useful supplement to their overall income.[42]

Reassurance and Support

While the 'life-enhancing' aspects of Freemasonry are adequate to attract members to it today, in the insecure and dangerous world of the eighteenth and nineteenth centuries the promises of brotherly support and prospect of generous charity in times of adversity undoubtedly played a major role in most individuals' decisions to become Masons. It cannot be over-emphasised that the growth and expansion of Masonry from the late seventeenth century took place in the context of increasing social and economic insecurity created by the process of industrialisation. Technological change and the movement from the countryside to the rapidly growing towns cast families adrift and required both men and women to reach out from broken familial connections to create new bonds of trust and mutual support with others in a similar position. Friendly and fraternal societies were founded everywhere and grew rapidly in size, the distribution and the diversity of their membership. Freemasonry was just one of many.

The correlation between insecurity and mutuality continued to hold true in the twentieth century, though now in a reverse direction. As increasingly centralised governments stepped in to provide a safety net for all—through health insurance, pensions and a widening range of care provisions—the need for independent mutual aid disappeared and the great benevolent orders withered and mainly died. The membership of Freemasonry tracked the decline, with a remaining rump surviving on the offer of entertainment and a suspicion of improved business networking opportunities. In this context, Masonic ritual finds its relevance not in its ancient and mystical origins but in its peculiar ability to reinforce Judaeo-Christian teachings about brotherly love and charity within a delineated group. Similarly, the attributes of respectability and reputation promoted by Freemasonry helped to promote the lifestyles that were necessary to retain a grip on prosperity and prevent an economic and social slide. Again the shift to state-sponsored social security helped to promote more liberal social attitudes and undermined the concept of 'respectability' within the vulnerable working class.

Networks
Everyone has a network of family, friends, associates and acquaintances that can be accessed for information, advice and help. Those networks are key to our life experience, guiding and facilitating our every action and reaction. Equally, those with the widest, wisest and most influential networks are the ones who are likely to make the best decisions and progress furthest in life, personally, economically and socially. In the rapidly changing Victorian world numerous new, semi-formal, extended networks began to appear. The most influential were 'old boy' school networks, which, in their various forms, included all of those 'that mattered' in industry, commerce and politics. Their influence was demonstrated recently in analysis of the future careers of those that attended elite private schools in England between 1897 and 2016 which found that they were very many more times likely to achieve top positions in all sectors of public and private life than those that attended other schools.[43] Exclusive clubs and societies reinforced and further extended their reach.[44] At the other end of the social scale, trades unions, trade associations, Nonconformist churches and local and regional groups connected people with wide-ranging skills and experience. Most of these networks, however, were closed and difficult, if not impossible, to join. The unique contribution of Masonry was to provide a way to

link them together and unleash their potential as sources of reliable information, contacts and collaboration. No one could ever become an 'old boy' of a school that they had not attended but a Mason might call on a brother to use those contacts to advise or assist his own endeavours. This facility was not limited to the Mason's own lodge, but applied to any other lodge that he might visit or perhaps correspond with. Even in today's world, with its almost limitless access to information via electronic systems, such personal contacts prove extremely useful in every aspect of life. In the new and anonymous, evolving towns of the nineteenth century, they were indispensable for all but the most mundane everyday affairs. With their wide social and occupational membership, lodges brought together extensive local, regional, national and, in some cases, international networks, providing unparalleled information exchanges and webs of personal contacts and introductions.

The level of assistance given through networks undoubtedly varied considerably. At one extreme it could be simply information on where to go or who to ask, suggestions of opportunities, an introduction, a personal favour, a guarantee of character. At the other it could be a job offer, a joint business venture, or an agreement to collaborate on a range of issues. Such potential opened the way for charges of conspiratorial advantage and corrupt dealing. Examples of the latter have been greatly celebrated in anti-Masonic literature[45] but those of the former—almost certainly a far greater number—remain hidden and virtually untraceable. Masonry, like most other orders, clubs, 'old school' associations and societies, undoubtedly struck a difficult balance between what economists refer to as cost-reducing 'transaction charges' and 'rent seeking' behaviour.[46]

Financial support
There were four sources of financial relief for Masons: individual brethren, lodge funds, PGL charities and UGLE charities. They all conformed closely to the understanding that they were providing temporary and discretionary *charitable* relief and not assured *benevolence*. The payment of Masonic lodge dues did not bestow any entitlement to sickness, unemployment, death or other benefits of the kind that were acquired as of right by membership of friendly or benevolent societies. The Masonic aim was to facilitate self-help, so that the recipient might regain sustainable independence. Charitable donations were rarely made to the same person more than once or twice. The only exceptions were those that would clearly not be able to become independent in the medium or long term, such as the old and the orphaned. In this latter respect it is useful to consider the main charitable providers in reverse order, starting with the UGLE, continuing to PGLs and then to ordinary lodges and individual brethren.

Arrangements for charitable relief were among the very earliest activities of the first Grand Lodge, established in London in 1717, and continued with both the Ancient and Modern Grand Lodges through the eighteenth century. Most activity was concerned with giving occasional charity to individuals but the key enduring development was the establishment of charities to support the children of dead brethren or those in severely diminished economic circumstances. What was to become the Royal Masonic Institute for Girls (RMIG) was started in 1788 and its partner, later the Royal Masonic Institute for Boys (RMIB), established its first school, in North London, in 1857. While the girls' charity started its own school—essentially an orphanage—the boys' charity simply provided grants for clothing, maintenance and education costs in various unconnected private schools. By the last quarter of the nineteenth century there were several hundred children attending these schools in the London area. The administration of occasional adult relief was regularised after the union of the Ancient and Modern lodges in 1813 by the formation of a Lodge of Benevolence, with a Board that met monthly to consider representations. More sustained relief for old and incapacitated Masons began in 1833, outside the immediate jurisdiction of UGLE, with the foundation of 'an Asylum for Aged and Decayed Freemasons' but was finally brought in-house by the formation of what became the Royal Masonic Benevolent Institution (RMBI) in 1842, which focused on providing annuities for out-relief in a Mason's own home.[48] A small residential home continued to be maintained but only small minority entered it.[49] Taken together, the RMBI, RMIG and the RMIB were often referred to as the Grand Charities. In addition to the charities under the UGLE, some of the side orders, with their own Grand Lodges, also established aid funds. The Mark Masons had one of the largest, established in 1869[50] and, as with the UGLE charities, this was split between occasional benevolence, annuities and educational assistance.[51]

Like UGLE, many but not all PGLs established funds both to distribute occasional relief and also to provide longer term help to those that were either old and incapable or needed orphan care and/or educational assistance.[52] In Cornwall, for example, the PGL established a 'Committee for the Relief of Indigent Brethren'[53] and another for 'Masonic Scholarships' around the mid-century. After 1864 these were amalgamated to become the Cornwall Masonic Annuity and Benevolent Fund. Similarly, by the last decades of the nineteenth century, the PGL of Devonshire had the Fortescue Annuity Fund and the Devon Masonic Education Fund; Warwickshire, the Warwickshire Masonic Benevolent and Pupils Aid Fund; Durham, the Hudson Benevolent Fund and the Durham Education

Fund; West Lancashire, the Educational, Hamer and Alpass Provincial charities; and East Lancashire, the East Lancashire Systematic Masonic Educational and Benevolent Institution.[54]

These organisations did not simply collect monies for their own charitable activities but also had the dual function of co-ordinating bids from their province for monies and annuities distributed by the Grand Charities. The distribution of monies by the Grand Charities was by votes, employing a form of 'subscriber democracy' common to many other charities.[55] Votes were purchased by individual Masons and lodges according to a formula—5 shillings purchasing one vote for one year and 5, 10, 50 and 100 guineas proportionately more on a continuing basis.[56] Larger donors were given prestigious titles like Vice-President or Patron, and their names were published in annual Provincial Yearbooks. The monies paid for the votes made up an important part of the income of the charities. In theory the voters could express a personal opinion about which candidates they favoured but it became a common practice for provinces to try to co-ordinate their local votes to maximise successful outcomes for local candidates. Provincial officials might then also co-ordinate with their opposite number in other provinces to organise vote 'swaps' to further maximise their successes. All provinces admonished those with votes within their jurisdiction to send their forms uncompleted to the local secretary so that he might achieve the optimum outcomes. The Report of the Provincial Fund for Northumberland in 1892 clearly illustrates the importance of such collaboration and the frustration of Provincial officials when individuals did not co-operate.

> The Committee have to express their regret for many of the votes having been withheld from them at the recent elections. In a few cases, as usual, this arose from the careless oversight of voters not signing their voting papers immediately on their receipt, and *at once* handing or forwarding them to the proper vote collectors of their respective lodges, or to the Secretary of this committee. But at the same time, several brethren sent away the votes for candidates altogether outside of our own Province. The right of every Brother to exercise his privilege in voting is, of course, admitted! But brethren—when solicited by friends to vote for candidates away from our own Province—they would find it vastly to their advantage to first consult the Secretary of its committee ... Who would materially aid them through their ability to affect *exchanges* of votes in all three institutions [the Grand Charities] and in this way protect the Province from any loss of votes.[57]

By contrast, the a meeting of the PGL of East Lancashire in 1900 noticed with satisfaction the outcome of elections for their candidates to the RMIB and declared that their representatives had done their work 'right well in the way in which they obtained the return of votes formerly borrowed from them and borrowed votes from other Provinces'.[58]

In provinces without separate charities of their own, the function of co-ordinating votes for the Grand Charities was handled either by the PGL itself or by some other body or committee set up specifically for that purpose. In Northamptonshire and Huntingdonshire, for example, it was strongly suggested that votes should be sent to the Provincial Secretary so that 'they may be polled, exchanged, or lent on behalf of the Province'.[59] Similarly, in Leicestershire, the 'Leicester and Rutland Masonic Charity Association' was set up, not to run its own major charitable funds but 'to awaken the interest and enlist the sympathies of the Craft within this Province in the Great Masonic Charities, to increase the voting power of the local charity organisation'.[60]

The beneficial effects of persuading as many local brethren as possible to purchase votes and then carefully to plan their distribution, were illustrated in annual report of West Lancashire's Provincial Secretary in 1892:

> Seven years ago we were very weak in votes of these institutions
> [the Grand Charities] having only 1,500 boys and girls and 1,500
> Benevolent votes, whereas we now have 4,100 boys and girls and
> 3,200 Benevolent votes and are getting a much better return.[61]

The Province of Devonshire was more explicit. In their annual report for 1879 it was observed that, by careful planning and collaboration with other provinces, they had been achieving a higher return from the Grand Charities, in terms of the number of annuities and educational grants, than they had been contributing. They were even greater recipients when account was taken of the length of life of some of their annuitants—one man having already received a total of £453, another £315, and another £273. One widow had received over £300 and all continued to receive their annual stipends of £40 for men and £32 for widows. All of this, they concluded, was due to the hard work of their Committee of Petitions which had 'judiciously manipulated' their voting power at the various elections, as well as the support of other provinces without whose help they surely would have been unsuccessful. In this respect they recorded their sincere thanks to the provinces of Cornwall, Cheshire, East Lancashire and North and South Wales. Devonshire was so grateful for its good fortune that it agreed to make special one-off donations to the RMBI of 100 guineas, the RMIB of 50 guineas, and the RMIG of 20 guineas.[62]

The absolute necessity for organisation in the election of candidates for the Grand Charities was reflected in the distribution of annuities between the provinces. All provinces saw some of their propositions to the RMBI accepted over the years but there were those that did much better than others, and it was not in proportion to their number of lodges or members (see Appendix 8). On the example of 1900, some provinces did very well, achieving an outcome of around one annuity for roughly every three lodges, while other provinces with a large number of lodges, such as West Lancashire, did very poorly. Suffolk appears to have been particularly successful with an average of one annuity to every two lodges. The success rate in proportion to the Province's total membership was more variable, with one to every ninety-five in Suffolk but elsewhere it was as low as less than one in three hundred. Even then, however, it was high enough for every Mason to be aware of someone who had been successful in securing his own old age and/or that of his widow. If he narrowed the numbers down to the minority of lodge members that were ever likely to be in real need of an annuity, the individual chances would seem much higher, particularly if linked to the additional help handed out by the provinces themselves.

However, one thing does appear to be incongruous in these returns. How did the London lodges do so well when they had no provincial structure to co-ordinate their bids? Part of the answer appears to be provided by the behaviour of many of the members of lodges in the provinces around London—Berkshire, Buckinghamshire, Middlesex, Surrey, etc. With improved rail connections, many of their members commuted to work in London and were also members of London lodges. They sometimes chose to exercise their votes on behalf of their London lodges rather than their home lodges.[63] Similarly, the RMBI took action to compensate for the disadvantages of London lodges by skewing the distribution of votes. In London, the Master of every lodge was given two votes for every male proposition and one for every female, whereas in the provinces only the PGM received votes—again two for male candidates and one for female. Votes were also distributed in the same way for Royal Arch Chapters, which could also join in the selection process. The significance of these compensatory arrangements was reflected in the outcomes for the RMIB elections, where no such compensatory provisions operated. There, in the elections for 1901, all twenty vacancies were filled from the provinces with nothing for the London lodges.[64]

The relative importance of the Grand and Provincial charities can be illustrated in terms of the funds that they had at their disposal. The Grand Charities were clearly the largest recipients of contributions. Their sources of income were wide ranging, including the UGLE's own funds, PGL funds, individual lodges and members, the proceeds of special festivals, bequests and, of course, the purchase of votes. The individual sums contributed varied considerably, from the £1,958 sent by Leicester and Rutland to the three Grand Charities between 1896 and 1900, to the £140,000 raised by a West Lancashire Festival for the RMIB in 1898. All told, the Grand Charities received a total of nearly £500,000 during the last five years of the century.[65] In 1900, the RMBI supported 207 male and 248 female annuitants, of whom twelve male and twenty female were resident in their 'asylum' in Croydon, near London.[66] The Board of Benevolence also made grants to occasional petitioners, relieving 330 of them in 1897 with a total of £8,835, or an average grant of £26 15s each.[67]

No single PGL could hold a candle to this, but taken together they no doubt commanded considerable sums and provided substantial support. In tiny Cornwall, for example, with a Masonic population of not much more than 1,500 for much of the late nineteenth century, the Cornwall Masonic Annuity and Benevolent Fund received £6,748 between 1864 and 1888, or an average of £281 a year. Out of this it paid £1,316 to male annuitants; £193 to widows; £70 in grants of occasional relief; and £540 in educational grants. Total administration costs amounted to only £281; the balance of £4,348 was invested in bonds with a small sum at the bank. As the recruitment of Masons in the Province accelerated, so did the fund's income and in the next ten years the total income received increased by £4,538, or at an average of £454 a year. The surplus invested funds then stood at £5,600. The number of annuities and educational grants had been increased accordingly, with eleven of both, but widows now considerably outnumbered men, at eight to four.[68] In much larger West Lancashire, with nearly eight thousand Masons, the Educational, Hamer, and Alpass Provincial charities received an annual income of £3,786 in 1899 and had invested funds of £35,000. Between them they assisted 180 children with educational grants, and twenty-three aged men and sixty-three widows with grants and annuities.[69] If the charitable activities of the side orders are added to these sums, the totals grow still larger. For example, in the last thirty years of the century, the Mark Benevolent Fund distributed £5,000 in relief and aided eighty-eight children at a cost of £6,000. In 1900 it also maintained six aged brethren and nine widows with annuities of £26 and £21, plus a £5 Christmas bonus.[70]

LODGES

The charitable activities of individual lodges are hidden within their many thousands of account books. It is most unlikely that any single or small group of lodges could ever have commanded the amounts of money mastered and deployed by the Grand Charities and Provincial enterprises, and they were certainly in no position to take on continuing commitments to providing for the old or orphaned. Nevertheless, taken together they undoubtedly played a critical role in meeting the everyday ad hoc needs of Masons and their families in temporary difficulty or distress. Myriad small grants were constantly being made to widows; to members trying to recover from health problems; to mitigate losses through fire or disaster; to help with the purchase of clothing in order to find a new job; to assist with emigration and moves to other areas; as contributions to disaster funds and at a host of other events where Masons and their families turned naturally to their brethren for assistance. Indeed, in this context, the Grand and Provincial charities addressed only a small tip of an otherwise submerged iceberg of Masonic care.

There are all sorts of indicative pieces of information to support this supposition. Most particularly there is an extended discussion below of the role of Masonic lodges in assisting migrant brethren and those in hazardous occupations that took them far from home—and a form of assistance that was considered so generous and available that it bred a specialised group of fraudster who made a living by acting as Masonic impostors.[71] On a more local basis, PGLs often reported critically on the number of lodges within their jurisdiction that failed to contribute as they thought appropriate to Provincial charities and the Grand Charities. In Devonshire in the late 1890s, for example, the Grand Lodges heard that twenty-two out of its nearly fifty lodges had contributed nothing to the Province's Fortescue Fund for that year and thirteen had made no contribution for the last four years. It may have been that some of those were impoverished but more likely that they used their funds in other ways.[72] In this context, it should be noticed that lodges, like individual Masons, the UGLE and PGLs, also contributed generously to special and occasional funds set up to relieve Masonic brethren caught up in overseas disasters, such as the Chicago Fire and the Boer War,[73] and many contributed frequently to 'outside' organisations that would tangentially benefit Masons, such as the Miners' Hospital in Cornwall.

INDIVIDUAL MASONS

What has been said about the total value of the acts of relief and assistance provided by lodges probably applies even more to those of individual Masons. As has been suggested above, these were probably the most common form of Masonic aid. From simple advice and favours, to small loans, gifts and forgiven debts, Masons were sworn to help and assist their brethren and the limited available evidence suggests that they did so generously. Here, however, there are no surviving receipts other than anecdotal accounts. One such, reported in the *Freemasons' Chronicle*, may serve to illustrate. At a meeting of Cornubian Lodge in Hayle, Cornwall, in the summer of 1867, 'a brother from Hungary was admitted, and having told the tales of his misfortunes, the funds of the lodge were lightened a little to help him, and the members also responded, and testified in a practical manner their sympathy'.[74] The role of individual Masons in supplying direct financial aid to travelling brethren will be further discussed below.

Through its many different channels, Freemasonry could collect and dispose of very large charitable funds to its members and their families. They preferred occasional discretionary aid but they were prepared to commit to longer-term support for those young and aged unable to be independent. How far this acted as a major attraction for Masonry, however, remains a moot point. Firstly, how widely known were the Masons charitable activities? This undoubtedly differed between areas. Variations in charitable giving between individuals, lodges, and PGLs, together with the unequal outcomes produced by the voting system in the Grand Charities, meant that the visibility of charitable outcomes differed widely across the country. In London, for example, without its own regional charitable structures and achieving little success in attracting grants from the Grand Charities, the many thousands of aspiring Masons would have seen scant evidence of Masonic charity. By contrast, in parochial Cornwall, most of the smaller total number of Masons and their friends would have heard of the, albeit minimal, quantity of widowed and orphaned being cared for by Masonry, and the opportunities for occasional support when in need appear to have been widely understood. Secondly, different socio-economic groups would have shown greater or lesser interest in the need for charity. The large middle-class membership of most lodges would have been aghast to imagine themselves ever to be in need of charity. Of course, they could and did fail in business, become victims of fraud, suffer from debilitating disease and physical misfortune, live beyond an age when they could make provision for themselves or their families, but these were the exceptions not to be contemplated. Similarly, the social, political and economic elite who joined Masonry in large numbers during the late nineteenth century—the landowners, clergy, politicians, bankers and merchants—would have found little in the concept of emergency support. For these middle- and upper-class groups, the act of charitable giving—a mark of social position—was more important than the security of the knowledge of becoming a potential recipient.

For the upper working class, however, it was a very different matter. Economic security was wafer thin and potential disaster for the whole family ever present. Hundreds of thousands joined burgeoning friendly and benefit societies for their sickness and death benefits, and it is unlikely that the large numbers of working-class Masons that were also Oddfellows, Foresters, Rechabites, etc., were indifferent to the charitable support that they could receive from Masonry. Indeed it might be argued that they were attracted to Masonry because the kinds of assistance offered actually complemented that insured elsewhere. Many orders offered occasional relief but the Masons did it particularly generously. It will be argued below that for some—particularly the vulnerable, those travelling or those working away from the security of home—the prospect of such support was widely known and a major factor in attracting men to Masonry. Similarly, Masonic educational grants and assistance to orphaned or impoverished children would have been admired and its annuities for the old provided an unusual prospect of security, being rarely copied by others until the twentieth century.[75] Actuarially they provided a serious challenge, particularly for long-lived widows, and were difficult for benevolent societies to guarantee. The RMBI calculated in 1900, for example, that in the previous year eighteen male annuitants had died who had received between them £4,200, and twenty-two females, who had received a total of £8,840. Several individuals had received £600 or more.[76] Annual subscriptions during men's working lives would have been prohibitive for such insurance and they could only be provided by the Masons as and when charitable income permitted.

Comparative Advantages

While it is convenient to list the attractions of Freemasonry, the best means of measuring their importance is in a comparative context. What other organisations existed that offered similar attractions, and how did they fare in attracting men's time and money? The most similar competitors were the major associated friendly societies, such as the Oddfellows and the Foresters. It is notable that they attracted far more members than the Freemasons but, as will be seen, tens and perhaps hundreds of thousands joined both. At one level they provided all of the things that Masonry offered and more; at another, they were clearly deficient in some areas. The contemporary who declared that 'The working man would find little in it [Freemasonry] to induce him to support it in preference to his club or Benefit Society'[77] may have been correct for the generality but a minority clearly thought otherwise. What is the evidence?

Activities and Offerings
Although there were important differences between them, all of the friendly societies enjoyed characteristics that were very similar to Freemasonry[78] and which may have been borrowed from it. They all had various systems of ritual

which conveyed concepts of morality and ethics, and harked back to an idealised past.[79] They worked in 'Lodges' (Oddfellows), 'Courts' (Foresters) and 'Tents' (Rechabites). They identified themselves as 'communities' with a sense of 'otherness' if not exclusivity. They offered networks of contacts and informal support where mutual trust provided the 'glue' that held the whole together.[80] They had local, regional, national and international dimensions. Although, as one commentator observed, people joined primarily 'to avoid the humiliation of pauperism and the need to accept charity',[81] they also offered facilities for 'entertainment' and social fellowship, both within the lodge and beyond, with annual festivals, church parades, picnics and sociable dinners. Members became trusted associates of supportive groups, expanded their networks of associations and frequently had the opportunity to mix as equals with others above their own social station. It is notable, for example, that in 1878 the membership of the Foresters, at a national level, included 17 peers, 4 bishops, and 172 MPs, including the Masons E.F.L. Gower who sat for Bodmin and Sir Frederick M. Williams for Truro.

It was a formula that had wide and enduring popularity and one that was not so much derived from Freemasonry as independently evolved alongside it. The Oddfellows provide a good example. Emerging first during the fashion for secret societies in the mid-eighteenth century, its initial activities were focused almost entirely on sociability and remained heavily centred on London.[82] Since a proportion of its early membership were Freemasons and as the Oddfellows took on various Masonic symbols and ritual structures, some tried initially to lay claim to similar ancient origins. It effectively lay dormant during the late eighteenth century but was reborn in a number of guises in the early nineteenth century in the industrial areas of the north of England. Although now focusing on the more mundane aspects of mutual assurance for the rapidly growing working class, it retained an amount of their previous rituals and structures.

The most successful and durable of the various Oddfellow orders was the Independent Order of Oddfellows, Manchester Unity.[83] This Order showed close parallels with Masonry, both in terms of its rituals and procedures as well as its institutional structures. Its guiding principles were Friendship, Love and Truth, and it emphasised brotherly love and charity in its various rituals. Like Masonry, its objective was to make its members wiser and better men, and it did so through a series of lectures linked to four degrees of initiation. They were: the First, or White Degree (charity); the Second, or Blue Degree (truth); the Third, or Scarlet Degree (knowledge); and the Fourth, or Gold Degree (science).[84] There were ceremonies for the opening and closing of lodges, and the use of a multitude of symbols, such as hand, heart, dove, olive branch, three rings, etc.[85]

As in Masonry, these ceremonies were adopted not simply for their esoteric meaning but to help bind members together, provide a means of identification and exclude intruders. Oddfellows lodges elected their own Master—the Noble Grand—and a Grand Lodge was ruled by a Grand Master and Grand Officers.

Though there were great similarities between the orders there were also major differences. They generally did not lay claim to the same continuous ancient lineage as the Masons,[86] preferring to look back to more recent origins; they introduced auxiliaries for women and young people; and they favoured guaranteed assurance over prospective charity. The great nineteenth-century friendly societies had largely found their initial inspiration in the small local 'penny clubs' that proliferated in the eighteenth century. In these clubs, members contributed small sums on their visits to the lodge to provide a common fund to relieve those in occasional distress. From the 1830s, however, the Oddfellows, like the other benevolent societies, began to phase that out in favour of a system of periodic dues, collections and initiation charges. By paying regular sums according to actuarially assessed tables, members could begin to assure themselves of the receipt of fixed amounts during periods of sickness and the death of themselves and their wife. In other words they began to provide what we might now recognise as collaborative social security. The working classes quickly began to flock into membership. By 1838 the Manchester Unity already had around 40,000 members, mainly around the Manchester area, and by 1845 this had increased to nearly a quarter of a million in 3,690 lodges scattered across the country.[87] Approximately 15% of these were ordinary labourers and 47% skilled or semi-skilled workers.[88]

By contrast to the occasional voluntary charitable contribution made by the Masons, the regular guaranteed benefits offered by the friendly societies placed them in an entirely different legal position. Since they needed to accumulate and maintain large funds to meet future commitments, they could be subject to fraud by their administrators. By the end of the eighteenth century it was thought prudent to introduce legislation that would enable them to register in order to obtain legal identity and protection. The Act of 1793 also established some supervision of the rules and administration of registered societies by the justices of the Quarter Sessions. Further legislation through the nineteenth century extended and tightened the regulations, and provided for greater transparency by the publication of detailed returns of their activities.[89] Freemasonry escaped all of this and lodges remained subject only to the stipulation that they make annual returns of their members to the Quarter Sessions—a requirement that remained in force through to the mid-twentieth century.

Broad occupational data for the Ancient Order of Foresters suggests that a great preponderance were also from skilled and semi-skilled manual occupations together with a large number of clerks and those involved in trade and hospitality.[90] There are no reliable estimates of the national participation rate in benevolent/friendly societies, but regional studies suggest that it was already very high by the third quarter of the nineteenth century. In her study of Glamorganshire, for example, Jones estimated that around one in every five of the county's population in the 1860s, regardless of age or sex, was a member of a registered friendly society and that for men alone it may have risen to almost 90%. Evidence from other local studies suggests that these conclusions were not wildly unusual, except possibly in London.[91]

Costs and Benefits

In terms of the comparative ease and costs of joining, annual subscriptions to sustain membership and the tangible benefits that could be expected, Freemasonry did not compare well with the major benevolent orders. The problems and expense were apparent from the outset. Individuals could not apply themselves but needed to be proposed by an existing member. That member needed to know, approve of and to trust them sufficiently to put up a one guinea[92] deposit to ensure that the candidate actually appeared on the night of their initiation. It was forfeit if they failed to appear without good cause. Thereafter the fees were incurred sequentially as the various stages of initiation were taken. These costs increased slightly after the mid-nineteenth century but those for the Lodge of Love and Honour at Falmouth, Cornwall in the late 1870s were as follows:

Proposition	£1 1s
First degree	£5 5s
Second degree	£1 1s
Third degree	£1 1s
Annual subscription	£1 0s

The total for a new member being initiated, passed and raised to the third degree of Master Mason, together with the first year's membership, was thus £7 7s, with the proposer receiving back his £1 1s. If a Lodge of Emergency was needed to conduct any part of the initiation, because the candidate was leaving the area or had some other call on his time, there would be an additional charge of £6 2s 6d. From this income, the lodge paid an initiation fee to UGLE of 17s 0d and to the PGL 5 shillings. Joining members, who had already become Masons in another lodge, paid one guinea if they were previously from an English constitution lodge or two guineas if from a lodge operating under another jurisdiction. Of this,

2s 6d and 1 shilling were paid to the UGLE and the PGL respectively,[93] These charges were identical or very similar for all of the lodges in West Cornwall and remained much the same over the whole period.[94] It effectively meant that simply to become a Freemason would have cost a working miner the equivalent of nearly two months' wages—a skilled craftsman more than a month's wages— and a professional several weeks' income.

Once a member, the 'running costs' of being a Mason were fairly low. The annual subscription, of around £1 paid in quarterly amounts, was a little less than what might be paid to the Foresters or the Oddfellows but additional costs associated with Masonry could bring the total up considerably higher. There were, for example, regular contributions of several shillings a year to benevolence, and entertainment could prove expensive. The Lodge of Love and Honour, for example, levied a charge of 5 shillings towards the cost of the dinner on St John the Evangelist's day, while Druids Lodge of Love and Liberality in Redruth charged visitors the full 10s 6d costs for the equivalent meal.[95] As the *Freemason* noted in 1894 in an editorial on 'The Cost of Masonry':

> the doors of our Society are opened indifferently to the men of rank and opulence, and the honest tradesman and mechanic or artisan of moderate means … the cost depends chiefly upon what the members, singularly or collectively, choose to make it, not upon any special rules or prescription pertaining to it.[96]

In return for all of these costs, Masons had no right to expect any tangible financial return. They might receive valuable help and advice from their brethren but the only monetary outcome was the possibility of a charitable grant in the event of death, disaster, old age or infirmity.

By contrast, the major benevolent societies were easy to join, affordable to belong to, and offered clear and guaranteed financial outcomes for a range of specified problems. Their members could claim relief under specific circumstance 'as of right', while Freemasons depended on the charity dispensed at the discretion of the lodge.[97] The costs of benevolent society membership generally varied according to the member's age and the level of insurance taken out. Thus, in the 1880s, an eighteen-year-old member of the Ancient Order of Foresters insuring an allowance of 1 shilling per week for sickness for the first six months would cost 1 shilling per annum; insuring for £1 per week would cost 20s 3d per annum. At age thirty-nine, the cost would be 1s 6d and 30s 4d respectively. Funeral benefit of £1 for a member would also vary, from 3¼d per annum at age eighteen to 10d at age fifty, and most would chose to multiply those figures for higher benefits. In that society, occupational dangers were rarely taken into account, but rates were varied accordingly 'rural, town district, city district', the lowest being for rural district. For an 'average' subscription in Cornwall it might be appropriate to take the sums paid by a thirty-year-old married male living in a town district. To ensure a sickness benefit of 12 shillings a week for the first six months off work[98] and 9 shillings a week for a second six months, together with a death benefit of £12 for himself and £8 for his wife, he would have to pay an annual subscription of 21s 6d.[99] The arrangements in the Manchester Unity of Oddfellows were similar but slightly more expensive: similar assurance for a thirty-year-old male in the 1880s approximated to 27 shillings per annum.[100] Unlike the Foresters, however, who admitted no new members over the age of thirty-five, the Oddfellows continued to recruit up to forty-five years of age and had some plans with slightly higher subscriptions for men in particularly hazardous employment. By the early years of the new century the average annual charge for those aged thirty appears to have increased to something around 30 shillings.[101]

Membership and Cross-membership
With clear cost-benefit advantages, the membership of benevolent and friendly societies expanded much more rapidly than Freemasonry and by the end of the century stood at around two million.[102] The relative importance of the different orders varied around the country, with the Independent Order of Oddfellows, Manchester Unity, being marginally the largest nationally. In Cornwall, however, cost advantages appear to have been particularly influential and the less-expensive Foresters soon outnumbered the Oddfellows almost two to one.[103] As Appendix 9 shows, the relative balance varied locally, with the Foresters only being exceeded by the Oddfellows in the main industrial towns of Truro, Redruth, Camborne and possibly Helston. Both orders faced a major challenge in the west of the county from the Independent Order of Rechabites, but their appeal appears to have been as much associated with their strict prohibition of drinking as by their respective membership costs.

Across Cornwall—as over the country as a whole—men and their families embraced the principles and practice of fraternity with ever-increasing enthusiasm. In every town, large and small, they often had a number of different options to choose between. Their choices reflected the relative costs and benefits, the attractions of the rituals performed, their existing friendships patterns, micro-local affiliations, etc.[104] At one level this greatly assisted the creation of social capital and cohesion, but at another it began further to divide communities. Most did not want, or could not afford, more than one affiliation—some societies even prohibited it—and different classes and groups deepened and narrowed their existing networking structures. Masonry vacuumed up the middle classes while the working classes increasingly lived and socialized with the brethren of their chosen benevolent order. However, these lines were never hard and fast, and there was much blurring at the margins. Many middle-class businessmen and professions looked for the added security of the assured benefits of benevolent societies; many of the more prosperous craftsmen and skilled workers became Masons in search of the benefits not bestowed to the same degree by benevolent societies. Some who wanted to reach out through multiple networks, such as politicians and other community leaders, maintained multiple networks. At a local level, cross-associational links were sometimes established to bring the various orders, church groups, etc., together.[105] Many of those that sought membership across the usual class divide often had experience of the other form of fraternity and some sustained it. Evidence of the joint membership of Masonic and Foresters lodges, for example, has already been presented below in Appendices 7 and 10. Unfortunately it is extremely difficult to produce more detailed analyses for specific lodges in particular towns because membership records for the various benevolent societies have not survived in the same complete and detailed condition as those for Freemasonry. However, some material can be pieced together for parts of Cornwall.

Around 1900 the largest benevolent societies in Cornwall were the Ancient Order of Foresters, the Independent Order of Oddfellows and the Rechabites, with roughly 7,800, 4,100 and 3,200 members respectively. It is possible that it had the most organised county in the country relative to population.[106] With just 2,000 members, Freemasonry was considerably smaller but was intimately connected with the other orders. Appendix 10 gives details of the members of the Masonic Fowey Lodge who also became members of Court Treffry of the Ancient Order of Foresters in Fowey. Overall, of the 243 men that joined Fowey Lodge between 1863 and 1900, sixty were, or became, members of Court Treffry indicating a cross-membership of around a quarter of the Lodge members. Of those with joint membership, the majority became Masons after a period of time as Foresters, suggesting that there were aspects of Masonry that were not provided by Forestry.

Unfortunately, it has not been possible to identify cross-membership of Masonic and Oddfellows lodges in Cornwall in the same detail, but it is probable that it stood at an equal level. While Freemasonry came to have the Prince of Wales as its Grand Master, the Oddfellows counted George IV as a member, its ritual was closely related and it had lodges in most major centres of population. Some even saw Oddfellowry as a direct adjunct to Masonry, deriving its name from the 'hod' carriers who worked with operative Masons in past times.[107] The second-largest Oddfellows lodge in Cornwall regularly met in Redruth's Masonic Hall and there were clearly close relations between the two groups throughout the nineteenth century.[108] Forestry probably stood socially a notch below the Masons and Oddfellows. Before leaving the subject of cross-membership, it is important to observe that it was not simply a two-way street between Masonry and the benevolent societies, but also between the benevolent societies themselves. Those that could afford it often had multiple memberships in order to access diverse network systems and the societies themselves also often collaborated for mutual help and support.[109] Industrial and community leaders might regard it as their duty to be represented in a wide range of benevolent and fraternal organisations.

Conclusion

Freemasonry had many and various offerings in the nineteenth century which worked in different combinations to attract different men in different places at different times. There is unlikely to have been any single factor that exercised a dominant influence over all potential members at any one point. Equally, it is highly probable that the factors that first attracted men to Masonry were not the same as those that caused them to stay. What they found on the inside of what was then a secretive organisation is likely to have been very different from what they initially observed from the outside. However, a particular combination of issues probably influenced some groups more than others. The aristocratic echelon were probably more swayed by the simple need to follow fashion and emulate royalty, while the middle class would have been attracted by the advantages that a Masonic identity bestowed in terms of respectability and reputation. Professionals and those involved in commerce might particularly have appreciated the networking potential, while clergy and politicians could have hoped to attract both attention and support. Entertainment would also have figured prominently for these groups, particularly the dinners held after regular lodge meetings as well as periodic festivals and provincial events. Lodges were famed for their food, drink and convivial companionship, and would have been seen not simply as a pleasurable way to spend an evening but also as a means of making and cementing new relationships. Of course these social activities normally would have appealed principally to the middle and upper classes with ample funds but the ability of lodges to tailor the frequency, location and cost of meals to members' resources also opened similar opportunities for craftsmen and artisans. Similar observations might also be made about the costs of other

Masonic entertainments such as outings, picnics and dances. It helped to be wealthy to enjoy the full benefits of Masonry, but it was not essential. The 'entertainment' value of nostalgia for a lost past and the possibilities of discovering 'hidden secrets' may have attracted the attention of men from a wide variety of backgrounds but it was probably a minority interest, and well down the list, for most.

The attractions of ritual are more difficult to estimate. At one level its practice could be regarded as simply as another aspect of the entertainment activities of Masonry, but at another it took on a clear significance of its own. Anyone who had experience of the meetings of skilled unions, friendly or benevolent societies might have gained an insight into such issues and been attracted to the extended and complex rituals of Masonry and its side orders. They might also have been drawn to the different forms of regalia, jewels and other ostentatious accoutrements offered by these orders as well as the high-sounding titles and rank that they offered. The regalia and jewels cost money—lots of it when constructed or ornamented with precious metals—but enabled the aristocracy and wealthy physically to display their position and dominance at the top of Masonry as in society at large. Rank similarly enabled the middle class to demonstrate their progression to ever greater things.

While there was much in Masonry for the upper and middle classes with the resources to enjoy it, what was in it for the financially stretched, respectable working class? They joined in ever larger numbers from the early nineteenth century and must surely have found powerful attractions that were not available elsewhere. From a comparison of Freemasonry with the other major fraternal and benevolent societies operating in the late nineteenth century it would appear that the working-class and lower-middle-class men that joined Masonry did not do so because it was much cheaper or offered better and more reliable benefits. Most would have been attracted by Masonry's 'other', largely qualitative, offerings. These could have included the opportunities to raise their social status, practice more complex rituals, provide access to hidden mysteries, widen their recreational opportunities, and numerous other narrowly individual and local issues. However, for some there was also one other very attractive and practical aspect of Masonry not shared to the same degree by other orders, namely its local, national and international support networks. These networks not only provided guidance and information, but also gave practical assistance in finding business contacts and jobs, assisting social assimilation and, above all, providing fallback temporary security for members and their families when on the move. Freemasonry was not unique in this respect. All of the benevolent societies, particularly the larger ones such as the Foresters and Oddfellows with thousands of affiliated branches across the country and much of the world, could offer similar linkages. Their members were commonly offered travel cards that enabled them to claim their usual benefits when away from home and they were provided with Masonic-like secret words, grips, signs and countersigns, and passwords to identify themselves.[110] However, unlike Masonry, they were usually time- and, sometimes, place-limited, and did not carry the same commitments to provide charitable relief under all circumstances. This will be the subject of the next chapter, which will show in some detail the importance of 'traveller relief' for working-class Masonic recruitment.

REASONS FOR JOINING, PART 2 OCCUPATIONAL: MUTUAL ASSURANCE, ACCESS AND NETWORKING

Mobile occupations and economic migration over short and long distances were well established long before the modern era. The movement of peoples was one of the earliest driving forces of civilisation, and the ancients had seen traders and merchants plying routes to the furthest reaches of Europe and Asia. By the medieval period, 'tramping artisans' regularly travelled throughout Europe and ironed out temporary regional imbalances in the supply of labour. Stonemasons, for example, had skills in international demand for building castles, churches and grand buildings of all descriptions, and as one project was completed they might necessarily move on to the next. The numbers involved in trade and shipping increased dramatically with the creation of European overseas empires in the sixteenth and seventeenth centuries, and the commercial revolution that accompanied it. The eighteenth and nineteenth centuries saw population explosions, spreading industrialisation, the relocation of jobs from rural to urban areas, new lands, resources and frontiers, and a transport revolution on land and sea that connected places faster and more cheaply than ever. Revolutions in communications, through rapid mail, telegraphy, newspapers and cheaply printed books and magazines made people ever more aware of distant opportunities. Largely sedentary old communities began to break down, new fluid ones were created, and travel and migration became a regular part of life, particularly for wage-dependent workers.

However, there was a problem—a major one. Travellers and migrants are subject to considerably greater risks from accidents, ill health, crime and disaster compared with those that stay at home. They are also without the support that they might commonly expect from family members and the community, and are unusually 'exposed' to the dangers they encounter. As we now are reminded by contemporary economic migrations, those making their way from village to town—and particularly from home to foreign countries—are particularly vulnerable to transport misadventures, exploitation by those that they meet en route and the constant fear of running out of money to obtain food and accommodation. On arrival they have problems finding work and housing; dealing with differences in languages, culture and religion; settling their families and generally integrating into their new social environment.[1] Even when they arrive safely and are settled in, they can be plagued by problems for the families that they have left behind.

Today, national governments and numerous well-funded charities do their best to alleviate many of these problems, particularly in the developed world. Rescue services and coastguards minister to the survivors of wrecked vehicles and vessels. Government agencies commonly provide food and shelter for those stranded on the road; they attempt to regulate exploitative practices by those that might provide work for new arrivals; and they develop extensive social services arrangements properly to settle and assimilate new arrivals.

During the second half of the nineteenth century, however, few if any of these 'safety nets' existed. In most places governments did little to secure the lives even of their own nationals and anyone who fell upon bad times necessarily had to rely on their personal resources or those of friends and family. They were often far away and uncontactable. Problems such as these were drivers for some of the earliest forms of state aid and the origins of the modern 'welfare state'. The State, for example, had long made limited arrangements for the care of the poor, old, orphaned and disabled, and collaborative friendly and benevolent societies emerged to provide private insurance for ill health, unemployment and death.[2] These, however, did little for domestic travellers and virtually nothing for those in international transit.

In this insecure world, Freemasonry offered some unusual and very reassuring benefits. Its key provisions were 'Brotherly Love' and 'Relief' which, along with 'Truth', made up its 'Three Grand Principles' to which all new members swore allegiance at their initiation. Today the commitment to 'relief' is generally taken to mean 'charity', and Masons and their lodges are one of the very largest sources of income for local and national charities as well as international emergency relief. In the eighteenth and nineteenth centuries, however, relief was interpreted very specifically as an expression of Masonic brotherly love and widely interpreted as a form of direct mutual assurance. As John Hamill put it in his history of Masonic charity, 'In simple terms our early brethren understood Relief to mean the alleviation of the suffering of a brother, or the dependents [sic] of a deceased brother, by giving money or sustenance until the circumstances improved.'[3] The support was usually in the form of small, one-off cash payments to those men and their families who encountered misadventure, as well as the opportunity to visit or join lodges after arrival. In those final destination lodges they could expect to receive advice and assistance in finding employment, long-term accommodation, local information and a range of other knowledge that would help them settle in. Such immediate and direct help is less necessary today, with donor and recipient usually being distanced by institutional charities, but it was very common until well into the twentieth century. Many groups of men in other organisations have made similar obligations of mutual assurance but none seem to have made it work more continuously and effectively as the Masons.

It will be argued here, firstly, that these many privileges of membership became widely known, inside and outside of the Craft. Secondly, that they helped to attract new members, particularly from the more mobile occupational and social groups, and greatly facilitated domestic and international migration. Thirdly, that they significantly improved the economic and social lives of Masons and their families after their arrival in new communities. Fourthly, that they made a significant contribution to the wider construction of social capital and the quality of life in receiving communities, especially in new and rapidly expanding frontier areas. The discussion will start by reviewing the mechanisms for charitable assistance for the travelling Masons and their families, and then move on to look at two large and particularly mobile occupational groups that benefited from migratory support. Much has already been outlined in the work of researchers such as Paul Rich and Jessica Harland-Jacobs,[4] but that will be extended here with material drawn from the archival material of lodges operating around the world and extended discussions held in the Masonic press.

Mutual Assurance and 'Tramping'

Today it is usual to think of Masonic charity in terms of the large central charities. The RMBI, RMIB and RMIG discussed above[5] had been transformed into, and complemented by, the Freemasons' Grand Charity, the Royal Masonic Trust for Girls and Boys, the Royal Masonic Benevolent Institution and the Masonic Samaritan Fund. These themselves have now been consolidated into one great Masonic Charitable Foundation, reflecting the modern 'distant' way of organising charity. In past times, however, immediate 'direct' charitable help and assistance between Masons was far more significant. With the amounts of money available to the large institutional charities limited until the end of the nineteenth century, this ad hoc charity, given either directly by individuals or organised through the lodges, was the most important way that Masons mutually assured each other in times of adversity. It was the kind of charity that was practiced before the evolution of the charitable institutions and which continued to operate actively alongside them for much of the nineteenth and early twentieth centuries.

Although it has now become uncommon, this form of charity lies at the heart of Freemasonry and a solemn obligation continues to be taken during the ceremony of initiation. Firstly, the initiate is advised:

> In a society so widely extended as Freemasonry, the branches of which are spread over the four quarters of the globe, it cannot be denied that we have many members of rank and opulence: neither can it be concealed that among the thousands who range under its banners, there are some who, perhaps from circumstances of unavoidable calamity and misfortune, are reduced to the lowest ebb of poverty and distress. On their behalf it is our usual custom to awaken the feelings of every new made Brother to such a claim on his charity as his circumstances in life may fairly warrant.

Then, following a test of his professed sincerity in pledging himself to such charitable giving, he is admonished:

> should you at any future period meet a brother in distressed circum- stances who might solicit your assistance ...... cheerfully embrace the opportunity of practising that virtue you have professed to admire.[6]

In the late eighteenth century, William Preston, one of the early authorities on modern Masonry, elaborated by declaring that:

> When pity is excited, the Mason will assuage grief, and cheerfully relieve distress. If a brother is in want, every heart is moved, when he is hungry, we feed him; when he is naked, we clothe him; when he is in trouble, we fly to his relief ... BROTHER, among Masons, is more than the name.[7]

The essential context of these commitments is that they applied not simply to the brethren of the lodge where they were made, but to all Masons everywhere. Thus Thomas Dunckerley explained:

> Let me travel from east to west, or between north and south, when I meet a true brother I shall find a friend, who will do all in his power

to serve me, without having the least view of self-interest: and if I am poor and in distress, he will relieve me to the utmost of his power, interest and capacity.

It is also important to stress that the promises extended, not just to the man, but also his family. As the Masonic newspaper *The Freemason* observed:

> The widow and orphan daughter of a Master Mason takes the place of the husband and father in the affections and good deeds of the Lodge ... If travelling at a distance from home, they find themselves sick and in want among strangers, they have but to make themselves known as the widow and orphan daughter of a worthy Master Mason ... To you are given all of the advantages of the Society, its shield of protection, its hand of relief, its voice of sympathy.[8]

A good example of such family support was reported in 1861. The widow of a Mason who had emigrated to Australia but died shortly after arrival, petitioned a local lodge in Sydney for the funds to return home with her children. Although the lodge had never actually seen her late husband, they raised over £20 to pay for the return journey.[9] Any prudent wife contemplating taking her family away from home might well decide that this more than compensated for her husband's long evenings at the lodge and festive board.

Clearly, direct personal assistance could, and did, take many forms. The most common was probably where the wealthier members of lodges assisted the less well off in times of emergency. In Cornwall, for example, Samuel Richards, a bootmaker, who was initiated into Lodge of Fortitude in Truro in 1872 and did well for some years, failed in business in 1881 and assigned all of his family's possessions to his creditors. The brethren of his lodge came together to raise £25 (the equivalent of more than £2,000 today) to relieve his immediate suffering and provide for some future income. But it was not only the working-class members of lodges that might need relief. Even the better off might themselves fall on hard times through ill health or business failure and look to their brethren for assistance. John Chandler, a City of London stockbroker, lost all of his business and personal property as a result of a commercial crisis in 1880, and looked to his brethren in Lodge of Felicity No. 58 to provide assistance. They collected funds not only to provide immediate sustenance for himself, his wife and seven children, but also to set up some business for him so that he might also recover an independent future.[10] However, while this kind of interactive relief between lodge members was probably very common, it is difficult to locate clear examples and even more difficult to quantify them. More easily identified are the charitable donations made to visiting brethren from other lodges who found themselves in difficulties while travelling. Where given by the lodge, these were usually recorded in lodge account books as 'road relief' or 'relief to a brother on the road'.

Unfortunately, there are not enough lodge account books still in existence to quantify accurately the amount of relief given in any particular region or period, and surviving proof of acts of charity between individuals is even more scarce. However, secondary evidence suggests that it stood at a high level, particularly in areas of frequent and rapid transit, and that it was particularly important for some very mobile occupational groups. At this point, it is necessary to step back and look at the means and methods commonly employed by travelling workmen in the eighteenth and early nineteenth centuries, and to give brief consideration to the practice of the 'Tramping Artisan'.

Before modern forms of cheap transport, travel for the less well off was principally on foot; it was slow and required frequent overnight stops. The workmen's practice of 'tramping' has been defined as a process of 'moving from town to town to remove surplus labour from one market and seek employment in another'.[11] It was first brought to prominence by the historian Eric Hobsbawm who observed that there was 'hardly any trade society [guild or union] in the country which provided its members with benefits [that] failed to adopt it'. He went on to describe the operation of the system:

> The man who wished to leave town to look for work elsewhere, received a 'blank' or 'clearance' or 'document' showing him to be a member in good standing of the society. This he presented to the local secretary or relieving officer in the 'lodge house' or 'club house' or 'house of call' of the strange town—generally a pub—receiving in return supper, lodging, perhaps beer, and a tramp allowance. If there was work to be found, he took it; the 'call book' (if there was one) was of course kept at the house of call, an unofficial local labour exchange.[12]

A good example of the evolution and operation of the system has been provided by Musson in his history of association in the skilled printing trades. He showed that typographical societies had been established in most large towns across Britain by the early nineteenth century and that they were linked together by a complex of tramping relief. Arriving members might receive overnight relief or even larger sums if they stayed for a longer period. He was also able to estimate the numbers involved in 'tramping', showing how one society in Manchester relieved 340 arriving men in the difficult year of 1841. It occurred over long as well as short distances, with some tramping members performing what was effectively a 'grand tour' of the country, particularly in periods of depression when employment was scarce.[13]

For stonemasons this system had begun to evolve in the medieval period.[14] Eager not only to maintain control of entrance to the craft and the quality of workmanship, the emergent guilds also strove to balance the labour force. They helped to attract more workers from outside when new projects created a demand as well as to 'export' workers to other areas when employment dried up, so maintaining stable wage levels. They had nationally and internationally transferable skills and long-distance travel was probably common for many. To facilitate movement, those that travelled in search of work could expect temporary accommodation, food and other relief from lodges encountered en route as well as advice and assistance in finding a job on arrival.[15] Knoop and Jones referred to sixteenth-century Ordinances which had provisions that 'required Masons to receive and cherish strange fellows and to provide them with work—in many versions a "fortnight's work"—or failing work, to supply them with money to bring them to the next Lodge'.[16] Travel and movement was part and parcel of the operatives' life and facilitating it was one of the primary functions of the operatives' guilds.

When the modern form of 'accepted' Masonry emerged from the guilds in the late seventeenth and early eighteenth centuries it was logical for them to carry over the same tramping arrangements that saw contemporary evolution elsewhere. They would have proved particularly useful for those working-class members of the new lodges that did not have other skilled trade affiliations, and perhaps could be seen as a useful addition for those that did. During the eighteenth century it was probably carried forward and developed more by the socially varied 'Ancients' than the relatively elitist 'Moderns' but it had become a firmly established aspect of the Order by the early nineteenth century and continued as such into the early twentieth century.

The manner of seeking support while tramping, or when encountering misfortune, was by personal application to individual Masons or the Almoner of the nearest lodge. There was no guarantee of the sums that might be received, but in England during most of the second half of the nineteenth century, it was usually between 2s 6d and 10s 6d (half a guinea). The lesser sum approximated to an unskilled labourer's daily wage at the time and would have guaranteed a good short-term subsistence to a single man. Since multiple gifts might be received, and since further applications could be made to other Masons and lodges along the road, such amounts would be attractive even to the more prosperous members of the Order. They certainly compared very well with the levels of support that an impoverished traveller was likely to receive from the parish they were passing through. For example, when a Cornish miner with his wife and child were returning from an unsuccessful migration to the Durham coal mines in 1867, he was forced to apply to the 'Poor Box' while passing through Exeter. First he had to convince an examining Magistrate that they were a worthy cause and then they were given the minimum of one-way third-class tickets to Plymouth with just 2 shillings for their food and accommodation.[17]

Examples of how the system worked can be found widely in contemporary lodge account books, the Masonic press and recorded anecdotes. Thus the Minute Book of Royal Alfred Lodge, meeting at Diss in Norfolk, recorded that at just its second meeting in March 1771:

> a distressed brother, one George D'Sherinb, a native of La Lippe, Buckenbourg, in Westphalia, having been, with his nephew, shipwrecked in the Bay of Biscay, and lost all he had on board, and travelling through this town, on his way to London, was relieved with a donation of 10s and 6d, having produced his certificate of being a member of the Lodge of 'Good Faith', Paris.[18]

At the beginning of the next century, with the cessation of major hostilities at the end of the Napoleonic wars, lodges in the south-east of England were sometimes called upon to assisted returning soldiers in onward travel to their homes and families. On 12 May 1814, for example, Robert Attree, of Brighton's Royal Clarence Lodge, met ten Masons who were coming home after being held as prisoners of war by the French at Ostend. They fortunately all carried with them what one private soldier described as his 'passport', the certificate issued by his lodge. Having noted the numbers so that they could later be verified, the men were rested, fed and each given 5 shillings to see them on their way. Three were bound for Gosport in Hampshire, two to Ludgate and Wapping in London, another to Dover in Kent. The remainder had further to go—to Manchester in Lancashire and Great Yarmouth in Norfolk—and may no doubt have called on other lodges en route for further assistance.[19]

One of the best indications of the value of the system was the scale of its exploitation. As the generous Masonic charitable commitment to distressed travellers became better known, it acted as a recruiting sergeant not just for legitimate new members but also for cheats and frauds. All welfare schemes lend themselves to exploitation and properly regulating them becomes ever more difficult. They also arguably undermine personal responsibility and encourage a culture of entitlement among some, even the deserving. Masons everywhere became increasingly concerned about abuses of the system. This was not something that was unique to Freemasonry but was common to all associations providing traveller relief and support. For example, the typographical association, mentioned earlier, also became concerned about worthless and dissolute workmen exploiting the system, and the increasing number of 'professional roadsters'.[20] Evidence of fraudulent problems for the Freemasons can be found from the earliest days of the Order. In 1735, for example, Grand Lodge passed a resolution effectively trying to ensure that those joining were of reputable economic standing and not simply looking to benefit from charitable funds.[21] At a more local level, a letter from the Secretary of the Lodge of Probity in Halifax in 1816 expressed concern about relieving 'tramping or itinerant Masons', and complained that 'Of late we have had many Applications from Tramps, etc, for relief as they pretended they were seeking work.'[22] On 3 December 1823 Grand Lodge Quarterly Communications contained a report from the Board of General Purposes alerting lodges to a man calling himself Simon Ramus, who had been using a forged certificate to obtain financial relief, and also noticed Joseph Larkin, who was attempting a similar fraud under the name of Miles Martin.[23]

Such concerns became increasingly common and Freemasons, with their relatively well-off membership and strong commitment to charitable assistance, appear to have been an easy and lucrative target. From the mid-nineteenth century, articles and leaders in the Masonic press show a rising tide of concern about a small army of 'Masonic impostors', who wandered the country and plagued lodges and individuals as they tried to live off benevolence. If the number of complaints provides an indicator of the scale of the problem, it appears to have come to a peak around the late 1890s and early 1900s.

The general concern and complaint appears to conflate two significantly different types of 'impostor'. Firstly, there were regular, and perhaps lapsed, Freemasons who had taken to exploiting the system and secondly, there were men who had never been Freemasons but fraudulently claimed membership. The first group were sometimes described as 'Masons in name, vagrant in act' and the second simply as 'tramps', 'pretend Masons', 'cadgers'.[24] The first group were seen by many to be drawn from the rising number of what were thought of as 'second-class' men being introduced into Masonry—artisans, tradesmen, low-grade clerical staff and ordinary workers—who accounted for much of the growth of Freemasonry during the second half of the century.[25] They had probably made insufficient provision for themselves and their family, while being more likely to wander in search of work and to encounter difficulties as they economised on travel facilities, accommodation and food. The chances were high that that they would become applicants for charity rather than the source of it and, above all, to appear 'improvident' to the more economically and socially successful groups that still generally dominated Masonry in England.

A good example of this can be found in the complaints that were made about Scottish Masons. It was argued that their lodges were particularly lax in letting in 'unsuitable' men of limited means by pushing them through their initiation too quickly and not requiring them to pay regular lodge dues.[26] Many English lodges, who commonly congratulated themselves on their middle-class membership, were frequently aghast at the number of 'tramping Masons' from Scotland, who were often little more than 'artisans'. Senior Masons in the North of England saw Scottish migrants as 'the greatest tax upon us' and one Deputy PGM complained bitterly that their lodges were being inundated almost daily, with men arriving 'not in single files, but in battalions'.[27] The UGLE complained on several occasions to the Grand Lodge of Scotland about the practice of Scottish lodges accommodating unsuitable Englishmen who crossed the border to find what they saw as an easier way into Masonry,[28] while the Grand Lodge of Scotland itself noted that:

> complaints are being made of young men furnished with diplomas arriving in the Colonies who are utterly unable to pass a simple examination, arising from the fact that they had in some instances been allowed to receive the three degrees in one night.[29]

It is important to point out, however, that not all Scottish Masons were rascals and that the great majority of members were thoroughly respectable equivalents of their English brethren and made a major contribution to lodges, their communities and the success of Freemasonry worldwide. The holders of Scottish Grand Lodge certificates had earned respect everywhere and were properly accorded the same access to lodges through the English constitution (see Illustration 6). It is equally important to remember that English lodges also were not without blame in sometimes attracting 'marginal' candidates. As will be shown below, many maritime lodges took in mariners from other nations who might not have been able to obtain membership under their own constitutions.[30] Similarly, many English lodges were happy to accommodate working men who joined to assist in their own travels to other districts or overseas.

Unsuitable candidates that were rejected by 'regular' lodges sometimes turned to 'irregular' lodges for initiation—i.e. those not recognised by the Grand Lodges and excluded from equivalent membership. These might provide a possible 'backdoor entry' into Freemasonry, when welcomed by unwary lodge

Illustration 6   Scottish Grand Lodge Certificate

Every Grand Lodge produced certificates of their own design but they all incorporated many similar symbols and characteristics. This certificate from the Scottish Grand Lodge enabled its holder to seek admission to lodges under the English, Irish and many other national Constitutions, conditional on passing additional tests of signs and passwords. Movement between lodges was particularly common in British colonies where multiple parallel networks of lodges had been warranted. Men would frequently be initiated in lodges other than those of their own nationality depending simply on their locational convenience and availability.

officers, particularly in remote places. In 1859 and again in 1871, for example, the UGLE issued warnings about a spurious lodge operating in Stratford, Essex, calling itself part of the 'Reformed Masonic Order of Memphis, or Rite of the Grand Lodge of Philadelphia'. Members of this lodge had used their certificates (a facsimile of which was circulated to all English lodges) to try to become joining members of regular Masonic lodges.[31]

Even when men could prove their regular Masonic status they were often questioned very closely on the cause of the circumstance and if they were thought at all 'improvident' they were turned away. When William Hughan conducted a survey of lodge Almoners on the 'Masonic vagrant' problem in the last years of the century, he was told by some that between a third and a half were considered not to be 'deserving'.[32] Younger Masons in particular were urged not to be taken in and encourage the practice by making personal donations but to refer applicants to lodge Almoners. The magazine *Masonic Illustrated* declared that:

> It is not the Board of Benevolence, nor the Lodge Almoner who is responsible for the Masonic tramp. It is the private brother who finds it easier to part with five shillings or half a sovereign to get rid of his visitor than to take his name and address and then to make communication in the proper quarter.[33]

In response to the increasing administrative and financial burden that these kinds of claimants made on lodges, some of those in the larger industrial cities came together to provide one common respondent to applicants. In Warwickshire in the late 1890s, for example, the PGL strongly 'suggested':

1. That the lodges in every town in the Province should combine to appoint some resident brother as Almoner for that town.
2. That all Masonic vagrants should be referred to him for examination of their cases.
3. That the name and address of such Almoner should be sent to the Almoner of the Itinerant Fund in Birmingham, who would then see all claimants.
4. That the town Almoners should *at once* report to the Almoner of the Itinerant Fund the names of the applicants for relief, with the number of their lodge, date of their Grand Lodge certificate and other particulars, including the amount of relief given.[34]

The Province of Surrey made similar arrangements with the position of the overall Almoner closely co-ordinated with the Provincial Grand Secretary and the Secretary of the Provincial Charity Committee.[35] In Yorkshire, the eight lodges meeting in Leeds[36] established a local Masonic Relief Fund with just one Almoner to whom all travelling Masons were referred. That Fund raised a levy of 1 shilling per member from the lodges, which was sufficient to fund the relief given over a two-year period. In 1901 they recorded 40 acts of relief for 37 distressed brethren of whom 20 were English Masons, 10 Scottish, 3 Irish and 4 foreign.[37]

Poor and indigent Masons may have been a problem but outright impostors were an unacceptable affront. Some were simply seizing the occasional opportunity—such as a man who had borrowed a certificate from a friendly Mason to enable him 'in an itinerant manner to apply to lodges for relief'[38]—but many others were well-practiced and habitual offenders. In 1856, the Grand Treasurer of the UGLE claimed that he 'had found hundreds of pretend Masons who made a trade of it and lived by it'.[39] Again, numerous cases were reported in the Masonic press and that of the man calling himself J.B. Williams provides a good example. Following the customary procedure of circulating his description, The Freemason[40] described him as being 'of short stature, dark brown hair, no whiskers, carrying an umbrella in his hand, and dressed as the captain of a vessel at sea'. He claimed to have been shipwrecked, first landing in Hamburg and now making passage back to England.[41] Calling on the Brotherhood to aid his return, he carried with him a subscription book which purported to include the signatures of some of the Masonic fraternity in Hamburg and elsewhere, and more especially the signature of the British Consul at Hamburg. Back in Britain he paid a visit to a lodge in Berwick-upon-Tweed and called on the Almoner of the district. Not finding him in, and learning that he was away for some days, he forged the Almoner's name in the book and claimed that he had subscribed 5 shillings to his relief. Armed with this mode of deception, he then called on four Masonic ships' captains in Berwick-upon-Tweed, showed them the list of subscribers, boasting particularly of the Consul's signature. Three of them gave him a half sovereign each. The fourth captain, a Lloyds Agent, was intimately familiar with the Hamburg Consul's signature and looked up the details of the supposed lost ship. Finding none, he challenged the impostor who immediately fled.

Williams was lucky and appears to have got away, but many other fraudulent applicants were less fortunate. They were detained, prosecuted for fraud, and sentenced to significant terms in prison. Details of many of these malfeasants during the late 1890s were collected and published by James Pownall. Many of them were operating in those counties of northern and midland England which had a high population turnover, though he also refers to several fraudulent claimants operating in the South West and elsewhere. Overall, he estimates that there were about two hundred almost professional impostors going about the country over a five- or six-year period, though their impact on lodges and individual brethren was made far greater by the velocity of their circulation. To cover their activities they used a wide variety of aliases and, of those that were apprehended, several used 2 or 3 aliases, six had 4 or 5, four had 7 to 9, and one man used 12. Some were reported to operate over wide circuits, taking them three or four years to complete, while often using the same tried and tested stories. Under the circumstances, it was not surprising that they received often severe sentences when successfully prosecuted. Prison terms were common, ranging between fourteen days' and three months' hard labour.

Even this, however, seems not to have dissuaded practiced fraudsters who continued to see rich pickings for the taking. John Wilson, for example, prosecuted under several names, received fourteen days hard labour at Rochdale in August 1894, seven days hard labour at Cheadle, Staffordshire in August 1898, and fourteen days hard labour at Retford, Nottingham in January 1899. Although fraudsters rarely made off with more than a few shillings at a time, they were hardly likely to receive a sympathetic hearing from Masons such as John Valpy Thomas, Almoner for a lodge in Retford, Nottinghamshire, who was also a Superintendent of Police, or John Morton, Almoner for Huddersfield and district who was the Chief Constable of the West Riding of Yorkshire.[42]

Many impostors were foreign, sometimes from upper-class or aristocratic backgrounds, and had convincing stories of hardship. The *Masonic Magazine* reported in April 1867 on a Polish impostor, who pleaded that he had lost everything in the recent insurrection in his homeland. Another correspondent recorded that 'I have recently learned by experience that many Germans, Jews and Polish vagrants are in the habit of carrying on a regular trade out of public sympathy for the undeserved misfortunes of Poland'.[43] Not all impostors were men. Several members of at least one lodge were victimized by a woman, dressed in deep mourning, who falsely claimed to be the widow of a Mason who had died suddenly while travelling, leaving her destitute.[44]

If fraud was a problem among Masons journeying at home, it was an even greater problem for international travel journeys.[45] Everywhere unworthy Masons and impostors tried to take advantage of the system and their task was made the easier because of the chaotic conditions of new frontier areas. Everyone was a 'foreigner' or, at least, from far away: they came from different constitutions with slightly different signs, passwords and certificates.[46] Even if they had been properly initiated there were enormous difficulties in checking whether they were fully paid up in their home lodge and had not been excluded for some misdemeanour. However, international recognition and support for Masons was a cornerstone for the Order and could not be withdrawn or limited.[47] Travellers were particularly exposed when travelling overseas and Freemasonry was jealous of its international reputation. If it was to substantiate its reputation as the pre-eminent fraternal organisation, its charity guarantees should have no limitations.

Distance from the support of relatives and friends, exposure to unfamiliar food and diseases, and the possibility of descending to a level of abject poverty below anything that might be encountered at home, all raised the level of hazard. In a letter to the Grand Secretary in London, one Australian corre-spondent observed that 'a quarter part of the free community have been admitted Masons in England from the prevailing notion of the necessity of being so on becoming travellers'.[48] Lodge of Unity in New South Wales provides a specific example, with its Minute books of the 1840s regularly recording travelling Masons being provided with bed, breakfast and 5 shillings to continue 'up country' in their search for work.[49] Even in 1890, when the population of the Australasian colonies had expanded very considerably, the incidence of Masonic membership and the potential support for travellers remained very high. For example, in that year the white male population over the age of twenty-one in New Zealand stood at just over 150,000—the size of a medium-sized county town in Britain today. For that population, there were 87 lodges warranted under the English constitution, 50 under the Scottish and 15 under the Irish.[50] Unfortunately, there are few records of the overall sums paid out for 'tramping' relief, and they undoubtedly varied between lodges and over time, but again it is likely that they were substantial and placed a real burden on many lodges. In Canada in the mid-nineteenth century, lodges were already complaining bitterly about the charges on their limited means resulting from the 'numberless claimants' and 'indigent Brethren arriving from Britain'.[51] However, the problem of the reliable identification of worthy claimants appeared to be at its worst in the United States. Immigrants of multiple ethnicities and languages were pouring in from all parts of the world, and communications were difficult, if not impossible, between remote frontier districts thousands of miles apart. The scale of the problem there, and the responses to resolve it, will be the subject of more detailed discussion in Part 2 below.

So far, Masonic benevolence to travellers has been seen as a 'reactive' issue—waiting for those in distress to seek relief—but it was also sometimes 'proactive', contributing sums to assist the less well off to seek a better fortune elsewhere. Such generosity was partly designed to ensure that migrants did not become relief dependent when actually on the road; partly to fill a common Masonic charitable desire to assist men in restoring their own independence rather than to maintain them as charity dependants; and partly, like the old operatives guilds, to reduce localised 'surplus' population. Again, the Masonic press provides good examples of these motivations. In 1847, for example, the *Freemasons Quarterly Review* called on all English lodges 'to assist their poor brethren who are leaving their native country in search of employment and homes' because they 'often arrive as cases of real distress'.[52] Equally, a few years earlier the same paper printed an obituary of John Fearn, a tailor, who had been assisted to emigrate to Ohio in the United States by his brethren in Old Newstead Lodge No. 55 in Nottingham and with a grant of £20 from the Board of Benevolence. It had been hoped that a change of climate would restore his health and the ability to support his wife and seven children, but sadly he died within months. To their credit, his new brethren in America gave him a full Masonic funeral and extended their protection to his family.[53] Some years later, and in a similar vein, the *Freemasons Magazine and Masonic Mirror* reported that during the summer recess a member of a lodge in Deptford, near London, finding himself in suddenly reduced circumstances, successfully solicited local brethren for financial aid to emigrate to America. He received over £10 in voluntary donations over a few days and left immediately, not delaying to make formal application to the Lodge of Benevolence.[54]

This sort of activity chimed well with the national mood in the second half of the nineteenth century. There was a widespread view that migration should be used both to reduce areas of overpopulation at home and to provide much-needed human resources to exploit the potential of a rapidly expanding Empire. Local and regional 'Emigration Societies' were formed across the country to help finance and organise the migrants, with women and children often being identified as being particularly needed in the colonial frontier areas.[55] Many thousands of Cornish emigrants were financially assisted during the peak years of emigration after the 1830s, not only by local poor law authorities anxious to reduce the burden on local rates but also by organisations overseas looking for more people.[56] Freemasonry was not to be left out. Many lodges made contact with their local societies and 'receiving' lodges, particularly in Canada, became proactive in looking for immigrants. In the 1860s, the UGLE proposed to alleviate the burden on the Royal Masonic School for Girls by assisting some of their number to emigrate and, across the Empire, Masons encouraged movement, not just from Britain but between the colonies. In London, Grand Lodge encouraged the development of new 'Imperial Lodges' from the 1880s, which were specifically designed to bring together visitors from the colonies with those who might be considering future outward movement. Identifying opportunities and securing jobs, as well as familiarisation and settlement assistance were a focus of their activities.[57]

The problems of administering travelling relief were not confined to the Masons. It was noted in the last chapter that Freemasonry had competition domestically in the form of the friendly societies and many of these had extensive international connections. In a manner not greatly dissimilar to the Masons they used a 'card system' for identification. The *Manual of Oddfellowship* explained that if a brother was out of work, 'he was furnished with a card and funds to reach the next lodge. If unsuccessful there, that lodge provided for his progress, and so on until employment was found, when he deposited his card in the nearest lodge.'[58] Many Masons also joined these organisations for additional help and assurance when travelling.[59] A letter from the Secretary of the Lodge of Probity in Halifax, Yorkshire, in 1816 provides a glimpse into this multifaceted world. He wrote:

> a Tramp came to be relieved by my workmen and I recollected having seen him there about six months before, on the same errand. He informed me that he had travelled since the time he was here before, nearly all over the Kingdom, also Ireland and part of Scotland and he had saved money by it as he was an Orangeman and an Oddfellow. He had been relieved by them and he meant to be made a Mason when he got home, which was in the neighbourhood of Stockport.[60]

The Ancient Order of Foresters appears to have been less keen on assisting travelling members, normally providing only a 'trifling sum' when searching for employment and placing tight limits on the usual benefits that could be claimed while using travelling licences. Affiliated Courts, including those in colonies such as Australia,[61] could make advances to visitors and expect compensation from the member's home Court, but monies often did not arrive and had to be compensated from a central fund. Accordingly they required that those requesting a travelling licence should pay six contributions in advance and that the licence was only valid for six weeks from the date of the grant.[62] This was often well in advance of the date of actual departure and the licence might well have expired before arrival when travelling internationally. Looking at Appendix 10, it is no coincidence that a majority of those members of the Foresters' Court Treffry that later joined Fowey Masonic Lodge were itinerants with maritime connections.

When Burn wrote in the early 1840s, he observed that:

> until the last three or four years a sort of friendly connection existed between the society in this country and the American Oddfellows.

> From time to time, many of our brethren, from choice or necessity, emigrated to that country, and for a considerable time were allowed to take through their cards of clearance into the lodges in the localities where they might reside, and consequently they became entitled to all the benefits of the funds of such Lodges.[63]

Unfortunately, this had caused considerable financial problems for the American lodges. With far more British visitors coming in than their own members going abroad, they suffered a serious adverse 'balance of trade'. The British members left their initiation money and subscriptions at home, and made no regular contributions to their new temporary host lodges, so the practice was reluctantly terminated. No doubt the American lodges continued to provide non-pecuniary support to visitors, through friendship, job-finding and other aspects of settlement and local community absorption.[64] Much the same can be said for the Ancient Order of Foresters and its one-time subsidiary, the Independent Order of Foresters. Men who, like Joseph Malins and Emanuel Marsh, became Foresters in England, later emigrated to north America and joined courts there, no doubt receiving the same cordial welcome as those incoming immigrants who joined the Independent Order for the first time.[65]

Burn also provided some indication of the scale of the Oddfellows' support for domestic migrants. According to the accounts of the Board of the Manchester Unity for 1845, more than £72,000 was paid in travelling relief[66] for members in search of employment, out of a total income of £325,000.[67] More recently, Weinbren has shown that in the ten years between 1863 and 1872, well over 90,000 individual payments were made to travelling Oddfellows.[68] These figures also provide some basis for roughly estimating the total support provided by Freemasonry for its domestic migrants. At the mid-century, the number of Oddfellows was probably two or three times that of English Freemasons[69] but if the incidence of travelling was similar in both orders it would suggest that there were many thousands of applicants for Masonic relief each year. It should also be noted that, with so many of their members travelling, the benevolent societies were also open to exploitation by fraudsters,[70] though the incidence of this may have been lower than for Freemasonry.[71]

So far, attention has been focused on the financial relief of the 'poor and distressed Mason' as he travelled, alone or with his family, along regional, national and international highways. But Freemasonry offered the migrant far more than that. In particular it offered access at final destination—access to informed and reliable members of the local community who could advise on where to find work and reliable service providers; access to entertainment, fellowship and private spaces of refuge in sometimes tumultuous towns and ports; and access to respectable family members who could help your own family to settle in. For most migratory Masons, this was the principal advantage of membership. Relief was insurance for unexpected emergencies, hopefully never to be called upon. The need for effective networking at final destination, however, could make or break the success of any venture.

The importance that Masons attached to access to lodges at home and abroad, and the networking potential of their members, can best be demonstrated through case studies of three occupational groups. The first two will relate to mariners and metal miners, and focus primarily on lodges in Cornwall, where they dominated the membership of several lodges. They will be considered at some length. A third group was that of commercial travellers who were represented in lodges across the country. Their inclusion is designed to show that the mariners and miners were not exceptional among travelling men, and their story was shared by many other occupational groups. Mariners will be the first group to be considered and attention will be focused on the mercantile marine rather than the Royal Navy, even as the latter supported a larger number of lodges and played a major role in diffusing Freemasonry around the country and across the globe. The issues promoting their membership were very different, however, from those encountered in civilian lodges and their history must be left for consideration elsewhere.

Mariners

Mariners joined Masonic lodges in large numbers from the early eighteenth century.[72] By the end of that century they may have been the largest single occupational group represented in the Order. Like miners, they had a natural affiliation to band together because of the mutually experienced hazards of their profession. As Shackleton later put it, there is a natural 'brotherhood of the sea. The men who go down to the sea in ships, serving and suffering, [...] bring into their own horizons the perils [...] of their brother sailormen.'[73] Freemasonry provided a practical vehicle for expressing that affiliation and providing mutual assurance. It offered membership to a wide range of men, from the captains of vessels, through engineers, mates and boatswains, and even ordinary seamen and lowly stewards. By far the most numerous group within the lodges described themselves as 'ship's master' or 'master mariner', though sometimes the simple term 'mariner' might also have been used. In modern terms, they might be categorised as 'managerial'. However, some caution needs to be exercised here since 'ship's master' could cover everything from a lone fisherman to the captain of an East Indiaman. As far as can be seen, this 'managerial' group of master mariners greatly outnumbered other 'non-managerial' mariners in all English lodges. It may be that the explanation for this is not entirely financial. The master mariners certainly had higher incomes than other 'non-managerial' groups, but for some time they were also, rather oddly, at greater risk. Under the terms of the Merchant Shipping Act, ships' masters were not regarded as 'seamen' and were not entitled to statutory relief. Whereas shipwrecked ordinary seamen could expect their passage home to be reimbursed, ships' officers could not—or if they did, they had to travel in the lowest possible class together with ordinary seamen. Not until the beginning of the twentieth century was provision made for them to travel in superior classes, appropriate to their rank.[74]

Master mariners' enthusiasm for Freemasonry, and their strategic role in spreading it nationally and internationally, was noticed from the very earliest days of the Order. Shortly after its establishment in 1756, for example, the Grand Lodge of the Netherlands placed administrative responsibility for the establishment of lodges in all its overseas trading centres in the hands of Johan Hendrick Steendekker, a sea captain in the service of the Dutch East India Company.[75] Numerous other eighteenth-century maritime Freemasons are noticed in the extensive *Dictionnaire Des Marins Francs-Maçons.*[76] For England, Heiron's history of Old Dundee Lodge, No. 18, meeting at Wapping at the centre of the then port of London, provides details of the extent of the maritime involvement in the still evolving Order. That Lodge was admirably placed to recruit mariners and invented a special category of 'sea members' to accommodate them as early as the mid-eighteenth century. By 1810 more than three-quarters of the Lodge's 485 members gave that as their occupation.[77] In Scotland, the actual port of Dundee's 'Lodge Ancients No. 49' was equally active with mariners and from 1850 to 1875 drew somewhere between a third and a half of all of its initiates from maritime professions.[78] The numerous small ships involved in the Baltic and North Sea trades also produced large numbers of members for lodges such as Phoenix No. 94 and Palatine No. 97 in Sunderland as well as many other ports in the north-east of England. Similarly, in the South West, the Lodge of Love and Honour No. 75 in Falmouth, Cornwall, was strategically located to recruit mariners involved in the Atlantic and long-distance trades. As one of the lodges in this focused study on West Cornwall, it lends itself to special study.

During the nineteenth century, Love and Honour recruited nearly three hundred master mariners and senior ships' officers (see Appendix 11). Recruitment, which was already brisk during and just after the Napoleonic wars, fell off during the second quarter of the century, but revived powerfully to an explosive peak during the 1850s and 1860s. During some of those years the Lodge was initiating or progressing as many as twenty mariners annually. Most of them were young men, in their twenties and thirties, looking forward to a good future career and had young families to take care of. For reasons that are not readily explained—but in common with many other port lodges— recruitment fell off sharply from the 1870s. Most of the men being welcomed by the Lodge gave a local address in Falmouth, but during the peak years it attracted 'temporary residents' from ports at home and abroad. The domestic 'visitors' came mostly from east-coast ports, such as Shields, Sunderland, Hull, Yarmouth, and London, though Liverpool, Bristol and some small ports in Devon, Kent and Wales also contributed (see Illustration 7). Those coming from overseas were mainly drawn from the Baltic ports of Denmark, Sweden, Finland and Germany, but also Belgium, Spain, Portugal and particularly America. It would appear that almost any mariner going west or east across the Atlantic, or taking a southerly route down towards the Iberian Peninsula, the Mediterranean, or South Atlantic, might take the opportunity to call into Falmouth and seek out the local Masonic lodge. In these circumstances, initiation was often undertaken in a rush, at special emergency meetings. Correspondence between the Lodge Secretary and the Grand Secretary often requests the candidates' Grand Lodge certificates urgently, because the candidate is 'about to go to sea' or was 'sailing very soon'. To facilitate those leaving without their Grand Lodge certificates, Love and Honour often issued their own certificates to prove that the bearer had received the first degree (see Illustration 8).

Such haste and lack of careful consideration of candidates might have resulted from an excessive zeal by lodge members to accommodate all those that expressed an interest in Masonry, but it more likely suggests a financial concern. Lodges like Love and Honour were happy to take initiation fees without making sufficient efforts to collect annual subscriptions and regularly return them as members. As noted earlier, lodges were treating seafarers as irregular semi-detached members. UGLE did not like that interpretation, not least because it was costing them income. In 1876 the Grand Secretary took the Secretary of Love and Honour to task for failing to collect, and pass on, the usual 6d per member per quarter for Benevolence, and dismissed any suggestion that the Lodge had been given a special dispensation not to collect it.[79] A response from the Lodge Secretary gives an insight into the difficulties that lodges faced in conforming to 'normal' administrative procedures and how they saw their role:

> Lodges like 'Love and Honour' situated in seaport towns usually get a large number of emergency meetings called for the purpose of initiating seafaring men who may be about to proceed to sea,

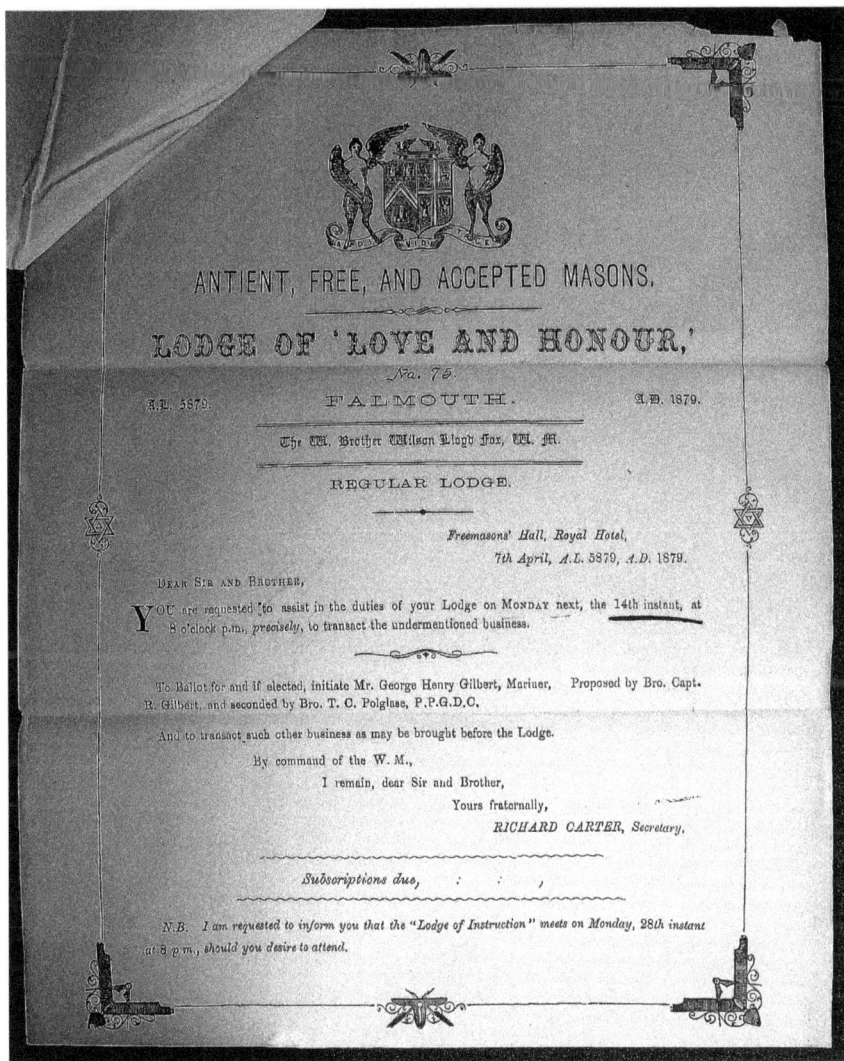

Illustration 7   Summons for Love and Honour Lodge, Falmouth, Cornwall

This was sent by the Secretary to all members of Love and Honour Lodge No. 76, to attend a meeting of the Lodge at the Royal Hotel, Falmouth on Monday, 14 April 1879 at 8.00 pm. The principal business of the meeting was to ballot for, and if elected, Initiate George Gilbert, a Master Mariner, normally resident locally. He was proposed by Captain R. Gilbert, another Master Mariner (probably his father or brother), who had been a member of the Lodge since 1873, and seconded by Timothy Charles Polglase, a Past Master of the Lodge (in 1873) and an honoured Past Grand Officer of the Province of Cornwall. The Proposer, Richard Charles Gilbert had originally been made a Mason in Prince of Wales Lodge No. 671 in Llanelli, South Wales and was likely to have been engaged in the coasting trade, possibly taking Cornish tin to the tin-plate works of South Wales. The Seconder, Charles Polglase was a local Falmouth ironmonger and had been a member of the Lodge for the last thirteen years. George Gilbert's ship sailed very shortly after his initiation.

Illustration 8   Love and Honour Lodge Certificate

This certificate, similar in design to a Grand Lodge certificate, was issued by the Lodge as a temporary method of demonstrating that the bearer had been properly initiated to the first degree of Freemasonry. It was intended to provide proof of initiation and to assist in obtaining a Grand Lodge certificate when the process of initiation was completed, possibly in another Lodge. It was given to John Gibson, a forty-year-old Master Mariner, from Blyth near Liverpool, on 10 November 1856. Gibson appears to have completed the second and third degrees of his initiation to Master Mason in Merchant's Lodge No. 241 in Liverpool and possibly Unanimity and Industry, Sumatra, and rejoined Love and Honour in 1869.

consequently they are not contributing members. We get them a Grand Lodge certificate which we think satisfactory. We are quite ignorant of being liable for the usual 6d per quarter to Benevolence. We cannot be expected to pay for them year after year without having seen them or without them having visited the lodge.[80]

The Lodge certainly seems to have found a way around the problem that had vexed them a generation earlier when they had complained of the requirement of seven days' notice for initiations. This they thought most unreasonable since people passing through could not be processed in time: 'They have frequently offered themselves as candidates, but in consequence of their short stay, they have been obliged to sail without it.'[81] The Lodge Secretary's request for a special dispensation for these unusual practices was firmly denied by the Grand Secretary, however, and the number of overseas and distant domestic mariner initiations fell off sharply thereafter.

Love and Honour was not alone in these disputes. Some years earlier, the Board of General Purposes had taken action against Royal Kent Lodge of Antiquity No. 20 in Chatham for initiating new members but not including them in returns or paying registration fees. The Board estimated that they had done this for more than fifteen years for upwards of fifty members and that Royal Kent now owed Grand Lodge £35 in unpaid subscriptions.[82] In their defence, lodge Secretaries argued that it was almost impossible to trace mariners after they had left port and that the usual administrative arrangements for lodges should not apply. It was an issue for itinerant Masons of all descriptions that plagued Secretaries, Grand and local, throughout the nineteenth century.

Once initiated, most of Love and Honour's new members were never seen again, rarely ever paying more than a fleeting visit. Under these circumstances the actual running of the Lodge devolved to a relatively small core of local residents. They were the usual mix of professional and those employed in the retail and service trades. A list of the Masters of Love and Honour Lodge from the mid-century provides a good example (see Appendix 12). Arguably these groups saw considerable personal advantage in the introduction of so many potential new lodge members, both as contributors to lodge funds, as well as potential new 'customers' for their commercial services.

While it might appear that the stay-at-home core members of maritime lodges were the clear winners out of this situation—freeloading on the financial contributions of absent mariners to run their lodges—it was precisely this group that the mariners wanted to access and network with. They were never going to enjoy the normal pleasures of lodge life, in terms of meeting regularly with local friends and colleagues, and enjoying their company, but they would want to be introduced to the more honest and reliable professionals on whose services they might have to depend. Thus the fifty or so shipbuilders, shipwrights, sailmakers, ships' carpenters and smiths that were members of the various Cornish coastal lodges would have been an attraction, as would the forty pilots and, from the early 1890s, increasing numbers of steam tug owners. They would also, of course, want to be able to meet the wider generality of the Masonic fraternity; to be sure of a welcome and the support of other Masons when arriving in foreign ports; and to find sanctuaries of calm familiarity in often chaotic and dangerous places. For some overseas applicants, such as those from Scandinavia, there was also the possibility that they were trying to find a 'back door' into Freemasonry which they could not access at home. All of them aspired to become part of what was clearly a very large and very economically and socially productive 'brotherhood of the sea'.

These attractions of Masonry can be illustrated from the annual membership returns and correspondence from lodges based around the world—in the North and South Atlantic, the Caribbean, the Mediterranean and the Pacific—all operating with Warrants from the UGLE. Several lodges have been researched: St Andrew's Lodge No. 732, working in Sydney, Nova Scotia; St John's Lodge No. 703 and Orphan Lodge No. 616 in Rio de Janeiro; Royal Lodge No. 207 and Sussex Lodge No. 621 in Kingston, Jamaica; Union Lodge No. 588, based in Floriana, Valletta, Malta;[83] and Yokohama Lodge No. 1092, working in Japan. What did new arrivals find when they visited one of these lodges? Firstly, the structure of the membership was all very much the same, including large numbers of merchants and their clerks, those involved in servicing ships and maritime trade, and the professional and business managers that supported the general economy of the town. The numbers of master mariners that were actual members varied somewhat—being higher in Union than in Yokohama Lodge for example—but all included other skilled maritime professionals, such as first and second officers, marine engineers, surgeons and pursers, as well as occasionally 'ordinary' seamen such as mariners, stewards, ships' carpenters and boatswains. They were a good place to look for, and perhaps find, additions to their crews.

Secondly, they could find seagoing and market intelligence. In ports with regular packet services—such as Halifax, Kingston and Rio—they could receive news and commercial intelligence from home, while 'tramps' coming in from all parts of the world could report on dangerous conditions or business opportunities almost everywhere. For example, Robert Colls, a master mariner, who joined St Andrew's in 1848, presented a certificate that was stamped to show that he had recently visited lodges in Tahiti and Montevideo. Similarly, Sussex Lodge

No. 621 in Kingston, Jamaica counted members with connections to London, Liverpool and Bristol in the 1840s and 1850s, and initiated the captains of at least two East Indiamen. Royal Lodge No. 207, also in Kingston, Jamaica, had its share of distant shipping interests but had a particularly large cohort of those who traded around the islands of the Caribbean. Most lodges also occasionally attracted a small number of naval personal—usually British but also American, like the Captain, officers and surgeon of the US Navy initiated in St John's No. 703 and Orphan Lodge No. 616, Rio de Janeiro. Consular officials added diplomatic information to the mix in Union and Yokohama lodges.[84] In all of these lodges, mariners could find entertainment and conversation on familiar issues and fellowship with like-minded men. As in so many other aspects of fraternal life at home and abroad, knowledge of what was available would have been advertised by travelling members of other orders, such as the Foresters, which also had extensions in the Caribbean.[85]

Thirdly, the 'stay-at-home' core of the lodge—the merchants, agents, customs officers, clergymen, tailors, sailmakers, physicians, etc.—would provide a reliable way in to the local economy and community, arranging for repairs and new cargo, re-victualling, and simply providing for personal services and accom-modation. Bills of Exchange due to members involved in trade with England enabled lodges to make payments to UGLE.[86]

Like Love and Honour, the core membership of these overseas lodges appears to have been small compared with the total numbers being initiated and joining. In Yokohama, for example, the regular paid-up membership in 1885 was just nineteen, which was considerably less than a third of those who had been initiated and joined in the previous ten years. All of the lodges appear to have been very much in the business of welcoming anyone who wished to be initiated, regardless of social status, with Union Lodge in Malta probably being the most active in recruiting master mariners (see Appendix 13). Many maritime initiates left immediately after their first degree and very few progressed beyond their second within the same lodge.[87] This tended to produce short-term benefits but also long-term problems. By boosting numbers and income, St John's Lodge in Rio de Janeiro was briefly able to offer additional 'assurance' benefits to members in the 1840s, raising money for a French Mason's widow whose house had been destroyed by fire and providing new tools for a goldsmith member who had fallen on hard times.[88] Similarly, Sussex Lodge in Kingston, Jamaica was able to establish a school for Masons' children for some years in the early 1850s, largely supporting the expenditure of £120 a year for forty pupils.[89] However, such local benevolence could only be supported out of initiation income. Subscription income was small and difficult to collect from a largely itinerant membership.

Thus the lodges often blossomed for a few years, but had insufficient local support when interest and recruitment declined, and frequently dwindled into closure.

It is impossible to overstate the importance that mariners, like all mobile men, placed on physical possession of their lodge certificates. In a world where they were always effectively a visitor, the certificate was an essential 'passport', without which they could neither gain access nor support. As James Rhymes, an initiate of Love and Honour, complained to the Grand Secretary's office in May 1856, 'my occupation being that of a Ship's Master and visiting foreign nations, I feel much at a loss not being forwarded my certificate—having been in the coast of Africa ever since I got the 3rd degree'.[90] As with the Lodge Secretaries in Cornwall,[91] the Secretary for St Andrew's Lodge wrote in May 1854 to ask the Grand Secretary to 'transmit without delay' four certificates for master mariners and merchants because 'I have had to appease the impatience and complaining of these brethren, who have expressed great dissatisfaction about the matter'.[92] Similarly in 1847 the Secretary of St John's Lodge in Rio wrote of the 'most pressing anxiety' for their Grand Lodge certificates felt by members in 'remote locations', particularly when they were likely to remove to even more remote locations.[93]

Sometimes the verbal tests of membership were carried out by the officers of lodges receiving visitors but they were an uncertain substitute for a certificate when visiting lodges under different constitutions and jurisdictions. The Secretary of Royal Lodge No. 207 in Jamaica observed in 1858 that some lodges might accept a verbal examination as sufficient for visitors, 'supposing the applicant, having been shipwrecked, had lost his papers', but 'we always decline to admit visitors without papers'.[94] On occasion, this could mean that joining applicants might even have to start the initiation process again, particularly where their new lodge did not easily recognise the 'proofs' given in tests of Masonic knowledge. Thus one mariner, who was initiated in a French lodge in Egypt was asked to take his first degree again before being admitted to an English constitution lodge in Jamaica. He then had to do the same again some years later when he applied to join an American lodge in New York. Progressing to Rio de Janeiro he was able to take his second degree in St John's English constitution lodge in the 1840s but had to take that again when he applied to join an American lodge in California. He finally managed to complete his third degree in that Californian lodge.[95] Apart from being time consuming, this process was also expensive with its multiple initiation fees, and nicely demonstrates exactly how prized Masonic membership could be.

To help to overcome the problem, many lodges, like Love and Honour, began to issue their own informal and temporary certificates, providing some authentication that the bearer had been through various degrees. This was particularly common for overseas lodges, where the delays between applying for and receiving Grand Lodge certificates could be weeks or months.[96] As early as 1788, Artillery Lodge in Halifax, Nova Scotia, was issuing letters of introduction for members, recommending them 'to all Regular and Warranted Lodges around the Globe wherever Providence may please to direct him'. St Andrew's and Royal Sussex in Nova Scotia, Sussex in Jamaica and St John's in Rio followed suit with their own certificates as did many other lodges. Indeed it appears to have become common practice, with Trinity Lodge in Elgin providing an example from a lodge under the Grand Lodge of Scotland. Endorsements of these certificates by the Secretaries of lodges that were visited often provide good evidence of the wanderings of those involved (see Illustration 9).

Illustration 9   Endorsed Lodge Certificate, Old Dundee Lodge, London

Issued by the Dundee Arms Lodge (later the Old Dundee Lodge), meeting at the Dundee Arms, Wapping, London, to Frederick Abell, who had received the three degrees of Freemasonry, on 14 January 1799. It was endorsed at least eight times during the next eighteen years in places such as Hamburg, Amsterdam and Minorca but many cannot be deciphered. Thomas Dunckerley, one of the most influential eighteenth-century Freemasons, had been an early 'sea member' of this Lodge.

Sometimes problems in the dispatch of certificates were eased by members returning to England and offering to collect them in person. A newly initiated member of St Andrew's Lodge in Sydney, Nova Scotia, for example, arrived in England after a voyage via the Mediterranean and went to the Grand Secretary's office to collect his certificate personally.[97] Finding that it still was not ready, he complained that it 'is really vexing as every travelling Mason, more particularly seafaring men, should have their certificate with them'.[98] Similarly in 1863 the Secretary of Union Lodge in Malta forwarded a message from Edward Petts asking for the swift dispatch of his certificate because 'I am leaving for the West Indies for several years and should have my certificate before I leave to enable me to attend a lodge, as I wish to become more enlightened in Masonry.'[99] George Holmes of St Andrew's similarly pestered the Grand Secretaries' office that he was 'now in Budleigh Salterton, Devon'—but nevertheless needed his certificate sent on urgently because he is 'uncertain how long he will remain'.[100] By 1876 the Secretary of Love and Honour was making use of telegrams to press the urgency of his cases.

The anxiety of recently initiated members to get their hands on their new 'passport' was more than matched by the near panic shown by established members who saw their certificates lost or destroyed. Cries that their certificates had been 'lost in a shipwreck' were commonplace and more exotic mishaps, such as 'lost while travelling with Bedouins and Arabs' and 'lost in a fire on a goods train from Cairo', were not unusual.[101] These members had first-hand experience of just how important these certificates were and they were desperate to have their Lodge Secretaries apply for replacements. A particularly interesting example of this is provided by an unhappy circumstance that occurred to a member of one of the few maritime groups that did not leave their home port but dealt on a daily basis with Masonic 'strangers', namely pilots. The heavy shipping traffic of the Fal estuary supported a considerable number of these expert seamen, who competed with one another for business. In a letter of 13 July 1882, Henry James, a Trinity Pilot and a member of Love and Honour, wrote to the Lodge Secretary asking him urgently to arrange for a replacement certificate, the original having been lost when he 'was run down and the cutter sunk by a steamer'. This necessarily begs the question, why did he have it on board the cutter? Did he need it in his daily work to somehow 'prove' his Masonic credentials—perhaps trustworthiness—to his client ship's masters? Was it an essential form of identity card for effective business networking? The answers are not clear, but a large number of pilots did seek and maintain Masonic membership. In 1875, for example, the Lodge of Love and Honour had fifty-six regular paid-up members of which twelve were pilots.[102] Mercenary motivations for the pilots' Masonic membership may also be indicated by their failure to join any of the side orders that other lodge members found attractive. Unlike master mariners, who rarely if ever had the chance to enjoy them, pilots were home based and might well have become members but seem to have regarded them as 'inessential luxuries'.

There are several other pieces of circumstantial evidence that suggest that mariners, more than most other groups, were narrowly motivated by the networking potential of Freemasonry compared with its other offerings. It is notable, for example, that none of the pilots, having obtained their certificates by becoming craft members, were sufficiently enthralled with ritual and rank to go on to become members of Mark or the Royal Arch—a very similar record to Master Mariners. Similarly, both groups completely eschewed involvement in running the Lodge, providing not a single Master during the period 1850–1900.[103] Perhaps most revealing however, is that the one group who had little or nothing to gain from improved networking at home or abroad—viz. fisherman—were conspicuous by their absence from Masonic membership. Unless they were camouflaged under the generic title of Master Mariner, there was not a single fisherman in any of the coastal lodges of West Cornwall at any point during this period. All of this should be compared with the capacity of Master Mariners to become members of other benevolent societies, with their guaranteed returns in times of adversity (see Appendix 10). In a more risky profession than most, they appear to have taken a particularly hard and clear view about getting an economic return from their financial outlays on fraternity and insurance.

Before leaving the issue of the attractions of Freemasonry for seafarers, brief attention must also be given to the central charitable funds that began to emerge during the nineteenth century. Perhaps not as immediately relevant as the facilities offered by individual Masons and their lodges, these grew rapidly from the mid-nineteenth century and many seafarers began to take advantage of them. Under the UGLE, a 'Fund of Benevolence', first established in the early eighteenth century, was managed by a 'Lodge of Benevolence' consisting of the Grand Master and past Grand Officers. This was separate from, and independent of, the Royal Masonic Benevolent Institution. The Board of Benevolence met monthly to consider applications for grants and received them from all classes of Masons and constituent lodges at home and abroad.[104] They included professional men, such as surgeons, architects, accountants, clergymen and the owners of once large businesses, as well as craftsmen, clerks, carriers, nurserymen and gardeners. In a world without public safety nets and still very little personal insurance, anyone who suffered major accident or physical or mental ill health rapidly took themselves and their families into absolute poverty. It was just a matter of time. In responding to such pleadings the Board was not simply showing compassion but also defending the institution of Freemasonry itself. If its claim to be a bastion of respectability and self-help was to be sustained, the public at large had to be shown that Freemasonry did its best to look after its own.

Perhaps because of the inherent insecurities of their occupation as well as their tenuous financial position, mariners were by far the largest occupational group requesting assistance around the 1850s and although their representation declined thereafter, they continued to appear throughout the last decades of the century. It is notable that the port lodges of the north-east of England were particularly well represented in the applications for charity, partly because of their large numbers of seafaring members but perhaps also because of their local knowledge of the potential of the Fund. The grants made by the Board were usually in the order of £5 or £10 but £15 and £20[105] were sometimes given, depending on the degree of need and to some extent the length of time that the petitioner had been a contributing lodge member (some left, rejoined, and moved between lodges, which might have reduced their time in membership). In accordance with the common practice followed by lodges and individual Masons, grants were made on an ad hoc basis and were designed to alleviate immediate problems rather than to provide for continuing support. The Board was underlining Freemasonry's role as a safety net, not as a benevolent institution, providing long-term insurance. As one correspondent of *The Freemason* put it, Masonry is not an institution 'where a man goes to receive certain monetary benefits or better a crippled condition, it takes care of its own when misfortune overtakes them'.[106] They were a last resort, not an insurance of first defence. In this context, the Board rarely entertained return or multiple applications.

Wherever possible the Board appeared to favour applications that facilitated men and/or their families restoring their independence by returning to self-sustaining employment. Thus numerous grants were made to master mariners to replace their navigational instruments lost in shipwrecks and widows sometimes looked for grants to help them establish small businesses. All of these issues are illustrated in Appendix 14, which provides details of the applications from mariners and their families that were considered by the Board of the Lodge of Benevolence between 1856 and 1859. The petitions have been divided into three groups: those from men suffering from injury and ill health; those for the replacement of lost or destroyed property; and those from widows on behalf of themselves and their children. Taken overall, not just to mariners, the Board of the Lodge of Benevolence was making over three hundred grants a year to distressed Masons by the mid-1880s, expending more than £9,000.[107] By this time, central charitable funds were also being used to help support the

Shipwrecked Fishermen and Mariners Royal Benevolent Society,[108] as well as the Royal National Lifeboat Institution. The presentation of lifeboats, such as the 'Albert Edward' based at Clacton-on-Sea during the 1870s, began a tradition of benevolence that continues to this day.[109]

Freemasonry offered a great deal to mariners both in terms of assurance if things went wrong, access to good and friendly society in ports around the world, and excellent opportunities for networking. Similarly, the Order benefited greatly from their numbers and support, and the facility that they provided for making it a truly international institution. Indeed, it might well be argued that the support of mariners and those connected with maritime trade was one of the most important driving forces in the expansion of total Masonic membership during the nineteenth century. The circumstantial evidence is certainly strong, with coastal provinces generally supporting significantly more lodges than inland provinces. As Appendix 15 shows, the 17 coastal provinces had a total of 677 lodges compared with 572 lodges in the 22 inland provinces, or an average of 40 lodges compared with 26. East Lancashire and West Yorkshire were the only inland provinces with any large number of lodges and without them the total for all inland lodges would be only 377, or just over half of that of the coastal provinces. The dominance of the coastal lodges is even more noticeable when looking at the coastal provinces. In Hampshire and the Isle of Wight, for example, Portsmouth, Gosport and Southampton supported twenty lodges with a total membership of 2,333 Masons in 1900, or 57% of the entire membership of the Province. Even more importantly, they accounted for a similar share of new initiates.[110] Similarly, in Devonshire, twenty lodges in Plymouth, Devonport and Stonehouse accounted for almost half of the Masons in the Province and most of the remainder were members of lodges in other port towns such as Brixham, Topsham, Exmouth, Teignmouth, Bideford, Barnstaple and Dartmouth.[111] Of course, these figures reflected large numbers of naval as well as general mercantile members, but the naval members all joined Freemasonry for much the same reasons of finding friendship and hospitality in distant and anonymous ports of call. In Cornwall, small and declining communities maintained relatively large numbers of both coastal and inland lodges by partnering their maritime trades with a highly mobile mining population.

Although Freemasonry was clearly very attractive to mariners it was far from being the only fraternal order that attracted their attention. The financial assurances that it offered were generous but not certain. As a charitable institution it could grant or withhold assistance at will, depending on third-party assessments of the problems. Many mariner Masons wanted more certainty and turned to benevolent societies for additional insurance. It is difficult to find surviving membership lists for the major benevolent societies to be sure of the general levels of joint membership, but the small port of Fowey provides some indicative evidence for the periods 1863 and 1900. Of the eighty-eight master mariner members of Fowey Lodge, thirty also became members of the Ancient Order of Foresters Court Treffry.[112] The master mariners were by far the largest occupational group among the Masons to establish joint membership, making up half of the total numbers joining both orders. This again suggests a pronounced predisposition by seafarers to insure against the insecurities of their trade as does their general propensity to join the Foresters before becoming Masons. Overall, two-thirds of the master mariners became Foresters before 'graduating' to Freemasonry while for the joint members as a whole the proportions were roughly equal. Whether this was common elsewhere remains open to question. It is notable that the master mariner members of Fowey Lodge were nearly all locally based and the incidence of multiple memberships—and benevolent society first—may have been much lower for those who spent most of their time away from their home port. Equally, however, it should be remembered that the Ancient Order of Foresters was only one of several benevolent societies that the master mariners and other lodge members might have joined and that overall joint membership might have been much higher.

Miners

What has been said about mariners and Masonry is equally applicable to Cornish metal miners. Large numbers were welcomed into inland mining lodges shortly before emigration in the same way that port lodges embraced seafarers. However, there were also important differences. While mariners rarely took an active part in their mother lodges, many miners—probably the majority—were happy to stay at home and to enjoy the usual pleasures and advantages of Freemasonry. Like most other initiates, the miners had numerous reasons for joining, but what were the specific attractions in terms of assurance and access? Two groups might be considered separately though clearly many men moved between them at different stages in their lives. Firstly, the stay-at-home miners.

As has been seen, the membership of inland lodges in West Cornwall was in most cases heavily dominated by men directly connected with mining. While many were ordinary working-class men, others were mine owners, agents, managers or involved in the operation of related businesses. Lodge membership was an opportunity to get to know either a current boss or potential employer. This could be of real importance, not simply in terms of gaining or securing employment, but also in making career progression. Unlike many other areas of industry, metal mining recruited nearly all of its managers from the ranks of successful, self-educated working men. There was little theoretical engineering knowledge necessary for mine managers until late in the nineteenth century and most were 'apprenticeship trained', learning their trade literally from the bottom up. Capable leaders of sub-contracting partnerships of miners could rise to being underground managers, surface managers and overall Mine Captain. The Captains of small mines could hope to progress to the management of larger mines if they proved successful in achieving and maintaining profitability.[113] Under such circumstances, Masonic lodges offered exceptional opportunities not only to become closely associated with those with the power to promote and employ them but also to find where future prospects might lie.

Similar observations could also be made for all of those already involved in senior management. They could hear of new or additional positions, access advice on new methods and machinery, and gather the consensus on the future of the mining and metal markets. Appendix 5 has already provided a snapshot of the range of lodge members holding managerial positions in 1883 but this can be considerably extended by looking at the full range of senior management involvement by lodge members over the long period 1859–1900 as a whole (see Appendix 16). It was common in Cornwall for the best managers to hold multiple positions contemporaneously as well as sequentially and to move frequently between posts. In general terms every mine had its own separate company but there were complex systems of shareholding and directorships which inter-linked mines.[114] Many of these mine owners and directors were themselves Freemasons and gave managers access to networks which extended deeply into the system of mine finance. These networks, with their connections to metal mines in other parts of the UK and overseas, favoured the recruitment of Cornish mine managers in a national, and rapidly expanding international, job market. Good examples of the Masonic links between management and ownership are provided by Sir Fredrick Martin, MP and Edward Carus-Wilson of the Cornish Miners' Bank. Martin, whose political activities no doubt helped account for his membership of Boscawen, Druids, Fortitude and Tregullow lodges, was a director of Boscaswell Downs Tin and Copper Mines Association (1871); a director of West Clifford United Tin and Copper Mining Company (1864); and a director of Leeds and St Aubyn Tin Mine (1869). Carus-Wilson, of Phoenix and Cornwall lodges, was connected through his bank to at least a dozen or so mines across Cornwall. Between them Martin and Carus-Wilson would have been effectively employers of several of the senior managers listed in Appendix 16.

It was not just mine managers who wanted to associate with their colleagues and employers that made lodge membership attractive. They had within their control several thousands of jobs for miners and craftsmen, commissions for builders and contractors, instructions for lawyers and barristers, and the sources of money that supported most of the business of shopkeepers, merchants, innkeepers and all of the others within the regional economy. Lodges became a focal point where most sections of the local community came together and it would have been difficult for anyone to have resisted the attractions of membership if it was offered.

None of this was peculiar to Cornwall and the South West. It can be demonstrated to varying degrees in mining communities everywhere. Experience in the lead-mining district of Cardiganshire in west Wales provides a good example. With just one major administrative centre in Aberystwyth, the town's only Masonic lodge, Aberystwyth Lodge No. 1072, became a magnet for the local mine managers. Warranted in 1865, a large number of its earliest members were responsible for the management of most of the district's largest mines (see Appendix 17). The close relationship continued through into the last decades of the century with these and other Lodge members, such as John Kitto, undertaking the management of large numbers of local mines. It was a natural choice for William Henry Williams of Boscawen Lodge in Chacewater to join Aberystwyth Lodge when he moved to take up a managerial post in Llanidloes in 1874. Similarly Richard Jones, a mine manager from Kimberley in South Africa, joined Aberystwyth Lodge when he arrived in 1884 and James Garland became a member in 1887 when he arrived back from Spain.[115] Overall, Aberystwyth Lodge was acting as a venue for the same kind of Cornish domination of mine management as was often seen in many overseas and colonial districts.

The access and networking that Freemasonry offered in Cornwall was not confined to the miner's own lodge, but extended to all of those across the Province and elsewhere. This was particularly important in a county riven with fierce local loyalties. Families from one small town would famously have little to do with those from a close neighbour. Masonry provided the passport to cross those boundaries, either as a visitor or as a 'joining member' if the opening and closing of mines forced men to move. Opportunities for intraregional networking were also provided by membership of side orders.[116] For example, Boscawen Mark Lodge, meeting in St Day, drew miner members from Scorrier, Truro, Redruth and Perranporth, while Hayle Royal Arch Chapter, meeting in Hayle, drew mine agents and engineers from Camborne, Redruth, Truro, Penzance and St Ives.

Those that remained in Cornwall would become well embedded in their lodges and would be well placed to look for help and support if their high-risk occupation resulted in disabling accidents or ill health. This might be forthcoming not simply from their brethren and lodges but from Provincial sources such as the Cornwall Masonic Annuity and Benevolent Fund as well as the central funds of the Lodge of Benevolence. By the end of the century the Cornwall Fund was paying regular annuities between £10 and £30 to aged Freemasons and widows as well as making grants for the education of sons and daughters (often orphans).[117] In June 1898, the Board of Benevolence awarded £10 to the widow of James Kempthorn, a 51-year-old miner with nearly twenty years membership of True and Faithful Lodge, Helston. More impressively, Richard Rich, a 64-year-old mining agent of One and All Lodge meeting in Bodmin, petitioned in October 1879 for relief after he lost 'all of his property in consequence of the depressed state of Cornish mining'. A Past Provincial Grand Warden and a member of the Order for thirty-six years, he was awarded the exceptional sum of £100 to care for himself and his family.[118] Of course, local residents were also in a position to join other friendly and benevolent societies to provide more certain insurance against accident, illness and death. The Cornish Unity Philanthropic Association, based in St Just, recruited many miners, as did the larger Oddfellows and Foresters societies, but more of this below.

While Masonic membership might have appeared as a useful opportunity for occupational and social advancement at home, for many miners and mine managers it also proved a seductive route into emigration. Lodges such as Boscawen in Chacewater, Druids Lodge of Love and Liberality in Redruth and Tregullow Lodge in St Day, all had a continuous turnover of men, coming and going overseas. Between 1860 and 1899 more than a quarter of the new recruits to those three lodges found employment overseas, with the proportion rising to 45% for those giving their occupation as miners and 39%, mining engineers. Inspection of the membership records of overseas lodges finds them popping up everywhere. Quincy Lodge No. 135 and Keweenaw Lodge No. 242 in the Michigan Upper Peninsular copper district, for example, counted Cornish joining members from Boscawen, Fortitude, Cornubian, Tregenna and True and Faithful lodges.[119] Equally the Cornish lodges saw many men joining from lodges in overseas mining districts (see Appendix 18). There was every opportunity to discover the advantages that Masonry had to offer the migrant and also evidence that joining before leaving might be easier than when overseas, in lodges dominated by foreign nationals or earlier arrivals.[120] This is well illustrated by the number of applicants for initiation in Cornwall giving their occupation as 'gold miner'. As was noted earlier, there was no commercially mined gold in Cornwall and using this job description implies that they had returned from a previously successful visit to gold districts overseas and probably intended to go back again. Although it was not impossible to join lodges while overseas—John

Hosking, Josiah Treweek, John Tregay and Edward Trevaskis were initiated in Golden Star Lodge, Deadwood, for example, in the 1880s[121]—it was almost certainly easier to obtain a 'Masonic passport' when at home. Becoming a Mason in their home town could also have been seen as a way of demonstrating their new-found economic success.

At the same time as they were bringing in returnees, the lodges also received frequent visitors from overseas—men that were already Masons and were familiar with the opportunities and advantages offered by Masonic membership in distant mining districts. Their stories and first-hand experience added colour and validity to the long-term activities of emigration agents and others who had long been promoting an outward-looking predisposition with the county.[122] During the 1860s and 1870s, lodge visitors came mainly from the principal gold- and silver-mining districts of Australia, and Mexico, California and Nevada in the United States—particularly the well-established Cornish enclaves around Nevada City and Grass Valley in California and the Virginia City/Comstock area of Nevada. These remained important during later decades but now visitors increasingly arrived from new developing mines in Idaho and Montana as well as South America, and particularly South Africa (see Appendix 19). By comparison, exposure to visitors from other parts of Britain was less common. There was some regular interchange with lodges like Bedford in Tavistock, which drew on the copper-mining communities in the Tamar valley, but very few appeared from further afield.[123] Overall the exposure of members of the mining lodges, like the maritime lodges, to constant international experience helped to foster an outward-looking perspective in Cornwall that was unlike most other parts of the UK—an internationalism that gave the county the reputation of 'West Barbary', connected more to the transatlantic world than to the rest of Britain.[124] It was in this world that a kind of a collective Cornish identity emerged, often more Cornish than the Cornish at home, and one in which Masonic lodges everywhere played an important role.

For the several hundred that were considering migration, the motivations appear to be very similar to those of mariners. Several forces were coming together to create this moment. Firstly, the local mining industry began a long terminal decline from the late 1860s and, with limited alternative employment, many saw some form of outward movement as inevitable. Secondly, the skills that mine managers, engineers and miners had acquired at home were in increasing demand in the world's new mining districts. Thirdly, returnees and visitors could provide personal recommendations and introductions. Fourthly, the power and influence of Freemasonry in mining communities overseas was growing and becoming well known. Fifthly, the Cornish community generally had become well acquainted with overseas migration from early in the nineteenth century and letters, personal reports and family members that had gone earlier, made the whole process less formidable.[125] In other words, rather like mariners and sea-going lodges, miners knew mining lodges, at home and overseas, to be excellent sources of information and to offer worthwhile networking opportunities into local economies and communities.

Knowledge of the advantages of Masonic membership for migration was not confined to the lodges and soon many men clamoured to join, often when their plans for departure were already well advanced. Like Love and Honour and the maritime lodges overseas, the Secretaries of the mining lodges were constantly bombarding Grand Lodge for the urgent dispatch of Grand Lodge certificates because the new brethren were 'going abroad', 'about to emigrate', 'leaving the country in a few days', etc.[126] In February 1893 the Secretary of Tregullow Lodge followed the precedent of Love and Honour in pressing the urgency of his case with a telegram, asking for no less than eight certificates because the brethren were 'leaving Friday morning for Africa'.[127] It is remarkable that the Grand Secretary's office was usually able to comply, given the level of staffing at the time. It is also testament to the efficiency of the Post Office that letters and documents could be delivered within twenty-four hours to and from this distant part of the country.

There is no doubt that these 'passports' were as essential to the miners as the mariners. A particularly good example is provided by the membership of St Andrew's Lodge in Sydney, Nova Scotia in the mid-1860s. Here miners coming in to work at the newly discovered gold mines on Fall River joined Master Mariners in petitioning for membership in a ratio of almost three to one. Fifteen miners were initiated between 1863 and 1868, as many as all of the other occupational groups taken together, including mariners.[128] The insecurities faced by the miners were legion: dangers of travel from home to port; long-distance ocean shipping; difficult overland travel to points of final destination; primitive conditions, disease and social anarchy in frontier mining communities. Although eased by the development of railways and steamships during the period, which made travel faster and more secure, many of these problems never went away. Miners were also worried about parents, wives and children left at home and how they would fare if the flow of funds that they regularly sent were interrupted or cut off. When they finally found work at their destination it was a particularly hard and hazardous trade. At every point they took great comfort from having the help and support of the far-flung Masonic network available to them.

While there were those eager to seek initiation the inland Cornish mining lodges, like the coastal lodges, were happy to accommodate them, even when these men were about to leave and might not return for some time. The lodges bestowed degrees in emergency meetings and Past Masters were often among the proposers of men of whom they knew little, other than their desire to become Masons before they left the country. Lodge Minute Books, such as those for Boscawen Lodge in Chacewater, provide innumerable examples. For example, on 26 January 1866, two Past Masters of Boscawen Lodge nominated W.H. Northey, 'miner, late of California, and now residing in Perranzabuloe', because he is 'to leave England shortly and is desirous of becoming a freemason'. Similarly, at a meeting on 27 April 1868, Francis Trezise was proposed for membership. A mine agent, late of the United States of America, he also was 'about to leave England for California, and was desirous of being made a Freemason previous to his leaving'. Nothing had changed a generation later. In January 1883 the Lodge balloted for a new member who was 'shortly about to leave again for America' and in 1887 Hector Burnett was proposed—a 28-year-old gold reduction foreman, 'late of Brazil and now temporarily residing in Redruth'. With all of this experience and enthusiasm for emigration, it is not surprising that Bros Tonkin and Robson, the Lodge's Senior Warden and Senior Deacon respectively, announced their resignation on 28 February 1870, because they were 'leaving for Chile in a few days'.

Again a financial motive might be inferred. As a correspondent of the *Freemasons' Magazine* commented in 1866, 'Some lodges, much in debt and shackled by a baroness [*sic*] of funds, consider the fact of five guineas entrance fee too powerful a temptation to be even prudently careful as to the character and position of candidates.'[129] Overall, initiates were charged £7 7s[130] for all three degrees and this would have been attractive to lodges struggling to survive in depressed and shrinking communities. With average earnings for miners and most working men at £1 per week or less during the third quarter of the century,[131] there were relatively few local men with the financial resources to become Masons and a constant flow of members abroad who represented a haemorrhaging of membership subscriptions. The lodges had to run fast with recruitment to stay still with membership numbers. When in 1883 the PGM enquired why the total number of brethren in Cornwall had fallen during the last year he was told that:

> There were many brethren absent from some lodges ... The numbers in one lodge had declined [by more than] 50, and this had arisen from many brethren engaged in mining, mining engineers and others, having gone abroad. Other brethren were at sea. The names of those were returned but they are not reckoned now as subscribing members.[132]

In some lodges a quarter or more of their income came from members overseas, some of whom had been gone for more than ten years, and at least one lodge historian has concluded that they were 'virtually in the business of exporting Freemasons'.[133] It is remarkable that, given all of the other costs of emigration, so many men were prepared to 'invest' a sum in acquiring Masonic identity which was the equivalent of two month's work and around twice the cost of steerage passage to America.[134]

With all of these opportunist initiations, and comings and goings of old and new members, it is not surprising that the PGL became increasingly concerned about the 'quality' of members. At a meeting in July 1875 the PGM complained that 'We do not want a man to join because he thinks having a square and compasses over his door will help him in business.'[135] Again in 1883, the Grand Secretary told a meeting of the PGL—with some significant understatement—that 'he feared there had been some precipitation in accepting candidates'.[136] With more alarm his successor told the Lodge in 1896 that there was 'a feeling in the Metropolis that the status of Masons was not being kept up in Cornwall as much as it ought to be'.[137] In an editorial following its report of that meeting, The Freemason noted that the Grand Master had several times before expressed his desire that lodges should be more careful who they admitted. The editor understood that in a difficult economic climate lodges were anxious to add to their numbers and through that anxiety sometimes accepted anyone who came forward. However, he concluded that 'For our part we trust the advice will be followed strictly by all of the lodges both in the Province of Cornwall, to which in this instance it was especially offered, and throughout the country generally.'[138] This advice appears finally to have been heeded, with the Grand Secretary reporting to a meeting in 1900 that there had been significant reductions in initiations which 'showed that the lodges were beginning to appreciate the fact that Freemasonry should be regarded as a luxury and not as a benefit society'.[139]

While the Cornish may have led the charge in seeking Masonic membership to facilitate migration, they were far from unique. 'Gold fever' swept Britain and Europe after the widely reported gold rushes in California and Australia in the late 1840s and early 1850s, and men everywhere looked for opportunities to find their fortunes, not just in mining but also the numerous boom towns that sprang up to support the industry. Like the Cornish, these men were keen to 'hedge' the dangers of emigration for themselves and their families, whether they were accompanied or left them behind. For example, a letter from the Secretary of Friendship Lodge No. 277 in Oldham, Lancashire, at the heart of the cotton manufacturing district, pressed the Grand Secretary in 1852 for the urgent return of a lodge certificate for a newly initiated member about to leave England for the newly discovered gold 'diggings' in Victoria, Australia.[140] Similarly, at the other side of the country and about as far as it is possible to be from a mining district, the Lodge Secretary of St Peter's Lodge No. 1024 in Maldon, Essex, wrote on behalf of a recent young initiate that he was 'leaving soon for the Rock [sic] Mountains'. A year later the same Lodge Secretary wrote pressing the need for a certificate for a middle-aged clerk who was initiated and resigned on the same night, because 'he is leaving here next week for the Cape', no doubt attracted by the prospects of the booming towns on the recently discovered gold reefs of the Rand.[141]

Once the ball started rolling, the urgency of applications never diminished, stoked by a continuing series of gold rushes throughout the second half of the nineteenth century. Just before Christmas, on 23 December 1884, the Secretary of Blackwater Lodge No. 1977, also in Maldon, Essex, wrote urgently to Grand Lodge to send 'ten certificates as per form enclosed and if possible let me have them by Wednesday the 31rd [sic] December as some of the Brethren are about leaving for a distant land'. He would have had little chance of such service today but the Grand Lodge secretariat had clearly become well used to dealing with such requests and he plainly had reason to expect a positive response. Similarly, but with little less urgency, he wrote on 1 March 1886, 'Kindly let me have the certificates by the 16th of the month as two of the Brothers are going away to New Zealand.'[142] Such letters are a common occurrence in the returns for lodges across England during the late nineteenth century.

Commercial Travellers

So far attention has been focused on the advantages that Masonic membership could give to accessing lodges and networking systems in distant overseas ports and mining districts. However, the same case can be made for those who undertook much shorter distance movement within the United Kingdom. Mariners and miners were not exceptional in finding Freemasonry useful for an itinerant life. Many other occupational groups also organized their lives around constant movement, one of the most regular of which were commercial travellers, i.e. travelling salesmen and representatives. They were encountered in every lodge in West Cornwall and can be identified at some point in the history of virtually every lodge across the country. As has been seen in the analysis of lodge memberships, there was nowhere better for them to meet the full spectrum of the owners and managers of every commercial enterprise in town and to establish an easy rapport with them. Examples abound but a few outside of Cornwall might be mentioned. There were two in the 1860s and 1870s in

Bedford Lodge No. 282, meeting in Tavistock, Devon; five in the 1870s and 1880s in Philanthropic Lodge No. 107, meeting in King's Lynn, Norfolk; two during 1871/3 in Royal Jubilee Lodge No. 72, meeting in Fleet Street, London; one in 1877 in Sir Watkins' Lodge No. 1477, meeting in Mold, Denbighshire; one also in 1877 in Aberystwyth Lodge No. 1072, meeting in Aberystwyth, Cardiganshire; two in the 1880s in St Peter's Lodge No. 1024, meeting in Maldon, Essex; four during 1902/4 in Earl Spencer Lodge No. 1420, meeting in Battersea; and two or three in Lodge of Probity No. 61 in Halifax in every decade of the second half of the century.[143] No less than fifteen joined Britannia Lodge No. 139 in Sheffield between 1839 and 1860.[144] Neither were they confined to England. Again, a random sample finds them in Johannesburg Lodge No. 2313 in South Africa; Rising Sun Lodge No. 1401 and Otentosama Lodge No. 1263 in Japan; and Corinthian Lodge No. 770 in Bendigo, Australia. These commercial travellers were all full members of the lodges mentioned. Many others no doubt visited as their Master Mason status permitted.

The meeting places of some Masonic lodges also underlined the relationship between local Masons and commercial travellers. Many, such as St John's Lodge No. 70 in Plymouth, held their meetings in local commercial hotels which were the usual hostelries for travelling salesmen[145] and many travellers advertised for work in the Masonic press. By the 1890s Masonic travellers had become so numerous in major commercial centres that they started to establish special interest lodges of their own such as the Commercial Lodge No. 1391 in Leicester, the Travellers Lodge No. 2609 in Chester, the Commercial Travellers Lodge No. 2631 in Liverpool and the Loyal Travellers Lodge No. 2733 in Birmingham. In the years around the turn of the century, similarly named commercial traveller lodges were established in London (No. 2795 in 1899), Preston (No. 3493 in 1910) and Newcastle (No. 3700 in 1913). The number grows even larger when taking account of lodges with non-specific names, such as Davie Lodge No. 3721, established in Exeter in 1914 principally by commercial travellers. English lodges overseas usually accommodated commercial travellers in general town lodges, where they often congregated in significant numbers. In Bendigo, Australia, for example, twenty-four commercial travellers joined Zenith, Golden and Corinthian lodges during the 1860s, 1870s and 1880s, and in nearby Ballarat, six joined Yarrowee Lodge alone in the 1880s. In sociological terms, these single-occupation lodges gave their members the opportunity to 'bond' and 'bridge' to customers in other local lodges.

Of course, those self-describing as 'commercial travellers' were only a fraction of the total number that pursued mobile occupations. Many of the large numbers of 'agents' and 'merchants' also travelled constantly, and in addition featured significantly in lodge membership everywhere. One particularly famous example of this was the well-known Masonic historian William Hughan. During his enormously productive lifetime, he travelled extensively and joined—or was given membership of—numerous lodges, being variously described as a warehouseman, commercial traveller, draper and merchant. If only a small proportion of these large generic groups were itinerant, the overall numbers of Masons availing themselves of the assurance and access facilities of the Craft would have been of major significance.

Clearly the core membership of the vast majority of Masonic lodges was mainly static and not geographically mobile. Even during the period of rapid industrialization, most people lived and died in their home town or district. Stability was far greater than it is today. Nevertheless, the evidence suggests that the many that did move were aware of the benefits that being a Freemason could bring, were often eager to obtain membership and that many lodges were more than happy to oblige them, whatever their social and economic status. However, it would be a mistake to conclude that men only became Masons for mercenary reasons. As has been seen, the Order had numerous other attractions that came to figure prominently in men's lives. The problem was that, being a largely secretive organisation, most of its other offerings remained hidden until a new member had passed through all of the stages of initiation. Equally costs were unknown, not simply in terms of dinners but expected contributions to charity. To a large degree therefore, the decision to accept an invitation to join had to be taken on trust—much as it still does today. At one level, this would suggest that Freemasonry found it hard to grow as it was not able to fully advertise its wares. However, the size and success of any organisation depends not on how many people it persuades to become members, but how many it retains. During the nineteenth century, most of those that joined had an experience that persuaded them to remain members for many years. Large numbers played an active role in the development of their lodges and many of those lodges became key players in creating community 'social capital' through involvement in local government, the administration of justice, the construction of schools and hospitals, and various forms of social care.[146] This will be considered in more detail in later chapters.

From all of this it seems reasonable to conclude that while there are many reasons why men became Freemasons, for many, particularly those in mobile occupation or those planning migration, the reassurance that it provided while travelling and the access to support and networking opportunities at final desti-nation featured very high on their agenda. This is still recalled in the final toast at the end of every Masonic dinner—the nine o'clock toast:

To all poor and distressed brethren,
Wherever they are dispersed,
Over land, sea, or in the air.
A speedy relief from their suffering,
And a safe return to their native land, should they so desire.

As the editor of *Masonic Illustrated* commented in 1905, this toast 'has more meaning when it is recited by expatriated Englishmen, 5,000 miles away from home and civilisation, than it has when drunk at the social board of a London lodge'.[147] All of this considerably eased and facilitated the process of internal and international migration. It significantly improved the economic and social lives of Masons and their families after their arrival in new districts, and made a significant contribution to the wider construction of social capital and the quality of life in receiving communities.

After this long review of all of the reasons *for* joining Freemasonry and the advantages that membership bestowed, it is perhaps useful to look at why men *did not* seek or gain membership—why the Order was not bigger than it actually was? Many of the answers are simply the obverse of issues already raised above but they are worth briefly noting. For example, a commitment to a belief in God was required, which became more difficult to make in an increasingly secular age. It was a secretive organisation and unless a man knew a Mason he was unlike to appreciate what he was missing. Equally, a lack of knowledge made many suspicious of the costs involved, not just in terms of fees and dinners, but contributions to charity, assistance to fellow brethren, etc. Also, unless he knew a Mason, a man was unlikely to receive an invitation to join. Furthermore, the Mason that he knew would have to be able persuade another of the rectitude of his candidate before an effective proposal could be made. Any whiff of criminality or impropriety would sink the proposal before it was formally submitted. Suspected narrow self-promotion, socially and economically, might have been rejected by many. Some perceived flirtation with the occult, which was a serious problem in a Cornish culture steeped in superstition. Religious groups sometimes regarded Freemasonry as a form of heresy to be condemned and avoided, and a strong tradition of temperance took hold in the county from the 1840s which did not sit easily with alcohol-fuelled lodge dinners.[148] Poor behaviour by less constrained Masons attracted public opprobrium and led to the PGL to call for stricter standards for those admitted, and a move of lodge meetings from their traditional home in taverns and hotels to their own purpose-built Masonic rooms and halls.[149] These issues are still be encountered first-hand when recruiting initiates to the Order today. Finally, many men were probably perfectly contented with a fraternal home in one of the other quasi-Masonic friendly societies, with their similar entertainments, guaranteed returns and provisions for family membership of one form or another.

Pursuing this line of inquiry, it would also seem appropriate to ask whether these uncertainties, sensibilities and rejection of Freemasonry incurred costs by those who did not join in terms of damaged careers or social progression. In academic terms, this amounts to whether a counterfactual argument can be constructed to test and evaluate the advantages of being a Mason by looking at what happened to those that were not members. What was the level of comparative advantage achieved? Unfortunately, it has not been possible to develop a methodology to conduct such an investigation, particularly in terms of socio-cultural impact. At best, it is possible only to refer to the overall careers of those that were not Masons. While some may have suffered, others appear to have performed perfectly well. In the context of the mining sector, for example, the various generation of the family that ran the immensely prestigious and influential international consultancy of John Taylor and Sons rarely appear to have shown any interest in becoming Masons. Similarly, Henry Montague Rogers and Oliver Wethered, the highly successful Cornish mining investors of the late nineteenth and early twentieth centuries,[150] never became members of a Masonic lodge. It is highly likely that many other examples can be found but it has not been possible to ascertain what proportion of the total they may have been and the degree to which their progression may have been frustrated by non-membership. Further research is necessary.[151]

CHAPTER 6

INTERNATIONAL COMPARISON: THE WESTERN UNITED STATES

Introduction

The previous chapters have looked at the organisation and structure of Freemasonry in Britain. They used a particular case study of Cornwall in the south-west of England to explore in some detail what can be discovered about this supposedly secret organisation—how it grew, which social and economic groups belonged to it, and how it related to the broader social analysis of Britain during the period. Attention was then given to why men became Masons—what did it offer, what did it cost, how did it compare with other similar fraternal societies? It concluded that there were many and varied experiences but that Masonry's offerings of reliable help and security were particularly attractive to men in mobile occupations, such as mariners and miners. They flocked to the Order in large numbers during the second half of the nineteenth century. This chapter will continue that discussion by exploring in more detail the relationship between Masonry and migration, but looking at it from the point of view of the receiving countries rather than outgoing or home countries. It will again look primarily at miners and mining communities, and those men and their families who moved to frontier districts, and it will focus on the particular experience in the Western mining districts of the United States. The following chapter will consider the experience in other parts of the world.

The inward flow of migrants to frontier mining areas took place in at least two stages. The first was that of the 'boomers' who rushed into new districts shortly after the first discoveries and used simple hand techniques to work shallow rich deposits. They founded new urban communities which, if the mines survived, became the focus of future mining operations. The 'second wave' came to provide labour and expertise for deeper, more difficult mining and the complex ore separation and smelting processes required to produce marketable metal. The kinds of support that migrant miners required differed somewhat depending on the phase of development in which they were involved.

The travels of the 'boomers' were the most hazardous. They launched out into unsurveyed lands with extremes of terrain and climate, and indigenous populations that were often resentful, occasionally aggressive and sometimes murderous. Their travelling companions were often worse still. They took a blind jump into the unknown—no one could tell how it would turn out. Although there had been earlier gold discoveries around the world, none had produced a sudden mass movement of people on the scale seen in Australia and California in the 1840s and 1850s. Very few could have had any real perception of how life would be in large communities in remote areas, several thousand miles beyond the settled frontier. If anything, accumulated experience showed that it was impossible to predict outcomes from 'rushing' and that the conditions for travel frequently deteriorated further as time went on. Under such circumstances the view of the 'boomers' as audacious gamblers has become an integral part of the historical interpretation of all of the rushes, from Sutter's Creek to the Klondike.

Whereas the 'boomers' looked primarily for aid and security in travel and had to create a new fraternal infrastructure at final destination, a 'second wave' of migrants might look less for support in transit and more for a welcome on arrival. They needed networks and introductions to those that might offer jobs, advice on housing and assistance to wives and children on what to do—and not to do—in the town. Those with funds to invest needed reliable and informed information on investment opportunities, which was a precious commodity in a world where the popular description of a mine was 'a hole in the ground with a liar at the top'.[1] In their many and various forms the lodges and their rituals also provided effective spaces for physical and spiritual sanctuary from the turmoil of emerging urban communities. They provided islands of the old and familiar from the world left behind, opportunities for exclusive socialising, entertainment and arguably helped to mould more moral, disciplined and productive characters.[2] Above all, they offered continuity and familiarity within the new and chaotic towns of the frontier, principles to hold on to, attitudes to share, something of the East and the Old World in the New World.

The Cornish were among the first waves of 'boomers', or 'Argonauts' as they were known in the Californian rush of 1849, and they were particularly visible in the second wave. However, they were far from the only, or even the main, group of arrivals. They were heavily eclipsed in number by men and women drawn from all existing settled areas and by incomers from other parts of the world. In the United States, for example, they came in very large numbers from the settled areas of the East Coast and the Midwest, from Europe, Mexico, Latin America and China. Like the Cornish, they all perceived the hazards and diffi-culties of such migration and cast around for the means of insuring themselves, or 'hedging' against those dangers.[3] This helped to produce an enormous growth of fraternal and benevolent organisations of all kinds during the years from the mid-century. As in Britain, membership of these organisations—acquired before, during or after migration—provided highly effective ways of ensuring trusted companionship, effective care and support for self and family, and successful integration at a final destination. The Masons may have shown the way but far greater numbers—both men and women—increased the membership of other orders into the millions. Together these orders helped incomers to take a full part in building the new communities, joining with the churches to promote morality, stability and continuity in otherwise anarchic conditions. As Rodman Paul observed, 'Three moveable institutions were universal on the mining frontier—saloons, churches, and fraternal lodges.'[4] Much has been written about the first two of these, but very little about the latter.[5]

The Freemasons may have been just one of many orders providing mutual support for this vast migration but their already long-established and wide network of lodges, together with their reputation as a powerful and elite organisation, put them ahead of the game. From well before the gold rushes, migratory Masons carried their fraternity along with them and called upon it whenever need arose. They might band together in mutually supportive groups, providing familiar and dependable company. They could rely on help and assistance en route either from the lodges in towns through which they passed or from fellow brethren encountered on the road. They should have been able to identify people that they could trust for information and advice in an otherwise highly insecure environment. Wives and families left behind in the care of relations would have the additional assurance of fraternal support. Fraternal networks could facilitate communications as well as help guarantee financial transfers from the new mining districts back to dependants at home.[6]

Once in the new mining districts, everyone was an outsider but they were already part of an extended family. As will be seen, that family was multinational and, to a degree, multi-ethnic. In every district Masons were among the very earliest to arrive, often having identified each other while travelling. They established lodges within months of arrival and from the outset became a focal point for the economic and social development of the community. Membership could be seen to bestow benefits in terms of networking and mutual support, and seeking admittance to the Order could be viewed as one of the very best ways for a man to protect and advance the prospects of himself and his family.

To give substance to these claims, this chapter will start by looking at the overall context of the growth of fraternal societies in the United States during the nineteenth century and will then move on to continue the focus on

Freemasonry and Freemasons. A series of case studies of Masonic lodges and their host communities in various parts of the American West will indicate in more detail how they might have facilitated incomers and assisted in longer-term community development. Occasional comparative glances at the Independent Order of Oddfellows will help to widen the discussion to the broader issues of fraternal activity and impact.

Growth and Expansion of Fraternal/Benevolent Societies

The first, most enduring, and generally the largest fraternal institutions were imported from abroad during the eighteenth and early nineteenth centuries. The Ancient Order of Free and Accepted Masons, the Independent Order of Oddfellows, the Ancient Order of Druids, the Ancient Order of Foresters and the Independent Order of Rechabites had all been successfully transplanted from Britain to the United States by the 1840s and their 'lodges', 'encampments' or 'tents' were flourishing everywhere.[7] As the frontier moved west, one or more of these groups would establish themselves in every town, almost from the date of first settlement. In 1843 the London-based *Freemasons Quarterly Review* attempted to outline the contemporary phenomenon of the rapid spread of Masonry in America for its readers.

> The tide [of migration] presses onward: a part now rushes into the Floridas, and another towards the rocky mountains. More or less of Masonic knowledge accompanies this motley crowd of human life in its rush into the wilderness. As the population becomes dense, churches and schools are erected, a post office is established; the blacksmith, the wheelwright, and the merchant, cluster around the church and the school house ... After a little time, there are Masons enough in the settlement to form a Lodge, and a dispensation or warrant being obtained from one of the nearest Grand Lodges, the Light of Masonry begins to shed its rays before the stumps of the old forest trees have disappeared from the fields around ... Masonry harmonizes with the principles, the habits, and the propensities of the people, and lodges are added, until, for the convenience of the officers, and possibly from that innate love of independence which accompanies the American everywhere, they form a constitution, separate from their Mother Grand Lodge, and with her concurrence, commence a regular form of government over the Masons in the territory.[8]

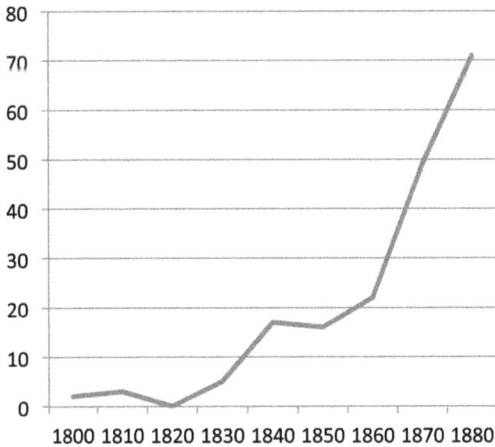

Figure 6   Chronological Establishment of National and International
Benevolent and Fraternal Organizations in America, 1800–1890

From the mid-century, 'home bred' organisations such as the Knights of Pythias and the Benevolent and Protective Order of Elks began to multiply rapidly and the total number of new organisations established each decade increased regularly until the end of the century (see Figure 6). By the end of the century these, and hundreds of other smaller local organisations, had around five million members—almost one in five of the male population. The rapid expansion of members was driven not only by the self-interest of individuals but also by the support of employers and politicians. They saw these institutions—unlike organised labour—as bastions of the status quo, promoting ideals of thrift and 'self-help', and stabilising families and communities.

The Expansion of Freemasonry and the Independent Order of Odd Fellows

Establishing the profile of growth over time and breaking down the numbers by organisation is difficult before the collection of regular data at the beginning of the twentieth century. At that time, however, the largest organisations were the Freemasons and the Oddfellows—known in the US as 'Odd Fellows'—with a roughly equal membership of around one million, followed by the Knights of Pythias with around 600,000 and the Red Men with about 350,000.[9] Together, they represented around 60% of the total. Periodic earlier estimates of the numbers of Freemasons were made by contemporaries from lodge membership returns made to the various State Grand Lodges from the beginning of the

Table 9   The Approximate Number of Masonic and Odd Fellows'
Lodges and their Members in the USA, 1800 1905

Date	Masonic Lodges	Odd Fellows' Lodges	No. of Freemasons	No. of Odd Fellows
1800	347	?	16,000 est.	?
1840	700	155	32,000	11,166
1850	1,835	2,400 est.	66,142	175,000 est.
1860	4,406	3,547	193,763	173,818
1870	7,194	3,867	443.898	298,637
1880	9,308	7,172	536,867	456,942
1889	10,088	8,400	609,463	545,300
1905	?		989,176	111,634

Source: FM, 23 August 1890, p. 94; Noel P. Gist, Secret Societies: A Cultural Study of Fraternalism in the
United States University of Missouri Studies: A Quarterly of Research XV, 4 (October 1940), p. 42;
Theo. A. Ross, Odd Fellowship: Its History and Manual (New York, 1888) pp. 660–61.

century. These undoubtedly include a level of double counting as Masons moved
around and joined different or multiple lodges but they provide a general view
of the scale and particularly the growth profile of the Order (see Table 9).

After slow growth during the early decades of the century, the orders began
to expand at an accelerating rate from the 1840s, doubling in that decade and
trebling in the next. They then slowed slightly but generally continued strongly
through the rest of the century. The largest numbers were in the main population
centres of the East Coast and Midwest but the rate of expansion was particularly
strong in the West. In California, for example, the number of Odd Fellows
increased from less than a thousand in the early 1850s to more than 20,000
by the late 1870s.[10] It is probable that the growth of the other major orders
followed a similar profile of expansion, making this genuinely a 'Golden Age of
Fraternity'[11] at the high point when as many as 40% of the US male population
may have been a member of one or more orders.[12]

The Wider Attractions of Fraternal Membership

The main drivers for the growth of the orders were the improved opportunities that they offered for social interaction, within and beyond the lodges, and
the chances to insure against the economic vicissitudes of life.[13] The relative
importance of these attractions varied between the different orders, with the
Freemasons particularly stressing the former and others a varied balance of the

two. The focus for social interaction within the lodges was the learning, rehearsal and performance of rituals. To one degree or another, most orders looked back to some utopian past which they celebrated, and took inspiration from, with rituals of varying levels of complexity. Some have seen the Freemasons as providing the original model for all of these orders, with others adopting, adapting and evolving their own stories and interpretations. This 'moral theatre' could also be seen as an important form of entertainment to leaven life in dull frontier communities. Ritual also created the foundations for 'rank'—the acquisition of elevated titles such as 'Grand Officer' and 'Grand Sire'—which bestowed enhanced 'fraternal status' on men of modest circumstances in everyday life. Outside of the lodge, periodic picnics, parades, parties and dinners offered further engagement, not just for members but also their wives and families. The nature of the financial 'insurance' offered by the orders[14] differed significantly. Most, such as the Odd Fellows, could be classed as 'benevolent organisations', providing some level of cover 'as of right' by making regular monthly charges for guaranteed returns at death or during sickness. A few—most notably the Freemasons—were less formal, providing only 'charitable' relief by discretionary donations to cover unexpected emergencies or to help members back on their feet after a life crisis.

The benevolent organisations, offering guaranteed returns, varied in the sums they charged and paid out, and many orders provided for different levels of cover for their members depending on how much they could afford. Some had regular contributions and some varied their contributions according to the calls made upon them at any particular time. In the late 1870s, the Independent Order of Foresters—which had seceded from its British parent the Ancient Order of Foresters in 1874[15]—was said sometimes to have made assessments that were so high that a member might have been paying the rent for a good house, though $9–10 a year was more probable.[16] Common levels of insurance for members included free medical assistance, weekly sickness benefits (frequently around $5, diminishing after an initial period), death benefits (usually around $50) and some provision for an endowment that would provide an annuity in old age. The Freemasons, who offered no certainty of relief but the possibility of financial assistance to help members get back on their feet, were expensive to join but inexpensive to belong to. Initiation fees varied between districts and lodges but were usually $75 or more—paid in advance—for the first three degrees necessary to become a fully-fledged Master Mason,[17] while annual dues might be only around $3.[18] Lodge finance was thus largely based on bringing men into the Order rather than continuing subscriptions. For example, Nevada City Lodge's hundred new entrants in 1852, not all requiring all three degrees, probably earned the Lodge around $5,175. Some went to benevolence and still more was accumulated from individuals' voluntary contributions.[19] On the urban frontier, the orders also often used their resources to provide facilities for their members that were not yet available from emergent town authorities. With the ever-present prospect of death, for example, and the pressing need for a proper Christian burial, the provision of cemeteries was given a high priority. The imperative duties of the American Odd Fellowship, for example, were 'To visit the sick, to relieve the distressed and to bury the dead.'[20] With such pressing concerns, the first major expenditure by Escurial Lodge in Virginia City was to purchase land for a Masonic cemetery,[21] while a generation later, in May 1898, the first meeting of 120 Freemasons at Lake Bennett in the Klondyke focused on a similar essential requirement.[22] In Deadwood, South Dakota, Golden Star Masonic Lodge, Dakota Lodge of the Knights of Pythius and lodges of the Independent Order of Odd Fellows in nearby Lead and Central City, came together in 1877 to patent several acres of land to provide a cemetery for themselves and other members of the community, including Jews and Chinese. When Mt Moriah cemetery was refurbished in 1914, the Masons went to the considerable trouble of marking out their section as a 'celestial lodge', complete with a tyler (the grave of George S. Jackson) two pillars (Boaz and Jachin), a Worshipful Master (the grave of Otto F. Parnell) and an altar.[23]

While all of these provisions for an uncertain future were desirable, it was probably the urgent needs of the present that took pole position on the gold seekers' list of priorities. Most fraternities—certainly those affiliated to extended national and international organisations—offered informal help and support to travelling brothers: the Freemasons were among the best known for this. In Europe, lodges frequently joined with local emigration societies in making charitable grants to less well-off brethren to pay the initial costs of emigration, so accommodating the principle of sustaining members' self-sufficiency. As early as 1838, the Board of Benevolence in Nottinghamshire, England, gave a grant of £20 to assist one of the local brethren to emigrate to the United States[24] and in 1847, a lodge in Offenbach, Germany, issued a circular calling upon Masons everywhere to contribute to emigration charities to assist poorer brethren to escape unemployment. Some years later a lodge in Deptford, near London, reported that 'One esteemed brother ... being reduced in circumstances caused by events entirely beyond his control, having solicited aid to assist him to emigrate to America, in a very few days had the sum of £10 7s given to him.'[25]

It was not just in getting started that the lodges were helpful. In 1853 *The Freemasons Quarterly Review* assured its British readers that 'thousands lament that they were not possessed of an advantage, before they left their homes, which opens a sure road to success for them upon their arrival in a strange land',[26] When asking the rhetorical question 'Why do men join the Masons?', a correspondent of the London-based *The Freemason* explained that it was 'for the same reasons that they join other organizations, for profit, for social intercourse, from curiosity' but most particularly:

> many men join because they think that it is a good thing to belong to an Order as universal as Masonry is, and which gives him the privileges of visiting kindred lodges all over the world, with his Masonry as a practical letter of introduction to those who would otherwise be strangers.[27]

For the more adventurous travellers, opportunity also became reassurance. A correspondent of another weekly observed that:

> wherever a ship sails, or a railroad runs—there is a Masonic lodge, there is a Brother's home. No accident will befall him that will deprive him of his friends. All of his travelling companions may die or desert him, or he may be robbed of all his money, but still the Freemason is among his relations, and may always find relief from his distress. This is, to a traveller, the *summum bonum* of Masonry.[28]

More specifically *The Freemason* told its readers that, in America, a sick and needy foreign Mason would be 'visited by a brother, assisted financially and, if death should ensue, he will be buried with respect and reverence in the Masonic cemetery'. They added that the Masons of California were particularly generous to charity and the support of members.[29] All of this was well established long before the 1849 gold rush. Lipson, writing of New England around the turn of the century, observed that 'Among the explicit appeals of Masonry were its advantages for a physically and socially mobile population',[30] and lodge visitors' books everywhere give testament to the regular comings and goings. At just one meeting in 1842, for example, Galena Lodge, in Galena, Illinois recorded visitors from lodges in Iowa Territory, England, Ireland, Indiana, Boston (Massachusetts) and New York.[31] Later, in the 1880s, Golden Star Lodge No. 9 in Deadwood, South Dakota, welcomed visitors from mining districts across the United States and Canada and on several occasions played host to incomers from Ireland (for example, David Norris, from Royal Blue No. 754, Coleraine), Scotland (George Cruickshank from Oban Lodge No. 180) and England (S.G. Burn from Whitwell

No. 1390, Cumberland). John Bawden and William Vincent from True and
Faithful No. 318 in Cornwall visited frequently, sometimes accompanied by
their fellow countryman Josiah Oates, who now gave his affiliation as Escurial
No. 7 of Virginia City, Nevada.[32]

For the travellers who had fallen on really hard times, or who had exhausted all
of their travelling funds, the lodges also proved an invaluable source of financial
relief. As back home in Britain and elsewhere, members of an affiliated order
could call on the local lodge and, with proof of membership, receive small sums
of money to cover the costs of a meal, short-stay accommodation and perhaps a
ticket to the next town. It was an invaluable network for a 'tramping brother'.
There are no central records of the sums paid out for 'tramping' relief, and they
undoubtedly varied between lodges and over time, but it is likely that they were
substantial and placed a real burden on some lodges. In the 1850s, for example,
the Canadian lodges complained bitterly of the charges on their limited means
of the 'numberless claimants for Masonic benevolence' arriving from Britain.[33]
Some years earlier, the Odd Fellows had suspended relief for all but domestic
members when they began to face similar burdens.

Given the considerable financial pressures that could be inflicted by the great
migration on small Western lodges, it is not surprising that it became commonplace for them to try to recover expenditures from the mother lodges of the
travelling brethren. In 1881, for example, St John's Lodge No. 18 of Pioche,
Nevada, tried to bill Druids Lodge of Redruth, Cornwall, for the $135 they
had spent on burying Matthew Rogers of Druids when he had died penniless in
Pioche, claiming that 'owing to other matters of the same sort we are in financial
straights'.[34] Similarly, in 1884 the Grand Lodge of Arizona paid close attention
to a dispute between a lodge in Montana and another in Illinois following a claim
for the repayment of monies spent on a travelling member of the Illinois lodge
for sickness and distress while in Montana's jurisdiction. They concluded ruefully
that while lodges did usually ask for such reimbursement, they customarily let
the matter drop if monies were not forthcoming.[35]

So common and so valuable were the fraternal 'handouts' that the whole
system became increasingly subject to fraudulent claims. This is an issue already
discussed above for Britain,[36] but in North America it was far worse, with
numbers growing particularly rapidly towards the end of the century. In frontier
districts the odds were stacked heavily in favour of the fraudsters. Everyone was
a 'foreigner' or, at least, from far away: they came from different constitutions
with slightly different signs and passwords; and certificates could easily have been
lost or forged[37] (see Illustration 10). Even if they were genuine members there
were considerable difficulties in checking whether they were currently paid up

Illustration 10   An American Grand Lodge Certificate, Missouri, USA

A certificate issued for Bro. Laurence Murphy of Montezuma Lodge, Santa Fe, New Mexico, under the authority of the Grand Lodge of Missouri, on the completion of his Third Degree of Initiation to Master Mason, dated 18 March 1871. The Grand Master of Missouri had claimed Masonic jurisdiction of what was to be the Territory of New Mexico in 1847 and it remained under their jurisdiction until the formation of the Grand Lodge of New Mexico in 1877. Montezuma Lodge was chartered in August 1851 as No. 109 on the roll of Missouri but, as the oldest Lodge in New Mexico, it became No. 1 on the new roll of the Grand Lodge of New Mexico.

in their home lodges and properly entitled to help. The opportunity was there for a free-for-all and everyone suffered. The Odd Fellows, the Foresters, the Druids and every other friendly society and fraternal order had their problems but it was probably the Masons that suffered the most.[38] Their far-flung network of lodges made it particularly difficult to validate claimants and it rendered them particularly subject to fraudulent abuse.

To tighten their procedures, the lodges tried a two-pronged approach. Firstly, many began to issue special 'travelling certificates', authenticating the holder and demonstrating his currently paid-up status.[39] This was as useful for the legitimate travelling Mason in a suspicious world as it was for the receiving lodges. Secondly, the North American Masons began to experiment with a system of national reporting of suspicious persons and already proven frauds. In 1877, for example, the Masonic Lodge of Relief in Baltimore, Maryland, circulated a poster to other lodges warning of an English Masonic impostor going by the name of Herbert Sydney. Claiming to be a portrait painter from Langthorne Lodge, Stratford in Essex, he had successfully obtained money in Baltimore over several weeks and would no doubt soon try to attempt the same swindle elsewhere.[40] In 1885 such arrangements were put on a more regular footing when a number of Masonic organisations met in Baltimore to organize the General Masonic Relief Association of the United States and Canada, in order 'to establish a central organisation for the purpose of facilitating the discovery and exposure of persons travelling about the country and imposing upon the charities of Masons'.[41] They accumulated a central register of the names, appearances, stories and sometimes photographs of impostors which were speedily distributed by telegram. These were circulated in monthly updated 'Warning Circulars' to subscribing lodges[42] that no doubt saw them as a sound money-saving investment (see Figure 1). Over the twenty-seven years from 1885 to 1912, the circulars recorded 4,833 'unworthy cases' including many multiple offenders.[43] Adding those to unknown and unreported frauds produces an average of around several hundred each year. This would have been only a very small fraction of the total number of applications made by genuine Masonic claimants.

A Case Study of Nevada City Masonic Lodge, California

General observations are useful but the optimal approach to understanding the advantages of fraternal/benevolent society membership is to study the orders at grass-roots level. In this context it is easier to appreciate their economic and social contributions to both the individual and community, and to obtain a sense of their 'inspirational' role in the construction of civic capital. By examining the membership of particular lodges in specific communities it is possible to be more positive about their role in such issues as advancing the economic outcomes of migration, providing sources of social security and promoting—or undermining—social, racial and ethnic cohesion.

Unfortunately, identifying communities for which data for multiple societies is available is far from straightforward. It is usually best to start with Freemasonry since, as in Britain, it provides the most regular and comprehensive membership information. Lodge membership lists were regularly published for most states in the annual *Proceedings* of their Grand Lodges and it is possible to derive a long and continuous series. Comparative material for other societies, however, is far more sporadic and dependent mainly on the random survival of manuscript data. Good background studies of communities against which the specific fraternal data can be cast are still more difficult to find.

Nevertheless, useful examples can be found across the mining West, of which Nevada City in California is one. California had seen the arrival of Freemasons and Odd Fellows even before the discovery of gold, and when the 'world rushed in' there were soon adequate numbers to form lodges in most of the emergent communities. By April 1850 the Freemasons were sufficiently well represented to establish their own Grand Lodge, six months before the State of California was itself admitted to the Union.[44] The Odd Fellows delayed their break with the Eastern authorities that warranted their first lodges, but they too established a California Grand Lodge in 1853.[45] Both had headquarters in San Francisco and both counted many thousands of members by the end of the decade. From the 1860s these early orders were also being joined by the Knights of Pythius, the Improved Order of Redmen, the American Order of Foresters, the Grange, the Benevolent Order of Elks and numerous others. So ubiquitous were they that even those outside of the orders—or excluded from them—were tempted to form their own groups to lampoon their rituals. They gave birth to *E Clampus Vitus* whose antics became a feature of many mining camps across California.[46]

The rush to Wolf Creek brought the first Argonauts to the Nevada City area in 1849. Though the settlement was still in the most rudimentary stage of development, a Masonic lodge was established the following year and the Independent Order of Odd Fellows followed in 1853. A short distance away, the Grass Valley community established their own lodges around the same time. Mann's excellent study of the overall social structure and evolution of these towns provides the crucial contextual background.[47] The deconstruction of lodge membership and interpretation of their role in the community will focus on the better documented Freemasons with comparative reference to the Odd Fellows.

Nevada City's Masonic lodge was established with a warrant from the Grand Lodge of Wisconsin and was initially known as Lafayette No. 29. Following the foundation of the Grand Lodge of California it was renamed and renumbered as Nevada Lodge No. 13, reflecting seniority of its original foundation in the state.[48] The number indicates the order of its foundation, standing in line with several other neighbouring towns such as Grass Valley, North San Juan, Rough and Ready, Orleans Flat, Truckee, Washington and Red Dog. With men pouring into the area, Nevada No. 13 was able briefly to claim that it was the largest lodge in California—larger even than San Francisco Lodge No. 1—not only welcoming those who were already Masons, but initiating and progressing well over a hundred new members in 1852 alone.[49] So great was the demand for admission that a second lodge was established in the city in 1853, though this lasted only for three years as Nevada Lodge continued to 'control the field'.[50]

Although it is possible to find the names of the Lodge members during the early years, it is difficult to trace much detailed information on their background. This becomes possible from 1860, however, with the regular decennial censuses, providing details of origin, age, marital status, occupation, etc. By that point, the first wave of the 'rush' was well past its peak, and many of the less successful and more footloose had undoubtedly moved on to other frontiers. Nevertheless, more than half of the members of the Lodge in the mid-1850s were still there in 1860.[51] An analysis of the Lodge structure in that year provides a useful reflection of those who looked to this particular fraternity for support and succour during both the early influx into the district and its rapid transition to larger-scale corporate mining.

At the beginning of 1860 the Lodge had ninety paid-up members, of which sixty still lived in the vicinity and can be found in the census returns. The great majority of the identifiable group were mature men in their thirties (69%), though there was a sizeable cohort in their twenties (22%). Fewer than one in ten was over forty. This suggests that in the very early days of the Lodge most of its members were in their twenties or early thirties (initiations for those under twenty-one years were rarely agreed exceptions), and that they were therefore fairly representative of the Argonauts as a whole as a youthful group. This was probably also true of their marital status in the early 1850s, with a predominance of bachelors; though by 1860 just over half of the identifiable members (56%) were married. This likely reflects the 'maturing' of the members and perhaps their relatively successful economic status.

The geographical origins of the Masons show a different balance from those of the Californian population as a whole.[52] By 1860, the Lodge members seem to have consisted mainly of men from the Northern and Eastern states of New York, Ohio, Pennsylvania, Massachusetts and New England rather than the Midwestern and Southern states. Of course, many of these men might already have moved from their place of birth to the Midwest, and used that as their 'jumping off base' for the gold rush. As has been seen, Nevada Lodge was established by men from Wisconsin, though none gave this as their place of birth. It is equally possible, however, that the Northern and Eastern states, with their long-established and widely dispersed networks of Masonic lodges, gave men from those areas a greater appreciation of the support and potential advantages of membership, and that this may have exponentially attracted them to lodge membership at their point of arrival.

It is not so much the regional origins of the Lodge's members that really distinguishes it from the rest of the Californian population, however, as the very large proportion of native-born Americans among its members. Comparing the nationality structure of the Lodge with that calculated by Mann for Nevada City as a whole, 72% of the Masons were American compared with just 54% of the residents of the city.[53] To put it another way, those who were foreign-born accounted for almost half of the city's population but only just over a quarter of the Lodge's membership. In this context, Freemasonry appears as a non-representative, heavily skewed, 'nativist' organisation. This picture is considerably moderated, however, if the Chinese residents of the district are removed from the equation. Freemasonry, like most other fraternities and social and political organisations of this period, excluded the Chinese[54] and if the structure of the Lodge is compared to the non-Chinese population of the city, there is a much closer match. Under such circumstances the domestic-born population rises to a much closer 64% for the city compared to 72% for the Lodge. The Lodge remains a relatively conservative, domestic-dominated organisation but not so greatly out of line with its host population.

The same cannot be said for the balance of origins of the foreign-born within the Lodge. While in the city as a whole, men from the British Isles accounted for 23% of the non-Chinese foreign-born, in the Lodge they only constituted 14% of the identified membership. Those from greater Germany and Scandinavia, however, accounted for 11% of the Lodge membership but only 9% of the non-Chinese city population. The reasons for this are probably both religious and socio-economic. A large part of the British component of the population were Irish and would have been excluded/self-excluded because of their Catholic faith and low-skilled position in the labour market. The Cornish, in particular, were keen to separate themselves from the Irish, who they saw as a low-wage threat to their niche advantage in employment.[55] Similarly, those from Southern Europe would not have embraced—or have been embraced by—Masonry, though their numbers in the city were low at this time. By contrast, Protestant and more highly skilled Germans and Scandinavians, would have known Freemasonry as an economically and socially elitist organisation at home and would have been eager to become members. Those who were already Masons would have been keen to sustain their membership and those that were offered initiation in America would have seen it as a fortuitous opportunity to integrate with the Anglo-Saxon establishment. It may be significant that the turnover of foreign-born members of the Lodge was much higher than that of the domestic-born population: though the numbers of identifiable foreign-born members doubled from seventeen to thirty-four between 1860 and 1870, only one was a member in both years. It suggests that Masonry was a particularly useful facilitator of continuing long-distance migration.

As might be expected, the identified occupations of sixty-four members of Nevada Lodge showed a strong orientation towards mining and mining-related activities, but also reflected the overall diversity of the local economy. Around half declared their occupations as miner, mill-man, or craftsmen—such as black-smiths and carpenters—with direct connections to mining or alluvial working, while the other half included a miscellany of town agents, merchants, manufac-turers, bankers, and legal and medical professionals. Hotel and storekeepers were also represented, as were clerks, post and telegraph operators, sheriffs and farmers. Even the lowest economic orders of 'labourer' produced three members, possibly men who had fallen on hard times or only recently arrived in the district. The largest and most glaring omissions from membership, however, were female workers of all descriptions. They were then, and still are, excluded from membership of regular Freemasonry and had to rely either on represen-tation through their husbands or joining related orders—such as the Eastern Star[56]—many of which later acquired considerable influence in their own right. The effect on the general economic and social welfare of women—particularly single businesswomen—resulting from their exclusion from fraternal and many benevolent societies[57] is an under-explored aspect of women's history and can only begin to be appreciated from a clearer understanding of the benefits of membership afforded to men.

Interpretation of employment data to obtain an impression of the social status of lodge members is fraught with difficulty. Many of the occupational categories—particularly 'miner'—could encompass a very wide range of experience, from a poverty-stricken employee to a wealthy mine owner, possibly with his own large labour force. A simple 'blue-' or 'white-collar' division of the occupations thus creates wide possibilities for error. However, accepting

Table 10   The Declared Total Asset Value of Members of
Nevada Lodge (Total Real and Personal Estate)

Year	No. of Members Declaring	$0 – $999	$1,000 – $4,999	$5,000 – $9,999	$10,000 – $14,999	$15,000 – $19,999	$20,000 – $29,999	$30,000 above
1860	27	4	13	5	1	2	1	1
1870	51	13	18	7	5	0	1	7

such risks and simply classifying the mining affiliated and some other small groups as 'blue-collar', and most of the urban occupations as 'white-collar', produces a predominance of blue-collar workers in a ratio of roughly 6:4. This is significantly different, however, from that calculated by Mann for Nevada City males as a whole at 9:1. It is suggested, therefore, that the Lodge members were disproportionately drawn from the upper quartile of their host society and that many were probably part of the city elite.

This last conclusion is supported by the personal and estate values declared by some members in the censuses of 1860 and 1870. Although the latter date is considerably beyond the early gold rush years it has been included to give some impression of the dynamic of asset acquisition that might be backward projected for the years before 1860. Thus Table 10 shows that the average asset value of members of the Lodge was growing quickly in the 1860s and that, even at the beginning of that decade, many Lodge members already had acquired significant personal wealth. Indeed, if these returns are compared with those calculated by Mann for the city as a whole they reveal that the Lodge, which had only 3% of the local male population, includes four of its twelve wealthiest citizens in 1860, assessed in terms of a declared asset value of more than $10,000. A similar relationship was maintained in 1870, when seven Lodge members were counted among an elite city group of twenty-one citizens declaring similar asset values.[58] Identifying the richest members of the Lodge also underlines the hazards of social categorisation by occupation. In 1860 they included the expected banker and attorney but also two 'miners'. Similarly, in 1870, three of the seven described themselves as a 'miner' with one of them, George Jacobs, declaring an asset value of $80,000. By contrast, in both years there were several 'miners' who declared their total net worth—real estate and personal estate—at $1,000 or less.

It is unclear how well Masonry served the foreign-born members of the Lodge. On the one hand it might be noted that in 1860 only two of the seventeen foreign-born members reported total assets in excess of $1,000 while by 1870 this number had increased to eleven out of thirty-four. However, only one of the original seventeen was still in the Lodge at the latter date, the rest having moved on. If they had all done as well as the single survivor—Charles Klingenspor, a miner from Germany—they would clearly have prospered. His declared assets had increased from nothing to over $2,000 during the intervening ten years.

Comparison of Nevada City Masonic Lodge with Others in Virginia City, Nevada and Virginia City, Montana

How typical was Nevada Lodge? Did its membership differ significantly from that of other Masonic lodges in western towns at a similar stage of development? To examine this question, two lodges in other districts have been chosen for an abbreviated comparative analysis: Virginia City Lodge in Virginia City, Nevada and Virginia City Lodge in Virginia City, Montana. Both lodges were established in the early 1860s by some of the earliest arrivals in the district and both grew rapidly thereafter.[59] The multiplication of lodges in neighbouring districts facilitated the foundation of independent Grand Lodges in Nevada in late 1864 and Montana in early 1866. However, conducting a direct comparative analysis of the membership of these lodges presents a problem. Background information on the membership of the two Virginia City lodges must be derived from the 1870 census. By that point they were at about the same distance in time from the first rush as Nevada Lodge had been in 1860, but Nevada City had now matured into a twenty-year-old community. For effective comparison it is therefore necessary to cast the 1870 data for the Virginia City lodges against the 1860 data for Nevada Lodge. This should produce results with an approximate level of acceptability.

The first observation is that all three communities appear still to have been experiencing the same rapid population turnover, with just over a third of the lodge members being untraceable within the state on those census years. Masons continued to have a high velocity of circulation, no doubt facilitated by the Masonic network. Secondly, the lodges were dominated by young men, the great majority being in their thirties. Those in the Virginia City lodges were marginally older, in their late rather than their early thirties, but they probably included many men who had first moved to California in the 1850s and had since progressed on from one district to another (see Figure 7). Thirdly, all three lodges had a roughly equal division of married and single men, with only a slight preponderance of single members. This was at considerable variance from the communities as a whole, where married men made up only a small percentage of the population and suggests that Masonic membership was considered to have particular advantages for migrant families.

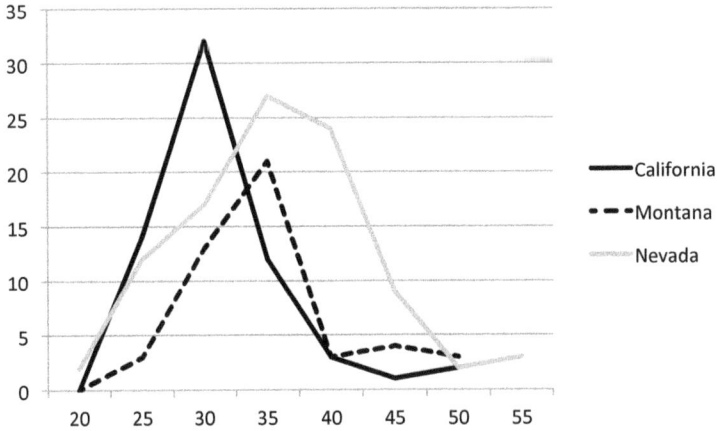

Figure 7　Distribution of Members by Age Group in Three Lodges
Total numbers by age groups 20–24; 25–29; 30–34, etc.

Fourthly, all three lodges were dominated by native-born Americans but between a third and a quarter of the traceable membership was foreign-born. Nevada Lodge had the smallest share of foreign-born members at around 28%, but both Virginia City lodges stood noticeably higher with Virginia City, Nevada, recording 40%. As in Nevada Lodge, California, the great majority of the foreign-born members were from the British Isles and greater Germany, with a smaller number from elsewhere in north-western Europe[60] and Canada (see Figure 8). All of the lodges apparently excluded the large Chinese and South American groups in their host communities as well as Native Americans. Representatives from Southern and Eastern Europe remained a great rarity and the French were not much in evidence.[61] This may have been because of the strong representation of Catholics among those national groups and because established French Freemasons were not acceptable to American Freemasonry.[62] Like Nevada Lodge, the Virginia City lodges drew the great majority of their native-born members from states in the Northeast and northern Midwest, in that order. Neither attracted even the small numbers that Nevada Lodge received from the southern Midwest (see Figure 9). Again this may simply reflect the more populous character of the Northern states, though it is possible that Freemasonry was less well represented in the South, with its lower level of urbanisation.

Fifthly, the occupational structure of the lodges in Montana and Nevada also generally reflected that observed in Nevada City. The dominance of mining-related groups was less pronounced but everywhere they embraced members from all sections of the economic community. The principal non-mining groups

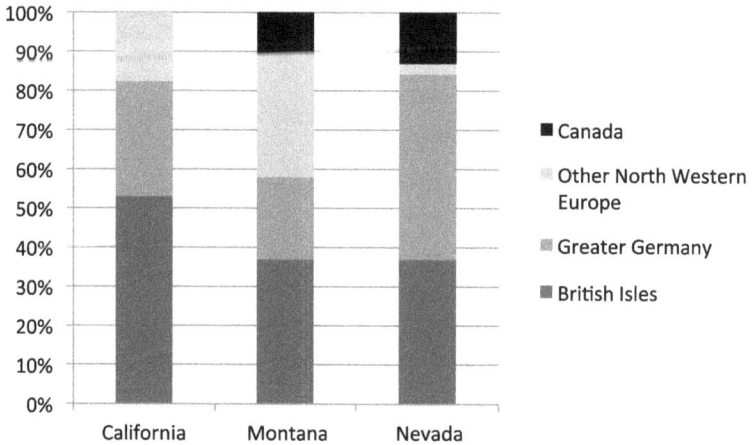

Figure 8　Origins of Foreign-born Lodge Members in Three Lodges (%)

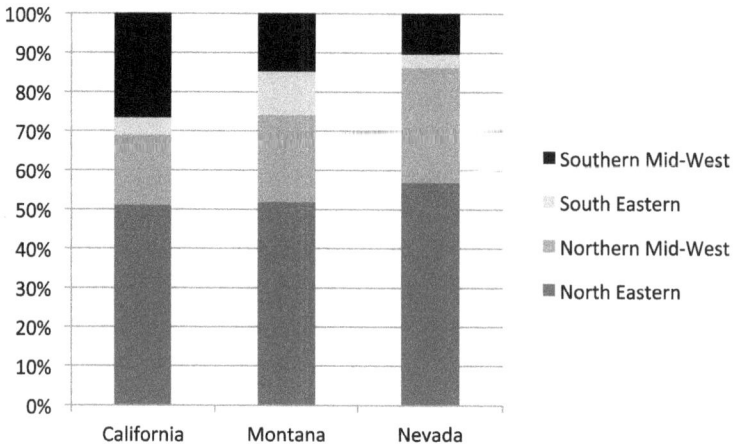

Figure 9　Origins of Domestic-born (%)

were comprised of those engaged in mercantile and retail activity, followed by professionals and finance, and government employees. Hospitality and services generally made up the next largest category, followed by tradesmen and craftsmen. Except in Virginia City, Montana, agriculture and husbandry were virtually invisible, probably reflecting the difficulties of accessing the towns for evening meetings, particularly during the main winter Masonic season (see Figure 10).

Finally, recorded real and private estate valuations underline the elite position of some lodge members but also reflect the wide diversity of wealth and economic

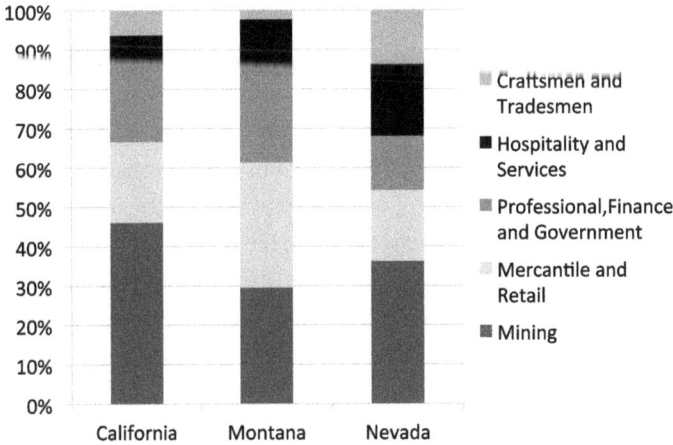

Figure 10 Principal Occupations by Category in Three Lodges (%)

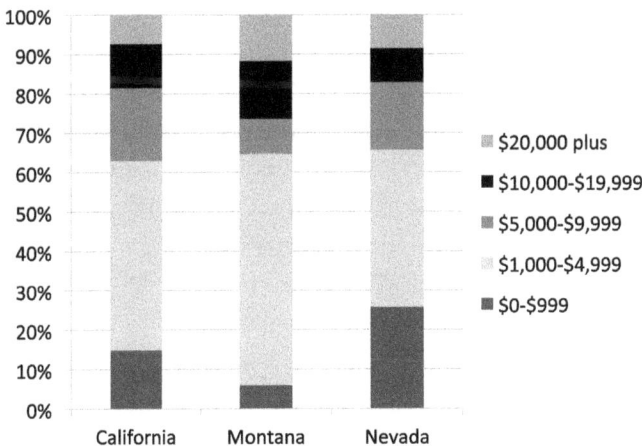

Figure 11 Total Asset Values, by Category in Three Lodges (%)

status of the membership as a whole. Figure 11 shows a remarkable similarity between the lodges in the distribution of the total asset values of declaring members. Personal and estate assets of between one and five thousand dollars appear everywhere to have been the most common, suggesting a membership that was generally quite well off, and economically and socially successful. However, they also welcomed some of very modest means and an equal number of the most successful in the community. They accordingly provided a platform for dialogue across much of the occupational and social spectrum, though one which was largely confined to certain ethnic and religious groups.

Comparison with Towns with Multiple Lodges

Before leaving the issue of the comparative structure of lodge memberships, it is useful also to consider whether towns with multiple lodges may have seen different patterns of membership. Whether multiple lodges (a) gave increased overall opportunities for joining and (b) whether there was a 'divisioning' of members between lodges, reflecting different occupations, social groups, ethnicity, etc. This cannot be done for Nevada City, which had only one lodge, but it is possible for the Virginia City area in Nevada. Here there were three lodges operating in 1870—namely Virginia City and Escurial in the city itself, and Silver Star Lodge in neighbouring Gold Hill. In that year they were all of a very similar size, with between 120 and 140 members each (Nevada Lodge had 125 in that time) and together the three lodges had just over 400 paid-up members. Nearly all of these members were drawn from Storey County[63] and probably accounted for around 6% of its adult male population in that year, again similar to Nevada City.[64] The population of the district was still highly mobile and only around two-thirds of the members can be traced in local census returns—almost identical to the 63% traceable for Nevada Lodge in 1860. Over a third had left and could not be found anywhere else in the state.

Firstly, a look at the structure of membership over the three lodges taken together, compared with Nevada Lodge. How did greater 'availability' affect membership? Like Nevada City, the great majority of members were in their thirties, though there was a far larger cohort in their forties and fifties. As previously noted, this may be because they included many men who had first rushed to California in the 1850s and had since moved on from one district to another. Such an explanation of 'footloose' mature men would also explain why the three lodges had a much lower number of married members (42%) compared with Nevada Lodge (56%). Most members were native-born, again drawn mainly from the Northern and Eastern states, but there was a much bigger group of foreign-born, amounting to over 46% of the total. This approximated to the ethnic distribution in Storey County as a whole, where the population was almost equally divided between native- and foreign-born. As in Nevada Lodge, many of the foreign-born were from Germany and Scandinavia, but here most came from the British Isles, with the English and the Irish being in roughly equal numbers. This, however, may disguise a shifting balance between the two groups during the 1860s.[65] Certainly data for Storey County as a whole shows a marked inflow of British immigrants during that period which reversed an earlier dominance of Germans and Scandinavians. James has estimated, for example, that by 1870 there were 7,817 males in Storey county, of which around

elevation, moral and social support, etc., but did indeed also allay some of the economic risks of migration to self and family, and improve the chances of success at intermediate or final destinations. There is, however, a need to exercise an element of caution in this particular conclusion. Masonic lodges appear to have become relatively elitist establishments in many communities. They did not simply assist members to become successful, but also became an order with which the successful wished to be associated. A straightforward analysis of the wealth of members does not necessarily reflect accurately their long-term economic and social mobility. It has not been possible to exclude the successful late joiners for this analysis but it is clear that even if Masonry did not help 'make' them, they helped to 'make' Masonry. The tendency for the rich and successful to 'ball together' within an organisation that stressed the value of work, education, honesty, diligence, reliability and mutual support was likely greatly to improve the life chances of all of those involved. This was true in the settled and civilised urban communities of the East and Europe—it was doubly true in the anarchic, unregulated mining towns of the Western American urban frontier.

One of the most useful aspects of comparative analysis is that it enables indicative evidence to be gathered to fill in some of the gaps in the story of Nevada Lodge. No information has been found, for example, on the turnover of lodge membership there or the proportion of members that travelled as existing Masons compared to those that simply joined the Order after arrival. Similarly, what were the economics of lodge membership: how much did membership cost, where did the lodges get their money from, how did they spend it? The better-documented experience of Escurial Lodge, operating alongside Virginia Lodge in Virginia City, Nevada, provides some suggestions. A history of the early years of that Lodge[68] shows that by the end of 1867, more than three-quarters of those that had joined the Lodge during the its first three years of operation were still paid-up members and the great majority continued to reside in the vicinity of Virginia City. Of those members in good stead who had already moved on, two were in California, one in South America and two back in Wales. Similarly, more than 90% of the joining members between 1864 and 1867 migrated as fully or partially initiated Masons, many completing their initiation by taking the third degree within the Lodge.[69] In its first two years of working, the Lodge charged an affiliation fee to joining members of $3 but this was soon abandoned in the interests of recruiting as many locally resident Masons as possible.[70] Thereafter, all of its income was derived from a charge for every degree given to advancing initiates. Over the four years the Lodge received $6,825 from bestowing degrees, compared with just $326 from the early affiliation charges and $3,333 from annual dues. The Lodge was thus making more money from admitting and advancing new Masons than it was receiving from current members—an indication of the popularity of the Order and the demand for membership. Some indication of the reasons for that popularity is found in the Lodge's expenditures. From a total income of $11,170 over the four years it spent $9,835. A substantial but undisclosed amount went on the purchase of land on the edge of town for a Masonic cemetery and the rest mainly on benevolence to its own and passing Masons. A proper burial and provision for those left behind was clearly a top priority for most members.

Comparison with the Independent Order of Odd Fellows

As has been seen, Freemasonry was not the only nor the largest fraternity to take root in the early western mining communities. The Independent Order of Odd Fellows, first introduced into Northeastern states from Britain in the early part of the century, became a major expansionary force after breaking with its Manchester-based parent in 1842. At least one contemporary observer saw a close symbiotic relationship between the two orders stretching back into the 1820s. Jacob Norton, writing about anti-Masonry in America, argued that Masonic unpopularity (following the Morgan affair)[71] was one of the primary causes of the success of the import of Oddfellowry from England. He declared:

> Oddfellowship aided Masonry in recovering its popularity. Oddfellows made no especial religious display in their public processions, hence they excited less prejudice among the pious and impious, and hence those that were biased against Masonry did not scruple to join the Oddfellows.

Having embraced Oddfellowship, erstwhile Masons then began to change it from the inside, introducing additional degrees and 'mysteries' on the Masonic model. Norton continues: 'when once Oddfellows acquired a taste for mysteries, they were then tempted to pry also into Masonic mysteries. Thus as anti-Masonic prejudices began to decline, Masonic popularity was finally revived.'[72] In California, small numbers of Odd Fellows began to operate informally, even before independence, and the first Charter to establish a lodge in the territory, issued in Philadelphia, was brought to San Francisco in 1849. Activity expanded rapidly and by 1853 there was a sufficient presence to institute the State's own Grand Lodge. In Nevada and Montana the development of Odd Fellowship also paralleled Masonry, with early lodges working under charters mainly from California. Wildey Lodge No. 1 was instituted at Gold Hill, Nevada in April 1862

Table 13   Membership of the Independent Order of Odd Fellows Compared
with the Number of Freemasons: California, Nevada and Montana, 1874

State	I.O.O.F. Lodges	I.O.O.F. Members	Masons Members
California	217	18,007	10,965
Nevada	25	1,943	1,373
Montana	5	171	550

and the State organised its own Grand Lodge in Virginia City in January 1867. Just a few months later, Montana Lodge No. 1 was instituted in Helena and the Grand Lodge of Montana was established in July 1874.[73] Table 13 shows the position of membership in the three states in 1874 compared with the number of Freemasons. All three of the case study cities just considered saw the foundation of Odd Fellows lodges, but that in Virginia City, Montana was considerably later in the profile of the community's development. It was also much less durable, not being instituted until 1875 and closed in October 1882. Indeed, Odd Fellowship in Montana as a whole never seems to have taken a strong hold, with only just over six hundred initiations into the Order across the whole state during its first ten years,[74] and total numbers counting little more than a third of those in Nevada in the mid-1880s.

A lack of surviving records has made it impossible to trace the membership of all of the Odd Fellows' lodges in, or near to, the three study communities, so it is unclear how their socio-economic structure compared with the local Masons. However, partial evidence has been found for Oustomah Lodge No. 16, founded in the vicinity of Nevada City in 1853. It provides general indicative evidence of the differences from, and similarities to, the local Masons, and the levels of interaction between them. Membership data is much less detailed and complete than that for Nevada Masonic Lodge but some manuscript records can be found for the years after 1858. Their most interesting feature is the high level of joint membership that is indicated for the two lodges. Over a number of years, fifty-seven members of Nevada Masonic Lodge also became members of the I.O.O.F. This reflects the same experience found by Klages in his study of fraternity in Harriston, Ontario[75] as well as in many British towns. It probably resulted from similar causes, such as a liking for ritual, a desire for wider fellowship and access to different networking opportunities. However, a common explanation could also probably be found in the comparative economic benefits put forward by different fraternities. As previously noted, the Masons offered the opportunity to seek charity from the lodge in times of personal or family economic adversity, while the Odd Fellows offered sickness, unemployment and death insurance as of right. Put the other way around, the Odd Fellows and many other fraternal groups offered the opportunity to ensure against the present dangers and pitfalls of life, while Masonry offered improved networking and the chance to advance economic and social prospects. The evidence for such conclusions is provided by the background of the joint members. Many appear to have become Odd Fellows first and to have joined Masonry later, presumably when their economic circumstances improved. A similar pattern was noticed for Masonic and Foresters lodges in Cornwall.[76] With the minimum cost of initiation in the constituent Masonic lodges of the Grand Lodge of California set at $75, this was no small hurdle.[77] Overall, the average socio-economic status of dual members appears to have been lower than the average for Nevada Lodge alone, being dominated by less well-off miners and millmen (see Table 14).[78]

It is important, however, not to see a simple social/economic distinction between the Masons and the Odd Fellows. As has been seen, there were many economically disadvantaged Masons and there were equally many very well-off and powerfully connected Odd Fellows. Large numbers of white-collar workers also became Odd Fellows without seeking Masonic membership, including

Table 14   Occupations of Nevada Lodge Members Joining the Independent Order of Odd Fellows, Oustomah Lodge No. 16, 1858–1880

Occupation	Percentage
Blue Collar (Total of 51)	
Miner/Millman	22
Craftsmen	5
Transport	0
Agriculture	2
White Collar (Total of 30)	
Mine Manager/Engineer	0
Hotel/Saloon Keeper	1
Clerks	1
Post/Sheriff/Telegrapher	0
Shopkeepers/Dealers	1
Health Related	4
Attorney/Judge/Banker	5
Agents/Merchants/Manufacturer	5
Others (Total of 19)	11

attorneys, bankers, merchants, and legal and medical professionals. Aaron Sargent, for example, one of the founders of Oustomah Lodge, was a newspaper publisher who became a district attorney, state congressman and US senator but remained a major figure in Odd Fellows' affairs.[79] Like Masonry, this, and probably many other fraternal groups, acted as a major networking hub on its own account, attracting many leading community figures and contributing importantly to the construction of civil society throughout the district. However, it is best to see the various fraternal groups as having widely overlapping membership structures, creating highly complex, interwoven networking systems, as those with the resources joined several different fraternities and other organisations to consolidate their position within the local, state and nationwide elites. For example, Henry Clay Frick, a partner of Andrew Carnegie and Chairman of United States Steel Company in the late nineteenth century, had become a Mason in 1872 at the age of twenty-three but steadily increased his other affiliations as his business success increased. When he died in 1919 he held life membership in sixty-seven clubs and associations, with those including 'National' or 'American' in the title predominating.[80]

From the evidence presented here it is clear that fraternities, in their many different forms, had the potential to play a significant role in facilitating the movement of migrants within and between continents, and in helping them to settle and integrate on arrival. Such societies and orders would have appeared particularly attractive to those whose quest was unusually hazardous and uncertain, such as the Argonauts and other gold seekers of the second half of the nineteenth century. Taking the specific example of Freemasonry, which had a particularly extended national and international network of lodges, all with clear obligations to assist travelling brethren, it can be shown that: (a) lodges were established in new urban mining communities within months of the earliest arrivals; (b) they were established by existing members who had probably availed themselves of the network as they had travelled to the gold fields; (c) the turnover of their membership was high, suggesting onward movement of members to new mining districts and other lodges; (d) they rapidly expanded their membership with new arrivals and especially new initiates who wished to take advantage of the various benefits offered; (e) most memberships were young men, in their twenties and early thirties, and a large cohort were unmarried; (f) most were nationals of the country but also included large numbers of first-generation immigrants from Great Britain, Germany, Scandinavia and other parts of Protestant north-western Europe; (g) by occupation they were mainly miners and those connected with the mining industry, though they reflected the entire business spectrum of the communities they served; (h) they were of widely varied economic status and wealth, though a tendency of the wealthy to seek membership to promote economic success meant that the lodges came to be generally representative of the economic elite of their host community; (i) many members, particularly the less well off, also became members of other fraternal organisations, especially those that offered insurance against accidents, illness and death; (j) the lodges offered advantages not just to their membership but to the wider construction of social capital in the community—or, as Robert Putnam has put it, they offered both a 'private good' to their members and a 'public good' to society at large through the promotion of civic virtue.[81]

CHAPTER 7

OTHER INTERNATIONAL COMPARISONS: VICTORIA, AUSTRALIA AND SOUTHERN AFRICA

So far attention has been focused on the membership structure of lodges in the western United States. There clearly remains a question about how far these fraternal experiences were duplicated in the numerous other 'rushes' that affected districts scattered across several continents during the frenetic second half of the nineteenth century.[1] There are two main ways to make such comparisons. Firstly by direct comparisons with the formation and membership structure of other lodges and, secondly, by looking at the nature of their impact on local host communities—to what extent did they have similar effects? The direct comparisons with other 'rush' experiences will be focused on the gold mining districts of Victoria, Australia, centred on the towns of Ballarat, Castlemaine and Bendigo,[2] and the booming diamond and gold districts of South Africa, located near to Kimberley and Johannesburg. In both the Australian and South African mining districts new arrivals found difficult environmental conditions similar to those encountered in the western United States and generally comparable problems in community formation. These districts also provide examples from one of the earliest and also one of the last of the great mass mining migrations. Comparison of the activities and influences of lodges and Masons on host communities will include (a) the influence on social cohesions, (b) major acts of charity, and (c) involvement in political activity and the creation of social capital.

Comparisons of the Development and Membership of Lodges in Mining Districts of Australia and South Africa

Australia

Ballarat, Castlemaine and Bendigo were comparable in size and development to both Nevada City and Virginia City. The world began to rush in here from late 1850, partly prompted by the hope of repeating the California gold strikes of a year or so earlier. Rapid immigration continued, in a series of pulses, for the next nine years, creating 'up country urbanisation'.[3] In many respects these districts had a similar experience to that in California, with a first stage of simple, small-scale partnership workings, followed by deeper, larger, capitalist enterprises. They saw a massive growth in the population of the mining districts from just a few hundred at the beginning of the decade to 30,000 adult males in 1852 and around 140,000 at its peak in 1858.[4] New urban communities sprang up and there was a scramble to create order and regulation.

There were, however, also some very important differences between the American and Australian experience. Whereas the development of the American districts largely took place without effective control by the Federal government which owned the land and its resources, the Australian districts emerged within the context of a colonial administration which claimed rights to the minerals on behalf of the Crown and invested a great deal of energy in trying to ensure their proper and controlled development. Similarly, whereas the 'world' rushed into California, in Victoria it was initially largely an 'inter-colonial rush' that populated the towns during the critical first two years of activity. Men—miners and others—came from New South Wales, New Zealand and Western Australia, and particularly South Australia and Van Diemen's Land. From the end of 1852 they were then joined by a great surge of immigrant 'cousins' from the industrial towns of Britain and north-western Europe. It was not until 1854, by which time many of the new communities had been firmly established, that other ethnic groups, such as the Chinese, began to arrive in large numbers. With a more regulated environment and a relatively 'high-quality', disciplined and homogeneous population,[5] it is not surprising that historians have seen Victoria's early development as 'more orderly than California'.[6] In this context, the development of fraternity here was less urgent than where it was needed as a bastion against anarchy and chaos, but it was more familiar and easily introduced. Freemasonry had become an organic part of Britain's empire and it flowed easily along the conduits of colonial control, carried by the army, the navy and a host of administrators.[7]

A basic network of Masonic lodges had been well established in Australia before the first gold discoveries and the Grand Lodges of England, Scotland and Ireland were happy, indeed competitive, to issue new warrants on demand. Their numbers and distribution varied widely. The UGLE warranted lodges in over a hundred towns across Victoria from the mid-nineteenth century, while the Irish established themselves in eighteen, mainly in and around Ballarat. The Grand Lodge of Scotland warranted seven, mainly in Melbourne[8] while the Bendigo area saw only English lodges. Unlike the United States, where the earliest lodges were warranted from neighbouring constitutions but soon broke away to establish their own State Grand Lodges, it was not until the 1880s that the various Australian provinces began to set up Grand Lodges themselves. The extensive presence of Freemasonry was very good for welcoming incomers, introducing new men into the Order, and generally maximising the influence of Masonry in the new emergent communities. Certainly Freemasonry became a major influence on the development of local government, not only in the new gold-mining towns, but also in major centres such as Melbourne. Most senior officials were members of the Order: most major civic occasions (such as foundation stone laying for courthouses, bridges, hospitals, etc.) were accompanied by large public Masonic processions and orations, and Masonic interest frequently spilled over into civic affairs. At one level the pre-existing Masonic structures greatly assisted the formulation of the new government agencies and perhaps introduced a strong element of moral rectitude into their affairs, but the symbiotic relationship also had potential downsides. As Barrett has concluded, 'Like lodges, municipal institutions were to provide opportunities for gaining influence, obtaining inside information and exchanging favours.'[9] Other fraternities, such as the Oddfellows, Foresters, and the Orange Order, also played a supportive role in civic affairs—and many men owed allegiances to more than the Masons alone—but the only real challenge to the Masons' dominance came from their own internal divisions. In the early years, the different nationalities tended to stick with their own lodges—English, Scottish and Irish—and imported and played out the same competitiveness as at home. These might also represent economic and class divisions—with the Scottish and Irish lodges probably being more 'blue-collar' than the English—and those rivalries often surfaced in civic affairs. Over time, however, the lodges became more mixed. By the great inrush of the early 1850s,[10] a much higher level of cohesion had emerged, although, as will be seen, marginal economic/class divisions on the pattern of the Virginia City, Nevada lodges, appears to have continued.[11]

The division of lodges by national administrative authority—English, Scottish and Irish—also creates problems for the historian. This research has been based only on the well-organised central archives of the UGLE and has focused on six of their lodges operating in the Ballarat and Bendigo gold districts during the 1850s—viz. in the Ballarat area: Lodge of Victoria No. 658; Yarrowee Lodge No. 713; Ballarat Lodge No. 717; and United Tradesmen's Lodge of Ballarat East No. 744. In the Bendigo area: Golden Lodge of Bendigo No. 641; and Corinthian Lodge No. 770 (see Appendix 20). Unfortunately, the membership returns that were sent back to UGLE were not entirely complete for these remote mining districts during the early stages of their development. They were often patchy, failed to be received or have been lost, and those for Yarrowee Lodge during the 1850s have completely disappeared. While this provides a problem for the historian, it caused consternation to the clerks of the UGLE in London, who saw their complex administrative arrangements, designed mainly for domestic use, breaking down for remote lodges on the other side of the world. Their complaints produced an informative response from the Secretary of Golden Lodge on 22 April 1857:

> From the peculiar circumstances of the population of the gold fields of Australia generally being of such a nomadic character, it has been hitherto extremely difficult to make complete returns. Within the last 15 months the community having assumed a more permanent character, since the formation of the townships—we are at length in consequence enabled to comply with the requirements of the Grand Lodge ... It is utterly impossible for ... a letter adequately to describe the many great difficulties that we, as the first Gold Fields Lodge, had to contend with in establishing this most flourishing branch of the Order ... a glance at the returns, more especially that of Brethren for whom the lodge do not require certificates in consequence of removal to other parts, will be sufficient proof of the continual changes taking place among us[12] (see Illustration 11).

Notwithstanding the difficulties, it has been possible to piece together the returns for around 440 men that joined five of the lodges (Yarrowee excluded) during the period to the end of 1859. Like the returns for domestic lodges, such as those in Cornwall, the data includes names, age at becoming a member, occupation and current residence. Unfortunately, the full range of this data is not available for all of the listed members. Unlike the data for the American districts, it does not include information on asset value or place of birth, but occasional comments on the recent origins of joining members gives a broad impression of the general direction of movement. It also provides a longitudinal view over the decade rather than a snapshot of membership in any one year, and thus perhaps gives a better view of the dynamics of lodge membership.

What does the data show? Firstly, as already noted, there was a fevered level of recruitment and turnover of members. In Corinthian Lodge No. 1072, for example, thirty-one men were initiated during the first five months of its existence but only around a quarter stayed long enough to take their Second degree. Similarly of the seventy-one initiates and joining members of Golden Lodge No. 924 during 1854 and 1855, nearly half had left by April 1857.

Illustration 11   Masonic Hall, Bendigo, Victoria, Australia

Bendigo experienced a major gold rush in the early 1850s and many Freemasons arrived along with the early pioneers. Golden Lodge was the first to receive its own warrant in October 1854. Amalgamating with Corinthian Lodge in 1872, it had an exceptionally large and wealthy membership. This opulent building was designed and built by William Vahland, a past Master of Golden Lodge, and his partner Robert Getzschmann, between 1873 and 1874, and provided public facilities in the form of a tavern, concert hall and large meeting room as well as a Lodge room, library, etc. When it opened it was one of the very largest buildings in the State of Victoria and demonstrated the power and influence of the Masons in the mines and local community.

Secondly, as in Nevada Lodge during its early years of development, the great majority of members were young, 70% being between the age of twenty-five and thirty-five. Very few were over forty and only one was over fifty. Name evidence suggests that, as in the Virginia City lodges, many were originally from Western Europe, particularly greater Germany, but included a few French, Dutch and other nationalities as well. A quantity of Scots and Irish also unexpectedly appear in the membership of these English lodges and there was a significant number of Jews in some lodges, many of them probably of central European origin.[13] Perhaps fifty or more of the members were not British or Australian born, suggesting a level of national mixing similar to that in the American lodges. Occasional notes appended to the returns of those existing Masons who were joining the lodge indicate their most recent residence. Thus there are numerous 'local' men coming in from lodges in Melbourne, Geelong and other surrounding areas in Victoria as well as neighbouring states, such as South Australia and New South Wales. Long-distance migrants were drawn from Lancashire, London, Bristol and Birmingham in England, and several came from lodges in Scotland and Ireland. At least three came direct from Canada (New Brunswick, Halifax and Ottawa) and seven declared their origins in the US including two miners, a carpenter, a hairdresser and a 'publican' (bar owner). They were, in every respect, a very disparate crowd, representative of the new mining communities but sharing little in common other than their Masonic identity.

The occupational structure of the five lodges over the decade also shows some general similarities with the American lodges but also some major differences. At the general level, the membership includes representatives from the broad range of the local economy, while at a more detailed level there are marked dissimilarities in the relative balance of the various groups. Thus, as in the American mining communities, the lodges included large numbers of miners and mine managers, but here they were not the dominant group, being outnumbered by publicans/ innkeepers, who rarely figured prominently in America. There were, of course, many from the mining-related professions and trades, such as speculators, share brokers, contractors, carpenters, smiths, merchants and clerks, as in Virginia City. However, the Ballarat and Bendigo lodges had a far stronger representation of storekeepers, retail trades (from butchers and bakers to bootmakers and tailors), professionals (from finance, law and medicine), government employees, and 'entertainment services' such as artists and musicians (see Table 15). The latter group would have found the networking opportunities offered by the lodges particularly useful in finding 'customers' for their services, as would the numerous auctioneers. Similarly, the lodges, as 'information exchanges', would have been highly beneficial for the journalists and perhaps those engaged in government service. Most surprisingly, there appears to have been very few mining managers and engineers, though the predominantly small scale of mining during this period may have kept their overall numbers down. As was common everywhere, there were very few farmers, though Corinthian No. 1072 and Golden No. 924 did list six 'vigneron', probably from Germany, who complemented the wine merchants in the lodge.

There are no obvious explanations for these divergences from the American experience but various options present themselves. Firstly, it is possible that the places and environments from which they were drawn did not have the same Masonic traditions among the working class as in America. Perhaps also the gold seekers in Victoria did not feel so exposed, so remote and isolated from friends and family, and so in need of support and sustenance. Secondly, it

Table 15   Principal Occupations of Members of
Five Lodges in Ballarat and Bendigo to 1859

Occupation	Number
Hospitality	52
Retail	42
Miners	40
Merchants	27
Professional/Management	27
Medical	22
Tradesmen	19
Government	17
Artists and Musicians	16
Clerks	15
Publishing	13
Food Preparation	11
Craftsmen	11
Auctioneers	9

may be that those who did look for 'insurance' found more positive guarantees in other fraternal or benevolent societies. For example, the Manchester Unity Independent Order of Oddfellows had established four lodges in the Ballarat district and six in and around Bendigo by 1860, and their membership increased rapidly.[14] Cusack has identified around forty fraternal and benefit societies operating in the Bendigo area during the second half of the century, concluding that the most affluent and influential were the Rechabites.[15] Founded in Salford, England in 1835, they had opened their first 'Tent' in Sydney, Australia, just seven years later. By the mid-1880s they counted 314 different 'Tents' in the Victoria district as a whole and had far more members than there were Masons.[16]

Thirdly, there may have been specialisation of trades and occupations between lodges of different constitutions. As already mentioned, there were non-English constitution Masonic lodges operating in this district that may have provided a home for a greater percentage of self-employed miners and other manual trades. For example, the Grand Lodge of Scotland established a lodge in Melbourne as early as 1843 and it had another working in nearby Geelong by 1853.[17] The Grand Lodge of Ireland was particularly active, warranting two lodges in Ballarat in the early 1860s and later establishing them all around the area—in Buninyong, Clunes, Linton, Sebastopol, Smythsdale, Talbot and Taradale.[18] The 'English' Masons may possibly have evolved into a white-collar 'middle-class' minority, specializing in town activities, with blue-collar industrial workers congregating in the Irish constitution lodges. By the 1880s, however, the significance of origins was diminishing as the Masons of Victoria as a whole took control of their affairs under a newly formed and integrated Grand Lodge of their own. Fourthly, it is possible that the economic structure of the towns was very different—the Australian towns being larger, more diversified, more advanced and perhaps more 'rounded' in their development than Nevada City and the Virginia Cities of Nevada and Montana during their early stages of growth. The simplest explanation, however, may be that the data used here is skewed by the absence of membership returns for Yarrowee Lodge during these years, though later evidence suggests that it never had very many miners.

What is particularly odd, however, is that the picture changes dramatically, and looks far more like that of California and Nevada, if the period of analysis is extended from 1850s through to the mid-1880s and all of the new English constitution lodges in Ballarat and Bendigo are included.[19] During these years, miners, mining and mining-related activities emerge as the dominant group, with urban occupations such as the professions, retail and hospitality pushed into second and third place[20] (see Table 16). This is notwithstanding the growth in the size and prosperity of the towns, improved transportation and the introduction of a wider range of occupations.[21] The relatively small number of English-constitution Masons in Ballarat compared with Bendigo suggests that some at least may have joined Scottish and Irish lodges in the former town. Irish lodges, for example, had been established in Ballarat in 1862 and 1863, and though not particularly successful, saw some two-way movement with English lodges.[22]

Table 16   Occupations of Members in Ballarat and Bendigo Lodges, 1854–1889

Occupation	Ballarat	Bendigo	Total
Miner	26	187	213
Mine Agent, Manager, Engineer	28	109	137
Hotel/Innkeepers and Publicans	50	94	144
Draper, Storekeeper	39	102	141
Merchant	35	62	97
Accountant, Banker	29	63	92
Baker, Blacksmith, Butcher, Carpenter	18	72	90
Legal, Medical	39	46	85
Clerks and Government	24	74	98
Police, Teachers	14	56	70

Precisely who the 'miners' were—working men or rich owners/investors—is again not clear, but Blainey's conclusions echo those for California and Nevada: 'Bendigo was a dusty democracy in which the wealthy capitalists sometimes worked underground and humble miners sometimes owned mining shares.'[23]

The experience of the gold districts of Victoria was repeated in other Australian mining communities, including the coal towns of New South Wales. McEwan has shown that Newcastle, for example, was highly 'fraternal', with at least forty different 'lodges' of one description or another being established during the second half of the nineteenth century. As well as the Masons, they included four different orders of Oddfellows as well as Druids, Rechabites, Sons of Temperance, Free Gardeners, Foresters, Buffaloes, Ancient Britons and the Protestant Alliance Friendly Society.[24] Similarly, Lay noticed that in the Bathurst district many Cornishmen were members of the Masons as well as several other fraternities, including Orangemen.[25]

Southern Africa

Events in the South African colonies followed a generally similar pattern, though with important local variations. Masonry had been established in the colony well before the mining booms and was already extending itself outwards from Cape Town by the mid-century. The expansion speeded up rapidly with the first major influx of miners between 1869 and 1871, not as a result of a quest for gold, but for diamonds. By 1875 there were twenty-two English constitution lodges and twenty-one Netherlandic lodges, with a total membership of 2,281 members.[26] Shallow-surface diamond mining employed much the same primitive hand techniques as those used for gold in the US and Australia, and attracted much the same kinds of 'boomers'. The distribution of the diamonds, however, was far more concentrated than those gold deposits, and working was focused in and around what became four large holes—New Rush, Dutoitspan, Bultfontein and Old De Beers—located near what are now the cities of Kimberley and Beaconsfield. The numbers of miners that could be accommodated was large but much less than that seen in many of the previous gold rushes, being counted in a few thousands rather than tens of thousands. Nevertheless, the rough and temporary camps that rapidly sprang up followed a pattern similar to mining frontier towns everywhere[27] and they very quickly spawned their own Masonic lodges. These lodges reflected the national origins of the earliest arrivals, being not just British—English, Scottish and Irish—but also Dutch. However, their membership soon became multinational and there was much crossover between them. Arthur Hodge, mentioned above in the context of Cornish Lodge, provides a good example. When he moved between Kimberley, Jagersfontein, Cape Town and various other places, he also moved seamlessly between English and Scottish constitution lodges. When he joined Pilgrims Lodge No. 738 (Scottish Constitution) in Lydenburg in 1894, he reported that its membership was mainly Dutch and that it worked either in English or Dutch, depending on the choice of the Master of the Lodge.[28]

One of the earliest of the diamond district lodges was Cosmopolitan Lodge No. 1409, warranted by the UGLE in Voormtzigt, near Kimberley, and consecrated in August 1872. The Lodge's early returns were not well kept but, as expected, the great majority of its large membership were given as 'digger', interspersed with periodic 'diamond buyers' and those that serviced the town. As mining and the urban community developed during the later 1870s and 1880s, however, the number of 'diggers' gradually declined and gave way to more professionals and tradesmen. Overall the membership was mainly English, but it also included men such as Denis Doyle, a founder member and probably Irish, as well as Berhardt Weinand—both given as 'digger'. Surprisingly there were few, if any, Cornishmen during the early years, perhaps because they preferred the immediate and ready money of gold mining rather than the need to sell diamonds of variable quality. The first Cornish miner to join the Lodge was William Spargo, in 1883. Two other Masonic lodges also operated in Kimberley from an early date—the Richard Giddy Lodge No. 1574, warranted in 1875 and Charles Warren Lodge No. 1832, warranted in 1879. They also included numerous mining men, not the least of whom was Charles Algernon Moreing, who added Richard Giddy Lodge to his list of London lodges in 1882.[29]

This situation remained somewhat similar when South Africa progressed to gold mining from the late 1880s. Gold had been mined in several districts from the 1870s but the big breakthrough came following intensive prospecting of the Langlaagt farm area, just west of modern Johannesburg, in 1886.[30] Yet again, an 'urban frontier' was created in a remote, sparsely populated area and, as with the discovery of diamonds fifteen years earlier, the finds produced a fevered interest. However, there was no immediate massive influx of independent miners: the new deposits outcropped over only a relatively small area; they were of a low grade; and the district had severely limited water supplies that frustrated simple washing operations. The Main Reef needed to be developed at depth and the required heavy investment was beyond the capacity of individuals and small partnerships. When large underground mines were finally constructed, the bulk of the workforce was made up of immigrant black labour from surrounding areas of Southern Africa, together with imported Chinese workers.[31] European, American and Australian miners were recruited principally to provide underground supervision and general management. Of these latter groups, around half were Cornish, attracted either directly or indirectly from other overseas mining districts.[32] Development of the industry proceeded rapidly and in the ten years after 1888 the total value of the gold produced increased from less than £1 million to over £15 million a year.[33]

The size and diversity of the city of Johannesburg increased along with this expansion and most of the people shaping that growth had long experience of booming mining towns elsewhere. Kennedy has shown, for example, how miners from Ballarat and Bendigo, as well as the other Australian mining districts of Mt Lyell, Mt Morgan and Broken Hill, flocked to the Rand and soon outnumbered local Dutch-born 'Hollanders' living in Johannesburg.[34] By the end of the 1880s the population of that city was already in excess of 20,000 and the first English constitution Masonic lodge—Johannesburg Lodge No. 2313—was warranted in May 1889. With a demand for membership that it simply could not accommodate, leading members of that Lodge, supported by members of Cosmopolitan Lodge now living in Johannesburg, petitioned for a charter of a second lodge, which became Gold Fields Lodge No. 2478, warranted in May 1893. When Gold Fields was consecrated in October 1893, the ceremony took place in the presence of 350 Masons, including forty-nine Past Masters of other lodges, and was 'generally acknowledged to have been the most successful Masonic function that has ever been held in South Africa'.[35] Both lodges initially met in the Johannesburg Stock Exchange Hall while their own Temple was being built.

Johannesburg Lodge was comprised mainly of middle-class professionals, merchants, speculators and tradesmen drawn from the burgeoning town economy. It also recruited a number of mine managers, engineers, contractors, metallurgists, assayers and other mining professionals—but not miners and skilled craftsmen. It is difficult to be sure of the origins of initiates but most appear to have been British, with some Australians and Americans. Early joining members included two musicians (Harold Stidolph, from the Lodge of Good Fellowship No. 276 in Chelmsford, Essex and Robert Heath, from Druids No. 589 in Cornwall) and two assayers (Robert Hall, from Mount Edgcumbe No. 1544 in Cornwall and John Williams, from Caradoc No. 1573, in Swansea, South Wales). These were a rarity, however, with most joining members coming from other lodges in Southern Africa.

Gold Fields Lodge appears to have been formed to provide a venue that was more ethnically and socially diverse. It still had a preponderance of members with British origins but more Dutch, German and, in particular, Jewish members. Many, perhaps most, of its members had a professional/managerial/

middle-class background, but it now also included 'blue-collar' workers such as miners, stonemasons, plumbers, carpenters, blacksmiths, builders and store keepers. Above all, it appears to have placed a much greater focus on the mining industry. In its first eight years of activity, over fifty mine managers, engineers and miners either joined or were initiated, together with an almost equal number of speculators, prospectors and government mining officials. Many were joining members from English domestic lodges but many others came from Scottish, Irish and Dutch constitution lodges, as well as English constitution lodges in Australasia and Southern Africa. By the late 1890s there were thirty-seven Scottish lodges, forty-four Irish and more than twenty Dutch lodges operating in South Africa. They were not nationally exclusive and often operated as an entry point to Freemasonry for working men who found the English constitution less welcoming.[36] As was commented in *The Freemason*, the English lodges were the most numerous, but 'the Scotch the most lenient as to the qualification of the candidates'[37] (see Appendix 21).

It has not been possible to investigate the full networking potential of Johannesburg and Gold Fields lodges but it was clearly very considerable given the presence of such powerfully connected members as George Richards, the Managing Director of Consolidated Gold Fields (Johannesburg), John Hays Hammond, the eminent American mining speculator (Gold Fields and Columbia, Johannesburg) and no less a celebrity than Cecil Rhodes.[38] Certainly, so great were the attractions that the numbers seeking initiation often could not be accommodated by the normal working of the lodges. Thus shortly after its foundation, Edward Letchworth, the Master of Gold Fields, wrote to London asking leave to 'ease' its working. As he explained:

> In a floating population like this, circumstances are continually arising which would cause me as Master of the Lodge to be beset with demands for degrees to be given within the prohibited dates, and unless I have dispensation from the Worshipful Grand Master, I should be unable to comply with the most urgent demands.[39]

While these two large lodges, often with more than two hundred paid-up members, offered excellent 'bridging' opportunities into every part of the local community and economy, many migrants probably found them intimidating, expensive and challenging. For a more relaxed environment they might well prefer, or also enjoy, the smaller and more intimate environment of men of similar occupations, origins and financial means. In many new mining districts these fraternities were organised outside of the confines of Masonry, but in

Johannesburg they found expression for the Cornish in Lodge of Cornwall No. 3490. Formed in 1910, possibly also as a response to the difficulties caused by the multinational membership of the larger lodges during the Boer Wars, this was comprised almost entirely of ordinary working men—miners, craftsmen, foremen—and a very few mine managers. In the early years, they were nearly all joining members from Cornish lodges, but as time went on they began to initiate new Cornish non-Masons as well as some from other parts of Britain. As part of its remit to provide a welcome for new arrivals, the Lodge worked closely with the South African Cornish Association. They were particularly active in putting on social events, such as banquets and concerts, and also organised temporary accommodation and employment advice. The leadership of Lodge and Association were often synonymous. Henry Young, originally from St Ives, was the first Master of the Lodge as well as President of the Association; G.L. Vincent, one of the founders of the Lodge, became the Association's Treasurer; S.U. Pearce and M.A. Rodda, both Lodge members, became Branch Chairmen of the Association.[40]

CHAPTER 8

THE INFLUENCE OF FREEMASONRY: MEMBERS AND THEIR COMMUNITIES

So far discussion has focused on the first two of the four research questions set out at the beginning of this volume—namely, who were the men that became Freemasons and what were their motivations in seeking membership? A series of answers have been suggested for the 'who' part of those questions, in terms of occupational and social class, nationality and ethnicity, etc. Similarly, a wide range of motivations for joining have been suggested, with a particular emphasis on the opportunities for economic and social networking as well as 'assurance' in times of adversity. This section will move on to consider the second set of questions, namely what did Freemasonry do for its members, both functionally and morally and, more broadly, what did it do for the communities in which it operated?

General Acts of Charity

As well as the individual acts of charity and support for their members that already have been discussed above, Masons also frequently subscribed large sums in wider acts of charity which relieved some that were not their own members and/or benefited the wider community by significantly reducing burdens that would otherwise have fallen upon it. A circular from a group of recently established California lodges in the early 1850s clearly illustrates the latter kind of event.[1] It observed that when the Argonauts rushed into California in the spring and summer of 1849, most men came 'lamentably unsupplied with any other means of providing for their necessities other than their capacity for labor'. In the Fall of that and the subsequent year, large numbers were compelled to leave the remote Sierra mining districts and retreat to Sacramento for medical advice and attendance in sickness. Many of the sick and destitute were Masons and 'they naturally and of right made their condition known to the Brethren, then established in that place'. With no municipal government then in place, the local lodges set up their own hospital. Aggravated by the cholera epidemic that swept over the city in 1850,[2] demand for its services grew rapidly and by the end of 1851 the local lodges estimated that they had paid out over £32,000 in relief to brethren 'coming in upon them from all parts of the civilized world'. This had created severe financial difficulties for some of the brethren, but 'no sick destitute and suffering brother had been permitted to suffer or die in their midst, uncared for'. Even allowing for hyperbole, it is clear that the local Masons had not only honoured their commitment to other brethren but had shouldered a large part of a burden that would otherwise have fallen directly on the rest of the community. By now appealing to other lodges outside of California for assistance in compensating that burden, they also acted as a conduit for importing welfare funds.

A similar American example of Masonic benevolence in times of adversity was seen in Chicago after the disastrous fire of October 1871. Apart from other damage which included the homes and businesses of many of the four thousand Masons resident in the city, the fire destroyed eight Masonic Halls and left eighteen of the thirty-one lodges in the city 'homeless'. The Grand Lodge of Illinois immediately set up a Masonic Board of Relief, which received nearly $60,000 in cash from Masonic lodges across America, as well as Canada, Newfoundland, Central America and England. The Grand Lodge of California alone sent $5,000. In Kentucky, the Masonic Widows and Orphans home threw its doors open and offered temporary accommodation to the bereft widows and children of Chicago Masons. As one correspondent concluded in the *Masonic Magazine*, the charity showered on the Chicago brethren meant that 'the hungry were fed, the naked clothed, the sick ministered to, the dead buried, and the penniless workmen furnished with new tools of their trade'. In addition to the help offered to individuals and families, substantial aid was also given to the lodges to assist in rebuilding and refurnishing and, when all was done, there were still residual funds that were returned pro rata to the subscribers. The local Masons were relieved and pleased, and the wider populace suitably impressed.[3]

In South Africa, the same 'closing of the ranks' to provide support for distressed and displaced brethren was displayed during the Second Boer War of 1899–1902.[4] Largely a consequence of a flood of gold-seeking miners into the semi-independent Boer Republic of the Transvaal, it caused major disruption and loss for families on both sides of the conflict—and many were Freemasons. Even before hostilities broke out, there was a flight of mainly British families from the area into the British Cape Colony and lodges there were being called upon for assistance.[5] When the fighting began in October 1899, the numbers increased exponentially.[6] Overall, it was estimated that there were around five thousand English-constitution Freemasons in nearly a hundred lodges across South Africa in the late 1890s, with perhaps another one thousand in Scottish-constitution lodges.[7] Approximately half of that number were rendered homeless and without any means of supporting their families, and their relief was clearly beyond the capacity of the others. An immediate call for assistance from Masons across the Empire was sent out by George Richards, the Grand Master for the Transvaal District. Contributions came in from all directions.[8] In England, the South African Masonic Relief Fund was set up by the UGLE and within months it had received donations of more than £6,000—over £1,000 coming from its own funds and the remainder from Provincial Grand Lodges, single lodges and private individuals.[9] A sum of five guineas was a standard contribution from lodges, while individuals often gave a standard 5 shillings.[10] Special gatherings were held to co-ordinate contributions and further sums of several tens of pounds raised.[11] By November 1901 the Fund stood at £10,000 and even though the fighting had largely subsided, it was decided to keep it open. Monies were distributed via the District Grand Lodges in South Africa with a careful eye, not simply to provide casual relief but, in the usual Masonic manner, 'to help the unfortunate amongst our brethren to help themselves'.[12] Cornwall, the home of many of those who had migrated to the mines of South Africa, was particularly affected by requests for help from those that made it back or remained stranded in the war zone. Their PGL established its own Masonic War Fund which stood at £473 by November 1900.[13]

Contributions also were made to the numerous non-Masonic charities set up to relieve the wider suffering in the war, such as the Transvaal Refugee Relief Fund, *The Daily Telegraph* Shilling Fund, the Patriotic Fund and the Mansion House Fund.[14] Precedents for such contributions were well established from efforts made to relieve other emergencies earlier in the century.[15] Lodge members in South Africa no doubt also contributed to the efforts made by their various national associations, such as the Cornish Association of South Africa, various Irish, Caledonian and Cambrian societies, and the Yiddish Landsleit fellowship.[16] In all of these efforts, Masons received encouragement from the knowledge that many generals leading the fighting, such as Lords Kitchener and Roberts, as well as many of their officers, were themselves members of the Order.[17]

In all of its charitable activities, both individual and general, Freemasonry can be seen as an important conduit for the redistribution of wealth, from the wealthy and well off to the destitute and temporarily deserving poor.

Civic Engagement and the Creation of Physical and Social Capital

Almost everywhere, members of Masonic lodges involved themselves in local and national political and charitable institutions, and played a leading role in the construction and evolution of their communities. These issues have been touched on before in the context of the analysis of the occupational structure of lodge membership but need further development to indicate the real level of lodge engagement in community development. In addition to those that owned and operated local businesses in and around the towns—shops, hotels, mines, mills, etc.—the lodges included the men that financed and managed the physical and cultural infrastructure—the roads, utilities, newspapers, theatres and institutions of state. Even with very limited information on the occupations of the members of many lodges in California, Nevada, Montana and Idaho, it is possible to identify numerous examples of such involvement. For example, Nevada Lodge in California, Escurial in Nevada, Red Mountain in Montana and Boise No. 2 in Idaho all had representatives of the men that built and operated the transport infrastructure—viz. toll roads, livery stables and coach lines. Similarly, though less commonly, they included the suppliers and operators of water facilities and the telegraph system. Bankers were ubiquitous, providing the services that facilitated payments, mobilised local savings and imported essential capital from afar. The owner of the theatre in Virginia City, Nevada, was a member of Virginia Lodge; a billiard hall keeper in Helena belonged to Helena No. 3; and newspaper owners and editors were prominent in Silver Star Lodge in Gold Hill, Nevada, Idaho No. 1 in Boise, Idaho, and King Solomon's Lodge in Tombstone, Arizona. Similarly, Gold Fields Lodge in Johannesburg, South Africa, Golden Lodge in Bendigo, Australia, and Otentosama Lodge in Japan, all included members who owned and/or managed newspapers and theatres. Everywhere there were clergymen, musicians, artists and photographers, and many of the lodges, particularly in Japan, included teachers. Together they helped to import the trappings of civilisation, ensured the effective education of the next generation, and encouraged the integration of all sections of the community. Of course, the Masonic lodges themselves, together with all of the other fraternal organisations, provided a major part of the social infrastructure of the new towns, with their entertainment, educational, family support and sports activities.

The civic engagement of lodge members stood at an equally high level. Again, nearly every lodge counted government employees of some description, from humble clerk, through regulatory inspector, to member of the local, state and sometimes national assembly. Thus Virginia Lodge, Nevada, Virginia City, Montana and Victoria Lodge, Bendigo all included the County Clerk or Recorder. County and Territorial Treasurers were members of Escurial, Nevada, Virginia City, Montana and Shoshone Lodge, Idaho. Inspectors of Mines, Revenue and other regulations were members of Owyhee Lodge, Idaho, Gold Fields Lodge, South Africa, and Ballarat and Golden lodges in Australia. In the early Japanese lodges, a large number of the European and American members were in the employ of the Japanese government and many provided Consular services for their own governments. Thus, Otentosama Lodge counted the Consuls for the British, US and French governments; Rising Sun Lodge in Kobe, a British Consul; and Nippon Lodge in Tokyo, the US Consul. Members of many lodges were elected mayor of their city, some became representative to the State legislature and a few progressed to the national level, with Victoria Lodge in Bendigo providing an early member of the Provincial Assembly. Thus the lodges of the Keweenaw provided one State Representative and two Congressmen;[18] King Solomon's Lodge in Tombstone, Arizona provided the town's first Mayor;[19] and Yarrowee Lodge in Ballarat provided at least eleven Members of Parliament and thirty mayors during the nineteenth and early twentieth centuries.[20] In England, the Masonic lodges of Sheffield included forty-seven members of the city council between 1843 and 1893 and, at the other end of the country, St George's Lodge in Exeter provided seventeen mayors of that city during the nineteenth century, with two or more in every decade.[21] Whether this level of engagement was because lodge members thought it their duty to seek public office, or because those that sought office thought it beneficial to become lodge members, remains an open question. It is clear, however, that the networking potential of Freemasonry would have assisted election, and it has already been noted how Cornish members of Parliament often thought it in their interests to maintain multiple lodge memberships.

Of all of the different sectors for civic engagement, the administration of law and justice was most common among lodge members. It is not clear why, but perhaps they were attracted by the rigid moral attitudes of Masonry and its strict interpretation of tradition. As has been seen, there were large numbers of lawyers and attorneys in many lodges, and policemen (constables, sergeants, inspector and superintendents), sheriffs (deputy, senior, US Marshall), court officials, justices of the peace, local and superior court judges all figured prominently. This was as true of the lodges in the Western towns of the US (e.g. Nevada Lodge, California; Montana Lodge No. 2 and Nevada Lodge No. 4, Montana; and Idaho Lodge No. 1, Idaho) as it was in West Cornwall, Australia (e.g. Golden, Victoria and Corinthian lodges) and South Africa (e.g. Gold Fields Lodge). The zeal of the Masonic desire to enforce law and administer justice may well have expressed itself in the vigilante activity that took place in many of the frontier mining towns of the American West, and even in some of its large cities. San Francisco, for example, experienced major vigilante activity in the mid-1850s,[22] and in 1855 alone, forty-seven men were executed in California by self-appointed groups of citizens. Those men frequently organised formal trials, made careful arrangements for the presentation of evidence and assembled independent juries.[23]

Little direct evidence has been discovered of Masonic involvement in these events but similar activities in Montana from the early 1860s have been investigated in great detail. Here, before the arrival of external forms of law and order, Masons have been shown to have led most of the emerging mining communities in administering extra-judicial justice through ad hoc and 'people's courts'.[24]

Early vigilante activity took place in Bannack, Beaverhead County, and Virginia City, Maddison County. Gold had been discovered in Grasshopper Creek, near the current town of Bannack, in the summer of 1862 and further, bigger discoveries were made just to the east, in Alder Creek, in the spring of 1863 (see Illustration 12). Men flooded in to this remote area from both the East and the West, and Bannack was quickly joined by new communities at Nevada City and Virginia City. By midsummer 1863, Alder Gulch was estimated to have

Illustration 12   Masonic Lodge and School Room, Bannack, Montana, USA

The town of Bannack sprang up after the discovery of gold in Grasshopper Creek in 1862 and the Masonic Lodge in the town was formed shortly thereafter. The town is famous for its response to robbery and banditry. The local Freemasons formed a Vigilance Committee and arrested and hanged the town Sheriff, Henry Plummer, on suspicion of his leading the gangs. It is now a ghost town and preserved as a National Historic Landmark, managed as a Montana State Park. This Masonic Hall was erected by the Masons in 1874. As was common, the Lodge meeting room was upstairs, to avoid prying eyes, and the ground floor was made available for a schoolroom and community facility.

a population approaching two thousand, many of whom were acquiring considerable portable wealth, not simply from mining but also mine supply and urban services. Such wealth in an environment far from any civil authority and system of justice attracted numerous 'road agents', who preyed upon the trade and traffic both within and between the communities as well as links to the outside world, either south to Salt Lake City or north to Fort Benton, the head of navigation on the Missouri river. Many were robbed and intimidated, and many were killed. Although contemporary estimates of over a hundred murders are probably an exaggeration, there was clearly a developing security crisis. Inspired and partly informed by earlier events in San Francisco in the 1850s, a 'Vigilance Committee' was formed by local citizens in December 1863 and led by prominent Masons such as Nathaniel Langford, Paris Pfouts, Wilbur Sanders, Jeremiah Fox and William Clark, to mention but a few. During the next two or three months they caught, tried, and hanged twenty perpetrators. Regular criminal justice finally reached the area with the appointment of Hezakiah Hosmer (also a Mason) as Federal Territorial Justice, towards the end of 1864. Vigilante arrests and killings then briefly stopped but when it became clear that the authorities did not yet have the means to maintain peace and security, they were again revived and by the end of 1865 the vigilantes' number of lynchings had risen to thirty-five. With extrajudicial killing now firmly established as part of the culture of Montana, vigilante action of one form or another was revived periodically through the rest of the century and continues to be honoured to this day.

These Masons' zeal for the exercise of justice has often been criticised as excessive. However, some of the same men have won universal praise for the efforts, just a few years later, in conducting the first exploration of the Yellowstone area and promoting its establishment as the first US National Park. The original initiative for this enterprise came from a meeting of Langford and Jay Cooke, the latter of whom was extending his Northern Pacific Railroad into Montana Territory and was interested in the tourist potential of the spectacular scenery that had been sporadically reported by hunters and other travellers. It was agreed that Langford would organise a small expedition to investigate the Yellowstone and Firehole river districts in the summer of 1870. A small nine-man party was quickly put together and took the name of the Washburn–Doane expedition, after the names of the leaders of the military escort that gave protection against hostile Indians. At least half of the civilian party were Masons, including Langford and Cornelius Hedges (past Grand Masters of Montana), Hezekiah Hosmer (Grand Secretary) and Samuel Hauser (the Governor of the Territory). James Stuart, another Mason from Deer Lodge, was involved in the early planning of the enterprise, but obliged to withdraw before it left.[25] Setting out on their enterprise in August, Hedges recorded in his diary that all was a public commotion, 'running around, saying goodbye, talking with Masons' [26] En route to their starting point, the expedition also stopped briefly at Gallatin Lodge No. 6 for Langford and Hedges to settle a Masonic dispute. Following the successful completion of the expedition, Cornelius Hedges formally proposed the permanent protection of the district as a National Park and in 1872 Nathaniel Langford became its first Superintendent, starting a system of National Parks which continues down to the present.[27]

With their direct connections into all aspects of their host communities, Masonic lodges and their members were clearly able to wield considerable levels of influence throughout political and civil society. In some areas it was regarded as all-pervading, with the churches that saw it as a malevolent influence being outspoken in their criticism. Rev. Van Der Lingren of the Dutch Reformed Church declared darkly in 1862, for example, that it was 'well known that there is no city on God's Earth that is so completely under the influence of Freemasonry as Cape Town'.[28] Substantiating the actual levels of influence achieved is, however, a difficult and complex task. Fortunately, two detailed studies of mining communities in Australia provide a useful guide to what might have been a common experience in many other early mining districts. They are Barrett's study of the origins of community and local government in the State of Victoria, and Wickham's closer look at the role of Freemasonry in the Ballarat District.[29]

Freemasons, as well as members of other fraternal lodges, such as the Oddfellows, were firmly established as a major presence in the political structure of Melbourne by the second quarter of the nineteenth century. Masons controlled the Market Commission, which laid the foundations for local government in Melbourne; their processions were a feature of all civic occasions; and the first Mayor of Melbourne was a Mason who frequently wore his Masonic regalia when officiating in office. On many issues the only constraint to their power was the competition between the members of different lodges, as the English, Scottish and Irish constitutions vied with each other. The fraternities were certainly not shy of their influence and no doubt used it to attract members. However, Barrett suggests that the real power lay with individual members, rather than the corporate body of the lodges themselves. He concluded that:

> It would be misleading to assume that the Masonic Lodge, the Oddfellows Lodge, or any other organisation was manipulating the council. It was probably nearer the truth to say that certain individuals were manipulating various organisations, including lodges as well as the council.[30]

With the discoveries of gold in the early 1850s, Masonry followed the rush of people into the interior of Victoria and continued to dominate the development of towns and communities everywhere. Much of the success of the Order was due to the arrival of large numbers of already-active Masons from England, who occupied many of the new positions of management and government authority. Barrett provides several examples. In East Collingwood, the first town clerk was a prominent Mason and most of the councillors were drawn from the Masonic lodge. Masonic connections to members of the legislative assembly helped them to obtain funding for an essential bridging of the river Yarra—Andrew Clerk, the Surveyor-General, was the PGM. Similarly, Zetland Lodge exercised a powerful influence in the development of Kyneton, with its members being prominent on the council as well as office-holders in the mechanics' institute, the hospital, the cricket club, the racing club and the volunteer Kyneton Mounted Rifles. Through the latter organisation they exercised a law-and-order influence not greatly dissimilar from the vigilantes of Virginia City, Montana, suppressing riot and civil disorder.[31]

Wickham continues the story from the 1850s through to the end of the century, focusing closely on what had now become the large town of Ballarat and its district. By the early 1890s more than fifty lodges of English, Scottish and Irish constitutions had been established within a thirty-mile radius of Ballarat, and they made up a little more than a third of all of those operating within the State. With another 180 Oddfellows lodges and many other affiliations, it had probably become the world's most intensively fraternal district relative to the male population.[32] Everywhere members of the different fraternities competed with each other for influence, but the Masons maintained their established leadership in most aspects of the community's economic and social development. They were prominent in the formation of the Stock Exchange and Mining Exchange, and were the driving force behind the formation of the Chamber of Commerce, the Ballarat School of Mines and the Ballarat Mechanics' Institute. A combination of need and social convention also encouraged them to take an active role in the organisation of non-Masonic charities. On the one hand a lack of public provision of adequate poor relief meant that there was often a major need for charitable assistance, while on the other, active involvement in charitable organisations gave status and authority. Thus in the 1850s they played a major role in fundraising for the Miners' Hospital, the Ballarat Benevolent and Visiting Society (providing relief to the destitute), and the Ballarat Benevolent Asylum, while in the 1860s they supported the Ballarat Orphan Asylum and the Ballarat Female Refuge. Most of these and other similar charities were also actively supported by the Oddfellows, Foresters and other fraternities but the Masons usually took the leading managerial role, with up to two-thirds of the membership of most committees being Freemasons. As Wickham suggests, it became a social 'badge of success' to be on the hospital, benevolent home or orphanage committees[33] and the Masons were glad to claim it. On every occasion, the Freemasons demonstrated their prestige and influence in the community, organising gardening societies, picnics, balls and parading in full regalia during every civic celebration, and they played a strategic role in encouraging the integration of non-British immigrants into the community. Taken together with the activities of all of the other fraternities, their role might, as Barrett suggests, be considered as that of an independent 'fourth tier' of institutions, standing equally alongside the other great tiers of local, state and national government in the formation of modern society.[34]

There have been very few studies of the role of Freemasons in civic affairs in Britain that could match those conducted for Australia, but they are far from unknown. Prescott's brief overview of 'Freemasonry in the Victorian City' suggests a very similar pattern of Masonic engagement in the creation of social capital.[35] In Manchester, for example, many of the city council members were Masons and they took a leading role in the gas, finance and technical instruction committees. Similarly in Merthyr Tydfil, Freemasons played a leading role in the development of civic culture.[36] Everywhere Masonic halls were among the great civic buildings[37] and Masonic lodges played a major role in raising the finance for many other ventures, such as the construction of the Chapter House for Liverpool Cathedral in 1906 and Truro Cathedral thirty years earlier. In his more recent study of Freemasonry in Harwich, Reilly has shown how leading local Freemasons were involved in the private companies that developed gas and water services, as well as the work of the Harwich Town Council, which planned and oversaw the improvement of harbour and rail facilities. As in Australia, they also took leading roles in elite leisure organisations, such as the Royal Harwich Yacht Club, the Essex Volunteer Regiment, the Harwich Institute, the Choral Society, etc.[38]

Of particular significance in increasing involvement in civil society was the emergence of 'class lodges' for men with special related interests, such as civic offices, particular businesses, old school affiliations, sports activities and religious groups.[39] Some of these had been around for many years, such as Westminster and Keystone Parliamentary Lodge founded in the early eighteenth century, and the Bank of England Lodge in the mid-nineteenth century, but they really came of age in the later Victorian and Edwardian period.[40] Thus London County Council, all of the London Boroughs[41] and most provincial local authorities established their own lodges, as did responsible agencies such as the Metropolitan Water Board, many universities,[42] schools, and Westminster Hospital. There were also numerous lodges that acted as a focus for single large business enterprises. By the 1930s, class lodges had become ubiquitous in the City of London and other large commercial towns throughout the country.[43] For the middle class and most middle managers, Masonic membership had become the norm rather than the exception. As Prescott concludes, the new elites of public officials expressed their social solidarity by adjourning to their Masonic lodge at the end of the day's work or at the end of periodic committee meetings.

These examples of the ways in which Freemasonry influenced the development of civic and civil society were also reflected in the role that the closely associated Orange Order played in shaping the municipal culture of Toronto, Canada. William Smyth's account of that subject holds up an interesting mirror.[44] In Toronto the influence of Freemasonry was eclipsed by the role of Orangeism, possibly because the Masons had restricted membership to the better-off classes and not opened to a wider membership, as in Australia.[45] Nevertheless, Orangeism represented much the same Protestant, Anglo-Saxon tradition as Masonry and it had a considerable crossover of membership. Originating in Ulster, Northern Ireland in 1795, the Order derived much of its ritual, symbolism and organisational structure from Freemasonry[46] and, again following a familiar pattern, it was introduced into Canada by Regiments with travelling lodge warrants. The numbers took off with high levels of immigration from Ulster following the end of the Napoleonic Wars, though the lodges also came to include many Scottish, English and Canadian members. The Orange Order emerged as a distinctive power block within local government in the 1840s and 1850s, and for the next hundred years virtually all of the Mayors of Toronto were Orangemen. As Smyth concludes, by the early twentieth century, 'Orange parades in Toronto usually included the premier of Ontario, the mayor of the city, several judges, senior administrators, managers and civil servants, including the chairman of Ontario Hydro and the Toronto Transit Commission.'[47] The Orangemen may have been the dominant force but they did not have it all their own way. Smyth quotes one observer in 1872 who suggested the municipalities may have been Orange but the railroad companies were Masonic, and Government employees a mixture of both. Overall, he suggests, 'the leading citizens preferred the social networks of the Masonic Order'.[48]

Social Cohesion

The membership of Masonic lodges during the late nineteenth and early twentieth centuries may well have reflected the range of local economic activity but it did not in any way properly represent the sexual, social, racial and ethnic mix. Women were excluded and found a voice only through their husbands or fathers. The poorest labouring classes were not invited and could not have afforded membership if they had been. Indigenous peoples were not represented, and those of African, Chinese, Latin American, Mexican and most others of non-European origin were not normally admitted. It would not be correct, however, to say that membership was confined only to the white community because large numbers of Europeans also were not invited, or chose to exclude themselves, particularly those from Southern and Eastern Europe. Masonic lodges in the West of America and the mining districts of Australia and South Africa were very predominantly Protestant with north-western European origins.[49] Catholics mainly excluded themselves because of threats of excommunication that were in force from the early eighteenth century. Many, often most, of the members were born elsewhere within the country and migrated to the mining districts while others were usually first-generation incomers. Jews were sometimes invited to become members, but there was a strong argument that membership should be confined to Christians, and Mormons were commonly rejected.[50]

While this clearly had the capacity to be highly socially divisive, there were some mitigating factors. Firstly, the societies in which the Masonic lodges operated were very different. In Cornwall, with its high preponderance of Nonconformists and a very low ethnic and racial mix, only the absence of women prevented them from closely reflecting the spread of the community. Similarly, in many of the new frontier districts the great majority of first incomers were native-born whites and immigrants from north-western Europe. Women and children usually came later to join husbands already established there. Similarly, poor non-white labour mainly arrived with a second stage of mining development, when small-scale independent mining was beginning to give way to larger-scale corporate enterprise and a demand for wage labour.[51] At this stage in their evolution, the increasing ethnic and social division of mining communities resulted from a whole range of reasons, of which Masonic membership was only one. Freemasonry was as much a victim of that social fracturing as a cause of it, as it struggled to maintain the economic 'quality' of those that it wanted to admit.

Secondly, it could be argued that the very exclusivity of Freemasonry was useful in encouraging other groups to develop their own fraternal and benevolent societies, with costs and offerings that were more suitable to their membership. An excellent example of this can be found among the African-American community. Excluded from regular Freemasonry by a 'whites only' policy in America, they used an original warrant issued by the English Grand Lodge in 1784 to establish a widening network of 'parallel' black Masonic lodges across the USA, the Caribbean and South America.[52] As a correspondent of the

American Masonic journal *New Age* explained, 'negro' Masonry had its own 'mirror' structure to white Masonry:

> From the first degree to the Order of the Knights Templar, the 'Colored Brother' finds *his* York Rite, Blue Lodges, Royal Arch Chapters, Councils and Commanderies ready to receive him, while in the Scottish Rite he can become a member of lodges of the Fortieth Degree, Chapters, Consistories and Supreme Councils.[53]

Even in the West, with its small black populations, the 'San Francisco Negro Masons of the Olive Branch Lodge' were operating in the late 1850s[54] and, out on the frontier, Prince Hall Masons established their first lodge—Rocky Mountain No. 1—in Colorado in 1867. By 1876 they could organize their first Grand Lodge for the territory, with a jurisdiction embracing what became Wyoming, Montana, Utah, New Mexico and Arizona, and during the next thirty years established twenty-three warranted lodges.[55] Prince Hall Masonry, however, was only part of a much wider and deeper tradition of mutuality within the black community. Excluded from most other 'white' fraternities yet facing particularly severe economic and social problems, they organised a large number of secret and benevolent societies which, alongside the church, honed identity awareness, organisational skills and community leaders.[56] By the early twentieth century, one investigator estimated that there were between 250 and 300 such societies in New Orleans alone, providing a wide range of services, such as medical assistance and support with burial costs.[57]

In a similar way, the excluded female members of Masons' families came together around 1850 to establish their own semi-Masonic Independent Order of the Eastern Star.[58] In the rapidly growing Finnish communities, women often joined men in fraternal religious and cultural organisations, such as temperance societies and community hall management.[59] The Catholics took the dramatic step of establishing their own semi-Masonic society, the Knights of Columbus, in the 1880s, in a desperate effort to counterbalance the seductive attractions of Freemasonry and the other, largely Protestant, fraternities.[60] The Chinese, who were probably the largest single group excluded from Freemasonry in most American and Australian mining camps, also supported their own fraternal and benevolent orders. Some of these 'Triads' and 'Tong' had traditions extending back to the fourth century in China and were imported into the mining camps by the first arrivals in the early 1850s. Although commonly associated in the popular mind with crime syndicates—which some were—the Triads often took the form of perfectly innocent friendly societies, providing death and sickness benefits on a

Illustration 13   Chinese 'Masons'

Chinese 'Masons' were often thought to be emulating European Masonry but were in fact celebrating their own ancient Tong and Triad fraternal traditions. These derived in various forms from the Hung Society, which spread rapidly through the United States, Canada and Australian from the mid-nineteenth century, and gradually evolved to become known as the Chinese Masonic Society, or Chee Kung Tong. A good example of a 'Chinese Masonic cemetery' can be seen in Goldfields Historic Cemetery, Bendigo, Australia. Chinese men were rarely, if ever, admitted to regular Free and Accepted Masonic lodges during the nineteenth century.

pattern similar to the Odd Fellows and Foresters (see Illustration 13). The Hung, otherwise Ghee Hin Society (meaning Justice and Peace Society), operated on principles very similar to those of Freemasonry, requiring its members to profess a belief in a supreme being, teaching a strict moral code, employing secret grips, signs and passwords as a means of recognition, and attempting to attract the better-off members of the community.[61] Sometimes described in the Western press as 'Chinese Freemasonry', the orders were firmly established in America by the mid-1870s and were reported to have over 150,000 members across the nation by the late 1880s. One press report suggested that the Yee Tong Hong Kong Lodge of San Francisco was the recognised leader of the orders, though they appear to have had no centralised structure, and a New York lodge, with a membership of around three hundred members by 1890, would have provided an important East Coast counter-weight. Very much in the tradition of the Freemasons, many of these societies issued their members with 'travelling cards' to assist transient members between lodges.[62] While the Triads and Tong were generally repressed by British colonial authorities in the Far East, they were tolerated and flourished in Australia,[63] with the possibility of some non-Chinese members.[64]

Thirdly, it should be noted that not all Masons were as personally exclusive as their Order. Many reached out to help create the large and all-embracing Noble and Holy Order of Knights of Labour in America from 1869. Drawing on the ritualistic traditions and 'secret knowledge' principles of a number of well-established fraternal orders, such as the Odd Fellows and the Improved Order of Redmen, the Knights embraced female, black and all other minority members. Here the strong ritualistic experience of black members played an important role in placing the Order on firm foundations. However, it was its acquired role as a labour organisation—almost a general trades union—that was the primary cause of its rapid growth in membership through to the mid-1880s. By that time it was estimated that almost a fifth of all workers were affiliated in some way. At that point its inclusiveness in terms of the spectrum of those that it included and the differences in their needs also became its greatest weakness. Failure effectively to represent and protect them during the severe economic downturn of 1886–87 and violent demonstrations caused a catastrophic loss of members, and the Knights ceased to be an effective force within a few years. It was, however, introduced into Australia in 1889, by members that included Freemasons, where it also enjoyed some initial success by reverting to its earlier ritualistic fraternal roots.[65]

The great proliferation of mutual societies in the increasingly hyphenated and sectionally divided America of the late nineteenth century provided a range of facilities catering for a spectrum of needs that never would have been conceived by one all-embracing organisation on its own account. For those with multiple memberships there were greatly widened opportunities for insurance, leisure and entertainment, and a potential for economic and social networking far beyond their own group. By pulling in most members of society, the various fraternities created opportunities for a kind of federated structure for social interaction and achieved more than any one group in isolation. As Murphy concluded in her study of Butte, Montana, multiple fraternities and voluntary associations came together 'to integrate communities by tackling projects, such as sanitation, recreation, and beautification, designed to benefit everyone'.[66] Extended networking potential increased the efficiency of local economic activity, and men and women from all parts of the community were given the scope for personal and social development that might not otherwise have occured.

Clearly it is essential to balance these claims of the positive effects of fraternity with more negative interpretation and experiences. A case study of the role of fraternal organisations in the bitter copper miners' strike of the Upper Michigan Peninsula in 1913–14 provides a useful example. It shows how, in the early stages of the development of mining in the district, orders such as the Freemasons and Odd Fellows brought together most sectors of the local population during the 1860s and 1870s, promoting a good level of communication and harmony. As in Nevada City, many men were members of both orders. However, while the population of the district increased rapidly from the 1880s with an influx of Eastern and Southern Europeans, the older fraternities continued to recruit mainly from the traditional domestic and north-western European ethnic base. These continued to have a close dialogue but to the exclusion of the new immigrants who found their fraternity in new, narrow and inwardly looking ethnic groups. To the extent that the older established groups represented most of the managerial power elite of the district, they became increasingly isolated from the larger semi-skilled and unskilled workforce with a consequent breakdown in the ability for information flows and dialogue.[67]

This scenario fits well with Rosenzweig's conclusions from a study of the role of Freemasonry in Boston during the early twentieth century. He suggested that the Masons saw the rising flood of new immigrants and the increasing power of the unions as a threat to the established order. They sought to protect that order by withdrawing inwards rather than reaching out and associated increasingly with conservative nativist movements.[68] More recently, Kaufman has gone even further in arguing that 'associationalism' in all of its forms had a broadly detrimental effect on social harmony because it provided the organisational apparatus for social segregation. Instead of helping the great 'American melting pot' to forge a homogeneous national American identity among new arrivals, the ethnically and sectionally divided fraternal organisations promoted hyphenated identities along ethnic, racial, religious and gender lines.[69]

These views are well reflected in the changing relationship between Freemasonry and Catholicism in America. Traditionally Masonry was open to Catholics and, even though there were various Catholic injunctions against membership from as early as 1738, many did become members. This situation changed significantly with the hardening of the Catholic injunction following the *Humanum Genus* promulgated by Pope Leo XIII on 20 April 1884. This proclaimed Masonic membership as a grave sin and provided for automatic excommunication for those Catholics that became members.[70] It was, however, also seen as a response by the Church to a rapidly changing industrialising world and a growing challenge to its authority. That claim to authority in turn led to an increasing retaliation to Catholicism within Freemasonry, which saw the Papal claim to catholic allegiance as a challenge to the authority of the State that Masons were sworn to uphold. As part of their reaction to the problems caused by the new waves of immigration from Southern and Eastern Europe, and the rising tide of nativism in America, many Freemasons became increasingly anti-Catholic. In August 1920 one correspondent of the Masonic *New Age Magazine* declared that:

> No avowed Roman Catholic should be elected or appointed to any office of public trust under the United States or under any State notwithstanding the admitted fact that they are honest and upright men and likeable good fellows. For the gist of the whole matter is that he owes his first allegiance to the Pope.

Other correspondents railed against 'Papist Poland' and 'Papist Austria', and denounced 'overwhelmingly Catholic Hungary' for closing Masonic lodges, confiscating their property, destroying their records and forbidding their meetings. Although acknowledging the prohibition on involvement in politics, many American Masons took the side of the British government against Irish home rule because it would give Irish brethren over to 'an intolerant, priestly despotism which probably, on the whole, exceeds that in any other European country'. Seeing an international Catholic conspiracy, they noted that the Senn Feiners had resisted conscription in the recent war, that Irish freedom agitation had the backing of 'German-hyphens' and that its success could mean the return of the German empire. They concluded that 'every Sinn Fein agitator is an enemy to American freedom and the cause of the Allies in arms'.[71]

Masons everywhere were very eager to make rules of inclusion and exclusion but also happy to modify or bend them. One such was the fundamental requirement for all Masons under the various British constitutions to express a belief in God. Initially this was a Judaeistic God but over time it was modified to a more all-embracing belief in a monotheistic Supreme Being: 'The Great Architect of the Universe'. This accommodated membership by those who adhered to other deistic religions, such as Islam. It was this flexibility that enabled the King of Afghanistan famously to be made a Mason by Lord Kitchener using the Koran rather than a Bible to take the oath. It was, however, one of the reasons why the Catholics and the Calvinists objected to Freemasonry. This requirement was dropped by much of European Freemasonry during the second half of the nineteenth century, leading to difficulties in inter-Grand Lodge relations.

Until the mid-nineteenth century there was greater harmony over the restriction of Masonic membership to men of white, European origin, though again, exceptions were always possible. Note has already be been made of Prince Hall Masonry and even lodges in the United States and South Africa, who took the convention particularly seriously, showed a preparedness to at least consider 'bending' it. During the eighteenth and early nineteenth centuries, the strongest prohibitions were against slaves, with every candidate for admission to an English lodge being asked to confirm that he was 'born a free man'. This began to alter, however, following the abolition of the slave trade in 1807 and, more particularly, the abolition of slavery in the Caribbean and South America from the 1830s. Principle and pragmatism drove the changes. On the one hand many Masons became part of the anti-slavery movement out of conviction,[72] while on the other, many lodges became aware of the need to embrace freed slaves who had become commercially successful and politically influential. Thus as early as 1839 the Secretary of Friendly Lodge No. 239 in Jamaica enquired of the Grand Secretary whether it was permissable to initiate a man as a Mason who was born a slave but freed immediately after his birth: 'We have several here who are now gentlemen of the first respectability, being members of the Assembly, Aldermen of this City and holding Her Majesty's Commissions as Officers.'[73] Following a sustained agitation, principally from overseas lodges, the UGLE altered the requirement for a candidate to confirm that he was 'born a free man' to 'I am a free man' in September 1847. This represented a profound attitudinal change in many colonial lodges as plantation owners became prepared to sit as equals with men who had previously been their 'property', and ex-slaves were prepared to engage with men who previously had been their masters. Unfortunately, some American Grand Lodges preferred to break relations with UGLE rather than accept the new arrangement.

Similar changes also took place in India and for similar reasons. A white European background was adhered to by all lodges during the eighteenth and early nineteenth centuries, with only exceptions to admit men of remarkable 'quality' and importance, such as the 8th Nabob of the Carnatic of Arscot in 1788. However, as the Empire expanded and became increasingly reliant on Indians for its administration and commercial success, pressure grew to admit middle-range civil servants, professions and merchants, particularly those drawn from the Parsi community. As the author of one study put it, 'they were a perfect class of collaborators', because they not only had economic interests embedded in British rule but were also a vulnerable ethnic minority in India.[74]

Manockjee Cursetjee, an Assistant Collector of Customs, claimed to have been the first to be initiated, in 1842, having travelled to Paris following rejections by an English constitution lodge in India. In 1843, however, the sympathetic Scottish constitution Grand Master of Western India, James Burnes, issued a dispensation for a new lodge to admit Indians—Rising Star of Western India No. 342 (SC)—which met in the Town Hall of Bombay.[75] A random sample of English constitution lodges in India shows that Bangalore Lodge No. 1043 was admitting Indians from the early 1870s and that Mysore Lodge No. 1841 was fully integrated by the late 1880s.[76]

In Britain, many Indians were becoming members of English lodges by the turn of the century but the first to be installed into the chair of an English lodge was Abdeali Shaikh Mahomedali Anik. A Bohra Muslim, he was installed into the Chair of Wantage Lodge No. 3178 in November 1917, supported by 'many of his Hindoo, Parsee and Christian brethren'.[77] Born in Surat in 1860 he had established himself as a successful merchant in London in 1901. As well as his Craft activities, he was also an active member of the Royal Arch, Mark, Royal Ark Mariners and Secret Monitor side orders.

Almost everywhere, Freemasonry accommodated changing economic arrangements and social relationships. Letters from the Secretary of Otentosama Lodge in Japan to the Grand Secretary of UGLE in 1872 provides a particularly good insight into the pragmatism of the time. The Secretary declared that he had received several enquiries about membership from Japanese men and sought guidance on whether they might be admitted. He noted that some Japanese men had been initiated in Paris and Washington in recent years but that many of the brethren in Yokohama 'view the idea with horror, as I am sorry to say that there is a tendency to include the Japanese in the generic term "nigger"'. Others, however:

> who have had the opportunities of becoming acquainted with Japanese gentlemen entertain no objection to welcoming them into Freemasonry. For myself, I do not like dealing in generalities ... Leaving aside the question of nationalities as a matter of which Freemasonry takes no cognisance, we should deal with individual candidates as we do with those of our own or any other country.

He further noted that 'large numbers of the upper-class [Japanese] believe in a Supreme Being' and recalled that in the 'Lodge of the Star of Eastern Irish' in Bombay he had seen a Parsee and a Mohamedon obligated at the same time, the former on the scriptures and the latter on the Koran. He concluded that he had personally been intimate friends with a number of 'the better classes' for two years, and that he found them 'well bred, sociable and hospitable, ceremonious but without affectation; many of them exceedingly intelligent and unmistakably gentlemen'.[78] Unfortunately there is no record of the reply from the Grand Secretary though it is notable that no Japanese became members of the four English constitution lodges operating in Yokohama, Kobe and Tokyo before the end of the 1880s. This may not have been due to Grand Lodge negativity, however, but rather more the result of the opposition of local members and/or the rising influence of anti-Masonry in Japan, largely instigated by Catholic priests.[79]

In Africa, lodges generally remained steadfastly white until well into the twentieth century,[80] though those in parts of West and East Africa also began to admit administrators and some mercantile interests from the third quarter of the nineteenth century. For example, Lagos Lodge No. 1171 in Nigeria initiated F.D. Cole, the black chief clerk at the colonial hospital, in December 1868, just a year after the Lodge was warranted.[81] The colour line was particularly strictly drawn in South Africa, but as one correspondent of the American Masonic Journal *Philalethes* observed in the 1940s, 'visiting foreign Brethren who are not European are, of course, hospitably received'.[82] The triumphant international expansion of Freemasonry through most of the nineteenth and twentieth centuries was based clearly on the principle that functionality in the management of economic, social and political relations trumped racial prejudice.

Improvement of the Individual in Society

It is undoubtedly true that not all Masonic activity was beneficial to all sections of their host communities. It is equally undeniable, however, that Freemasonry at least aspired to maximise the potential of its members—morally, spiritually and civically. Through its core allegory with operative Masons, it constantly strove to make its members the building blocks of an honest and just society. Overall, its influence was similar to, and helped to reinforce that of, the Church and the military, all working together to push men in the right direction. It had its roots deep in the teachings of the Old Testament, robustly proclaiming the moral tenets of the Commandments and engendered a sense of discipline, rank and loyalty. To the extent that most other fraternities took their inspiration from Freemasonry, they also promoted similar aspirations among their members. Today, sociologists would say that through corporate purpose, self-discipline and comradeship they engendered 'muscular bonding',[83] perhaps displaying the characteristics of 'schicksalsgemeinschaft', or communities of fate or destiny.

They certainly had the clear objective of making men good even though the outcomes may have been variable. On the one hand, the constant rehearsal of Masonic ceremonies and recommitment to noble aspirations is likely at least to have made them better than they would otherwise have been—better to create, and fit into, civilised and regulated society. It also gave them practical transferable skills. The learning and performance of ritual encouraged the development of reading skills and memory, gave simple men a much greater awareness of language and its uses, and developed self-confidence and the ability to speak in public. Similarly, involvement in the running of the lodge taught the administrative skills necessary for an efficient secretary or treasurer, developed an appreciation of democratic processes, showed the importance of political negotiations in influencing committee decision-making and encouraged the acceptance of personal responsibility. For artisans and white-collar workers, the lodge, trade union and chapel worked together to produce class leaders and promote social and economic mobility.

Certainly some fell short in such noble aspirations, but at least the path was made clear and many, if not most, trod it. Where individuals might stray, peer pressure helped to steer a course of self-restraint. Intimate involvement with broad Protestant ecumenicalism[84] meant that wherever they turned, their community constantly stressed the cardinal Victorian virtues of thrift, self-help, self-discipline and loyalty.[85] Both ritual and the practical requirements of taking part in the running of the lodge promoted the importance of educational advancement[86] and instructed that they should be a loyal, peaceful and law-abiding citizen. Closer to home, wives might have reinforced the need for temperance and self-constraint, encouraging a night spent in the lodge rather than one in the saloons and the bordellos. It might be that some evidence of these effects can be seen in the patterns of crime encountered in many frontier towns during the initial unruly stages of their development. While violent crime and fracas was a common occurrence, usually committed by small minorities of socially excluded groups of roughs and bad men, the socially dishonest crimes of theft, fraud and burglary were widely constrained through the overall force of moral authority.[87]

Of equal importance to Freemasonry's positive influence on personal development was its role in preventing the emergence of negative generational, social and regional divisions in society and culture. Many would see this as a particularly contentious proposition, preferring to stress the wider social divisiveness of fraternity along racial, religious, gender and ethnic lines. Within the inclusive groups, however, the young, inexperienced, single and feckless were brought together in lodges with middle-aged, married and family men creating good role models and discouraging anti-social behaviour. Many stayed, played and worked together as they progressed through life, cementing relationships and building integrated, if sectional, communities. For the wives and families of members the numerous social functions organised by lodges—ladies' nights, picnics, outings, etc.—helped to bridge the often exclusive, separate public and private spheres of mining communities and extended social support mechanisms.[88] Although membership tended to favour the more economically successful, all economic and social groups were brought together in an egalitarian context that militated against the emergence of sharp social divisions. One Australian historian, writing of the development of the Mount Morgan community in Queensland, has spoken of their role in producing a 'fluidity between master and men' during the 1860s, 1870s and 1880s that delayed the evolution of confrontational union–employer relations.[89] Perhaps most pervasively and most importantly, the moral and cultural traditions of the 'Old World'—of urban Europe and the Northeast— were imported into the new world of the Western frontier, helping to constrain emergent differences and sustain a coherent national identity. In this respect, Freemasonry and many other fraternities and social orders worked alongside what Louis B. Wright classically described as the spiritual and secular agencies that civilised the frontier.[90] Of particular significance here was the essentially Protestant orientation of the fraternities, which conveyed, and helped to ensure, the ascendancy of the Puritan traditions of the Founding Fathers in western areas otherwise dominated by the numbers of Hispanics and Chinese. The 'invention' of the Knights of Columbus by the Catholic Church in 1882, specifically to provide a counterbalance to the increasingly seductive influence of the estab- lished 'Protestant' fraternities, gives testament to the deep social influence that they saw those organisations wield.[91]

Across the English-speaking world Freemasonry acted as a vehicle for exporting traditional religious and cultural values, which helped to facilitate dialogue and constrain the development of differences. Similarly, its increasing adoption of positions of rank and authority chimed with Victorian social attitudes and accommodated it to the military, which became one of its greatest supporters.

Increasing the Efficiency of Economic and Social Interaction

Throughout this discussion there has been reference to Masonic lodges as infor- mation exchanges—the Google of their day. They commonly included a wide range of the leading members of the community and local economy, and members and visitors could find ready answers to most enquiries relating to the social, cultural and economic life of the community. Similarly, sworn trust relationships

facilitated the performance of business without access to additional legal arrangements. This trust was built not simply on previous commitments but the real
and certain knowledge that transgressions against a member would be commu-
nicated throughout the Masonic community and would have serious detrimental
effects on all future commercial dealings. In the worst-case scenario, a member
might be excluded with disastrous consequences both for their business and
their whole family's standing in the community. Fair dealing between Masons
had some very powerful guarantees. Taken together with extended networking
systems it is likely that, in economists' terms, Freemasonry helped significantly to
reduce 'transaction costs' across local and regional economies while promoting
the formation of 'social capital', which improved the effective functioning of
societies in all of their institutional and cultural forms. Some historical evidence
for this was provided in a recent analysis of the performance of 412 companies
quoted on the London Stock Exchange between 1895 and 1902. It was found
that those quasi-private companies with Masonic managers or directors generally
found it easier to obtain credit than other similar enterprises and that they tended
to produce higher profits.[92]

Of course, these close relationships could also work to the detriment of
the community, or at least some sections of it. Again, in economists' terms, it
could encourage 'rent-seeking' behaviour. Non-Masons could find themselves
marginalised or excluded from some commercial and social engagements; there
were strong opportunities for collusion to exploit the wider public and its social
and political institutions; and systems of law and justice could be subverted for
private advantage. All of these things and more have been extensively addressed
in anti-Masonic literature and need no further exploration here. This, however,
leads to the central question: did the beneficial effects of Masonry outweigh
the negative effects? Interesting as it may be to debate such an issue, it is clearly
impossible to calculate anything approximating to an accurate answer. No one
can ever estimate the savings and efficiency improvements made in a myriad of
transactions and, by their very nature, no one can ever estimate the costs of essentially hidden and clandestine activities. However, it might again be argued that
well-intentioned men subjected to a continuous programme of moral guidance
and self-improvement are likely to have produced more positive outcomes than
negative ones.

CHAPTER 9

CONCLUSION

The rise and diffusion of mutual organisations closely tracked the progress of industrialisation in Western societies during the eighteenth and nineteenth centuries. Both developments facilitated and fed off the challenges and opportunities created by the other. On the one hand the migratory turmoil created by the movement of labour from old settlements to new anonymous industrial cities created a need for mutual self-help in a world with few alternative sources of welfare. All levels of society were vulnerable to the fluctuations of the new economic engine as well as to heightened risks of disease and disablement. The only salvation was through collaboration with new acquaintances in a similar predicament. On the other hand, mutuality raised money to relieve poverty, created networks that reduced business transaction costs, made major contributions to the construction of social capital, and facilitated the transfer of economic resources from old to new areas of enterprise.

In the twentieth century this symbiotic relationship began to break down. The helter-skelter growth of new towns slowed, stable communities emerged with established filial support relationships, commercial insurance companies provided a widening range of products and, above all, local and central government developed welfare provisions that provided a minimum safety net for all. Instead of the problems of organising their own provision, families could source it elsewhere or simply 'buy it in'. Whereas more than one in ten families in Britain, North America, Australia and other parts of the Anglo-Saxon world had some level of involvement in mutuality at the end of the nineteenth century, with some societies claiming millions of members, nearly all have now ceased to exist, or continue only in the form of profit-making companies.

Within this broad mixture of associations, orders and friendly societies, Freemasonry was neither the largest nor the smallest, but it was certainly the oldest, most stable and now longest lived. It started in its modern form towards the end of the seventeenth century, roughly contemporaneously with the end of the scientific revolution and the first stirrings of industrialisation. Several members of the Royal Society were early Freemasons as were many of the later captains of industry. During the early eighteenth century the Order grew as a wide range of social classes were attracted to an expanding selection of lodges, and it began a process of diffusion overseas, which took it to all parts of Europe and British and European colonies everywhere. It survived government restriction during the Napoleonic War years but numbers appear to have declined and subsequently failed to recover swiftly during the early nineteenth century. However, from the middle of that century, Masonry, along with some of the great friendly societies, such as the Oddfellows and Foresters, began to explode into life. Masonry had finally acquired the critical mass to elevate it from a small minority interest group with a total membership measured in thousands to one that began to be counted in hundreds of thousands. The peak years, like other mutual groups, were probably in the years around the turn of the twentieth century, although there were brief surges in membership after the First and Second World Wars. Although today much reduced in numbers from those heights, it remains a vibrant organisation in towns and cities—small and large—across the world.

The reasons for this unusual success and durability are to be found in the types of men that became and remained Masons, and the adaptability of the Order to accommodate changing fashions and requirements. The basic philosophical aspirations, secrets and organizational structure of the Order stayed the same but everything else adapted constantly to the evolving social and economic world that accommodated it. These issues were the primary focus of this discussion and reveal that Freemasonry had a range of functionality that was not enjoyed to the same extent by other mutual organisations which enabled it to make a unique contribution to the lives of its members and the communities they lived in. Freemasonry offered more than simple mutuality and those things continue to have appeal.

The initial focus of the discussion was the identity of the men that became Masons. The available archival sources for Freemasonry are extensive and far more complete than for any other mutual association. They provide details of the identity, age, occupation and residence of nearly every initiate and joining member of every lodge under the English Masonic constitution from the early eighteenth century to the present, and are generally available for the period through to the First World War.[1] Reviewing all of the material was beyond the time and resources available, and a specified study area was selected— West Cornwall. This is a clearly delineated geographical area with a range of small and large towns, and a mix of inland and port economies. Details of the membership of thirteen lodges and several side orders were extracted for a period from the mid-nineteenth century through to c.1900. Occupational infor- mation demonstrated that there were representatives from nearly all parts of the regional economy and it was used as a means of analysing the social structure of lodges. This varied between lodges, reflecting differences in the local economy, but everywhere included a wide social spectrum from the aristocracy and gentry, through commercial and professional groups, to artisans and the upper working class. Very few unskilled workers were encountered. Overall, middle-class professional and mercantile groups were in the majority but everywhere working-class members provided a large cohort and in some lodges they were in a majority. Random checks of these findings against the membership of lodges in many other parts of the country confirm similar conclusions, as does the analysis of particular lodge membership overseas, such as the western United States, Australia and South Africa. Freemasonry in the Victorian period, from its earliest origins in the early eighteenth century, was far from an exclusive middle- and upper-class organisation. Large numbers of ordinary working men also became members everywhere. Random observation of present-day Masonic lodges suggests that this remains true, with different lodges seeing variations in the upper-class/middle-class and lower-middle-class/upper-working-class mix.

It is difficult to compare these findings with the situation in other mutual societies because of a lack of comparable membership data. However, from occasional surviving records for some friendly society lodges in Cornwall and elsewhere, it would appear that their membership had similar broad occupational distribution but generally emphasised a predominance of working-class membership over the professional and middle classes. These differences may account for the relatively stronger performance of Freemasonry in the twentieth century. Middle-class groups were likely to be less interested in the welfare insurance provision offered by mutual organisations and therefore less susceptible to being lured away by emergent state and commercial insurance provision. They were also likely to be more interested in the other attractions of Masonry.

The reasons why men became and remained Masons were many and various, and no doubt they worked in different combinations for different individuals and groups in different places at different times. When investigating these issues it is important to remember that Masonry was a secretive organisation and what it was found to offer once a man had become a member was likely to have varied substantially from what it was perceived to offer while they were outsiders. It has been suggested, however, that the wide experience of men in other forms of pseudo-Masonic friendly societies and craft trade unions during the later nineteenth century would have given many a good insight and preparation for what might have been seen as a progression to Masonry. Certainly Victorians would have been more prepared for the functional and ritualistic aspects of Freemasonry than new members today.

The various attractions of Masonry were grouped together under a number of headings in Chapters 4 and 5. They could be roughly divided into two broad groups— improving quality of life and practical or functional. For many men, Freemasonry was, and is, a major source of conviviality and entertainment. Today there are many alternatives but in the dour industrial towns of the late nineteenth century it was one of the very few respectable sources of pleasure outside of the home. Masonic meetings centred around the performance of ritual—effectively a form of amateur dramatics—which gave opportunities to demonstrate prowess and gain status away from their real-world positions. Many found the ritual itself spiritually uplifting and elevating, much like church services, though not performed in a devotional context. The learning and practice of sometimes long and complex ritual roles could be undertaken at home and filled in time between monthly lodge meetings. The meetings themselves were commonly followed by dinners, which provided regular opportunities for social engagement, entertainment and drinking. The potential to join side orders further augmented these ritualistic and entertainment activities, as did attendance at periodic balls, outings, picnics, ladies' evenings, etc. For those with esoteric interests, the pursuit of Masonic secrets, hidden truths and ancient knowledge gave opportunities for study and research.

Masonic initiation also conferred respectability and reputation, which were the most iconic of Victorian virtues. The Prince of Wales himself was the Grand Master of the Order and there could be no greater stamp of social approval. But unlike joining a friendly society, men could not simply decide to become Masons as they needed to be invited and sponsored by influential friends. That invitation was seen as a guarantee that the new member was honest, reliable, truthful and upright—'one of us'. Such an accolade was not simply life-enhancing, for both the member and his family, but also offered highly significant practical advantages for employment and business activities, advancement in politics and the Church, and a wide range of social and cultural activities. That status was not hidden, as it became in the twentieth century with Masonry's retreat into secrecy, but publicly flaunted in the frequent Masonic parades which accompanied all major public events. Masons could be seen in the mutual embrace of the 'great and the good' of the community.

Such connections also conferred perhaps the most practical and useful attributes of Masonic membership, namely powerful networking connections. In the lodges of the mining districts of Cornwall, the lawyers, accountants, contractors and carriers could have access to the mine managers who might employ their services. Similarly, in port cities everywhere, lodges accommodated those that provisioned and repaired vessels, organised cargoes and provided a wealth of valuable information to home-based and visiting mariners. In the frontier boom towns of the United States, Australia and South Africa, lodges brought together the men that were at the forefront of shaping the local economy and urban environment, and provided privileged access to new arrivals who exercised their visiting rights. In a time before electronic communications and with limited circulation of newspapers, the lodges provided a rare 'information exchange' for local, national and international affairs, where first-hand experience could be substituted for rumour.[2]

Masonic lodges did not simply bring men together to create networks. They also guaranteed the strength and reliability of those networks. Each member was sworn to the very highest standards of honesty and integrity in dealing with his brethren, and to offering help and assistance wherever it was required. That commitment was not simply to other members of the same lodge, but to Masons everywhere, and it had inestimable value at a time when business was done on a handshake and it was essential to be sure of the honesty and reliability of business partners. Charles Moreing, a member of Westminster and Keystone Lodge discussed above, demonstrated the imperative of such honesty. He used over £50,000 of his own funds to cover the irregular activities of one of his partners and lent further sums to his other partners to assist them in maintaining the company's honour. One of those partners was Herbert Hoover, the future President of the United States. Public knowledge of such propriety greatly assisted them in their future business activities.[3]

For most members of most lodges—the men that stayed in and around the same communities for the greater part of their lives—the entertainment, respectability and simple local networking offerings of Masonry were probably more than sufficient to attract and retain them. In what was still a deeply religious age, many also no doubt derived considerable spiritual satisfaction from the Old Testament-based lodge rituals, which complemented their regular devotions in church or chapel.[4] They might also derive reassurance from their ability to call on the charity of other Masons, lodges and the funds administered by Provincial and Grand Lodges, should they encounter major problems in life. Middle-class members would probably have hoped that their own resources would suffice for most emergencies, but even they would know of others who had failed in business, been ruined by lost investments, or had suffered long-term illness or any number of unforeseen changes in their fortunes. Fallback support for wives and families had appeal for everyone, not just the working class. For those that could afford it, joint membership of the Freemasons and one or more of the various friendly societies, offered still greater security and the limited available evidence suggests that many took advantage of such arrangements.

For a minority of members—sometimes a large minority and occasionally a majority in some lodges—the attractions of Masonry took a very different order. Those with mobile occupations and those needing to be geographically mobile, could rarely enjoy its entertainment aspects. They were rarely present in their home lodge long enough to learn and take part in ritual; to progress through the various lodge offices; to acquire rank; to dine regularly with friends; and to enjoy other occasional activities organised outside of the lodge. Equally they were likely to derive little direct benefit from improved local reputation and reputable status. Their interest was far more in the extended networking opportunities provided by the Order and the potential for finding help and assistance if their hazardous lives encountered serious difficulties or disaster. In this latter sense, the support that families might receive could also have been of particular relevance.

Investigation of the membership of lodges in West Cornwall identified two very large mobile occupational groups—miners and mariners—who displayed a great propensity to seek Masonic membership shortly before, or during, periods of long-distance movement. Looking at mining and maritime lodges overseas provides a good indication of why they were so keen. For mariners—particularly those manning the regular packet ships from ports like Falmouth—Masonic membership gave access to a 'home away from home', or as *The Cosmopolitan Masonic Calendar* put it, to find 'brothers' not 'strangers'.[5] Lodges provided a familiar context, a haven from the tumult of dockside life, a place to meet friends and those with similar interests, to gather local intelligence and to access the providers of reliable services. In the event of misadventure such as injury, illness or shipwreck, fellow Masons could be called upon for help and assistance, and possibly a passage home. Lodges and Masonic charities in England might make grants to assist those wives and children left destitute. Similarly, migratory miners—not simply those escaping from failing Cornwall but also those engaged in a career that saw them frequently shift between the world's new mining districts—could claim assistance and friendship from those that they encountered in transit as well as help with finding a job and integration at final destination. The flow of return migrants through mining lodges in Cornwall often left many of their members more informed about affairs in distant mining districts than the London Stock Exchange, and lodge members who had gone before might pave the way for later migrants.[6] None of this was confined to mariners and miners. Members of other mobile occupations, such as commercial travellers, saw similar advantages in having a Masonic identity. No traveller who could afford the cost of membership would sensibly forego it.

Detailed studies of lodges in new mining districts in different parts of the world added depth and detail to these general comments. With men pouring in from Europe and distant settled parts of the new territories, lodges provided key physical, cultural and spiritual places to bring them together. Analysis of origins, occupational and financial circumstances demonstrated the ability of Masonry to assist bonding between men of similar backgrounds, while also facilitating 'bridging' to others of different nationalities and social status. Sometimes, as in South Africa, membership of different specialised lodges could further smooth these activities. Advice and assistance from the wives and families of established members would also help new arrivals to integrate into the rapidly emerging communities. Of course, Freemasonry was not alone in providing such resources. Many other fraternal and mutual organisations provided similar institutional facilities on a national, if not international, basis. They created a strategic focus for efforts to establish local government, plan town development, construct public buildings and utilities, organise charities to provide for the old and orphaned, sick and injured. Together with the church, they were the main vehicle for importing the ethics, biblical tenets, attitudes and social structures from the Old World into the New World. They provided a coherent conservative force in civilising the otherwise anarchic conditions of early boom towns.

Today, the power and influence of fraternal and mutual associations is just a shadow of what it was a hundred years ago. However, the 'archaeology' of this former glory is still clearly to be seen in the form of surviving lodge rooms and halls, civic buildings, the names of streets and bars in towns across continents. More often than not, the Masonic Hall was one of the very largest and most opulent structures built in most towns before the turn of the century. They were designed not simply to epitomise Masonic origins and values but also to make a public statement of the wealth, power and influence of its members. In that sense, they emulated the churches and cathedrals of 'old' Europe, which distinctly announced an unchallengeable temporal as well as spiritual authority. Nowhere was the significance of Masonic, or indeed any other fraternal identity, more strongly demonstrated than in death. The cemeteries of many towns had separate fraternal sections to continue the association in perpetuity and even those buried in more common ground frequently made use of fraternal iconography to signify their main achievement in life (see Illustration 14). Masons' wives and children, who frequently had been members of closely associated orders such as the Eastern Star, also proclaimed their symbols on family grave headstones and sculptures.

All of these positive comments on the force and influence of Masonry and fraternalism must also be qualified by looking at their negative aspect.

Illustration 14   A Cornish Freemason's Grave, Lead, South Dakota, USA

Masonic tombstones were a common feature of cemeteries in early mining communities throughout the western United States and in many other countries. They were sometimes scattered around municipal cemeteries but are often found in specific Masonic sections, originally owned and administered by the lodges themselves. Other fraternities, such as the Odd Fellows, did likewise. This grave of John Hosking and his wife bears the square and compasses of the Freemasons as well as the three rings of the Odd Fellows, indicating that he was a member of both fraternities.

Freemasonry may have oiled the wheels of community development but it could also introduce grit and sludge into the system. Issues of favouritism and corruption have already been mentioned and what bound some together also excluded others. Masonic lodges rarely accommodated men with non-European Protestant origins and left others to make their own separate arrangements. For example, African Americans were obliged to develop their own independent branch of Prince Hall Masonry; the Chinese took refuge in their traditional Triad associations; immigrants frequently developed their own exclusive ethnic associations; and Catholics finally established their own Knights of Columbus along quasi-Masonic lines. Many simply objected to Freemasonry on principle, refused to engage with its members and were often aggressively hostile. Although the various orders and associations occasionally came together, and some members established cross-memberships in various fraternal and mutual societies, they generally remained apart, inward-looking, frequently competitive and viewed each other from separate bastions. With their predominance of professional, managerial and skilled workers, and their constant reinforcement of traditional conservative values, they acted as a powerful organised counter-radical force, slowing change and the rising force of popular democracy.

If an overall judgement can be made, it seems likely that Masonry probably had a benign effect on societal consolidation during the early stages of community development but perhaps became more divisive as the range of immigrant groups diversified over time. Its one overriding asset was its pragmatism. Above all, Masonic lodges aspired to host not just good and worthy men but also those that had a strong economic or social influence in the community. When that embrace required them to lower their barriers to those that might otherwise have been excluded, they were content to do so.

These comments clearly bring the discussion to a final casting of account. What was the net contribution of Freemasonry to Western social and economic development in the eighteenth and nineteenth centuries? Was it, overall, a good or bad thing? Popular culture, then as now, usually jumps to a negative conclusion. Anti-Masonic writings were common throughout the period, with cyclical fevers of opprobrium. They produced numerous well-supported instances of favouritism, corruption, subversion, criminality and every other kind of detrimental influence. These examples could clearly be matched with equal accounts of exceptional kindness, generosity, charity, public service, community building and innumerable cases of increased social and economic interaction achieved through lodges. Such rebuttals have been far less common, however, with Masonry preferring silence to contentious debates. This is not the place to find specific examples of the positive contributions made by Masonry—many of these have already been mentioned in earlier chapters—but it is appropriate to review the general headings of the things that need to be considered and weighed in the overall balance.

1. The principles of charity and mutual support on which Freemasonry was founded assisted millions of men internationally to fulfil the primary responsibility of all members of society to ensure the sustenance of themselves and their families at all times, good and bad. As such, it also facilitated the laissez-faire prejudices of the Victorian State and assisted the emergence of a free-market economy.

2. It has been argued that the nature of regularly repeated Masonic ritual was likely to make Masons—as individual social and economic actors— more honest, reliable and charitable than they might otherwise have been. This would have improved their interaction with both Masons and non-Masons, and made the whole more sensitive and functional. They were more likely to become improved men than worse. As Baron Bielfield put it well, 'I did not expect, by becoming a Freemason, to be introduced to a society of angels, but of worthy men', and, he declared confidently, 'I have not been disappointed'.[7]

3. Taking part in lodge affairs gave experience of democratic processes, confidence in speaking publicly and the management of sometimes conflicting and competitive interests and personalities. Taking office as secretary or treasurer taught other functional skills that were trans- ferable to the workplace or charity administration. Skills and experience acquired in the affairs of Masonic lodges and other mutual organisations played a major role in the development of a wide range of other social, political and economic organisations.

4. Freemasonry, like other fraternal and friendly societies, provided a major source of entertainment for its members, adding considerably to the quality of life of the hundreds of thousands involved. This applied not just to male members but to all of their family. By promoting respectable behaviour it tended to make them all more useful contrib- uting members of society.

5. Masonic charity brought together funds for the relief of the old, orphans, the ill and destitute that would otherwise have remained inactive. Mutuality in all of its forms reduced reliance on the public purse and was of real advantage to all of those that were not members.

6. The creation of wide networks of trust within the business community— locally, nationally and internationally—improved information flows and

reduced the difficulties of conducting transactions. Put simply, business was made easier and more efficient,

7. By facilitating mobility, Masonry encouraged the redistribution of labour to match new areas of enterprise and to exploit newly discovered resources.

Taking all of these things together it would seem reasonable to conclude that the overall benefits of Freemasonry, like most other examples of mutual congregation, were probably positive and beneficial, with the many pluses generally outweighing the negatives.

What of the Future?

The central argument of this book is that Freemasonry, like other mutual and benefit societies, prospered when such organisations had economic and social utility. Masonry provided agreeable entertainment and personal improvement, but its overall costs were less than the economic advantages that could be gained. It already has been suggested that this relationship changed from the middle of the twentieth century. An increasing range of state-provided economic safety nets improved family security and negatively impacted on all forms of mutual assurance. New private institutions for saving and insurance provided those with surplus funds the means of assuring their own security in times of adversity. A more mobile 'commuter' society undermined localism and reduced the relevance of local networking. New business arrangements have substituted legal commitments for the 'gentleman's handshake' and the need for personal trust relationships is much reduced. An increasingly secular society has reduced the numbers of men that would profess a belief in a 'supreme being', the bedrock of English regular Freemasonry.

It has not stopped there. New undermining forces continue to appear. Sophisticated electronic communications and social media platforms are now busily undermining face-to-face relationships. Access to internet database information systems puts the individual in direct touch with whatever he needs to know about suppliers and customers, and greatly reduces the need for traditional networks. Professional associations, guaranteeing levels of competence with national and international standards of quality control, consistently reduce the need for trust in the individual. The practical needs once served by Freemasonry have largely disappeared. Of course there is the ever-present possibility that centralised state socialism will collapse under the weight of its top-heavy welfare state systems and require the revival of some forms of small group co-operative effort,[8] but currently this seems a distant prospect.

Today, therefore, Freemasonry exists in a different world and has lost most of its nineteenth- and early twentieth-century relevance. It might now be regarded as a franchising operation with less to offer and a dwindling customer base. Grand Lodges issue and confirm warrants to groups of men to form lodges, in return for annual royalties paid on the membership of those lodges—currently set by the UGLE at a membership fee of £39 and benevolence contribution of £17. These have increased significantly over time as a share of total lodge fees as the Grand Lodges struggle to cope with the costs of large central facilities that were expanded during period of peak membership and cannot now easily be reduced. The UGLE also becomes increasingly remote from its constituent lodges. The active members of Grand Lodge—the effective 'rulers of the Craft'—remain a remote and self-selecting group, largely drawn from elite public schools and the lodges of Oxford and Cambridge universities. It is increasingly unclear from where they draw their authority. Freemasonry's long association with royalty is now becoming tenuous but no progress has been made in engaging the support and approval from ordinary lodge members through open democratic processes. A lack of forums for open debate deprives policymakers of the experience at grass-roots level.

What the membership receive for their contributions, other than simple participatory theatre and social dining, is increasingly unclear. Unsurprisingly, membership continues to contract. Most lodges are now more eager to recruit new members than to find cause to exclude them. Some of the reasons for this have just been discussed, but there are also many others. The average age of membership is now much higher, with a majority in most lodges beyond the age of retirement. Their interest in, and/or capacity for, the use of Freemasonry for business networking purposes is thus greatly diminished. In the age of the individual, where social obstructions to personal happiness and fulfilment are increasingly rejected, the Victorian concept of 'respectability'—i.e. conservative family values of morality, self-restraint, modesty, piety and self-respect—has become less significant. Similarly today, 'reputation' is taken more to mean degrees of celebrity than a statement of personal conduct and general regard in the community. For many young adults a 'bad reputation' becomes a coveted badge of rebellion and rejection of undesirable traditional values.

The nature of Masonic charity has also changed dramatically since the late nineteenth century by being gradually 'anonymised'. It is no longer about a Mason fulfilling his obligation to a brother directly, but contributing to a general fund that is separately, and often distantly, administered. Since the late nineteenth century there has been an increasing 'disconnect' between the giver and the receiver, and for many, charitable contributions have become little more than a 'tax' collected during and after lodge meetings. Many Masons will still join a lodge when moving to a new area and receive a warm welcome, help and support, but that is unlikely to have any financial or business dimension. Similarly, most charitable monies are now passed to the national Masonic Charitable Foundation which no longer focuses closely on Masons and their families, but also distributes a large proportion of its income to a wide variety of non-Masonic charities. In recent years, such generosity has been second only to the National Lottery in charitable donations and it has provided important support for international disaster relief. However, while this may help to improve the public image of Freemasonry, it reduces the direct functionality of lodge charitable collections as far members are concerned. It may also have diminishing public relations effects, as many increasingly question the ethics of Freemasonry and other all-male closed societies, and see such donations as a camouflage to avoid open disclosure of their activities.

Lodges now are no longer simply the product of closely defined communities but their members are increasingly drawn from wide geographical areas, held together by particular sets of interests. 'Class lodges' of one description or another have been a great success and their emergence has been facilitated by improvements in rail, road and public transport facilities. Similarly, multiple lodges in larger towns now often broadly divide themselves by occupation, social class, nationality, recreational activity or some other basis. Visiting between lodges has grown more popular on a local and regional basis although welcoming international visitors has probably become less frequent. They have generally lost their once powerful influence in local politics and economic affairs but they frequently act as influential platforms to bring together multiple ethnic groups and to forge common values and virtues. Bridging the genders continues to prove a troublesome issue for Freemasonry but the emergence of parallel women's Masonry has reduced the difficulties.

In an underemployed and business-disconnected society—a trend set to increase with robotisation, expert systems and a greater longevity—'pleasure' maximisation replaces 'profit' maximization as the driving force in shaping men's behaviour. Today they become Freemasons mainly for social interaction and entertainment among friends. Once having become a member of a lodge they are encouraged to learn and practice ritual, and to advance through its offices. If they enjoy ritual they may seek membership of innumerable side orders and many/ most will aspire to the higher Provincial and Grand Ranks. They are motivated by closely focused 'intra-Masonic interests': pleasure, progression and enjoyment within a closed society, still largely shut away from the everyday world. A report on *The Future of Freemasonry*, published by UGLE in 2017, distils its view of what the Order currently does, and to what it should continue to aspire. It sees a combination of both the old and the new in a loose liberal alliance. Through increasing openness and transparency, it 'instills in its members a moral and ethical approach to life—including thoughtfulness for others, kindness in the community, honesty in business, courtesy in society and fairness in all things'. There are few references to its origins in exclusive mutual support, loyalty to the establishment of Crown and country, the pursuit of esoteric lost secrets and the other principles which underpinned its eighteenth- and nineteenth-century success. It is this flexibility of Freemasonry, and its ability to adjust and reinvent itself for a changing society, that has been the secret of its survival. Its essential duality, as a source of conviviality and entertainment on the one hand, and functional charitable assistance on the other, has enabled it to play up the one as the need for the other has declined—unlike its once more populous competitor mutual societies that disappeared along with the need for their dominant primary function. There is also the ever-present possibility, of course, that nostalgia for an idealised lost past proves as attractive for a new generation threatened by tumultuous change as it did for those that first developed Freemasonry at the beginning of the age of industrialisation. It is an ancient institution capable of continuity as much as it is of change.[9]

MEMBERSHIP OF CORNISH CRAFT LODGES AT YEAR'S END, 1863–1900

Lodge	1863	1870	1875	1880	1885	1890	1895	1900
Love & Honour	60	44	67	67	79	79	110	109
Mt Sinai	34	44	38	74	61	70	98	115
Fortitude	72	67	72	77	66	88	91	81
True & Faithful	11	21	32	55	45	53	63	73
One & All	32	49	89	80	65	62	80	83
Phoenix	50	60	64	70	56	60	50	56
Cornubian	34	60	95	89	74	76	76	89
Peace & Harmony	24	32	55	40	50	54	56	71
St Martin's	33	39	60	53	41	57	66	56
Loyal Victoria	17	27	61	60	56	55	65	70
Druids	31	45	104	100	82	93	94	97
Boscawen	24	58	119	54	47	58	64	79
Dunheved	16	14	30	45	38	22	29	28
St Matthew's	15	15	19	29	31	40	46	35
Meridian	15	21	57	72	61	54	60	56
Three Grand Principles		33	28	31	33	29	44	61
St Anne's		32	46	46	43	38	38	40
Fowey		45	58	73	60	59	42	41
Tregullow		25	47	25	35	47	75	101
Zetland		35	49	58	63	57	68	65
Carew		21	40	84	66	68	68	74
St Andrew's		38	49	45	43	35	46	53
Elliot		21	20	26	25	23	38	34
Tregenna		23	52	48	51	59	72	86
Fort			25	32	33	29	23	0
Duke of Cornwall			26	43	36	36	37	31
Mt Edgcumbe			31	55	56	81	76	118
St Petroc				20	38	36	37	42
Molesworth					26	29	40	47
Cotehele						32	48	69
St Michael's								35
Total	468	869	1433	1551	1465	1559	1800	1995
Average	31	36	53	55	50	53	60	64
Initiations		107	173	104	77		144	132

Source: W. J. Hughan, *Directory for the Provincial Grand Lodge of Cornwall* (annually from 1870)

NUMBER OF MEMBERS IN ROYAL ARCH CHAPTERS WORKING IN CORNWALL BEFORE 1900

Name	Place	Start date	1880	1885	1890	1895	1900
Druids Chapter of Love and Liberality	Redruth	1791					
The Chapter of Light and Truth	Penryn	1795					
Volubian	Falmouth	1810	?	27	34	33	32
Holy Mount	Penzance	1833	18	19	26	35	36
Royal Cornubian	Truro	1862	25	25	28	18	24
St Martin's	Liskeard	1864	26	22	25	30	35
Unity	Fowey		31	21	19	15	19
Rose of Sharon	St Day/Redruth	1867	26	17	?	19	56
Eliot	St Germans	1871	14	17	18	19	11
Mt Edgcumbe	St Austell	1874	25	29	23	16	11
Hayle	Hayle	1874	22	34	40	51	64
Zetland	Saltash	1876	?	11	9	13	19
Dunheved	Launceston	1876	13	10	?	0	0
St Petroc	Bodmin	1877	13	21	23	25	30
St Anne's	East Looe	1878	22	28	26	25	30
Valletort	Callington	1879	10	11	14	28	32
Total			245+	292	285+	327	399

NUMBER OF MEMBERS OF MARK MASON LODGES WORKING IN CORNWALL BEFORE 1900

Name	Place	Start date	1879	1890	1895	1900
Meridian	Millbrook/Redruth	1864	35	?	48	60
Fortitude	Truro	1865	50	28	34	33
Cornubian	Hayle	1865	49	?	46	41
Love and Honour	Falmouth	1866	18	?	30	30
Boscawen	St Day	1868	27	13	24	35
St Michael's	Helston	1874	22	25	22	38
Fort	Newquay	1877	21	25	?	erased
St Austell	St Austell	1881		31	17	18
Lebanon	Fowey/Lostwithiel	1884		18	14	erased
St Anne's	East Looe	1885		28	29	22
St Martins'	Liskeard	1887		27	29	34
St John the Baptist	Penzance	1890		29	41	35
Mt Edgcumbe	Camborne	1890			34	39
Total			222	224+	368+	385

LIST OF PROFESSIONS GIVEN BY INITIATES IN THIRTEEN WEST CORNWALL LODGES: ARRANGED BY SOCIAL GROUP

[Occupations as self-described]

Category 1 (Gentlemen, Property and Business Owners)

Banker	8			Captain	2
Clergyman, Rector/Deacon	3			Major	4
Foreign Consul	1			Colonel	2
Gentleman	162		Navy	Lieutenant	9
Hotel Owner/Proprietor	10			Commander	1
Justice of the Peace	1			Engineer	2
Manufacturer	(unspecified)	4		Midshipman	1
	Gunpowder	1		Surgeon	1
	Boot and Shoe	3	Plantation Owner		1
	Safety Fuse	1	Ship Builder		19
Member of Parliament	5		Ship Owner		2
Military Officer			Tin Stream Proprietor		2
Army	Lieutenant	7	Total		253

Category II (Professional, Managerial, Retail, Services)

Accountant		184		Land (Land Steward)	7
Agent	(unspecified)	36			
	Bank	1		Mineral	2
	Copper	1		Wine	1
	Estate	1	Architect		9
	House	1	Artist		11
			Auctioneer		12

Auditor		1
Author		2
Bank Manager		12
Boat Builder		1
Boot and Shoe Maker/Seller/Factor		13
Brewer		16
Broker	(unspecified)	4
	Mine	1
	Share	1
	Ships'	2
	Stock	3
Builder		83
Bus Proprietor		2
Cab Proprietor		2
Clergyman		59
Clerk of Works/Managing Clerk		1
Clothier		2
Coach/Carriage Builder		7
Confectioner		19
Contractor		10
Conveyancer		1
Curator		1
Dealer (Cattle, Coal, General, Horse, Provisions, Share)		8
Draper		88
Druggist/Chemist		35
	Analytical	1
	Metallurgical	1
	Pharmaceutical	1
Engineer	(unspecified)	192
	Borough	1
	Civil	17
	Electrical	1
	Gas	2
	Marine	7
	Mechanical	3
	Mining	62
	Sanitary	1
	Telephone	1

Esquire		9
Farmer/Yeoman		99
Grocer		163
Harbour Master		1
House Furnisher		2
Insurance Superintendent		1
Ironmonger		25
Jeweller		30
Keeper		
	Coffee House	1
	Boarding House	1
	Hotel	49
	Inn	75
	Livery Stable	1
	Restaurant	1
	Shop	3
	Store	3
Legal		
	Barrister/QC	5
	Solicitor	58
Licensed Victualler		8
Maltster		2
Man of Letters		1
Manager	(unspecified)	3
	Gas Works	5
	Grocers	1
	Outfitters	1
	Wine Bar	1
	Water Works	2
	Works	1
Mariner		
	Master	389
	Officer	4
	Tug Owner	4
Master		
	Monumental Mason	1
	Painter	1
	Smith	1
	Rope Maker	2

Medical		
	Practitioner	12
	Dentist	10
	Doctor	3
	Physician	2
	Surgeon	62
	Vetinary Surgeon	2
Mercer		7
Merchant	(unspecified)	155
	Cloth	1
	Coal	8
	Corn	2
	Diamond	1
	Egg	1
	Fish	1
	Provisions	1
	Seed	2
	Shoe	1
	Spirit	6
	Tailor	1
	Timber	1
	Velvet	1
	Wine	2
Metallurgist		1
Miller		8
Mine		
	Agent	180
	Captain	4
	Contractor	8
	Manager	4
	Prospector	1
	Purser	3
Mineralogist		1
Newsagent		1
Newspaper/Press Editor		3
Organist		4
Outfitter		18
Pawnbroker		1
Post Horse Proprietor		1
Principal of Private School		1

Printer and Stationer		2
Public		
	Borough Surveyor	3
	Civil Servant	2
	Coast Guard Chief Officer	3
	Collector of Taxes	1
	County Fire Officer	1
	Customs Controller	1
	Customs House Officer	1
	Customs Superintendent	1
	High Bailiff (County Court)	2
	Inspector of Mines	3
	Inspector of Schools	1
	Inspector of Weights and Measures	1
	Master of Workhouse/Union	4
	Police Inspector	3
	Police Superintendent	6
	Post Master	1
	Registrar of Births, Deaths and Marriages	1
	Sanitary Inspector	1
	Sheriff	1
	Surveyor of Taxes	1
Railway		
	Contractor	2
	District Manager	1
	Engineer	1
	Inspector of Works	1
	Station Master	10
	Superintendent	3
	Supervisor	1

Traffic Manager		1	Surveyor		13
Seedsman		1		Lloyds	1
Ships' Chandler		7		Mine	1
Superintendent/Supervisor		2		Roads	1
	Insurance	1	Watchmaker		2
	Telegraph	1	Wool Stapler		1
			Total		2,495

Category III (N) (Skilled Non-Manual Employees)

Agent			Military Non-Commissioned Officer			
	Cycle	1	Army		Corporal	1
	Explosive	1			Sergeant	1
	Insurance	7			Sergeant Major	4
	Medical	1			Drill Instructor	2
	Railway	2			Ordnance Depot	1
	Shipping	4			Paymaster	1
Bank Cashier		2	Navy		Artificer	1
Billiard Marker		2			Band Master	1
Bookseller		5			Boatswain	1
Butler		1			Boilermaker (HM Dockyard)	1
Cashier		3			Carpenter	1
Clerk	(unspecified)	20			Clerk	1
	Bankers'	7			Gunner	2
	Consular	1			Instructor	6
	Merchant	3			Master-at-Arms	1
	Post Office	2			Paymaster	1
	Solicitor's	11			Petty Officer	10
	Telegraph	6			Schoolmaster	2
Club Steward		1			Writer	1
Comedian		1	Organist			1
Commercial Traveller		39	Public			
Consular Clerk/Linguist		1			Beadle	1
Draughtsman		2			Coast Guard	12
Florist		1			Customs Clerk	2
Foreman		3			Customs Collector	1
Fruiterer		1			Customs Officer	6
Journalist		8			Excise Officer	7
					Overseer	2

Policeman/ Constable		7
Police Sergeant		1
Post Office Clerk		3
Post Office Sorting Clerk		1
	Rate Collector	1
Railway Clerk		2
Scrivener		1
Secretary		3
Teacher		
	School	57

Art Master	2
Music Teacher	2
Music Master	4
Music Professor	4
Teacher of Mechanics	1
Tutor	2
Telegraphist	9
Time Keeper	1
Tobacconist	1
Writer	5
Total	313

Category III (M) (Skilled Manual Employees)

Amalgamator		2
Artificer		1
Assayer		44
Bacon Curer		1
Bailiff		1
Baker		7
Blacksmith/Smith		50
	Ship's Smith	1
Bookbinder		1
Butcher		18
Cabinet Maker		12
Carpenter/Joiner		20
	Ship's	6
Cooper		7
Cordwainer		7
Crucible Maker		2
Currier		6
Cutler		1
Decorator		7
Diver		1
Dyer		2
Electrician		5
Engine Fitter		2
Farrier		1
Fitter		7

Founder (Brass, Iron)		14
Fruit Grower		1
Gamekeeper		1
Gardener		10
Hairdresser		7
Huntsman		1
Lime Burner		1
Machinist		3
Market Gardener		4
Mariner		37
	Mate	6
	Pilot	41
Mechanic		3
Millwright		1
Miner	(unspecified)	335
	Dresser	9
	Smelter	3
	Streamer	3
Moulder		1
Painter		13
Pattern Maker		5
Photographer		7
Piano Tuner		1
Plumber		3
	Brazier	1

Tin man	1	Silversmith	1
Printer/Stationer	24	Smelter	3
Railway		Stone Mason/Dresser	22
Engine Driver	3	Tailor	33
Engineer	1	Tin Dresser	9
Roper	1	Tin Streamer	3
Sadler	7	Tyler (Masonic?)	1
Sail Maker	7	Upholsterer	2
Shipbuilder's Assistant	1	Wheelwright	6
Shipwright	14	Wool Comber	1
Shoemaker	7	Total	870

Category IV (Semi-Skilled Employees)

Assistant	1		Fireman	1
Carrier	2		Guard	7
Chemist's Assistant	1	Student		
Coachman	1		Chemistry	1
Fisherman	2		Law	1
Grocer's Assistant	1		Medical	4
Labourer	3		Mining	12
Lay Assistant	1		Pharmaceutical	1
Millman	1	Overseer Assistant		1
Military		Pensioner		2
Royal Navy Seaman	1	Postman		4
		Steward (ship's)		1
Royal Navy Sickbay Attendant	1	Waiter		3
		Total		60
Railway				

Total Number of Members with Specified Occupation	3,991
Total Number of Occupations	357
Total Number of Members with no Specified Occupation	273

MANAGERIAL POSITIONS IN CORNISH MINES HELD BY MEMBERS OF MASONIC LODGES IN WEST CORNWALL IN 1883[1]

Lodge	Position	Mine
Boscawen, Chacewater		
Moses Bawden	Manager	Drakewalls, Gunnislake
Nicholas Clymo	Agent	West Seton, Camborne
James Craze	Agent	West Shepherds, Perranzabuloe
James Evans	Manager	Penhale & Barton, St Enoder
William Giles	Agent	Wheal Hope, Chacewater
John Gribble	Agent	West Tolgus, Illogan
George C. Hancock	Purser[2]	New Kitty, St Agnes
" "	Agent	West Polbreen, St Agnes
" "	Purser	Trevaunance United, St Agnes
Samuel Harris	Agent	West Vor, Breage
Thomas Richards	Agent	Hingston Down, Gunnislake
William Williams	Agent	South Condurrow, Camborne
Cornubian, Hayle		
Thomas Hodge	Manager	West Godolphin, Breage
" "	Manager	Wheal Grenville, Camborne
Richard Goldsworthy	Manager	Wheal Langford, Gunnislake
William Rowe	Agent	West Wheal Francis, Camborne
Druids, Redruth		
Charles Craze	Agent	South Frances, Redruth
Frederick W. Dabb	Purser	Wheal Jewel, St Hilary
" "	Purser	St Aubyn United, Gwennap
Stephen Davey	Manager	North Penstruthal, Gwennap
" "	Manager	South Penstruthal, Gwennap
" "	Manager	Cathedral Consols, Gwennap
Stephen Davey Jnr	Agent	" " "
Francis William Michell	Manager	Wheal Union
William Pascoe	Agent	South Crofty, Pool
Richard Pryor	Manager	Basset and Buller Consols, Redruth
Thomas Pryor	Purser	Wheal Peevor
" "	Purser	West Wheal Peevor, Camborne
" "	Purser	West Wheal Seton, Camborne
James Henry Reynolds	Purser	Wheal Basset

R.W. Rickard	Owner	Basset Valley, Redruth
William Teague	Manager	Carn Brea, Camborne
William Thomas	Agent	New Cooks Kitchen, Camborne
" "	Agent	West Wheal Frances, Camborne
William Tregay	Purser	Mount Carbis, Redruth
Thomas Trelease	Captain	North Herodsfoot, Liskeard
Thomas Trevena	Manager	Wheal Agar, Redruth
W.C. Trevena	Manager	Wheal Basset

Fortitude, Truro

James Nancarrow	Agent	Old Shepherds, Newlyn
Richard Southey	Agent	Wheal Jane, Chacewater
Charles Thomas	Agent	Cooks Kitchen, Camborne

Fowey, Fowey

| William Polkinhorne | Purser | Phoenix and West Phoenix, Callington |

Mount Edgcumbe, Camborne

Francis Hodge	Captain	West Basset, Redruth
" "	Agent	West Godolphin, Breage
Peter Temby	Captain	Herodsfoot, Liskeard

Mount Sinai, Penzance

Stephen Harvey James	Purser	Botallack, St Just
Richard White	Purser	Levant, Pendeen
William Vivian	Manager	Wheal Coates United, St Agnes

Phoenix Lodge of Honour and Prudence, Truro

John James	Agent	Mounts Bay Consols, Breage
William Henry Martin	Manager	Polcrebo, Helston
John Tregoning	Purser	Killifreth, Chacewater

Tregullow, St Day

| William Pascoe | Manager | New Fowey Consols, Tywardreath |
| John Nicholls | Manager | Violet Seton, Camborne |

True and Faithful, Helston

William H. Argall	Purser	Great Wheal Fortune, Helston
" "	Agent	Mounts Bay Consols, Breage
" "	Manager	Wheal Trebarvah, Marazion
John Rowe	Agent	Wheal Trebarvah, Marazion

REPRESENTATIVES FROM THIRTEEN WEST CORNWALL LODGES GIVEN ACTIVE PROVINCIAL GRAND RANK, 1890–1895

Name	Lodge	Profession	Grand Rank
Anderton, E.D.	Phoenix 331	Merchant	PGSec 1895
Angel, R.	Fortitude 131	Police Superintendent	PGStB 1892
Baker, W.K.	Tregenna 1272	Merchant	PJGW 1894
Bazeley, J.	Cornubian 450	Grocer/Draper	PGReg 1895
Brewer, J.	Druids 589	Station Manager	PJGD 1895
Bryant, C.	Phoenix 331	Bank Cashier	PGTreas 1893
Carne, J.M.	Love & Honour 75	Merchant	PSGD 1894
Carus-Wilson, E.W.	Phoenix 331	Banker	PGStB. 1894
Chegwidden, W.L.	Druids 589	Agent/Builder	PGSW 1895
Chilcott, S.H.	Phoenix 331	Solicitor	PGReg 1892
Chirgwin, T.	Fortitude 131	Accountant	PGS 1890
Colenzo, W.	Mt Sinai 121	Painter	PGStB 1893
Collins, W.J.	Tregullow 1006	Engineer	PGStB 1894
Colville-Smith, P.	Phoenix 331	Gentleman	PSGW 1895
Crewes, J.C.R.	Fortitude 131	Accountant	PAGSec 1890
Dale, W.	Mt Sinai 121	Solicitor	PGReg 1890
Dunstan, R.	True & Faithfull [sic] 318	Accountant	PGStwd 1892
Ellis, W.	True & Faithfull [sic] 318	Rope Maker	PGPurst 1891
Edgcumbe, W.H.	Cornish 2369	Deputy Grand Master	PGM
Edwards, E.	Fortitude 131	Hair Dresser	PGSwB 1890
Fraser-Frizell, R.	Fortitude 131	Clergyman	PGChap 1890
Graves-Sawle, Sir C.	Cornish 2369	Gentleman	DPGM 1890
Grylls, T.R.	Love & Honour 75	Banker	PGStB 1891
Hall, W.	Boscawen 699	Draper	PJGD 1893
Hawking, W.T.	Fortitude 131	Schoolmaster	PGDC 1892
Hughan, W.J.	Love & Honour 75	Merchant	PSGW 1892
Huxtable, E.	Phoenix 331	Clergyman	PGChap 1891
James, R.	True & Faithful 318	Accountant	PGTyler 1891
Johns, W.J.	Fortitude 131	Accountant	PJGW 1893
Jose, J.	Tregullow 1006	Gentleman	PJGW 1890
Kendall, Rev. T.S.	Fortitude 131	Clergyman	PGOrg 1892
Kistler, T.H.	Druids 589	Jeweller	PSGD 1891
Langdon, J.	Fortitude 131	Gardener	PAsGPurst 1890
Mack, T.C.	Fortitude 131	Accountant	PSGD 1891
Mockridge, G.R.	Mt Sinai 121	Superintendent Telegraph	PAGDC 1892

Monk, M.J.	Fortitude 131	Organist	PGOrg 1894
Petty, H.M.	Love & Honour 75	Clergyman	PGChap 1891
Polglase, J.P.	Love & Honour 75	Accountant	PAGDC 1893
Ratcliffe, A.E.	True & Faithful 318	Gentleman	PGReg 1894
Reed, G.G.	Love & Honour 75	RN Lieut	PJGW 1895
Retallick, J.	Boscawen 699	Commercial Traveller	PGStB 1895
Rodda, F.	Fortitude 131	Printer	PDGDC 1891
Rodda, R.	Druids 589	Accountant	PJGD 1895
Ross, J.J.	Mt Sinai 121	Army Major	PSGW 1891
Rowe, Richard	Mt Edgcumbe 1544	Mine Agent	PGDC 1894
Sampson, M.	Mt Sinai 121	Draper	PSGD 1895
Simpson, S.J.	Mt Sinai 121	Draper	PGOrg 1890
Staff, G.T.A.	Tregenna 1272	Surgeon	PSGD 1892
Taylor, T.	True & Faithful 318	Schoolmaster	PGTreas 1891
Timmsins, G.	Tregullow 1006	Inn Keeper	PGStd 1893
Tresidder, S.	Love & Honour 75	Accountant	PAGSec 1891
Trevenen, W.	True & Faithful 318	Solicitor	PGReg 1891
Wagner, W.	Cornubian	School Principal	PGS 1890
Wales, W.	Druids 589	Auctioneer	PGSofW 1893
Wearne, J.	Tregenna 1272	Printer	PJGD 1890
Willey, J.	True & Faithful 318	Grocer	PGS 1893

Definitions of abbreviations

PGM	Provincial Grand Master
PSGW	Provincial Senior Grand Warden
PGChap	Provincial Grand Chaplain
PGReg	Provincial Grand Registrar
PGDC	Provincial Grand Director of Ceremonies
PGSofW	Provincial Grand Superintendent of Works
PSGD	Provincial Senior Grand Deacon
PAGSec	Provincial Assistant Grand Secretary
PGOrg	Provincial Grand Organist
PGPurst	Provincial Grand Pursuivant
PAsGPurst	Provincial Assistant Grand Pursuivant
DPGM	Deputy Provincial Grand Master
PJGW	Provincial Junior Grand Warden
PGTreas	Provincial Grand Treasurer
PGSec	Provincial Grand Secretary
PGSwB	Provincial Grand Sword Bearer
PDGDC	Provincial Deputy Grand Director of Ceremonies
PJGD	Provincial Junior Grand Deacon
PAGDC	Provincial Assistant Grand Director of Ceremonies
PGStB	Provincial Grand Standard Bearer
PGS	Provincial Grand Steward
PGTyler	Provincial Grand Tyler

APPENDIX 7

THE SECRETARIES AND TREASURERS OF SOME CORNISH ANCIENT ORDER OF FORESTER COURTS: SHOWING THOSE WITH MASONIC AFFILIATIONS

Court 'One and All', No. 3470, Truro

Secretary	1867	Hugh T. Pearce	
	1869	Anthony Thomas Blamey	Initiated Fortitude Lodge, 1869
	1871	J.H. James	
Treasurer	1876	William Lake	Initiated Fortitude Lodge, 1862
	1879	William Kendall	" " " , 1879
	1890	Theophilus L. Dorrington	" " " , 1865
	1898	Richard Burrow	" " " , 1892

Court 'Riviere', No. 3843, Hayle

Secretary	1867	William Quick	Initiated Cornubian Lodge, 1873
	1877	George Stevens	" " " , 1872
	1889	Thomas William Vincent	" " " , 1892
	1893	M.A.C. Trebilcock	Mt Edgcumbe Lodge, 1884
Treasurer	1876	George Stevens	Initiated Cornubian Lodge, 1872
	1877	Thomas Mills	" " " , 1875
	1901	John Broad Williams	" " " , 1898

Court 'Druids', No. 3908, Redruth

Secretary	1867	Edward Harry	
	1872	John Polkinghorne	Founder of Druids Lodge, 1862
	1880	Richard Sobey Behenna	Initiated Mt Edgcumbe Lodge, 1886
Treasurer	1876	Richard Sobey Behenna	Initiated Mt Edgcumbe Lodge, 1886
	1880	John Polkinghorne	Founder of Druids Lodge, 1862
	1900	T.M. Samson	

Court 'De Dunstanville', No. 6321, Camborne

Secretary	1877	Alfred Richards	Initiated Boscawen Lodge, 1869
	1880	W. Cock	
	1883	Frank Bartle	
	1884	F.H. Richards	
	1889	Charles W. Eddy	
Treasurer	1877	John Charles Burrow	Initiated Mt Edgcumbe Lodge, 1877
	1890	John Bawden Vial	" " " , 1901

THE NUMBER OF ANNUITANTS OF THE ROYAL MASONIC BENEVOLENT INSTITUTION IN LONDON AND SOME PROVINCES IN 1900

District	Total Male Annuitants	Total Widow Annuitants	Number of Lodges	Number of Masons	Ratio Total Annuitants to Lodges	Ratio Total Annuitants to Members
London	76	94	488	32,000 *est.*	1:3	1:176
Provinces						
Cheshire	0	0	54	2,729	–	–
Devonshire	10	12	59	4,303	1:3	1:196
Essex	4	10	44	2,352	1:3	1:168
Hamp. & I of W	5	8	48	4,114	1:4	1:316
Kent	10	21	65	4,550	1:2	1:147
East Lancs.	12	7	113	7,345 *est.*	1:6	1:387
West Lancs.	0	0	121	7,910	–	–
Suffolk	5	6	22	1,045	1:2	1:95
West Yorks.	20	16	82	5,330 *est.*	1:2	1:148

Estimated membership figures based on an expected average of 65 members per lodge, as suggested by the West Lancashire figures.

Source: *Annual Report, Regulations, and List of the Governors and Subscribers of the Royal Masonic Benevolent Institution for Aged Freemasons and Widows of Freemasons 1890, 1895, 1900*

MASONIC, FRIENDLY AND BENEVOLENT SOCIETIES IN WEST CORNWALL: WITH MEMBERSHIP FOR 1886

Four Groups

Central, South: Truro, Falmouth, Penryn, Perranarworthal, Devoran
Central, North: Redruth, St Day, Camborne, Chacewater, Lanner, St Agnes
The Lizard: Helston, Porthleven, Lizard, Mawgan, Mullion
The West: Hayle, St Ives, St Just, Penzance, St Burian

FM = Free and Accepted Masons; OF = Manchester Unity of Oddfellows;
AF = Ancient Order of Foresters; OR = Order of Rechabites

Place	Order	Name	When Established	Numbers of Members 1886/7
Central, South				
Truro	FM	Fortitude	1814	67
	OF	Temple of Peace	1845	454
	AF	One & All	1860	367
	OR	Rose of the City	1881	23
Falmouth	FM	Love & Honour	1751	76
	AF	Pendennis	1861	400 *est.*
Penryn	FM	Three Grand Principles	1863	33
	AF	Unity	1863	270 *est.*
Perranarworthal	AF	Concord	1865	120 *est.*
Devoran	OF	Robartes	1862	230
Central, North				
Redruth	FM	Druids	1851	83
	OF	Cornubian	1858	316
	AF	Druids	1862	244
	OR	Hand & Heart	1881	240
St Day	FM	Tregullow	1865	37
Camborne	FM	Mt Edgcumbe	1875	56

Place	Order	Name	When Established	Numbers of Members 1886/7
	OF	Basset	1859	275
	AF	De Dunstanville	1877	106
	OR	One & All	1884	54
Chacewater	FM	Boscawen	1857	49
	OF	Florence Nightingale	1857	107
Lanner	OF	Lannarth	1865	72
St Agnes	OF	St Agnes	1845	187
The Lizard				
Helston	FM	True & Faithful	1800	50
	OF	Duke of Cornwall	1859	255
	AF	Penrose	1862	240 *est.*
Porthleven	OR	Star of the West	1880	39
Lizard	OF	Lizard	1879	39
Mawgan	AF	Pride of the South	1869	95 *est.*
Mullion	AF	St Melina	1866	140 *est.*
The West				
Hayle	FM	Cornubian	1848	64
	OF	St Aubyn	1870	80
	AF	Riviere	1862	210 *est.*
	OR	Jas Teare	1874	133
St Ives	FM	Tregenna	1869	52
	AF	Welcome All	1872	85 *est.*
Penzance	FM	Mount Sinai	1813	68
	AF	Queen of the West	1861	400 *est.*
	OR	Guiding Star	1877	300
St Just	OR	Lafrowda	1873	269
St Burrian	OR	First & Last	1885	91

CORNISH MASONS WITH JOINT MEMBERSHIP OF FOWEY LODGE NO. 977 AND COURT TREFFRY NO. 4184, FOWEY, 1863–1900

Name	Occupation	Initiated Fowey	Age	Joined Treffry
Abbott, William	Accountant	1865	21	1873
Bate, Richard	Master Mariner	1864	29	1865
Beale, Richard	Master Mariner	1866	24	1868
Beale, William	Master Mariner	1869	32	1867
Biddick, George	Master Mariner	1866	34	1873
Cann, Ralph T.	Surgeon	1896	33	1897
Clunes, James	Gentleman	1881	24	1879
Cossentine, Albert	Farmer	1882	31	1871
Couch, Nathaniel C.	Master Mariner	1864	29	1866
Davis, Alfred P.	Merchant	1881	21	1882
Davis, A. Percy	Surgeon	1872	21	1872
Dennison, Francis	Draper	1882	?	1880
Dingle, William	Master Mariner	1875	28	1871
Dyer, Charles	Master Mariner	1873	26	1873
Dyer, John	Master Mariner	1863	?	1876
Edwards, Richard	Master Mariner	1887	?	1875
George, Thomas	Master Mariner	1876	26	1870
Gully, Joshua	Master Mariner	1875	25	1870
Harvey, William	Master Mariner	1863	?	1870
Hawken, Charles	Blacksmith	1864	27	1863
Hawken, Henry J.	Master Mariner	1874	26	1873
Hockin, John	?	1879	?	1882
Isbell, John Pain	House Decorator	1882	40	1863
Johns, Joseph	Master Mariner	1874	?	1865
Luke, William T.	Master Mariner	1865	28	1883
Martin, William	Master Mariner	1876	24	1870
Mitchell, William	Miner	1887	33	1889
Moon, William	Shipwright	1865	40	1864
Murphy, Jeremiah	Master Mariner	1881	26	1875
Pearce, Samuel	Inn Keeper	1865	40	1865
Phillips, William	Station Master	1877	33	1867
Puckey, Joseph	Seaman RN	1879	26	1880

Rescorl, John	Master Mariner	1870	?	1865
Richards, Thomas	Master Mariner	1869	?	1873
Rundle, William	Merchant	1865	41	1873
Sadler, John	Master Mariner	1884	45	1881
Scantlebury, Thomas	Master Mariner	1874	38	1872
Sennett, Thomas M.	Schoolmaster	1879	24	1879
Slade, John	Shipbuilder	1864	?	1863
Slade, Thomas H.	Master Mariner	1893	?	1890
Slade, Thomas	Master Mariner	1863	?	1864
Slade, William Salt	Ships' Carpenter	1863	28	1863
Smith, Joseph	Master Mariner	1864	22	1871
Smith, William	Sailmaker	1884	?	1870
Stebbins, James	Master Mariner	1880	39	1872
Sweet, William	Blacksmith	1873	60	1863
Sweet, William T.	Butcher	1881	28	1875
Tadd, Samuel	Master Mariner	1881	?	1873
Tamblin, William	Master Mariner	1881	?	1873
Thomas, Samuel	Draper	1863	30	1865
Toms, James	Master Mariner	1864	36	1877
Toms, William J.	Master Mariner	1882	?	1876
Treffry, J. de Cressy	Merchant	1880	?	1877
Treffry, Spencer T.	Gentleman	1881	24	1877
Vincent, William	Master Mariner	1873	27	1864
Wellington, James	Chemist	1867	38	1864
Wellington, William	Petty Officer RN	1877	41	1865
Williams, Francis B.	Farmer / Butcher	1870	28	1873
Williams, Joseph M.	Innkeeper	1884	38	1883
Williams, John	Innkeeper	1879	32	1876

MARITIME MEMBERS OF THE LODGE OF LOVE & HONOUR NO. 75, FALMOUTH, 1801–1900[1]

[*NB Transcription problems may have resulted in the names of members being misspelt. Ages given where available.*]

Date	Name		Occupation	From[2]
1801	Charles White		Mariner	Falmouth
1801	Richard Harvey		Mariner	"
1801	Patrick Ryan		Mariner	"
1801	Richard James		Mariner	"
1801	Stephen Bell		Mariner	"
1801	William Horswell		Mariner	"
1801	Alexander Grey		Mariner	"
1801	Henry Fenner		Mariner	Flushing
1801	John Marston		Mariner	Falmouth
1801	John Wade	40	Mariner	"
1801	Charles Jenking		Mariner	"
1801	Thomas Dunstan	22	Mariner	"
1801	John Latham Clerk	26	Mariner	America
1803	Thomas Temple	32	Mariner	Devon
1803	William Gittins	28	Mariner	Kent
1803	Robert Formage	31	Mariner	Kent
1804	John Carpenter		Mariner	Falmouth
1804	James Jenkins		Mariner	"
1805	Charles Painter	23	Mariner	"
1805	Anders Jorgen Dahl		Mariner	Denmark
1805	Francis Pawson		Mariner	Falmouth
1806	David Williams		Mariner	"
1806	Jean Henry Schutt		Mariner	Denmark
1807	Richard Withiel		Mariner	Falmouth
1807	Robert Goodfellow		Mariner	"
1807	Edward Vinnicombe		Mariner	"
1807	James Renshaw		Mariner	America
1807	John Byng Nicholson		Mariner	America
1807	David Absolom	22	Mariner	Yarmouth
1808	Nathaniel Murphy	34	Mariner	
1808	William Jackson	35	Mariner	
1808	Thomas Hutchinson	27	Mariner	
1808	William Stratford	31	Mariner	Falmouth
1808	Thomas B. Sulivan	30	Captain RN	Mylor

1808	William Rogers	27	Capt. HM Packet, 'Chichester'	Falmouth
1808	Bartholomew James	57	Captain RN	Mylor
1808	John Haswell	32	Captain RN	"
1808	Nicholas Pocock	22	Captain HM Packet, 'Princess Mary'	Falmouth
1808	Samuel Cock	40	Lieutenant RN	Blackhead
1808	Robert Sibson	45	Mariner	Cumberland
1808	Richard L. Davis	44	Captain HM Packet, 'Manchester'	Falmouth
1810	Edward Lawrence	38	Captain HM Packet	
1810	Robert Tullock	30	Mariner	Falmouth
1810	John Williams	26	Mariner	"
1810	William James	32	Mariner	"
1810	Thomas Lawrence	40	Mariner	"
1810	Simon Davey	38	Mariner	"
1810	Henry D. Gibbon	36	Mariner	"
1810	Daniel Braily	35	Mariner	"
1810	John Foxton	35	Mariner	"
1810	William Futtock	42	Mariner	St. Mawes
1810	William McDonald	33	Mariner	Falmouth
1812	James A. Stevens	22	Captain of Packet	Falmouth
1812	John Britton	40	Captain of Packet	"
1812	Thomas Sampson	32	Captain of Packet	"
1812	Robert Burton	30	Mariner	"
1812	Peter T. Hill	36	Mariner	"
1812	Richard M. Teed	25	Lieutenant RN	"
1812	Abraham Illingworth	25	Surgeon RN	"
1813	Anthony Barker	26	Mariner	"
1813	Charles Sarle	24	Merchant	Lisbon
1813	Richard Crosby	23	Mariner	Falmouth
1813	John Quick	40	Captain of Packet	"
1813	James Wallace	25	Lieutenant RN	"
1813	Thomas Cooper	24	Mariner	"
1813	Henry Glanville	35	Mariner	"
1813	William Hodge	22	Mariner	"
1813	James Porteous	40	Captain of Packet	"
1814	John Button		Mariner	"
1814	Henry Granville		Mariner	"
1816	Richard Dunstan		Mariner	"
1816	John Bullock		Captain of Packet	"
1816	Robert Snell		Lieutenant RN	Mylor
1816	William E. Brown		Captain of Packet	Falmouth
1816	Peter Gilberg		Mariner	Holland
1816	John Norris		Mariner	London
1816	John Elliot		Mariner	
1816	Thomas Carter		Captain of Packet	
1816	Malachi Donellan		Lieutenant RN	
1817	William Richards		Mariner	Falmouth
1817	Thomas Jones		Lieutenant RN	
1818	Christian Sauerland[3]		Mariner	Denmark
1819	? Feliciano[4]		Mariner	Portugal
1820	Thomas Baldock		Captain of Packet	
1820	George Doherty		Surgeon of Packet	
1820	Thomas Valentine Cook		Lieutenant RN	
1820	William H. Box		Surgeon of Packet	
1820	James O'Connor		Surgeon of Packet	

1822	William James		Lieutenant RN	
1823	John Burrill	35	Mariner	
1826	Joseph Martyn	29	Gunner of HM Packet, 'Cygnet'	
1826	William Baynes	25	Mariner	Falmouth
1826	Robert Ede[5]		Captain HM Packet, 'Speldrake'	
1828	Barthol. Karsten[6]	50	Mariner	
1828	James Teague	33	Captain HM Packet, 'Kingfisher'	
1828	William Blamey	27	Captain HM Packet, 'Osborn'	
1829	Charles Ralph	22	Mariner	Falmouth
1830	John K. Martyn	23	Mariner HM Packet, 'Swallow'	
1835	Joseph Vivian	23	Commander of Merchant Ship	
1840	Fred. A.B. Sietzes[7]	32	Captain of Merchant Ship	Dordt, Holland
1841	Thomas Dunningham	28	Master Mariner	
1844	Thomas S. Beale		Captain Schooner 'Eliza Scott'	London
1845	John Harvey	30	Command of Brigantine 'Hope'	Liverpool
1845	Wm Hy Willoughby	30	Captain Schooner 'Maltas' (?)	Portsmouth
1845	George Penny		Master Mariner	
1845	Thomas Hiscock[8]		Command of Schooner 'Pidgeon'	
1846	George Penny[9]			
1846	Hy Bowker Downing	26	Command of Schooner	Liverpool
1847	John Pickering[10]	40	Ship's Master	
1847	Henry Whitehead[11]	38	" "	
1847	John H. Taylor	26	" "	
1847	Harry Lynch		Mate Brig 'Hume'	
1848	William Blair	34	Master Mariner	
1848	Christopher Bell		" "	
1848	Peter Gunderson	31	" "	Finland
1849?	? Enogrin		" "	Abo, Finland
1849?	Joseph Manning[12]	33	Mariner	
1850	Augustus Permion		Mariner	Germany
1850?	John Watson	30	Mariner	
1851	Edward Hosken	34	Master Mariner	Sunderland
1851	Kinick Berthelsen	36	" "	Copenhagen
1851	Thomas Aanensen		" "	Jersey
1851	Richard Pincher[13]		" "	London
1851	C. Johann Hasse		" "	Denmark
1851	Thomas Stevens		" "	
1852	Hendick Eddes	27	Master of 'Galliot Venillie'	Dordt, Holland
1853	Cornelius Ingerman	29	Commander of Brig 'Kormeet'	Rotterdam
1853	Albert Hangeland	26	Ship's Master	Norway
1853	James Rhymer	30	Ship's Master Brig 'Phoenetian'[14]	
1853	Albert Firth	27	Ship's Master Brig 'Amarath'	
1853	Joseph Shelford	26	Ship's Master	Liverpool
1853	George Hunter	32	Ship's Master	Sunderland
1853	Wm Crowell	33	Ship's Master	Sunderland
1853	John Lucas	22	Ship's Master	Shields
1853	John Middleton	28	Ship's Master	Shields
1853	John Boag	28	Ship's Master Barque 'Otodine'	
1853	Charles W. Weatherley	25	Ship's Master Barque 'Boadicia'	
1853	John Harrison	23	Ship's Master Barque 'Nairn'	
1853	James Cousens	37	Ship's Master Barque 'Druid'	
1853	John Cooper	36	Ship's Master	Dundee
1853	Thomas T. Jarvis	33	Ship's Master	Southwark
1853	Malcolm Campbell	26	Ship's Master	Scotland

Year	Name	Age	Rank	Ship	Place
1853	Thomas Parkin	38	Ship's Master		Sunderland
1853	Henry Thomas Cloake	28	Ship's Master		Sunderland
1853	Wm. Atkinson Robson	50	Ship's Master		Sunderland
1853	John Otter	41	Ship's Master Brig 'Edward Bennet'		
1853	James Cape	28	Master Mariner		Liverpool
1853	Michael Vowells[15]	36	" "		Falmouth
1853	Timothy Laing[16]		" "		London
1854	Jens A. Holmboe	25	Master Mariner		
1855	James Dennison	25	" "	Brig 'Victoria'	S. Shields
1855	Henrick Hoenke[17]		" "		Bremen
1855	Ralph H. Armstrong	23	" "		Northumb'lnd
1855	Peter Tait	30	" "		Falmouth
1855	James Adie[18]	33	" "	Barque 'Brothers'	Hull
1856	John Lenty[19]		" "		
1856	John Gilison		" "		
1856	John Gustav Regnell	29	" "	Brig 'La Plata'	Gottenberg
1857	William Smart		" "	Bark 'Francis Yates'	London
1857	Ambrose Gibson[20]	24	Mariner		
1858	Charles Donkin		Master Mariner		Falmouth
1858	Adolph C. Gieschen		" "		
1858	Johann G. Lange		" "		
1858	Jurgen Kroll[21]		" "		
1858	Christian L. Kohn[22]		" "		
1858	Charles Robertson		" "		
1858	David Cock		" "		Falmouth
1858	George Ellery		" "		Falmouth
1858	Louis Valentine Martin		" "		
1859	Escajadillo Vincent		" "		
1859	Hans Julius Andresen		" "		Denmark
1859	David Lewis		" "		
1859	Henry Strathen		" "		
1859	William Cooper		" "		Falmouth
1859	Euginis Maranelli		" "		
1859	Thomas Wilson Cases[23]		" "		
1860	Richard Gilbert		" "	Schooner 'Revenge'	Bristol
1860	Matteo Fabro		" "	Austrian ship from Venice	
1860	Daniel S. Stanwood	24	" "		USA
1860	Eric Ludwig Deurell	27	" "		Sweden
1860	Klaas J. Zanerdyk	30	" "		Groningen
1860	Douwe J. Zanerdyk	34	" "		Groningen
1860	William H. Valler[24]		" "		
1860	Christian M. Andresen	41	" "		Denmark
1860	Diedrich Herman Siefkes[25]		" "		
1860	? Hjorth[26]		" "		Bremen
1860	? Branfuhr		" "		Holstein
1861	August E. Didron	36	" "	Schooner 'Venus'	Stockholm
1861	Pehr D. Hogsham	48	" "		Sweden
1861	Andreas M. Pettersen	36	" "		Sweden
1861	Carl A. Svanljung	23	" "		Finland[27]
1861	William Simeston	28	" "		Kirkwall
1861	Henrick P. Bradhering	29	" "		Hamburg
1861	Jean J. Cassier	30	" "		Sweden
1861	Guiseppe Piaggio		" "		
1861	Heinrich H. Meyer	32	" "		Sweden

Year	Name	Age			Place
1861	Francisco Bussolino		"	"	
1861	Johann Sjolander	13	"	"	Sweden
1861	Peter H. Korff	24	"	"	Mecklenburg
1861	William P. Hutchinson	26	"	"	London
1861	Antonio Petravich	28	"	"	Austria
1861	Peter Stehr	25	"	"	Hamburg
1861	Henry H. Meyers	30	"	"	Belgium
1861	Daniel Mollier	39	"	"	Mecklenburg
1861	Heinrich Adolph Korne	28	"	"	
1861	Micheli A. Vucasovich	31	"	"	Austria
1861	Lars Johann Westerlund	33	"	"	Sweden[28]
1862	Herman Rasmers		"	"	Bremen
1862	Arthur Bracey	28	"	"	
1862	Eric L. Deurell		"	"	
1862	Fritz Pieper		"	"	
1862	T. Nicholas Sarowsky		"	"	Hamburg
1862	Thomas Casey		"	"	Falmouth
1863	Christian Baunbeck		"	"	Copenhagen
1863	William Donaldson	26	"	"	
1863	Cornelius W. Timmer		"	"	Holland
1863	Peter Jacob		"	"	Holland
1863	Erdman C. Freers		"	"	Hamburg
1863	D. van der Steene		"	"	Belgium
1863	Carl A. Svanljung		"	"	
1864	John Staples		"	"	
1865	Eugimo Gambaro[29]		"	"	Falmouth
1865	Macsimo Carranza	31	"	"	Spain
1865	Philip Bisson		"	"	Penryn
1865	Richard Pearce	42	"	"	Falmouth
1866	Elijah Wild		"	"	Falmouth
1866	Henry Smith	32	"	"	
1866	Caspar Bugdahl		"	"	Germany
1866	Adolphus Steigerstahl		"	"	Germany
1867	Sjoerd Schaafsman	28	"	"	Holland
1867	William Smith[30]		"	"	
1867	Jacob Rowe		"	"	Falmouth
1867	Francis J. Polglaze		"	"	Liverpool
1867	Christopher Minto	35	"	"	Sunderland
1867	Robert Fowler		"	"	London
1867	Edward B. Eastwich[31]		"	"	London
1867	Francois J. Storms	33	"	"	Antwerp
1868	Julius Rosenberg	36	"	"	Prussia
1868	Alfred Lietke	30	"	"	Prussia
1868	Peter Farquhar	31	"	"	Sunderland
1868	William Northey	37	"	"	Falmouth
1868	Edward Wilce		"	"	Truro
1869	William Bull	62	"	"	Falmouth
1869	Joh Gibson[32]		"	"	Blyth
1869	John James Ormiston	27	"	"	Kings Lynn
1870	Richard C. Gilbert[33]	23	"	"	Falmouth
1870	John Henry Sawle	29	"	"	St Mawes
1870	Samuel H. Soules	36	"	"	Bath, USA
1872	Johann H. Kluge	28	"	"	Germany
1872	Richard Skinner	40	"	"	

Year	Name	Age			Place
1872	Edward Wilse		"	"	
1873	John Cook	27	"	"	Liverpool
1873	Johann H. Lokander	21	"	"	Falmouth
1873	Soren Natvig	27	"	"	Norway[34]
1874	James Benney	25	"	"	Falmouth
1874	John Bibbings	29	"	"	Cardiff
1874	William Osborn	31	"	"	Yarmouth
1874	Robert Whitburn	24	"	"	Truro
1875	James George Leaity	23	"	"	Falmouth
1876	Charles S. Jarvis	24	"	"	Falmouth
1876	James Richards	31	"	"	Wales
1876	John Roskilly	44	"	"	St Stephens
1879	George Henry Gilbert		"	"	Falmouth
1882	Edward Yorker		"	"	Liverpool
1890	John Bevan Kendall	38	"	"	Falmouth
1893	Alfred Jarvis		"	"	Salcombe
1900	Robert O. Williams		"	"	Port Madoc
1900	George Woolcock		"	"	Falmouth

OCCUPATIONS OF THE MASTERS OF THE LODGE OF LOVE AND HONOUR NO. 75, FALMOUTH, 1850–1900[1]

Date	Name	Occupation	Date	Name	Occupation
1850	William R. Ellis	Auctioneer	1877	Arthur Harris	Surgeon
1851	George Passmore	Chemist	1878	Harry Tily	Solicitor
1852	Joseph Ellis	Tailor	1879	Wilson Fox	Solicitor
1853	John Williams	Surgeon	1880	Joseph Wallace	Innkeeper
1854/5	Edward Gilbert	Engineer	1881	William Rogers	Accountant
1856	John Williams	Surgeon	1882	Richard Carter	Hotelier
1857	Frederick Williams	Sailmaker	1883	James Polglase	Accountant
1858	William R. Ellis	Auctioneer	1884	George Carter	Trinity Pilot
1859	James Hicks	Tailor	1885	George Reed	Lieut. RN
1860	Henry Rusden	Mercer	1886	John M. Carne	Merchant
1861/2	Thomas Lanyon	Currier	1887	Samuel Tresidder	Accountant
1863	Henry Sleeman	Gentleman	1888	George Olver	Architect
1864	Theophilus Jones	Grocer	1889	William Anderson	Sgt Maj. RA
1865	John Vivian	Hotelier	1890	Thomas Grylls	Accountant
1866	Walter Newman	Druggist	1891	R.C.M. Pooley	Surgeon
1867	William Dunstan	Builder	1892	John T. Williams	Engineer
1868	William Pellowe	Baker	1893	Charles Deeble	Outfitter
1869	Francis Dinnis	Dealer	1894	Walter Gooding	Outfitter
1870	D.W. Tremewan		1895	Aaron Smith	Stable Owner
1871/2	Thomas Shilston	Shipbuilder	1896	Thomas Holder	Ships' Chandler
1873	Timothy Polglase	Ironmonger	1897	Wallace Sharp	Clerk
1874	Michael Little	Draper	1898	Bruce Gregg	Schoolmaster
1875	William Dunstan	Builder	1899	Albert Webber	Confectioner
1876	Thomas Webber	Merchant	1900	Joseph Buckley	Manager

MARINERS INITIATED AND JOINING UNION LODGE NO. 588, FLORIANA, MALTA, 1860–1869[1]

1860	William Clarke (34)	Master Mariner	
1860	John Hugh (42)	" "	Brighton, Sussex
1860	Edward Poole (30)	" "	Shoreham, Sussex
1861	R.A. Reay (31)	" "	South Shields
1863	Edward Petts (36)	" "	Southsea
1863	Joseph Glover (33)	" "	Liverpool
1863	Thomas Kemp (28)	" "	Newport, Monmouth
1864	Joseph Loughlin (34)	" "	Newport
1864	John Thomas Sherwin (28)	" "	Malta
1864	John E. Hills (38)	" "	Landport, Portsmouth
1864	John Smith (30)	" "	Shields
1864	William Mills (25)	" "	Shields
1864	Benjamin B. Sharp (36)	" "	America
1864	Robert R. Snow (32)	" "	America
1864	James Davenport (33)	" "	America
1864	Augustus Hatch (24)	" "	America
1864	Nathaniel Friezel (48)	" "	Nova Scotia
1864	Robert Diggins (24)	" "	Sunderland
1864	Samuel Harding (37)	" "	Padstow, Cornwall
1864	Richard B. Peak (29)	" "	Littlehampton, Sussex
1865	Rundle Harris (25)	" "	Fowey, Cornwall
1865	Richard Errington (32)	" "	Sunderland
1865	Jonathan Reinhardt Kraeft	" "	America
1866	Francis Overman (28)	" "	Malta
1866	Charles L. Lind (26)	" "	Malta
1866	Charles Nicholl (28)	" "	Sunderland
1866	James Mountain (34)	" "	Sunderland
1866	Robert Chambers (40)	" "	Sunderland
1866	Joseph Partridge (28)	" "	Liverpool
1867	Benjamin Moor	" "	Hull
1867	Francis Binnington (31)	" "	North Shields
1867	Charles Argent (36)	Mariner	Malta
1867	Stephen Belville (28)	"	Malta
1867	Benjamin Wilson (23)	"	Malta
1868	Ralph Harrison (29)	"	Sunderland
1868	Adam Wood (34)	"	North Shields
1868	Thomas William Jewison	"	Hull
1869	Richard H. Richards	"	Malta
1869	George Bagley (24)	Master Mariner	Essex

Letters in the Returns from Union, Malta

21 May 1858. 'Bro Remfry was shipwrecked at the beginning of this year and lost his private lodge certificate along with everything he had with him.'

9 February 1863. Letter from George Bradshaw. He has lost his GL certificate on the P&O ship Colombo when it sank. He desperately needs another, 'as it is very useful to us seafaring men'. He is writing from the Sailors' Home, Wells St., Tower Hill, where he is staying while fitting out another of the Company's vessels in the East India Dock.

17th November 1863. Letter from Edward J. Petts. He wants his certificate because 'I am leaving for the West Indies for several years and should have had my certificate before I left to enable me to attend a lodge as I wish to become more enlightened in Masonry.'

30th March 1869. Letter to introduce Bro. Francis Binnington, 'him having lost his certificate when the vessel which he commanded was run down in the English Channel'. He needs a new one—and this is the second such request—because the first was handed over to the Lodge secretary of a Lodge in North Shields and he failed to pass it on. Binnington now proposes to present himself at Grand Lodge in London to obtain a new certificate to, 'make sure of getting a duplicate, he having experienced great inconvenience for want of it'.

MINUTES OF THE BOARD OF THE LODGE OF BENEVOLENCE, UGLE LIBRARY AND MUSEUM MARITIME PETITIONS FOR RELIEF, 1856–1859

(NB. The purchasing power of £10 in 1850 would approximate to £900 today. All lodge members paid 2 shillings a quarter to benevolence as part of their membership.)

Petitions for Injury and Ill Health

March 1856. Ebenezer Johnson of Lodge No. 309, Brixham. While salvaging a wreck about four months ago he caught a severe cold that damaged his lungs. He cannot now find work but has a wife and four children. Receives 5 shillings a week from a Friendly Society. Given relief of £10.

July 1856. George Rochester of Lodge No. 624, North Shields. Joined from Ireland in 1854. A master mariner, he was now nearly blind and paralysed, with a wife and five young children. Given relief of £20.

July 1857. Matthew Le Marinel of Lodge No. 860, Jersey. He was initiated 1853 and paid into his Lodge for three years. He was shipwrecked in his vessel in November 1854 and has since been seriously ill and paralysed. He has a wife and several dependent children. Given relief of £20.

December 1857. Joseph Jeffrey of a Lodge in Connecticut. He was a ship's cook and met with an accident on the Sea Star during a voyage from Shanghai to London. This deprived him of his occupation and he is now unemployed. Given relief of £5.

February 1858. William Baglee of Lodge No. 111, Sunderland. A sail maker who joined from a lodge in Scotand [sic] where he was initiated in 1819. He had paid to his Lodge for 36 years. Now aged 79 he is unable to work but has a pension of 1 shilling a day. Given relief of £10.

May 1858. Charles Dix of Lodge No. 91, Gravesend. He was a river pilot who was initiated in 1848 and paid to his Lodge for seven years. He suffered severe injuries caused by the breaking of a towing hawser and is still disabled, with a wife and five children. Given relief of £10.

November 1858. William Dunn of Lodge No. 624, North Shields. He was initiated in 1843 and paid to his Lodge for 13 years. He was the captain of a vessel on its way to Havana in May when illness caused him to leave his ship. He returned home at great expense and is now destitute. Given relief of £15.

August 1859. Daniel McBeath of Lodge No. 548, Sydney, New South Wales. A master mariner initiated in 1855. He was engaged in the South Sea Trade when, in 1856, he had an accident that fractured his leg in three places. He had been under medical treatment ever since, and sent to England by the Masonic Board of General Purposes in Sydney. He was now in Kings College hospital in London having undergone the amputation of his left leg. He is destitute. Given relief of £20.

Petitions for Replacement of Property

March 1856. Robert Palmer of Lodge No. 95, Sunderland. He was wrecked off Cadiz on the 8th January and lost all of his clothing, charts and nautical instruments to a value of £120. To help him find employment. Given relief of £10.

March 1856 (same meeting). John Ditchburn of Lodge No. 111, Sunderland. He was shipwrecked near Bass Island in Furth-of-Forth [sic] on 7th February and lost everything. Now out of employment. Given relief of £19.

May 1856. Walter Martin of Lodge No. 111, Sunderland. Initiated in Lodge 214, Quebec in July 1841. He was the part owner of the Schooner 'Fairy Queen' which was lost 15th April. He lost all of his clothes, instruments etc to a value of £40. This was the third time that he had been shipwrecked. His ship had been insured but the insurers failed and a claim not paid. Given relief of £20.

February 1857. John Glen of Lodge No. 111, Sunderland. He joined from an Irish lodge in 1842. He was shipwrecked in Yarmouth Roads in January 1857 and lost all of his property and nautical instruments, to the value of £49. The second shipwreck in 17 months and now out of work. He has a wife and six children. Given relief of £20.

February 1857 (same meeting). Ferguson Gourland of Lodge No. 95, Sunderland. Shipwrecked off Sunderland in January. Lost all of his possessions. He has since been out of employment and is unwell. He has a wife and five children. Given relief of £7.

April 1857. Samuel Shillito of Lodge No. 111, Sunderland. A ship's carpenter and part owner of a small vessel wrecked in March. He lost everything he possessed. Given relief of £10.

December 1857. James Purse of Lodge No. 111, Sunderland. His vessel was run down in the Humber in October. His brother was killed and he lost all of the property that he had on board. He has a wife and six children. Given relief of £10.

May 1858. Joseph Butterfield of Lodge No. 203, London. He was initiated in Ireland in January 1854 and wrecked off the coast of Africa. He lost all of his property and instruments and was not insured. Given relief of £10.

May 1859. Samuel Turney of Lodge No. 232, Barbados. Initiated 1830. In 1852 he purchased the Bark 'Pactolas' but the Bark was lost with all of his property. Now cannot find employment and requests assistance to return to Barbados. Given relief of £10.

August 1859. Henry Phillips of Lodge in Scotland. Was Master of the Bark 'Canute' which was destroyed by fire in 1856. He lost all of his possessions and has been involved with an unsettled dispute with the owners. Given relief of £15.

Petitions from Widows

January 1856. For Henry Bransby of Lodge No. 813, Southwold. He sailed for New Orleans and died of yellow fever shortly after arrival. He left a widow and six children. Given relief of £10.

June 1856. For Alexander Jack of Lodge No. 95, Sunderland. He was initiated in 1842 and commanded a vessel sailing to Almeria in Spain but died in Almeria 5th April. He left a widow destitute. Given relief of £10.

August 1856. For John Harvey of Lodge No. 750, Liskeard. He was initiated in 1845 but died in Cape Town in January this year, leaving a wife and eight children. Widow requests assistance to start a small business. Given relief of £20.

October 1856. For John Thinkfield of Lodge No. 111, Sunderland. He was initiated July 1855. He sailed from Guernsey for London on 7th May and has not been since heard of. It is supposed that the ship foundered at sea and that the crew all perished. He left a wife and four young children, including a four-month-old baby. Given relief of £10.

October 1856. For Edward Warden of Lodge No. 111, Sunderland. He was initiated in Lodge No. 756, Malta, January 1848 and joined No. 111 in June 1848. He died in the East Indies in April, leaving a wife and six children, including a nine-month-old baby, with no other provision. Given relief of £20.

November 1856. For John Jenkins of Lodge No. 182, Plymouth. He was initiated 1822 and paid until 1839. He was a waterman and a pilot who died after a long illness leaving a wife but no dependent children. Given relief of £10.

January 1857. For Henry King of Lodge No. 238, Devonport. He was initiated 1844 and paid for eight years. He died in Singapore in August 1855. His wife and family are now in great distress because of the refusal of his employers to pay the balance of his earnings. Given relief of £10.

February 1857. For William Green of Lodge No. 95, Sunderland. He was initiated in 1855. The mate of the ship Riga, he was accidentally drowned in London in January 1857, leaving a wife and three children. Given relief of £10.

December 1857. For Christopher Anderson of Lodge No. 95, Sunderland. He was initiated 1854. Employed as an acting mate on the ship Reindeer and was accidentally drowned in the Hamburg River in September, leaving a widow. Given relief of £10.

February 1858. For Nicholas Westerberry of Lodge No. 748, Singapore. He was initiated in 1855. The captain of the ship Typhoon, he was shipwrecked in the China Sea in October and died, leaving a wife. Given relief of £5.

March 1858. For Joseph Fenwick of Lodge No. 56, Gateshead. He was initiated in 1850 and paid for five years. He died in September 1857 leaving a wife and four children. Given relief of £10.

December 1858. For William Beerling of Lodge No. 812, London. He was initiated in 1854. Employed as a master mariner, he died of sun stroke in Singapore in July. He left a widow and dependent children. Given relief of £10.

December 1858. For Robert Smith of Lodge No. 95, Sunderland. He was a master mariner who was initiated in Lodge No. 740, Calcutta in October 1852 and joined Lodge 95 in March 1854. He died in Calcutta in September 1858, leaving a wife and four children, including an eight-month-old baby. Given relief of £10.

February 1859. For William Gillan, from Lodge No. 279, Calcutta. He was initiated in 1837 and commanded a vessel belonging to the Government of Central America. After a long and disastrous voyage he died in Guayaquil, Equador in March 1858. Given relief of £100 [the largest sum recorded; possibly a mistake in the minutes].

February 1859. For John Horner of Lodge No. 111, Sunderland. He was initiated in Guernsey in 1856. A master mariner, he died in a wreck in Yarmouth Roads in January 1859, leaving a wife and eight children. Given relief of £20.

August 1859. For Philip Palot of Lodge No. 812, London. He was initiated in 1851 and paid until 1856. A master mariner he died from an attack of diarrhoea in Africa in December, aged 33 years. He left a wife and two children, and his wife asked for relief to help establish a small grocer's shop. Given relief of £15.

November 1859. For Nicholas Johnson of Lodge No. 111, Sunderland. Initiated in 1851, he died of sun stroke off Cape Florida in July. His wife died shortly after and his two orphans were destitute. Given relief of £10.

November 1859. For James Edgar Brown of Lodge No. 310, Liverpool. He was initiated in 1856. A master mariner, he died at sea June 1858, leaving a wife and three children. Given relief of £10.

December 1880. For John Pease of 1284, Topsham. He was initiated in 1871 and paid for eight years. A master mariner, he had been shipwrecked three times, during last of which misadventures, in February 1879, he had lost his life. His wife has now exhausted all of his savings and is left with no means of support and is in great distress. Given relief of £20, paid through the Exeter Bank.

Name and Location of These Lodges During These Years

[*The lodge numbers given in the returns for the 1850s were those that had been established in 1832. They were revised, to their current format, in 1863.*]

Lodge No. 91 was Lodge of Freedom, now No. 77, meeting in the Town Hall, High St., Gravesend.

Lodge No. 95 was St John's Lodge, now No. 80, and Lodge No. 111 was Phoenix Lodge, now No. 94. Both met during these years in Phoenix Hall, Queen St., Sunderland.

Lodge No. 182 was Harmony Lodge, now 156, meeting in the White Swan Inn, St Andrew's St, Plymouth.

Lodge No. 203 was Lodge of Sincerity, now No. 174, meeting in the Cheshire Cheese Tavern, Crutchfield Friars, City of London.

Lodge No. 232 was Albion Lodge, now No. 196, meeting in the Lodge Room, Bridge St., Bridgetown, Barbados.

Lodge No. 238 was Lodge of Friendship, now No. 202, meeting in the Lord Hood Hotel, King St., Devonport.

Lodge No. 310 was Mariners' Lodge, now No. 249, meeting in Hanck's Buildings, 42 Duke St., Liverpool.

Lodge No. 548 was Lodge of Australia, later No. 390, meeting in the Lodge Room, The Royal Hotel, Sydney.

Lodge No. 624 was St George's Lodge, now No. 431, meeting in the Commercial Hotel, Howard St, North Shields.

Lodge No. 748 was Lodge Zetland in the East, now No. 508, meeting in the Masonic Hall, The Esplanade, Singapore.

Lodge No. 750 was St Martin's Lodge, now No. 510, meeting in the London Inn, West St., Liskeard.

Lodge No. 279 was Lodge of Humility with Fortitude, now No. 229, meeting in Fort William, Calcutta, Bengal.

Lodge No. 812 was Yarborough Lodge, now No. 554, meeting in the George Tavern, Commercial Road East, London.

Lodge No. 813 was Lodge of Fidelity, now No. 555, meeting in the Town Hall, Market Place, Southwold, Suffolk.

Lodge No. 860 was Loge la Cesaree, now No. 590, meeting in the Masonic Hall, Museum St, Jersey [the Lodge worked in French].

APPENDIX 15

THE NUMBER OF LODGES IN COASTAL AND INLAND PROVINCES, 1900

Coastal Counties

County	No. of Lodges
Cornwall	31
Devon	59
Somerset	26
Dorset	15
Hamp. & I.o.W.	48
Sussex	33
Kent	65
Essex	45
Suffolk	22
Norfolk	18
Cheshire	53
West Lancashire	122
Lincolnshire	25
Monmouthshire	11
N. and E. Yorkshire	34
Durham	37
Northumberland	33
Total No. Provinces	*Total No. Lodges*
17	677

Inland Counties / Provinces

County	No. of Lodges
Wiltshire	12
Berkshire	17
Gloucestershire	17
Oxfordshire	12
Surrey	24
Buckinghamshire	20
Middlesex	42
Hertfordshire	24
Bedfordshire	7
Cambridgeshire	7
North'pton & Hunts.	16
Warwickshire	32
Heredfordshire	5
Cumb. & West'lnd.	22
Leicester & Rutland	14
Staffordshire	34
Shropshire	12
Derbyshire	27
Nottinghamshire	18
West Yorkshire	82
East Lancashire	113
Worcestershire	15
Total No. Provinces	*Total No. Lodges*
22	572

Source: *Freemasons' Calendar and Pocket Book for 1900* (UGLE)

LODGE MEMBERS WHO HELD SENIOR MANAGERIAL POSITIONS IN COPPER, TIN AND LEAD MINES IN CORNWALL AND DEVON, 1859–1900

Data has been derived from a comparison of the names of lodge members who gave their occupation as 'mine agent' in lodge returns with the returns of mine managers that were published annually in the *Mineral Statistics of the United Kingdom*. A full database of the latter is available in R. Burt *et al.*, *Mining in Cornwall and Devon* (2014). There is a clear possibility of error in matching names and conflating different individuals but every effort has been made to maximise accuracy. It is probable the inclusion of some wrong people is at least partly compensated by the exclusion of some of the right ones in terms of the overall conclusions of the exercise. It is also probable that the lodge members listed as 'Mine Agents' in the lodge returns that were not noted in the *Mineral Statistics* held more junior management positions in these or other mines.

Columns

Name of Lodge Member

Date of Birth from Lodge returns

Date of Initiation from Lodge returns

Comments from Lodge returns

Lists of mines in which senior positions were held, giving earliest and last date of reported employment. Taken from the *Mineral Statistics*. No information was published for the years before 1859.

Names with a * denotes evidence of their employment in management positions in British metal mines outside the South West.

Boscawen Lodge, Chacewater (from 1857)

Name	Date of Birth	Initiated
Abrahams, Henry South Condurrow 1870–1871	1834	1871
Bawden, John Dolcoath 1870–1876	1830	1870*

Bennetts, Henry   1847   1869
Carn Camborne, Newton, Pendarves United, Penhale and Lomax, Prince Royal, North Shepherds, Trebartha Lemarne, Trelawney, Hartley 1861–1902

Bray, William   ?   1857
Wheal Jane 1861–1864

Clymo, Nicholas   ?   1871
Camborne Vean, New Dolcoath, North Pool, Tolgus Consols 1860–1881

Craze, W. James   1828   1864
North Busy, 1862

Dower, Edward   1803   1865
Nangiles 1861–1864

Edwards, J.   ?   1867
Okel Tor 1861–1863

Evans, James   1830   1869*
West Basset, Budnick Consols, East Budnick, Great Chiverton Consols, New Chiverton Consols, Coit, Colquite & Callington United, Duke of Cornwall, Friendly, Levant, Park of Mines, Patty, Penhale and Barton, Prince Victor, South Providence, Rose and Chiverton, East Wheal Rose, West Roskear, St Agnes Consols, St George, Trevennen, Treworlack 1859–1886

Evans, James   1830   1869
Budnick Consols 1859–1860

Giles, William   1848   1891
Comment 'abroad 1893'
Creegbrawse, Hope, Wheal Jane, West Jane 1868–1881

Gill, Thomas   1841   1869
Sithney Buller, Sithney Metal, Great Vor 1859–1864

Hancock, William   ?   1864; Fortitude 1869*
North Chiverton, East Falmouth, Hony, East Hony, Old Treburgett, Wrey Consols 1859–1882

Harris, William   1849   1872*
Bicton, Lucy, West Lucy, Old Treburgett Emma 1872–1887

Nicholls, William   1842   1865
West Chiverton, 1880

Oates, W. Jnr   1841   1868
Comment: 'abroad 1882, 1890'
Basset and Grylls 1868–1873

Oates, W. J.   1860   1895
Wheal Jane 1911

Pascoe, William   ?   1866
Buller and Basset United, South Buller, South Crofty, Fowey, South Wheal Francis, Gonamena, North Grambler, Kehelland Consols, Leeds, Park of Mines, Polgear, South Providence, East Seton, West Seton, Old Tolgus United, and Wendron United 1859–1883

Pearce, Abel   1821   1870
Unity Consols 1859–1866

Richards, Thomas   1830   1876
Comment: 'abroad 1882'
East Boscaswell, Fursden, Hingston Down Consols, Wheal Kitty, Mary Great Consols, Prosper United, East Providence, Rosewarne United, Old Shepherds, St Ives Wheal Allen, Treloweth, Trefusis, East Trefusis, Trencom, Treweatha, Trungle, Tyringham Consols, East Devon Consols 1859–1884

Roberts, Thomas   1840   1867*
Mary 1859–1866

Rowe, James   ?   1871*
Boscean, Goonzion, North Lovell, Nangiles, Owles, Frankmills, Teign Valley 1859–1881

Tredinnick, John   1823   1864
Allen, Blencowe Consols, Great Briggan, Carzise, Fowey, Great Eleanor 1860–1880

Whalley, A.J.   1832   1871
Blackhay, Mount No. 1, Trebisken 1872–1878

Williams, Stephen   1825   1868
Harriet, Wheal Kitty 1859–1874

Williams, William Henry   1843   1868*
Clitters United 1900–1901

Druids Lodge of Love and Liberality, Redruth (from 1851)

Blight, John   1832   1876
Tresavean, Tresavean, Trevaunance, Creegbrawse 1859–1875

Browne, James   ?   1860
Buller,   Burra Burra, Caradon 1861–1877

Craze, Charles   1833   1872 (Cornubian Lodge from 1873)
Brea Consols, South Frances, New South Frances, West Shepherds, Great Work 1859–1887

Davey, John Jnr   ?   1853
Wheal Emma, Wheal Buller, Burra Burra and Copper Hill 1859–1869

Davey, Stephen   ?   1863
Cathedral, Wheal Kitty, North Penstruthal, South Penstruthal 1872–1885

Dawe, John   ?   1863
Carn Brea, South Carn Brea, Emily Henrietta, Henrietta, Great South Tolgus, Tywarnhaile, 1859–1869

Delbridge, John   ?   1861*
North Buller, Great Busy, South Crenver, Louisa, East Rosewarne 1859–1864

Higgins, William   ?   1863
Clinton, Penhalls 1862–1868

Martin, William   1824   1870*
Comment: 'in Africa 1893'
Basset, Carn Camborne 1868–1876

Michell, Edmund   ?   1860
Comment: 'from Boscawen'
Tresavean 1859–1871

Nancarrow, William   ?   1853*
East Basset 1859–1864

Odger, Williams   1824   1853
East Grenville 1862–1865

Odgers, George R.   ?   1860
West Dolcoath, Collins, Wheal Grenville, East Grenville, South Grenville, Nelson, West Perran
Great St George, Great Retallack, New Rosewarne, North Rosewarne, Trevellyan, West Trevellyan,
Trumpet United, West Wendron Consols 1859–1871

Parkin, William   1850   1889
Comment: 'in India 1894'
Girt Down 1874

Pascoe,W.H.   1838   1869*
Fowey Consols, New Fowey Consols, Pelyn Wood, Old Tolgus United, 1861–1907

Penberthy,William   1820   1874
Carn Camborne 1872

Pryor, Richard   ?   1863
Great Baddern, Basset and Buller Consols, East Basset, Boswarthen Penzance Consols, Cape
Cornwall, New Great Consols, Cupid, Damsel, New Dolcoath, Illogan Mines, Wheal Kitty, Penhale
and Lomax, Penhalls, Perran Silver-Lead Consols, Phoenix, St Just Amalgamated, St Just United,
East St Just United, Stray Park, New Towan, North Treskerby, Tryphena 1859–1887

Pryor, Thomas   ?   1884
Peevor, West Peevor, West Seton, Trelawney 1861–1893

Pryor, Thomas   ?   1863
Boys, Buller, West Caradon, East Carn Brea, Carn Camborne, Emily Henrietta, North Francis,
Gorland, Peevor, West Peevor, Perran Wheal Virgin, North Roskear, East Seton, West Seton,
Treleigh Wood United, Wheal Virgin Chiverton, Trelawney, Buller 1861–1893

Roberts,William   1845   1869*
Agar, East Agar, North Basset, West Basset, Camborne Consols, Carvennal, South Dolcoath,
Tywarnhaile 1859–1904

Teague,William   1847   1872
Anna Maria, Carn Brea, Christopher Consols, Illogan Mines, Wheal Kitty, Penstruthal Consols,
West Poldice, Wheal Seton, Tincroft, Great Work 1859–1908

Thomas,William   ?   1873*
North Balleswidden, Botallack, Botrea, Coates, New Cooks Kitchen, South Condurrow, New
Cooks Kitchen, Crenver and Abraham, West Frances, King Edward, East Margaret, Pednandrea
United, Penstruthal Consols, Phoenix, West Poldice, Trevethoe, Great Vor 1874–1913

Trelease, Thomas   1820   1864
Comment: 'going abroad 1864'. Not present 1863–1869
Alfred Consols, Great Briggan, Great Busy, East Caradon, Great Caradon, New Crow Hill,
Herodsfoot, North Herodsfoot, Great North Downs, Plushys, Trungle 1859–1887

Trevena,William Charles   1827   1871
Agar, Basset 1873–1887

Truran, Samuel George   ?   1873
In Sweden 1888. In Spain 1889
Wheal Rose, East Wheal Rose, Excelsior and Emily Henrietta 1866–1874

Vivian, John   1843   1872*
North Alfred, North Treskerby, Crenver and Abraham 1859–1876

Williams, John   ?   1859*
Charlestown United, South Dolcoath, Hender, Phoenix, Tremayne 1859–1898

Tregullow Lodge, St Day (from 1865)

Bawden, Thomas   1842   1870
Alfred Consols, Devon and Courtenay, New East Russell, St Just Amalgamated 1859–1874

Bray, Thomas   1847   1873
Wheal Jane, Great Lovell 1861–1872

Cock, Joseph   1818   1867
Poldice, West Poldice, Devon Kapunda 1859–1874

Dawe, John Jnr   ?   1863
Great South Tolgus 1862–1869

Grenfell, J. 1813 1865
Comment 'Going to Mexico' 1867
North Downs 1867

Hosking, Edwin 1825 1875
Carn Brea, Grenville, East Grenville, Rosewarne United, North Rosewarne, Treleigh Wood, Combe
Martin 1859–1876

Jewell, Joseph ? 1865*
Comment: 'joined Tregullow from California, USA'
Tolcarne, East Tolgus, 1859–1865

Johns, George 1816 1865
West Wheal Jewell, 1860–1874

Keast, J.W. 1851 1899
East Charlotte 1911–1913

Odgers, John 1854 1886 (Druids Lodge from 1885)
Clifford United, Tresavean 1859–1895

Pascoe, William 1821 1866
South Buller, Fowey, South Frances, Gonamena, North Grambler, Kehelland Consols,
Leeds, Park of Mines, Polgear, South Providence, East Seton, Old Tolgus United, Wendron United
1859–1883

Pryor, Joseph 1852 1874
Boys, Peevor, Prussia 1878–1881

Cornubian Lodge, Hayle (from 1838)

Bray, Alfred 1828 1874
Penberthy Crofts 1873–1874

Carkeek, Charles ? 1873
Comment. From Fortitude. Died 1874.
Carzise, New Frances, Gernick, South Gernick, New Metal, West Great Work 1859–1873

Goldsworthy, Richard ? 1874
Comment 'From War Eagle No. 6, Silver City, Idaho'
Bedford United, Tamar Silver Lead, Tamar Valley, North Roskear, South Ward 1869–1888

Hall, John 1831 1869*
New Carleen Vor 1876

Hollow, William 1838 1866
Carrack Dews, West Margaret, Providence, East Providence, Trebarvah 1859–1877

Martin, James ? 1868
Comment: 'from Royal Sussex 479, Nova Scotia'
Tincroft 1872–1880

Noell, Samuel Shepherd 1815 1850
Maria 1874–1875

Roach, Thomas 1822 1878
Millett, Polrose 1869–1879

Stevens, William 1818 1852*
West Fowey Consols, 1864

Sweet, John 1841 1873
North Rosewarne 1872

Thomas, William Henry 1831 1863
North Crofty, Carn Camborne, West Damsel, Pednandrea United 1860–1869

White, James   1834   1857*
East Blue Hills, West Metal, Uny, North Vor, Levant 1859–1893

Williams, Joseph   1831   1870
North Downs, South Tolgus 1859–1869

Woolcock, John   1844   1877*
Mellanear, Restormel Royal, Holmbush 1862–1877

Mount Edgcumbe Lodge, Camborne (from 1875)

Arthur, Henry   ?   1894
East Seton, and North Levant 1870–1879

Hodge, Francis   1853   1881
Basset, West, South Wheal Jane 1863–1881

Jennings, Joseph   ?   1899
From Lodge No. 2566 Bulawayo
Pool, East 1909–1913

Rowe, Richard   1848   1879
Comment: Managed 10 mines in the Isle of Man
Crane, 1868–1873

Temby, J.A.   1859   1887
Comment: 'going to South Africa' 1889
Black Dog, North Crofty, Gorland, Peevor, Peevor United 1897–1913

Lodge of Fortitude, Truro (from 1826)

Bawden, William   1817   1868*
Dolcoath, Camborne Vean, Hallenbeagle, West Perran Great St George, Trannack,
Tremadoc 1860–1872

Borlase, W.H.   1850   1874*
Golden 1872–1873

Nancarrow, James   1840   1865*
East Chiverton, South Chiverton, Old Shepherds 1864–1881

Vivian, Joseph   1810   1837
Abraham Consols, East Alfred Consols, Condurrow, South Condurrow, North Crofty, North
Dolcoath, Great Fortune, North Grambler, Hartley, West Wheal Kitty, Prudence, North Roskear,
East Seton, St Agnes Consols, West Stray Park, New Vor, North Great Work 1859–1876

Mount Sinai Lodge, Penzance (from 1813)

Davey, William   1801   1822
Trewavas 1840

Thomas, Arthur   1868   1891
Dolcoath, Great Hewas 1901–1915

Blight, John   ?   1863
Creegbrawse, Tresavean, Trevaunance 1859–1875

Eddy, William   1869
Boscaswell, East Boscaswell, and Pendeen Consols 1859–1879

White, Richard   1832   1891
Wheal Carden, Levant, North Levant, Pendeen Consols, Spearne Consols, and Wheal Vor 1858–
1902

James, Stephen Harvey   1822   1876
Botallack 1842–1887

Tregenna Lodge, St Ives (from 1870)

Martin, Richard   1830   1873
Wheal Basset and St Ives Consols 1872–1881

Pooley, Edward   1846   1873
Trelyon Consols 1859–1873

Pollard, James   1830   1873
East Vor 1864–65

Tonkin, John   ?   1874
Wheal Charlotte, New Charlotte, Balmynheer, Chytane, Dolcoath, Polhigey Moor, Parbola 1870–1876

True and Faithful Lodge, Helston (Warranted 1799)

Hosking, John   ?   1861
Charlotte United, Chiverton, Coldvreath, Ellen, Killevreath, Great Moor, East Pool, Prosper United, Speedwell Treverbyn 1840–1870

Roberts, William   1861   1893
Tywarnhaile and Wheal Leisure 1901–1908

Williams, John   1867   1896
Phoenix and Gooninnis 1889–1906

Phoenix Lodge of Honour and Prudence, Truro (Warranted 1810)

Michell, Theophilus   ?   1852
Wheal Busy, Besore, Falmouth, East Fortune, Hallenbeagle, Wheal Hope, Nangiles, Wheal Sperries and five stream works 1852–1857

Tregay, William   ?   1860
East Buller, New Chiverton, Grambler and St Aubyn, Maudlin, Mount Carbis, Pednandrea United, Prussia, Respryn, South Towan, North Treleigh Wood 1859–1885

Lodge of Love and Honour, Falmouth (Warranted 1751)

Verran, William   1825   1847
Emmens United, Wheal Florence, North Fortescue and Holmbush

Collins, William John   1820   1846
Wheal Ruby 1842

Fowey Lodge, Fowey (from 1864)

Merrett, Charles   ?   1864
Fowey Consols, South Fowey Consols and New Pembroke 1863–1876

SOME MEMBERS OF ABERYSTWYTH LODGE NO. 1072 INVOLVED IN THE MANAGEMENT OF CARDIGANSHIRE LEAD MINES IN THE 1860S

Name	Mine Name
James Bennets	Earl Lisburn's mines
John Boundy	Cwmsebon
Nicholas Bray	Llwynmalees
James Garland	East Darren; Vaughan
Peter Garland	Earl Lisburn's mines; Talybont
Robert Northey	Bwadrain; Blaendyffryn; Bwlchystyllan; Camddwr; Tynyfron
James Paull	Goginan; Cwmbryno
John Williams	Court Grange; Nanty

Source: UGLE Aberystwyth Lodge returns

SOME MEMBERS OF OVERSEAS LODGES JOINING CORNISH MINING LODGES, 1852–1901

[*Variable available data*]

Boscawen, Chacewater

1865	*from*	'an American lodge'
1872		'America'
1872		No. 16, Mexico
1872		Nevada, USA
1874		No. 128, Michigan, USA (2 members)
1874		No. 13, Nevada, USA
1875		No. 16, USA
1890		Venezuela
1892		Montana, USA
1898		No. 22, Montana, USA

Druids, Redruth

1866	*from*	Sardinia
1866		California, USA
1871		New Zealand
1874		No. 14, Nevada, USA
1875		No. 23, California, USA
1876		Brazil
1883		Cosmopolitan No. 1409, Kimberley, South Africa
1889		California, USA
1892		Burma
1893		Northern Star No. 1463, Ferazapore, Punjab, India
1896		No. 55, Victoria, Australia
1899		Charles Warren No. 1832, Kimberley, South Africa

Mount Edgcumbe, Camborne

1876	*from*	Owyhee, Silver City, Idaho, USA
1884		Cariboo No. 469, British Columbia, Canada
1888		Anchor of Hope No. 1093, Wellington, Madras, India
1890		Michigan, USA
1890		Amity No. 4, Silver City, Nevada, USA
1892		No. 43, California, USA
1892		No. 4, Nevada/Colorado, USA
1893		Unity No. 6, Pachuca, Mexico
1894		Unity No. 6, Pachuca, Mexico (3 members)
1894		Nevada No. 4, Colorado, USA
1895		Unity No. 6, Pachuca, Mexico
1896		No. 13, Silver City, Idaho, USA
1897		Mexico
1899		No. 2566, Bulawayo, Rhodesia
1899		No. 2778, Kalgoolie, Australia

Tregullow, St Day

1865	*from*	California
1872		Mexico
1876		California
1880		California
1880		West Indies
1886		Peru and Bolivia
1892		Chile
1892		Kimberley, South Africa
1900		United Tradesmen No. 744, Ballarat, Victoria, Australia
1900		Toltec No. 214, Mexico

MEMBERS OF FOREIGN LODGES WHO VISITED TREGULLOW LODGE, ST DAY, 1864–1901

Name	Date Visited	Parent Lodge
Joseph Jewell	16 Aug. 1864	Owen Lodge, No. 108 California, USA
William Clift	15 Sept. 1868	Maddison Lodge, No. 23, Grass Valley, California, USA
Joseph Michell	17 Nov. 1868	No. 133 California, USA
Jonathan Bawden	16 July 1872	Charity Lodge, No. 69, Real del Monte, Mexico
Charles Clift	19 Nov. 1872	Maddison Lodge, No. 23, Grass Valley, California, USA
Charles Barnett	17 Nov. 1874	No. 28 Colombia
Thomas Cook	17 Nov. 1874	No. 5 British Columbia, Canada
J.H. Hodge	16 July 1878	Silver Star No. 5, Nevada, USA
George Vincent	20 Jan. 1880	Maddison Lodge, No. 23, Grass Valley, California, USA.
Thomas Curnow	16 Sept. 1884	Bodie Lodge, No. 252, California, USA
James I. Dunstan	19 Sept. 1887	St John's Devonport No. 655, Australia
S. Trebilcock	17 April 1888	Morning Star No. 5, Montana, USA
E. Nicholls	17 April 1888	Lander No. 8, Nevada, USA
Richard Davey	16 July 1889	Butte No. 20, Montana, USA
W.H. Perry	20 Aug. 1889	Butte No. 22, Montana, USA
S. Jeffery	15 April 1890	Golden Star, South Dakota, USA
John Wellington	17 Feb. 1891	Butte No. 22, Montana, USA
Joseph Millett	21 July 1891	Philipstown No. 236
Thomas Spargo	21 July 1891	St John la Coquimbo No. 616, Chile
Zacharias Uren	17 May 1892	Athole Lodge, No. 591, Kimberley, South Africa
J. Chapple		Casilia Lodge, Valparaiso, Chile
Alfred Martin	21 June 1892	Crockett Lodge, No. 139, USA

William Hodge	21 June 1892	King Solomon Lodge, No. 9, Helena, Montana, USA
J.A. Richards	16 Aug. 1892	Penrhyn No. 258, California, USA
Peter Oppy	c.1890	Silver Bow, Montana, USA
R. Angove	8 Dec. 1892	Cosmoss No. 428, Shanghai, China
Thomas Bawden	20 June 1893	Cariboo Lodge, No. 4, British Columbia, Canada
John H. Pengelly	20 June 1893	Eagle Pass No. 626, Texas, USA
James H. Peters	16 Jan. 1894	Central City No. 22, South Dakota, USA
Frederick Brenton	17 July 1894	Hiram No. 1, Connecticut, USA
J.H. Combellack	21 Aug. 1894	Monitor No. 3, Montana, USA
W.G. Jeffrey	18 Sept. 1894	Butte No. 22, Montana, USA
Edwin Phillips	21 May 1895	Escurial No. 7, Virginia City, Nevada USA
Richard Opie	16 July 1895	Monitor No. 35, Walkerville, Montana, USA
H. Bennett	14 Jan. 1896	Butte No. 22, Montana, USA
R.H. Bartle	15 Sept. 1896	Germiston No. 2498, South Africa
E.W. Bartle	15 Sept. 1896	Germiston No. 2498, South Africa
James Gray	17 Nov. 1896	Southern Cross No. 528, India
R.W.T. Patterson	19 Oct. 1897	Union of Malta No. 407, Malta
A. Gregory	19 July 1898	Royal George No. 244, Krugersdorp, South Africa
Andrew E. Hand	21 Feb. 1899	Mount Moriah No. 24, Montana, USA
Frederick J. Scoble	16 Aug. 1899	Roodepoort No. 2539, Transvaal, South Africa
J.H.W. Paull	17 Oct. 1899	Germiston No. 2498, South Africa
G. Argall	21 Nov. 1899	Roodepoort No. 2439, Transvaal, South Africa
W.J.J. Morcom	21 Nov. 1899	Royal George No. 2643, South Africa
J.J. Trewern	21 Nov. 1899	Gordon No. 804, South Africa
Alfred Teague	21 Nov. 1899	King Solomon No. 887, South Africa
C.E. Gregor	21 Nov. 1899	Germiston No. 2498, South Africa
Simon Kinsman	20 Feb. 1900	Royal George No. 2643, South Africa
James Cocking	15 May 1900	Jackson No. 60, USA
Henry Jewell	21 Aug. 1900	Golden Thistle No. 744, Johannesburg, South Africa
Charles R. Williams	15 Jan. 1901	Toltec No. 214, Mexico

Source: Tregullow Lodge Minute Books, abstracted by Joseph Mills, Secretary. See also Mills, *Tregullow Lodge*, pp. 36–38.

THE FOUNDATION OF ENGLISH CONSTITUTION LODGES IN BALLARAT AND BENDIGO, VICTORIA, AUSTRALIA

Ballarat
Lodge of Victoria 658
  Consecrated 25 September 1858
  United with Yarrowee Lodge 713 in 1869
Ballarat Lodge 717
  Consecrated 2 October 1857
  United with Yarrowee Lodge 713 in 1869
United Tradesmen Lodge 744
  Consecrated 17 May 1858
  United with Yarrowee Lodge 713 in 1869
Yarrowee Lodge 713
  Consecrated 25 August 1857
  United with Lodge of Victoria and United Tradesmen Lodge in 1869

Bendigo
Golden Lodge of Bendigo 641
  Consecrated 1854
  United with Corinthian Lodge 770 in 1872
  Thereafter Golden and Corinthian Lodge of Bendigo 770
Corinthian Lodge 770
  Consecrated 21 December 1858
  United with Golden Lodge in 1872
  Thereafter Golden and Corinthian Lodge of Bendigo 770

SOME MEMBERS OF DOMESTIC ENGLISH CONSTITUTION LODGES JOINING GOLD FIELDS LODGE, JOHANNESBURG, 1893–1898

From Cornwall

William Bennetts from Tregullow Lodge No. 1006, St Day, *Miner*

John Blewett from Mount Sinai Lodge No. 121, Penzance, *Carpenter*

Samuel Dotson from Lodge of Love and Honour No. 75, Falmouth, *Miner*

Ernest Grose from Boscawen Lodge No. 699, Chacewater, *Contractor*

Charles Hosking from Mount Sinai Lodge No. 121, Penzance, *Miner*

Joseph Jeffery from Loyal Victoria Lodge No. 557, Callington, *Miner*

John Laity from Druids Lodge of Love and Liberality No. 589, Redruth, *Miner*

Henry Leigh from Lodge of Love and Honour No. 75, Falmouth, *Speculator*

James Polmear from Mount Edgcumbe Lodge No. 1544, Camborne, *Engineer*

John Pope from Cornubian Lodge No. 450, Hayle, *Mine Manager*

Samuel Tregaskis from St Petroc Lodge No. 1785, Padstow, *Miner*

? Warne from Cotehele Lodge No. 2166, Calstock, *Miner*

Other Parts of England

Solomon Barnett from Lodge of Israel No. 1502, Liverpool, Lancashire, *Auctioneer*

Edward Berlandina from Empire Lodge No. 2108, London, *Broker*

Thomas Butt from Lodge of Prudence No. 1550, Plymouth, Devon, *Miner*

Robert Foster from Newcastle-upon-Tyne Lodge No. 24, Northumberland, *Metallurgist*

Herman Goldbord from Lodge of Israel No. 1502, Liverpool, *Outfitter*

Emil Halle from Lodge of Israel No. 205, London, *Clerk*

Henry Heilbuth from Lodge Star in the East No. 650, Harwich, Essex, *Caterer*

Solomon Joel from Montefiore Lodge, No. 1017, London, *Financier*

William Mallock from Bolingbroke Lodge No. 2417, London, *Engineer*

Hyam Moss from Lodge of Sincerity No. 189, Plymouth, Devon, *Insurance Manager*

Charles de Pinna from Sir Hugh Myddleton Lodge No. 1602, London, *Agent*

John Walter from Montefiore Lodge No. 1017, London, *Clerk*

George Waiter from Hindpool Lodge No. 1225, Barrow-in-Furness, Lancashire, *Storekeeper*

Wesley Walter from Royal Navy Lodge No. 429, Ramsgate, Kent, *Carpenter*

Simon Weinberg from Friars Lodge No. 1349, London, *Cigarette Maker*

Herman Weinberg from Sir Hugh Myddleton Lodge No. 1602, London, *Cigarette Maker*

Michael Zoccola from Northern Counties Lodge No. 406 Newcastle-upon-Tyne, Northumberland, *Hotel Owner*

NOTES

Chapter 1   Introduction: Freemasonry—a Global Institution

1.   Yoshio Washizu, 'English Freemasonry—A Product of Club Movement?' *AQC* 130 (2017) pp. 163–90.

2.   Andy Durr, 'Chicken and Egg—the Emblem Book and Freemasonry: The Visual and Material Culture of Associated Life' *AQC* 118 (2005) p. 29.

3.   See, for example, Martin Gorsky, *Patterns of Philanthropy: Charity and Society in Nineteenth Century Bristol* (Woodbridge, 1999); Peter Clark, *British Clubs and Societies 1580–1800: The Origins of an Associational World* (Oxford, 2000); Malcolm Chase, *Early Trade Unionism: Fraternity, Skill and the Politics of Labour* (Farnham, 2000); Simon Cordery, *British Friendly Societies 1750–1914* (London, 2003). See also the earlier study by P.H.J.H. Gosden, *Friendly Societies in England 1815–1875* (Manchester, 1961).

4.   See, for example, the *Transactions of the Leicester Lodge of Research No. 2429, the Manchester Association for Masonic Research* and particularly *Ars Quatuor Coronatorum*, the *Transactions of Quatuor Coronati Lodge No. 2076.*

5.   John Goodchild, 'The Freemasons and the Friendly Societies: An Historical Study' *TMAMR* LXXXVI (1996), pp. 50–65.

6.   See pp. 79ff.

7.   For a review of the origins of Freemasonry, see Trevor Stewart, 'Aspects of Freemasonry in the Western Hermetic Tradition' in *The Stewart Papers: New Perspectives* (Hamburg, 2017).

8.   An easily accessible instruction to Freemasonry in Britain and America is provided in Alexander Piatigorsky, *Who's Afraid of Freemasons?* (London, 1997).

9.   It also takes no account of those lodges authorised by other European Grand Lodges.

10.   R. Burt, 'Segmented Capital Markets and Patterns of Investment in Late Victorian Britain: Evidence from the Non-Ferrous Mining Industry' *EcHR* 51/4 (November 1998) pp. 709–33.

Chapter 2   Cornwall and Cornish Freemasonry in the Nineteenth Century

1. See John Rowe, *Cornwall in the Age of the Industrial Revolution* 2nd edn (St Austell, 1993).

2. See Roger Burt, *The British Lead Mining Industry* (Redruth, 1984); Robert W. Randall, *Real del Monte: A British Mining Venture on Mexico* (Austin, 1972); and A.C. Todd, *The Search for Silver: Cornish Miners in Mexico 1824–1947* (Padstow, 1977).

3. See, for example, Marshall C. Eakin, *British Enterprise in Brazil: The St John d'el Rey Mining Company and the Morro Velho Gold Mine, 1830–1960* (Durham, North Carolina, 1989). Sharron Schwartz, *The Cornish in Latin America: 'Cousin Jack' and the New World* (privately published, 2016) provides an overview of the subject.

4. See John Rowe, *The Hard Rock Men: Cornish Immigration and the North American Mining Frontier* (Liverpool, 1974); Philip Payton, *The Cornish Miner in Australia* (Redruth, 1984); Patricia Lay, *One and All: The Cornish in New South Wales* (Queanbeyan, New South Wales, 1998).

5. For a detailed overview of all of these issues and further references, see Philip Payton, *The Cornish Overseas* (Fowey, 1999).

6. See Richard D. Dawe, *Cornish Pioneers in South Africa* (St Austell, 1998); Graham B. Dickason, *Cornish Immigrants to South Africa* (Cape Town, 1978).

7. Numerous examples can be found. William and Grace Andrew, for example, left Cornwall to wander through lead-mining districts in Scotland, South and North Wales, and Shropshire; the Trelours left West Cornwall to work in developing mines across Devon before moving north to the developing iron mines in the Barrow-in Furness area. See Michael Statham, 'Miners—A Mobile Workforce' *Welsh Mines Society Newsletter* 79 (Autumn 2018) pp. 12–24; Norman Hannan, *Travels and Heartaches of a Mining Family* (privately printed, 1984).

8. The membership figures have been taken from Appendix 9. They have often been derived for different years within the period and the population data relates to 1891. There may have been some double counting as some men were members of two or more orders, and some female members may have been included for some orders.

9. It has been suggested recently that the date of the formation of the Grand Lodge was 1721 rather than the long-accepted date of 1717.

10. Peter Davies also mentions the importance of sea routes in his study of the early foundation of lodges in South Wales: 'How Freemasonry Evolved in South Wales' *AQC* 129 (2016) pp. 41–92.

11. Douglas Williams (ed.), *Thread of Gold 1752–2002* (Truro, 2001) p. 30.

12. Joseph G. Osborn, *History of Freemasonry in West Cornwall, from 1765 to 1828* (Penzance, 1901).

13. John Lane, *Masonic Records 1717–1894* (London, 1895).

14. E.S. Vincent, *A Record of Freemasonry in the Province of Cornwall* (Truro: privately printed, 1959) p. 15.

15. See David Harrison and John Belton, 'Society in Flux:The Emergence and Rise of Middle-class Civil Society in Nineteenth Century Industrial North West England' in Andreas Onnerfors and Robert Peter (eds) *Researching British Freemasonry 1717–2017* (Sheffield: Sheffield Lectures on the History of Freemasonry and Fraternalism, 3, 2010) pp. 71–98; and John L. Belton and Robert L.D. Cooper, 'Scotland's Masons: Membership and Occupations of Freemasons 1800–2000' in Onnerfors and Peter (eds) *Researching British Freemasonry* pp. 99–126.

16. See *FMC*, 25 June 1898, p. 293.

17. *FM*, 23 November 1889, p. 229.

18. *FM*, 8 September 1883, p. 452.

19. *FM*, 19 January 1884, p. 27.

20. See A.K. Hamilton Jenkin, *The Cornish Miner* (London, 1948), Chapter IX.

21. *FMC*, 6 April 1867, p. 282.

22. *FM*, 17 July 1875.

23. *FM*, 3 October 1896, p. 520.

24. *FM*, 3 November 1900, p. 634.

25. K.B. Jackson, *Beyond the Craft* (Hersham, 1994).

26. C. John Mandleberg and L.W. Davies, *Royal Arch Masons and Knights Templar at Redruth, Cornwall, 1791–1828* (London, 2005) pp. 4–14.

27. Vincent, *Cornwall*, p. 60.

28. The minimum age for initiation into Masonry.

29. *FM*, 9 September 1891, p. 125.

Chapter 3 The Economic and Social Structure of Cornish Craft Lodges and Side Orders

1. These are held in the Library and Museum of the United Grand Lodge of England, 60 Great Queen St, London, UK.

2. The prejudicial effects of such exclusion may well have been a cause of the failure of many women's businesses. See Jennifer Aston and Paolo di Martino, 'Risk, success and failure: female entrepreneurship in late Victorian and Edwardian England' *EcHR* 70/3 (August 2017) pp. 837–58.

3. See R. Burt with R. Burnley, M. Gill and A. Neill, *Mining in Cornwall and Devon: Mines and Men* (Exeter, 2014).

4. *Census of Great Britain, 1851. Religious Worship in England and Wales.* Table G Religious Accommodation Provided for Each County of England and Wales.

5. The number of Catholics attending a service on the census day was less than 1,500 and probably remained no more than a few thousand before the end of the century.

6. *FM*, 20 November 1869, p. 222.

7. See Rowe, *Cornwall*, p. 261.36.

8. *FM*, 30 July 1870, p. 362.

9. *FM*, 31 January 1880, p. 55. The Wesleyan Rev. Richard Kennedy was thought to have been the first of that denomination to have been made the Master of a lodge anywhere.

10. *FM*, 29 May 1880, p. 247. See also Minute files in the PGL of Cornwall.

11. See Burt *et al.*, *Mining in Cornwall and Devon*, Appendix A4.

12. See for example, D.R. Mills and J. Mills, 'Occupation and Social Stratification Revisited: The Census Enumerators' Books of Victorian Britain' *Urban History Yearbook 1989* (May 1989) pp. 63–77. Other sources consulted included W.A. Armstrong, *Stability and Change in an English County Town: A Social Study of York 1801–1851* (Cambridge, 1974) pp. 209–37; W.A. Armstrong, 'The Use of Information about Occupation' in E.A. Wrigley (ed.) *Nineteenth Century Society: Essays on the Use of Quantitative Methods for the Study of Social Data* (Cambridge, 1972) pp. 215–23; C. Erickson, *British Industry: Steel and Hosiery* (Cambridge, 1986) pp. 11–24.

13. See below pp. 214–19.

14. See Harold Perkin, *The Rise of Professional Society in England Since 1880* (London, 2002), Chapter 2.

15. Roger Burt, 'Industrial Relations in the British Non-Ferrous Mining Industry in the Nineteenth Century' *Labour History Review* 71/1 (April 2006) pp. 57–79.

16. See R. Burt, *Cornish Mining* (Newton Abbot, 1969).

17. R. Burt, 'Freemasonry and business networking during the Victorian period' *EcHR* 56/4 (November 2003) pp. 657–88.

18. See Lord Amherst and Hamon Le Strange, *History of Union Lodge, Norwich, No. 52* (privately printed, 1898); Herbert Crossley, *History of the Lodge of Probity No. 61* (Halifax, 1888); and F.R. Worts, *The History of the Lodge of Peace No. 149* (n.d.).

19. See UGLE Lodge returns for Lists of Members 1851, 1861, 1871. See also David Harrison and Frederick Lomax, *Freemasonry and Fraternal Societies* (Addlestone, 2015) p. 16.

20. See *Lodge Returns*. Initiations 1883 to 1893.

21. Ibid.

22. See, for example, *Proceedings of the Provincial Grand Lodge of Cornwall* 4 September 1883.

23. Daniel Weinbren, 'Freemasonry and Friendly Societies' in Henrick Bogdan and Jan Snoek (eds) *Handbook of Freemasonry* (Leiden, 2014) pp. 387–406.

24. Ages were not given for many of those joining Royal Arch Chapters and this figure comes from around a third of the total.

25. This average is derived from the returns for just over 2,600 initiates.

26. F.W. Shepherd, *An Account of the History of Royal Arch Masonry in Cornwall from the Earliest Times to 1977* (Truro, 1977) p. 32.

27. A.K. Hamilton Jenkin wrote of a 'spirit of clanship' in Cornwall and it has been claimed that most Cornish families would rather travel to a town with their local

friends and family in a distant country, than move to another part of Cornwall. See A.K. Hamilton Jenkin, *Cornwall and Its People* (London, 1945) p. 127.

28. Lord Mount Edgcumbe was also a member of this Lodge.

29. Arthur C. Hodge, *The Odyssey of a Mason*. UGLE Library *Masonic Pamphlets 1872–1932* 10/26 (n.d.) B10MAS.

30. See Janette Rutterford, Dimitris Sotiropoulos and Carry van Lieshout, 'Individual investors and local bias in the UK, 1870–1935' *EcHR* 70/4 (November 2017) pp. 1291–320.

31. Sir Charles Graves-Sawle as Junior Grand Warden in 1887 and Edward Anderton as Junior Grand Deacon in 1896. See *Masonic Year Book: Historical Supplement* (UGLE 1964).

32. Much of what follows was drawn from Williams (ed.), *Thread of Gold*.

33. Though he was made an honorary member of Love and Honour.

34. *Kelly's Directory of Cornwall* (1883).

35. It is possible that this job description relates to 'market gardener' which was a rapidly expanding activity in Cornwall at the end of the nineteenth century and would have carried a higher economic and social status.

36. A similar process can be observed in the United States where fraternity helped to diffuse middle-class values across a wide range of social groups. See Mark C. Carnes, *Secret Ritual and Manhood in Victorian America* (New Haven, 1989) p. 31.

37. Rowe, *Cornwall*, p. 156. For an extended discussion of the role of Masonic lodges in Cornish industrial relations, see Burt, 'Industrial Relations'.

38. For an extended study of changing class relationships in Britain during the period, see David Cannadine, *Class in Britain* (New Haven, 1998) Chapter 3.

39. See A.N. Newman, 'The Contribution of the Provinces to the Development of English Freemasonry' *TLRL* (2002) pp. 14–30.

Chapter 4   Reasons for Joining, Part 1: Life-Enhancing and Reassurance—Social, Intellectual, Spiritual, Charitable

1. See Clark, *Clubs*; Chase, *Early Trade Unionism*.

2. John Timbs, *Clubs and Club Life in London from the Seventeenth Century Until the Present Day* (London, 1872). Eric Hobsbawm reflected on some of the causes of such bonding in *Bandits* (London, 1969).

3. J. Scott Kenny, *Brought to Light: Contemporary Freemasonry, Meaning and Society* (Waterloo, Ontario, 2016) pp. 42–44.

4. He continues that 'The respectable man was a good man, and also a pillar of society. He might be poor, he might be rich; it really made no matter which.' Geoffrey Best, *Mid-Victorian Britain 1851–75* (London, 1971) p. 282. See also F.M.L. Thompson, *The Rise of Respectable Society: A Social History of Victorian Britain 1830–1900* (Cambridge, Mass., 1990).

5. See Simon Cordery, 'Friendly Societies and the Discourse of Respectability in Britain 1825–1875' *Journal of British Studies* 34 (January 1995) pp. 35–58.

6. See W.J. Hughan, *Autobiography* (Manuscript, Library and Museum of Freemasonry) (n.p., n.d.) and Richard Gan, 'Frederick Binckes: The Rise and Fall of an Outstanding Victorian Freemason' *AQC* 128 (2015) pp. 155–96.

7. See John S. Wade, '"Go and do thou likewise": English Masonic Processions from the 18th to the 20th centuries' *AQC* 122 (2009) pp. 75–120; J. Mark MacAlpine, 'Nineteenth Century Masonic Processions in Shanghai' *AQC* 128 (2015) pp. 197–212.

8. Simon Gunn, *The Public Culture of the Victorian Middle Class: Ritual and Authority in the English Industrial City 1840–1914* (Manchester, 2007) p. 1. Unfortunately, he makes no reference to the parades of Masons or the ritual activities of other major fraternities or friendly societies.

9. *FM*, 30 July 1870, p. 362.

10. See *Cornubian and Redruth Times*, 23 April 1880, p. 5 and 21 May 1880, p. 4; *FM*, 8 May 1880, p. 203 and 29 May 1880, p. 247. The Masons raised large sums of money for the construction of the cathedral.

11. Clark, *Clubs*, pp. 330–31. In a survey of active Masons carried out in America in the 1970s, nearly two-thirds of those questioned thought that what they most liked was the fellowship and enjoyment they gained from lodge meetings. See J. Wilson, 'Voluntary Associations and Civil religion: The Case of Freemasonry' *Review of Religious Research* 22/2 (December, 1980) pp. 125–36.

12. David Stevenson, *The Origins of Freemasonry* (Cambridge, 1990) pp. 186–89; Margaret C. Jacobs, *The Origins of Freemasonry: Facts and Fictions* (Philadelphia, 2006) p. 50.

13. See James Webb, *The Flight from Reason: The Age of the Irrational* ((London: 1971) and Alex Owen, *The Place of Enchantment: British Occultism and the Culture of the Modern* (Chicago, 2004).

14. See N.H. Webster, *Secret Societies and Subversive Movements* (London, 1955) and Harrison and Lomax, *Fraternal Societies*, pp. 130–37.

15. See above p. 39.

16. See Jackson, *Beyond*, pp. 73–78 and A.C.F. Jackson, 'Rosicrucianism and its effect on Craft Masonry' *AQC* 97 (1984) pp. 115–50.

17. See Jackson, *Beyond*, p. 73 and Richard Gan, Susan Snell and David Peabody, 'Robert Wentworth Little: A Duplicitous Freemason, Wordsmith and Mystic' *AQC* 130 (2017) pp. 107–44.

18. Jackson, *Beyond* gives brief details of many of these orders and others. See also Ellic Howe, 'Fringe Masonry in England 1870–85' *AQC* 85 (1972) pp. 242–95. Howe saw the emergence of these orders as the product of 'a widespread contemporary public interest in spiritualism and alleged mediumistic phenomena' (p. 243).

19. Ibid., pp. 245, 281.

20. For a history of this order, its beliefs and rituals, see Robert A. Gilbert, *The Golden Dawn Companion* (Wellingborough, 1986) and *The Golden Dawn Scrap Book: The Rise and Fall of a Magical Order* (York Beach, Maine, 1997); and Ellic Howe, *The Magicians of the Golden Dawn: A Documentary History of a Magical Order 1887–1923* (London, 1972).

21. Anthony Charles Fuller, 'Anglo-Catholic Clergy and the Golden Dawn: The Ritual Revival and the Modern Magical Order 1887–1940' (Ph.D. diss., University of Exeter, 2009) pp. 186–87.

22. For a detailed discussion of the secrets and esoteric aspects of Freemasonry, see Fabio Venzi, *Freemasonry: The Esoteric Tradition* (Addlestone, 2016).

23. For a full, well-informed and highly accessible guide to Freemasonry, see S. Brent Morris, *The Complete Idiot's Guide to Freemasonry* Masons (New York, 2006) which also contains a good bibliography.

24. Charles Moore's *New Masonic Trestle Board* was published in various editions in Boston from the 1840s.

25. This was particularly common in the United States. See S. Brent Morris, 'Itinerant American Masonic Lecturers' *AQC* 121 (2008) pp. 1–19.

26. Mary Ann Clawson, *Constructing Brotherhood: Class, Gender and Fraternalism* (Princeton, 1989) pp. 228–30.

27. It is notable that many Freemasons became professional entertainers and, equally, entertainers were attracted to Freemasonry. See J.F. Ashby, 'Freemasonry and Entertainment' *TMAMR* LXXXIX (1999) pp. 39–63.

28. Lynn Dumenil, *Freemasonry and American Culture, 1880–1939* (Princeton, 1984) pp. 32–42.

29. Jason Kaufman, *For the Common Good? American Civil Life and the Golden Age of Fraternity* (Oxford, 2002) p. 46.

30. Carnes, *Secret Ritual*, p. 14.

31. *The Complete Manual of Oddfellowship: Being a Practical Guide to its History, Principles, Ceremonies and Symbolism* (privately printed, 1879) p. 18. For Oddfellows' ritual also see *The Lectures Used by the Manchester Unity or Independent Order of Oddfellows* (1846).

32. Daniel Weinbren, *The Oddfellows 1810–2010* (Lancaster, 2010) p. 67.

33. See below p. 228.

34. Andy Durr, 'Rituals of Association and the Organisation of the Common People' *AQC* 100 (1987) pp. 88–108 and 'From Fraternal Groups to Trade Unions' *Freemasonry Today* 24 (2003). For examples, see D.C. Cummings, *An Historical Survey of the Boiler Makers' and Iron and Steel Ship Builders' Society* (Newcastle-upon-Tyne, 1905) and A.E. Musson, *The Typographical Association, Origins and History up to 1949* (Oxford, 1972).

35. Weinbren, *Oddfellows*, p. 71.

36. The Ancient Order of Foresters retain a large number of membership registers that might be matched with Masonic Lodge records for other parts of the country but this has not been attempted here.

37. For a detailed discussion of regalia and rituals in American fraternities see Harriet W. Macbride, 'The Golden Age of Fraternity' *Heredom* 13 (2005) pp. 117–49.

38. See Roger Burt, 'Who were the Mark Masons? A Look at Some Lodges in West Cornwall during the Victorian Period' in Andrew Prescott (ed.), *Marking Well* (London, 2006) pp. 171–80.

39. The career of William James Hughan provides a particularly successful example.

40. R.J. Hall, *Lodge of Love and Honour No. 75, Falmouth: A History from 1751 to 2001* (Falmouth, 2001) and J. Mills, *Tregullow Lodge No. 1006 1864–1990* (St Day, 1990).

41. Today 'fantasy role play' commands the interest of millions of devotees in the artificial worlds of electronic gaming. That, like the activities within the lodges and chapters, is essentially the practice of sociability through gaming, the only significant difference being that it takes place through digital connectivity rather than physical presence.

42. For an extended discussion of this subject, see C. John Mandleberg, 'Past Grand Rank' *AQC* 126 (2013) pp. 71–94. One of the influential appointments to Past Grand Rank was Sir Charles Warren, Metropolitan Police Commissioner in charge of the 'Jack the Ripper' enquiry.

43. See Aaron Reeves, Sam Friedman, Charles Rahal, 'The Decline and the Persistence of the Old Boy: Private Schools and Elite Recruitment 1897 to 2016' *American Sociological Review* 82/6 (2017) pp. 1139–66.

44. Tim Heald, *Networks: Who we Know and How we Use Them* (London, 1983) p. 18.

45. See, for example, Stephen Knight, *The Brotherhood: The Secret World of the Freemasons* (London, 1984); Martin Short, *Inside the Brotherhood* (London, 1989).

46. See also the role of 'class lodges' below p. 183.

47. In the eighteenth century there were two Grand Lodges in England—the Ancients and the Moderns—who united to form the United Grand Lodge of England in 1813.

48. For an extended discussion of English Masonic benevolence, see John Hamill, 'And the Greatest of these is Charity: The Development of Masonic Charity' *AQC* 108 (1995) pp. 162–74.

49. *FM*, 26 January 1884, p. 41.

50. For the origins of this fund, see Gan, 'Binckes', pp. 170–72.

51. *The Freemasons Calendar and Directory for the Province of Somerset 1899–1900*; *FM*, 1 September 1888, p. 507; *FM*, 19 February 1898, p. 81.

52. For a general discussion of the role of PGLs, see A.N. Newman, 'The Contribution of the Provinces to the Development of English Freemasonry' *TLRL* (2002) pp. 14–30.

53. *Provincial Grand Lodge of Cornwall*. Minutes of meetings.

54. See *The Devon Masonic Directory for 1899*; *The Freemasons Calendar for the Province of Warwickshire 1900–1*; *The Freemasons Calendar and Directory for the Province of Durham 1899*; *The West Lancashire Masonic Calendar 1899–1900*; *Calendar for Masonic Meetings in East Lancashire 1899–1900*.

55. See Weinbren, *Oddfellows*, p. 53.

56. The arrangements for votes for the RMBI grants. See *Masonic Calendar and Directory for Northamptonshire and Huntingdonshire 1899–1900.*

57. *Masonic Calendar for the Province of Northumberland 1893* p. 41.

58. *FM*, 8 December 1900, p. 714.

59. *Masonic Calendar and Directory for Northamptonshire and Huntingdonshire 1899–1900* p. 100.

60. *The Freemasons Calendar and Directory for the Provinces of Leicestershire and Rutland 1899.*

61. *West Lancashire Masonic Calendar 1899–1900* p. 29.

62. *FMC*, 23 August 1879, pp. 136–37. For the total income of the RMIB 1850–90, see Gan, 'Binckes', p. 193.

63. This problem reflected back in turn on the election outcomes for those provinces, giving poor results and great cause for concern. See *Masonic Calendar and Directory for the Province of Middlesex 1901* p. 114.

64. *MI*, 1 December 1901, p. 51.

65. See *West Lancashire* and *Leicester and Rutland* calendars.

66. *The Freemasons Calendar and Directory for the Province of Essex 1900.* Eligibility for an annuity was an age of at least sixty years, at least fifteen years' lodge membership, and a means test for cash and property of less than £32. New admissions were made to the Croydon home from a panel of previously approved applicants as spaces became vacant. *FM*, 6 January 1900, p. 1; *FMC*, 27 May 1893, p. 25.

67. *FM*, 1 January 1898. p. 3.

68. *FMC*, 8 January 1989, p. 19; *FMC*, 19 February 1898, p. 81.

69. *West Lancashire* calendar.

70. *Calendar of Durham* and *Calendar of Somerset. Masonic Calendar and Directory for the Province of Surrey 1900* p. 197.

71. See below p. 94.

72. *FMC*, 30 July 1898, p. 50.

73. *FM*, 20 January 1900, p. 31.

74. *FMC*, 22 June 1867, p. 485.

75. W.T.C. Blake and J.M. Moore, *Friendly Societies* (Cambridge, 1951) p. 22.

76. *Annual Report, Regulations, and List of the Governors and Subscribers of the Royal Masonic Benevolent Institution for Aged Freemasons and Widows of Freemasons 1900.*

77. *FMC*, 20 January 1894, p. 17.

78. See Clark, *Clubs*, p. 348 and D. Weinbren, 'Beneath the All-Seeing Eye: Fraternal Order and Friendly Society Banners in Nineteenth and Twentieth Century Britain' *Cultural and Social History* 3/2 (April 2006) pp. 167–91; G.W.S. Davie, 'Loyal Order of Moose and Freemasonry' *AQC* 119 (October, 2006) pp. 106–28.

79. See Nob Doran, 'Risky Business: Codifying Embodied Experience in the Manchester Unity of Oddfellows' *Journal of Historical Sociology* 7/2 (1994) pp. 131–54. See also *Rules of Court 'Tower' No. 5349 Branch of the St Austell United District of the Ancient Order of Foresters Friendly Society. Held at Newquay, Cornwall 1907*, p. 13.

80. See the discussion of the role of trust in Carolyn Downs, 'Networks, Trust, and Risk Mitigation during the American Revolutionary War: A Case Study' *EcHR* 70/2 (May 2017) pp. 509–28.

81. R.W. Dodman, *The Social Aspect of the Manchester Unity of Oddfellows* (Stamford, 1894) p. 4.

82. J. Burn, *An Historical Sketch of the Independent Order of Oddfellows, Manchester Unity* (Manchester, 1845) p. 19.

83. There were at least twenty other orders with Oddfellows in their title, mostly with purely local affiliations. See <http://en.Wikipedia.org/wiki/Odd_Fellows> [accessed 3 October 2019].

84. See *The Lectures Used by the Manchester Unity of the Independent Order of Oddfellows* (June 1846).

85. *The Complete Manual of Oddfellowship: Being a Practical Guide to its History, Principles, Ceremonies and Symbolism* (1879) p. 11.

86. The Oddfellows had made a claim to roots going back to the Romans but this was later dropped. The Ancient Order of Foresters imagined origins in the Robin Hood era.

87. Burn, *Oddfellows*, pp. 35, 109.

88. Weinbren, *Oddfellows*, p. 67.

89. Legislation was enacted in 1818, 1829, 1834, 1846, 1850, 1875 and 1896. See Blake and Moore, *Friendly Societies*, pp. 5–8 for a brief outline of the requirements of the various Acts.

90. Audrey Fisk, *Mutual Self-help in Southern England 1850–1912* (Southampton, 2006) pp. 145–50.

91. See Dot Jones, 'Did Friendly Societies Matter? A Study of Friendly Society Membership in Glamorgan, 1794–1910' *Welsh History Review* 12/3 (June 1985) pp. 324–49.

92. A guinea was equal to 1 pound and 1 shilling, which today would be £1.05.

93. W.J. Hughan, *By-Laws and Regulations of the Lodge of Love and Honour No. 75* (Falmouth, 1877). See also *By-Laws of Tregullow Lodge, St Day, Cornwall* (Redruth, 1879); *By-Laws of Cornubian Lodge 450, Hayle* (Truro, 1869) and *By-Laws of Druids Lodge of Love and Liberality 589, Redruth* (Redruth, 1852). Although Masons could apply to visit other lodges they had no automatic right to join them. A vote of the current membership needed to be taken, resulting in no more than two black balls.

94. This was not always the case in other parts of the country with some lodges asking for much higher entry fees to ensure exclusivity, such as the 20 guineas charged by Quatuor Coronati No. 2076 in the 1880s. No principle of Masonic equality was broken—it remained open to all, just like the Grill Room at the Savoy.

95. Ibid.

96. *FM*, 27 January 1894, p. 37.

97. *The Monthly Magazine of the Independent Order of Oddfellows, Manchester Unity Friendly Society* XVII (New Series Nos. 25–36, January to December 1886), p. 325.

98. The average weekly wage for a miner in Cornwall at this time was around 18 shillings per week. See Burt, *British Lead Mining*, p. 165.

99. Francis G.P. Neison, *Ancient Order of Foresters, Report upon The Additional Statistics Deduced from the Original Records of the Sickness Experience (1871–1875) of the Order: New Tables of Contributions and Benefit* (Leeds, 1886) pp. 41, 53.

100. *Rules for the Independent Order of Oddfellows Manchester Unity Friendly Society 1887* (Manchester, 1887) p. 47.

101. *Rules of Court 'Tower'*, p. 13.

102. This included the membership of the three main Oddfellows orders (viz. Independent (Manchester Unity), National Independent, and Grand United) as well as the Ancient Order of Foresters, Independent Order of Rechabites, Loyal Order of Ancient Shepherds, United Order of Free Gardeners and the United Ancient Order of Druids. There were also numerous other smaller orders. Roger Logan, 'The Role of Friendly Society Orders in British Society 1793–1911, with Special reference to the Ancient Order of Foresters Friendly Society' (Ph.D. diss., Kingston University, 2003) p. 83.

103. In 1900 the number of Foresters stood at 7,780 and the Oddfellows at 4,102. Burt, 'West Cornwall Masonic Lodges', p. 33.

104. The Ancient Order of Shepherds specialised in offering additional benefits to those who were already members of other societies. See Jones, 'Glamorgan', p. 332.

105. Fisk, *Self-Help*, pp. 159–65.

106. Ibid., p. 111.

107. *Complete Manual*, p. 17. The author rejected the authenticity of this explanation.

108. *Directory and List of the Lodges composing the Independent Order of Oddfellows (Manchester Unity) Friendly Society 1899–1900* p. 14.

109. See Fisk, *Self-Help*, pp. 159–65.

110. Weinbren, *Oddfellows*, p. 71. The separate orders of Rechabites in Britain and the America concluded an agreement in 1883 that they would extend insurance to all of their members on a mutual basis. British members travelling in the United States would receive American levels of benefit, with the sums being recouped from their home Tent. See Robert Highet, *Rechabite History* (Manchester, 1936) p. 178.

Chapter 5   Reasons for Joining, Part 2: Occupational—Mutual Assurance, Access and Networking

1. See C.G. Pooley and S. D'Cruze, 'Migration and Urbanisation in North West England circa 1760–1830' *Social History* 19/3 (1994) pp. 339–58.

2. See E.P. Hennock, *The Origins of the Welfare State in England and Germany, 1850–1914* (Cambridge, 2007).

3. See Hamill, 'And the Greatest of these is Charity'.

4. See Paul J. Rich, *Elixir of Empire: English Public Schools, Ritualism, Freemasonry and Imperialism* (London, 1989); *Chains of Empire: English Public Schools, Masonic Cabalism,*

Historical Causality, and Imperial Clubdom (London, 1991); Jessica L. Harland-Jacobs, *Builders of Empire: Freemasonry and British Imperialism* (Chapel Hill, 2007).

5. See p. 69.

6. *Emulation Ritual* (London, 1991) pp. 93–94.

7. William Preston, *Illustrations of Freemasonry* (London, 1867 edn) pp. 15–16.

8. *FM*, 25 March 1871, p. 127.

9. *FMMM*, March 1861, p. 167.

10. *Minutes of the Board of the Lodge of Benevolence*, December 1880, July 1881. Library and Museum of UGLE.

11. Richard Price, *British Society 1680–1880: Dynamism, Containment and Change* (Cambridge, 1999) p. 49.

12. E. J. Hobsbawm, 'The Tramping Artisan' *EcHR* New Series 3/3 (1951) pp. 299–320, also in his *Labouring Men: Studies in the History of Labour* (London, 1964) pp. 42–63.

13. Musson, *Typographical Association*, pp. 26–27, 50–52.

14. Douglas Knoop and G.P. Jones, *The Medieval Mason: An Economic History of English Stone Building in the Later Middle Ages and Early Modern Times* (Manchester, 1933) pp. 219–20.

15. These arrangements were sometimes encountered across Europe. See, for example, M.H.D. van Leeuwen, 'Guilds and middle-class welfare, 1500–1800: provisions for burial, sickness, old age, and widowhood' *EcHR* 65/1 (2012) pp. 61–90.

16. Knoop and Jones, *Medieval Mason*, pp. 219–20.

17. *Western Times*, 6 December 1867.

18. *FM*, 18 May 1878, p. 253.

19. Royal Clarence Lodge, Subscription and Account Book 1813–1850, East Sussex Record Office M.S. MAS 9/3/1. See Durr, 'Chicken and Egg', p. 29.

20. Musson, *Typographical Association*, p. 51.

21. Andrew Prescott and Susan Mitchell Sommers, 'Searching for the Apple Tree: Revisiting the Earliest Years of English Organised Freemasonry' *Heredom* 25 (2017) p. 134.

22. Thomas W. Hanson, *The Lodge of Probity No. 61 1738–1938* (Halifax, 1939) p. 232.

23. The full Minute reads: 'A Report from the Board of General Purposes was read, stating that an Individual, calling himself Simon Ramus, had been endeavouring to impose upon Brethren, and to obtain pecuniary Assistance, under colour of a fabricated Certificate, stating him to have been a Member of the Lodge No. 353, formerly No. 280, but which Certificate had been detained from him by the Lodge No. 283, and transmitted to the Grand Lodge. And, also, that another Individual calling himself Miles Martin, but supposed to be one Joseph Larkin, had, in a similar manner, been endeavouring to impose upon Brethren, under colour, a Certificate from the Grand Lodge of Ireland, and a certificate from the Lodge No. 145, at Norwich, but which Certificates had been detained by the S.W. of the Lodge No. 779, and transmitted to the Grand Lodge: the Board stated, that

they were induced to make this report with a View to guard Brethren against further Attempts at Imposition by those individuals, although their means were, in a great Measure, destroyed by the Detention of the Certificates.' These events were referred to by George Oliver in his editorial notes to the 1867 edition of Preston's *Illustrations*, p. 16, in which he also noticed that, 'Masonic imposters [*sic*] are [now] very numerous'.

24. *FMC*, 22 June 1901, p. 296; *FMM*, 10 August 1867, p. 107.

25. See Roger Burt, 'The Membership of West Cornwall Masonic Lodges during the Victorian Period or Why did Men become Masons' *TLRL* (2008) pp. 30–35 and Margaret Jacobs, *The First Knowledge Economy: Human Capital and the European Economy 1750–1850* (Cambridge, 2014).

26. *FM*, 19 September 1874, p. 564; 7 September 1878, p. 443.

27. *FMM*, 12 September 1868, p. 212.

28. *PUGLE*, Minutes of the Board of General Purposes, 1 June 1859. The Grand Lodge of England was particularly concerned about the Scottish practice of progressing candidates through all three degrees of initiation in one evening and requested that Scottish lodges be required to impose on English candidates the same time intervals between degrees as those that pertained in England.

29. *Proceedings of the Grand Lodge of New York*, 1896. Reporting on the *Proceedings of the Grand Lodge of Scotland*, p. 149.

30. See below p. 230.

31. *PUGLE*, 7 December 1859 and 6 December 1871. See also Andrew Prescott, 'The Causes of Humanity: Charles Bradlaugh and Freemasonry' *AQC* 116 (2003) pp. 60–63, for further background on this issue.

32. *FM*, 30 November 1901, p. 620.

33. *MI*, June 1905, p. 10.

34. *Calendar for Warwickshire 1900–1*.

35. *Calendar for Surrey 1900*.

36. They were Fidelity, Philanthropic, Alfred, Excelsior, Goderich, Defence, Zetland, and Prudence.

37. *FM*, 12 December 1901, p. 295.

38. Grand Lodge suspended a member of a London lodge for loaning his certificate for this purpose. See *PUGLE*, Minutes General Purposes, 4 March 1896.

39. *Masonic Observer*, December 1856, p. 7.

40. *FM*, 17 December 1870, p. 659.

41. The shipwrecked story was a good one, difficult to verify in the short term and helping to explain the absence of a certificate. It was used by Masonic fraudsters everywhere. See, for example, a report of American Masonic impostors in Ireland with similar stories. *FM*, 15 January 1876, p. 26.

42. James William Pownall, *List of Names of Masonic Impostors and other undeserving persons, who make a practice of habitually seeking assistance from the Almoners' Funds in different parts of the country* (Ashton-under-Lyne, 1902).

43. *MM*, 13 April 1867, p. 290.

44. *FMM*, 30 November 1867, p. 428.

45. The *FMQR*, June 1852, p. 143, commented particularly on the problems already being encountered in Boston, Massachusetts.

46. The *MM*, July 1881, p. 30, greatly regretted, 'the readiness with which American Masons are swindled' and observed that, 'there is no way by which the Masonic Order can close its doors against brazen imposters [*sic*]'.

47. It is notable that the concept of reliable 'friends', particularly away from home, was extremely important in the eighteenth and nineteenth centuries, and would have been particularly significant for less well-off Masons. See K.D.M. Snell, 'Belonging and Community: understandings of "home" and "friends" among the English poor, 1750–1850' *EcHR* 65/1 (2012) pp. 1–25.

48. Library and Museum of the Grand Lodge of England 21/C/1 (Australia) Freemasonry prospered considerably in the early Australian colonies and played a major role in the development of the economy and civic government. See B. Barrett, *The Civic Frontier: The Origins of Local Communities and Local Government in Victoria* (Melbourne, 1979) pp. 27, 44–46.

49. Bob James, *They Call Each Other Brother: Secret Societies and the Strange Slow Death of Mateship in Australia 1788–2010* (New South Wales, 2010) p. 51.

50. *PUGLE*, Minutes of the Board of General Purposes, 4 June 1890.

51. *FMMM*, 1 March 1856 p. 170; July 1857, p. 527.

52. *FMQR*, 31 December 1847, p. 123.

53. *FMQR*, 30 September 1840, p. 65.

54. *FMMM*, 24 October 1868, p. 14.

55. See, for example, The Female Middle-Class Emigration Society (1862–86) and The Women's Emigration Society (1880–84). See also J. Bush, 'The right sort of woman: female emigrators and emigration to the British Empire 1890–1910' *Journal of South African Studies* 3/3 (1994) pp. 385–409.

56. See Payton, *Cornish Overseas*, p. 87 and Jim Faull, *The Cornish in Australia* (Melbourne, 1983) p. 22.

57. Harland-Jacobs, *Builders of Empire*, pp. 248–52.

58. Ibid., p. 19.

59. James suggests that, once in Australia, many Freemasons left Masonry and joined other benevolent societies with more 'guaranteed' insurance arrangements. See Bob James, 'British Freemasonry—Fact or Fiction?' *TMAMR* 99 (2009) pp. 87–98.

60. Hanson, *Lodge of Probity*, p. 232.

61. There were over 1,200 members of Foresters' Courts in South Australia in 1861. See *The Foresters' Miscellany and Quarterly Review*, October 1862, p. 258.

62. *General Laws of the Ancient Order of Foresters Friendly Society* (1875) pp. 39–40.

63. Burn, *Oddfellows*. These arrangements appear to have been in operation since the foundation of the Order in the US in 1819.

64. Weinbren, *Oddfellows*, p. 68.

65. See Oronhyatekha, *History of the Independent Order of Foresters* (Toronto, 1894), which provides detail of many British immigrants joining the Order during the later nineteenth century.

66. This figure probably included the members' 'insured' relief for sickness.

67. Burn, *Oddfellows*, p. 155.

68. Weinbren, *Oddfellows*, p. 70.

69. See Burt, 'Membership of West Cornwall Masonic Lodges'.

70. See James, *They Call Each Other Brother*, p. 67.

71. *FMQR*, August 1900, p. 72.

72. There is no full listing of these lodges but a large number are included in K. Cochrane (ed.), *A Collection of Histories of Lodges with a Nautical Connection, Together with Summaries of the Various Grand Lodge Histories* (1989) UGLE Library and Museum A 50 COC. He lists forty-seven lodges under the United Grand Lodge of England as well as several others under the Grand Lodges of Scotland and Ireland. The book is mainly concerned with naval lodges but also includes several civilian lodges. For maritime lodges and Masons in France, see also Cécile Révauger and Éric Saunier (eds), *La Franc-maçonnerie dans les ports* (Bordeaux, 2012).

73. Ernest Shackleton, *South!: The Story of Shackleton's 1914–1917 Expedition* (London, 1922) p. 128.

74. See the Merchant Shipping Act 1894, section 742, for a definition of 'seamen'. *The Guild Gazette: A Journal of the Merchant Service Guild* (Liverpool) No. 6 (December 1899) pp. 1–2; No. 7 (April 1900) p. 9.

75. Steendekker was appointed Foreign Grand Master and given the power to constitute lodges, subject to ratification by the Grand Lodge of the Netherlands. See A. T. Penman, 'Freemasonry in South Africa' *AQC* 80 (1967) pp. 280–86.

76. *Dictionnaire Des Marins Francs-Maçons: Gens de Mer et Professions Connexes aux XVIIIe, XIXe et XXe siècles* (Nantes, 2011). See also Andrew Prescott, 'The Cross-Currents of the Union' *TLRL* (2013–14) pp. 158–68, for the participation of Swedish mariners.

77. Arthur Heiron, *Ancient Freemasonry and the Old Dundee Lodge, No. 18* (London, 1921) p. 241. Dunckerley had held membership in this lodge as a sea member before transferring to the regular category. See p. 89. See also Andrew Prescott, 'Relations between the Grand Lodges of England and Sweden during the Long Eighteenth Century' *JRFF* 3/2 (2012) pp. 185–222.

78. Belton and Cooper, 'Scotland's Masons'.

79. UGLE Love and Honour Lodge Returns, 10 October 1876.

80. Ibid. Letter, 10 October 1876.

81. Ibid. Letter, 12 February 1819.

82. *PUGLE*, Minutes of the Board of General Purposes, 7 August 1860.

83. There were three other English lodges working in Malta during the last part of the nineteenth century, but Union Lodge appears to have been the preference for

the great majority of civilian mercantile members. See D. Timson, 'Freemasonry in Malta' *TLRL* (1967–68) pp. 81–90.

84. The American Consul was a member of Union Lodge and the British Consul was a member of Yokohama.

85. See A. Ramsay, 'The Roots/Routes of the Ancient Order of Foresters in the Anglophone Caribbean' *History in Action* 2/1 (2011) pp. 1–13.

86. UGLE Sussex Lodge No. 621 Returns, 1839.

87. One initiate from Union Lodge, Captain W. Williams of the Barque 'Glencairn', was raised to a Master Mason in 1860, but later joined Cornubian Lodge, giving his address as the Foundry, Hayle. See UGLE Union Lodge Returns. Letter, 3 January 1864.

88. See Lodge Minutes, December 1844 and the Lodge of Emergency, November 1849.

89. UGLE Sussex Lodge Returns. Letter, 25 May 1852. For a general overview of the development and role of Freemasonry in Jamaica, see Jackie Ranston, *Masonic Jamaica and the Cayman Islands* 2 vols (London, 2017).

90. UGLE Sussex Lodge Returns. Letter, 2 May 1856.

91. See Burt, 'Membership', pp. 65–66.

92. UGLE Lodge returns correspondence, 22 May 1854.

93. UGLE Lodge returns correspondence, 8 May 1847.

94. UGLE Lodge Returns. Letter, 10 November 1858.

95. *FMC*, 5 May 1917, p. 148.

96. The Grand Secretary received constant complaints about these delays.

97. This was common practice for the members of many overseas lodges. See, for example, lodge correspondence from Sussex Lodge No. 345 in Kingston, Jamaica.

98. UGLE Lodge Returns, St Andrew's Lodge No. 118, now No. 1 on the roll of the Grand Lodge of Nova Scotia, 6 July 1849. The returns for this lodge include a temporary travelling certificate endorsed by numerous lodges visited by the bearer, including Rio de Janeiro and several in the Caribbean.

99. UGLE Lodge Returns, 17 November 1863.

100. Ibid., 29 March 1853.

101. UGLE Union Lodge Returns, correspondence, 21 May 1858; 13 March 1865; 2 June 1865.

102. A total of 28 pilots became members of Love and Honour, mainly in the 1860s and 1870s. See Lodge Returns.

103. Hall, *Love and Honour*.

104. See Hamill, 'And the Greatest of these is Charity', p. 164.

105. These sums appear trivial today but it is suggested that £10 in the 1850s produced a purchasing power equal to around £900 today.

106. *FM*, 15 September 1894, p. 3.

107. *FM*, January 1886, p. 3.

108. *FM*, September 1883, p. 4.

109. Ibid., December 1870, p. 6 and February 1879, p. 9; *FMC*, January 1877, p. 13. See also Prescott, 'Causes of Humanity', p. 61.

110. *Masonic Calendar for the Province of Hampshire and the Isle of Wight 1901–2*, p. 73.

111. *Devon Directory 1901*.

112. See p. 228.

113. See Burt *et al.*, *Mining in Cornwall and Devon*, Appendix A4.

114. Ibid.

115. UGLE Aberystwyth Lodge No. 1072 returns and R. Burt, P. Waite and R. Burnley, *The Mines of Cardiganshire: Metalliferous and Associated Minerals 1845–1913* (Exeter, 1985). Numerous British migrants joined lodges in Spanish mining districts, particularly those such as Linares, which were dominated by British companies. 'Santiago' Garland was one of their members, as well as John Barker, Thomas Davey, Julian Evans, Walter Pool, John Gorman, Alfred and Thomas Hancock, R. Kendall and J. Langdon. See Francisco López Villarejo, *Masonería y Sociedad en Linares, 1882–1894* (Zaragoza, 1989) Appendix 1.

116. See above p. 41.

117. Hughan, *Directory of the Provincial Grand Lodge of Cornwall* (1900).

118. UGLE *Minutes of the Board of the Lodge of Benevolence*.

119. Lodge records. Michigan Technological University Archives and Copper Country Historical Collection, Houghton, Michigan.

120. There is also evidence that some overseas lodges were ready to 'blackball' foreign applicants for membership. Thus Thomas Pearce, Jonathan and Joseph Curnow, Jonathan Mitchell, Alfred Kinsmen and T.J. Bawden were all rejected by Quincy Lodge in the 1870s and 1880s. Ibid.

121. Golden Star Lodge Account Book, Box 3, Folder 30, Homestake Adams Research and Cultural Center, Deadwood, South Dakota.

122. See Payton, *Cornish Overseas*, p. 19.

123. See, for example, *Boscawen Lodge Minutes Books, 11 Volumes, 1857–1990*, Cornwall Record Office, Truro. AD 1576.

124. See Lawrence L. Price, 'West Barbary': Or Notes on the System of Work and Wages in the Cornish Mines (1891) reprinted in Roger Burt (ed.) *Cornish Mining: Essays on the Organisation of Cornish Mines and the Cornish Mining Economy* (Newton Abbot, 1969) pp. 111–206.

125. See Payton, *Cornish Overseas*.

126. UGLE Druids Lodge returns.

127. UGLE Tregullow Lodge returns.

128. UGLE St Andrew's Lodge No. 118 returns, 1863 to 1868. All of the miners were 'fast-tracked' so that they passed through the three stages of initiation in the minimum time permitted.

129. *FMM*, 29 September 1866.

130. Hughan, *Love and Honour*. The charge for all three degrees was set at 7 guineas.

131. *Parliamentary Papers* 1890–91 [c6455], p. 43. Return of Rates of Wages in the Mines and Quarries.

132. *FM*, 8 September 1883, p. 452.

133. See Geoffrey Stobie, *Boscawen Lodge No. 699: A History 1857 to 1994* (1995) p. 5. The process went on into the twentieth century.

134. See John Killick, 'Transatlantic steerage fares, British and Irish migration, and return migration' *EcHR* 67/1 (February 2014) pp. 214–30. It should be remembered, however, that many migrants received financial assistance for their fares.

135. *FM*, 17 July 1875.

136. *FM*, 8 September 1883, p. 452.

137. *FM*, 21 September 1896, p. 522. This ominous rumbling probably originated from the Cornish Lodge No. 2363, which met in London and had a membership that included many of the elite Cornish Masons who were represented in both the Grand and Provincial Grand Lodges. See *FM*, 21 February 1891, p. 109.

138. *FM*, 3 October 1896, p. 520.

139. *FM*, 3 November 1900, p. 634.

140. In this instance the Lodge Secretary was more sceptical than his better-informed Cornish brethren who had advised that it was probably a 'wild goose chase'. He had observed that the candidate's family, 'was already well supplied with the precious metal'. UGLE Lodge Returns, Letter, 29 April 1852.

141. UGLE Lodge Returns. Letters, 17 February 1886 and 29 November 1887.

142. UGLE Lodge Returns. Letters, 1 March 1886.

143. Hanson, *Lodge of Probity*, pp. 351–78.

144. John S. Wade (ed.), *A History of Craft Freemasonry in Sheffield 1761–2017* (Sheffield, 2017) p. 28.

145. See *Exeter Pocket Journal 1857*, p. 213 and C.P. Hosgood, 'The Knights of the Road: Commercial Travellers and the Culture of the Commercial Room in late-Victorian and Edwardian England' *Victorian Studies* 37/4 (1994) pp. 519–47.

146. See, for example, Graeme Turpie, 'Freemasons in the Community' in David Beagley (ed.) *Gold and Blue: Freemasonry and Community in Bendigo 1854–2004* (Bendigo, Victoria, 2004) pp. 53–59.

147. *MI*, June 1905, p. 10.

148. Many of these issues were discussed in W.J. Hughan, 'A History of Freemasonry in Cornwall' *FMMM*, in parts, 29 September 1866, p. 246 to 31 August 1867.

149. All of the lodges in West Cornwall were sensitive to these issues and moved to their own lodge rooms between the early 1860s and the late 1870s.

150. Rogers and Wethered chaired the companies that ran two of the largest Cornish tin mines operating during and after the First World War.

151. This will be greatly facilitated by the details of all men that became Masons in lodges under the English, Scottish and Irish constitutions, which are now available via Ancestry.com.

Chapter 6   International Comparison: The Western United States

1. See Dan Plazak, *A Hole in the Ground with a Liar at the Top: Fraud and Deceit in the Golden Age of American Mining* (Salt Lake, Ut., 2006). See also George G. Rice, *My Adventures with Your Money* (Las Vegas, Nev., 1986).

2. See Carnes, *Secret Ritual*. Similarly, Greever observes that the fraternal organisations frequently provided the centre for social life in the mining towns. William S. Greever, *Bonanza West: The Story of the Western Mining Rushes 1848–1900* (Moscow, 1963) p. 180.

3. This is a use of the financial concept of hedging, where payments are made to make provision against future difficulties.

4. Rodman W. Paul, *Mining Frontiers of the Far West 1848–1880* (Albuquerque, 2001 edn) p. 213. Oddly, however, the story of fraternal lodges has received little attention from Western historians. Ronald M. James in *The Roar and the Silence: A History of Virginia City and the Comstock Lode* (Reno, 1998), makes a few oblique references to fraternities and social clubs but Elizabeth Jameson in Chapter 4 of *All that Glitters: Class, Conflict and Community in Cripple Creek* (Urbana, 1998), provides the only western urban study to give them significant notice. Richard E. Lingenfelter in *The Mining West: A Bibliography and Guide to the History and Literature of Mining in the American and Canadian West* 2 vols (Lanham, Md., 2003), notices no significant study of the subject.

5. It is notable that while churches and saloons have regularly featured in the Western film genre, lodges and fraternities are conspicuously ignored, notwithstanding the membership of many of the writers, directors and actors.

6. See, for example, Malcolm J. Rohrbough, *Days of Gold: The California Gold Rush and the American Nation* (Berkeley, 1997) pp. 40–48, 62; Price, 'West Barbary', pp. 162, 182.

7. See Noel P. Gist, *Secret Societies: A Cultural Study of Fraternalism in the United States*. University of Missouri Studies: A Quarterly of Research, XV, 4 (October 1940) pp. 31–32.

8. *FMQR*, 31 March 1843, p. 111.

9. See the *Statistics of Fraternal Societies* 1904, following. See also Louie B. Sarmiento, *The Odd Fellows* (n.l., 2019).

10. Theo A. Ross, *Odd Fellowship: Its History and Manual* (New York, 1888) p. 647.

11. W.S. Harwood, 'Secret Societies in America' *North American Review* 164 (May 1897) pp. 620–23.

12. Albert C. Stevens (ed.), *Cyclopedia of Fraternities* (New York, 1907) p. xvi.

13. For a recent survey of the range of factors promoting fraternalism during the late nineteenth and early twentieth centuries, see Kaufman, *For the Common Good?*

14. See Gunther Peck, 'Manly Gambles: The Politics of Risk on the Comstock Lode, 1860–1880' *Journal of Social History* 26/4 (Summer 1993) pp. 701–23 (pp. 707–09).

15. Oronhyatekha, *Independent Order of Foresters*, p. 9. The Independent Order continued to enjoy close relations with the Ancient Order and shared a common ritual.

16. Warren Potter and Robert Oliver, *Fraternally Yours: A History of the Independent Order of Foresters* (London, 1967) p. 49.

17. These were the early rates set by the Grand Lodges of California and Montana for lodges within their jurisdiction. See *Proceedings of the Grand Lodge of Montana*, 24 January 1866, p. 15.

18. See Anon, *History of Freemasonry in the City of Galena, Illinois* (Galena, 1874). Miners' Lodge 273, 1858, p. 69.

19. The new initiates to Nevada Lodge consisted of some men who were being initiated from the start and some who had already begun the three-degree process of initiation elsewhere. Of the total, there were 37 initiates (needing three degrees), 33 'Entered Apprentices' (needing two degrees) and 30 'Fellow Craft' (needing one degree).

20. Grand Lodge of the Independent Order of Odd Fellows, State of Nevada, *Manual of Instructions* (undated) p. 10.

21. *Roll of the Members of Escurial Lodge No. 7 F & AM, Virginia City, Storey County, Nevada also a Short History of the Lodge to December 1st 1867* available in the Bancroft Library.

22. *FMC*, 23 July 1898, p. 40.

23. The altar took the form of a small obelisk, topped with a closed bible, with a square and compasses. The base listed the names of eighteen Masons buried within 25 feet of the monument. The roads in the cemetery were also given Masonic names, such as Solomon, Jachin and Boaz. Today the cemetery's principal claim to fame is as the last resting place of Wild Bill Hickok and Calamity Jane.

24. *FMQR*, 30 September 1840, p. 65 and 31 December 1847, p. 123.

25. *FMMM*, 24 October 1868, p. 14 and also 1 September 1858, p. 604.

26. *FMQR*, 31 March 1853, p. 17.

27. *FM*, 10 August 1895, p. 456.

28. *FMC*, 15 June 1895, p. 262.

29. *FM*, 12 January 1892, p. 12.

30. Dorothy Ann Lipson, *Freemasonry in Federalist Connecticut 1789–1835* (Princeton, 1977) p. 244.

31. Anon., *Freemasonry in the City of Galena*, p. 30.

32. Golden Star Lodge Visitors Book, Box 16, Folder 10, Homestake Adams Research and Cultural Center, Deadwood, South Dakota.

33. *FMMM*, 1 March 1856, p. 170.

34. UGLE Druids Lodge returns, Letter, 22 November 1881. The claim was rejected by Druids Lodge as excessive.

35. *Proceedings of the Grand Lodge of Arizona*, 1884, p. 28.

36. See above p. 140.

37. The *MM*, July 1881, p. 30, greatly regretted, 'the readiness with which American Masons are swindled' and observed that, 'there is no way by which the Masonic Order can close its doors against brazen imposters [*sic*]'.

38. *FMQR*, August 1900, p. 72.

39. This echoed the established practice of many maritime lodges.

40. *Masonic Imposter Broadside. D.K. Osbourne & Co., Baltimore, MD, 1877*. Scottish Rite Masonic Museum and Library, Van Gorden-Williams Library and Archives, Lexington, Mass., A2002/118/1.

41. Jeffrey Croteau, 'Brotherly Deception' *Cabinet* 33 (Spring 2009).

42. Lodges subscribed on a per capita membership basis of a few cents per member.

43. Croteau, 'Deception'.

44. For a general history of Freemasonry in the United States and its organizational structure, see Mark A. Tabbert, *American Freemasons: Three Centuries of Building Communities* (Lexington, Mass., 2005).

45. Ross, *Odd Fellowship*, p. 394.

46. See Greever, *Bonanza West*, p. 63; G. Meier, *Gold Camp Foolery: E Clampus Vitus*.

47. Ralph Mann, *After the Gold Rush: Society in Grass Valley and Nevada City, California 1849–1870* (Stanford, 1982).

48. Annual returns of the membership of all Masonic lodges in California thereafter were published in the *Proceedings of the Grand Lodge of California*, 1850 and following.

49. Nevada Lodge was to become one of the leading forces in Californian Masonry, producing two Grand Masters, one Senior Grand Warden, two US Senators and two Justices of the California Supreme Court. See Granville K. Frisbie, *Gold Dust and Trowels: Nuggets of Freemasonry in the Gold Rush Days of California* (San Francisco, 1977) p. 113.

50. For the origins of Nevada Lodge, see Orval Bronson, 'Freemasonry and Some Luminaries of Nevada Lodge No. 13 F&AM' *Nevada County Historical Society Bulletin* 57/2 (April 2003) pp. 1–4.

51. Nearly all of those that left the Lodge each year generally did so by 'withdrawing', i.e. after having paid their fees up to date. Very few lost their Masonic status by being excluded. This would imply that they generally wished to remain Masons and would probably seek another lodge at their next destination.

52. See Karen Clay and Randal Jones, 'Migrating to Riches? Evidence from the California Gold Rush' *JEcH* 68/4 (2008) pp. 997–1027, for an analysis of the limited censuses of 1852 and 1854.

53. Mann, *Gold Rush*, p. 238.

54. See Liping Zhu, *A Chinaman's Chance: The Chinese on the Rocky Mountain Mining Frontier* (Niwot, Colo., 1997) p. 88.

55. See Ronald M. James, 'Defining the Group: Nineteenth Century Cornish on the North American Mining Frontier' in Philip Payton (ed.) *Cornish Studies* 2nd ser.

No. 2 (1994) p. 41. The Cornish displayed no similar hostility to their other Celtic cousins, the Welsh. With a rapidly expanding coal industry at home, the Welsh were less prominent in overseas mining districts and a long-standing symbiotic relationship across the Bristol Channel in the mining and smelting of Cornish copper had established mutual respect for their different skills. See Elwyn T. Ashton, *The Welsh in the United States* (Hove, Sussex, 1984) pp. 99–100. The Burra Burra copper mining township in South Australia, provides a particularly good example of Cornish miners and Welsh smelting workers living harmoniously in adjoining communities. See Ian Auhl, *The Story of the 'Monster Mine':The Burra Burra Mine and its Townships 1845–1877* (Burra Burra, Australia, 1986). Similarly, the Welsh worked alongside the Cornish in Nevada City and many other mining camps across the USA. See Alan Conway (ed.), *The Welsh in America: Letters from Immigrants* (Cardiff, 1961) p. 236.

56. The Order of the Eastern Star was established in Massachusetts in 1850 and introduced into the Western states by the early 1870s. See Susan Sommers, '"Hidden in Plain Sight". The Order of the Eastern Star in the Historiography of American Women's Associations' *JRFF* 4/1–2 (2013) pp. 160–79.

57. Zanjani makes brief reference to the difficulties caused for women entrepreneurs by their exclusion from the clubs and other spaces where potential investors could be found. See Sally Zanjani, *A Mine of Her Own:Women Prospectors in the American West 1850–1950* (Lincoln, Nebr., 1997) p. 6.

58. Mann, *Gold Rush*, Table 13, p. 236.

59. An informal meeting of Masons took place in Virginia City, Nevada as early as 1860 but it was not until 1863 that the first lodge was formed there, with a warrant from the California Grand Lodge. An early lodge at Bannack in Montana failed and the first permanent and surviving lodge was established in Virginia City, in Beverhead County, in 1863, with a warrant from the Grand Lodge of Kansas.

60. Those members from other parts of Europe included one or more men from France, Belgium, Norway, Denmark, Switzerland and Poland.

61. R.H. Limbaugh and W.P. Fuller, *Calaveras Gold:The Impact of Mining on a Mother Lode County* (Reno, Nev., 2004) p. 101, note that the French generally kept themselves apart in Californian mining communities. Their absence from lodges may have been a cause and/or effect of that attitude.

62. Both English and American Freemasonry required a professed belief in a 'supreme being' as a prerequisite for membership but several European Grand Lodges had become secular by the last quarter of the nineteenth century.

63. Named after a prominent local Freemason.

64. For details of the membership of Nevada lodges, see the published annual *Proceedings of the Grand Lodge of Nevada*, Grand Lodge of Nevada, West Street, Reno, Nevada.

65. James, *The Roar and the Silence*, p. 95.

66. Ronald M. James, 'Home Away from Home: Cornish Immigrants in Nineteenth Century Nevada' *Cornish Studies* 2nd ser. No. 15 (2008) pp. 1–28.

67. There is evidence that some other ethnic groups joined unions specifically to counter the preferential treatment afforded by Cornish mine managers to their countrymen. See James, 'Defining the Group', p. 36.

68. *Roll of Escurial Lodge.*

69. There are three degrees in the process of initiation to becoming a full member of a lodge as a Master Mason. The majority had achieved that status before they 'affiliated' to the Lodge but a number of others either completed their initiation by taking the third degree in Escurial Lodge or were introduced and taken through all three degrees. Overall, the Lodge itself had initiated/conferred the first degree on sixty-seven candidates, most of whom probably stayed, but some had clearly moved on. The unaccounted fourteen members of the Lodge were its founders, and therefore already well-established Master Masons. Ibid., p. 8.

70. There was concern in all of the Western territories that many of the incomers were Masons who sustained their membership of their home lodge, and chose simply to visit and not become permanent members of the lodges in the new towns. Many took steps to make it obligatory to join local lodges after one year's residence.

71. William Morgan was a Masonic impostor who was said to have been murdered by Masons in New York in 1826. His death, or disappearance, resulted in a major reaction against Masonry and a sharp fall in its total membership in the next decade.

72. *MM*, May 1879, p. 523.

73. Ross, *Odd Fellowship.*

74. *Proceedings of the Grand Lodge of I.O.O.F of Montana* 1882 and 1886.

75. Gregory Klages, 'Freemasons and Orange Order Membership in Rural Ontario during the Nineteenth Century' *Ontario History* C III/2 (Fall 2011) pp. 67–88.

76. See above p. 82.

77. It should be noted that many incomers had been made Masons under other jurisdictions at significantly lower cost.

78. From membership records of Oustomah Lodge held in the Doris Foley Library, Nevada City.

79. *Fifty Years of Odd Fellowship in California* (California, 1899).

80. Frick was made a Mason in King Solomon Lodge of Connellsville, Pennsylvania. See George Harvey, *Henry Clay Frick: The Man* (privately printed, 1936) p. 370.

81. Robert D. Putnam, *Bowling Alone: The Collapse and Revival of American Community* (New York, 2000) pp. 19–22.

Chapter 7   Other International Comparisons: Victoria, Australia and Southern Africa

1.   See W.P. Morrell, *The Gold Rushes* (London, 1940).

2. For a general review of the development of this district, see Charles Fahey, 'Peopling the Victorian Gold Fields: From Boom to Bust, 1851–1901' in Keir Reeves, Lionel Frost and Charles Fahey (eds) *A World in Search of Gold* Australian Economic History Review, Special Edition, 50/2 (July 2010) pp. 148–61. NB Until 1891 Bendigo was known as Sandhurst; the modern name of Bendigo has been used here throughout.

3. See Weston Bate, *Victorian Gold Rushes* (Melbourne, 1988).

4. Geoffrey Blainey, *The Rush that Never Ended:A History of Australian Mining* (Melbourne, 1969) pp. 42, 60.

5. High quality in terms of literacy and skills. See Bate, *Gold Rushes*, p. 30.

6. Blainey, *Rush that Never Ended*, p. 42.

7. Harland-Jacobs, *Builders of Empire*, pp. 51–60.

8. See Lane, *Masonic Records 1717–1894*; George S. Draffen, *Scottish Masonic Records 1736–1950* (Edinburgh, 1951); Philip Crossle, *Irish Masonic Records* (Dublin, 1973).

9. Barrett, *Civic Frontier*, p. 27.

10. In 1853, the *Argus* newspaper reported that 'We are told that there are upwards of two thousand Freemasons, chiefly recent arrivals, now in Melbourne, many of whom were persons of influence at home, and who now occupy here positions of great responsibility.'

11. See above p. 154.

12. UGLE Golden Lodge of Bendigo No. 641, membership returns.

13. See M. Butcher, 'Anti-Semitism in the Early Bendigo Lodges' in Beagley (ed.), *Gold and Blue*, pp. 39–46.

14. Thomas Collins, *List of the Lodges Composing the Independent Order of Oddfellows (Manchester Unity) Friendly Society, for 1892–3* (Manchester, 1892) pp. 222–23.

15. E.F. Cusack, *Bendigo:A History* (Melbourne, rev. edn, 2002) p. 185.

16. *Independent Order of Rechabites. Directory and General Reference Book for 1887–8* (Manchester, 1887). Some of the Rechabites' records can be found in the University of London Library, Senate House. Reference MS 1158.

17. Draffen, *Scottish Masonic Records*.

18. Crossle, *Irish Masonic Records*, p. 95.

19. UGLE Lodge returns for the Ballarat lodges—viz. Ballarat, United Tradesmen, Victoria, and Yarrowee lodges—for the years 1855–87 list 628 members. Returns for the Bendigo lodges—viz. Corinthian, Eaglehawk, Golden and Zenith—for the years 1854–89 list 1504 members. Many did not list their occupation. Returns to the UGLE were phased out from 1883 with the formation of the independent United Grand Lodge of Victoria.

20. See R. Burt, 'Masonic Networking by Migrating Cornish Miners' in Beagley (ed.), *Gold and Blue*, pp.13–18.

21. For example, in the food preparation trades fishmongers, grocers, confectioners, cordial makers and tobacconists appear after the 1850s.

22. Crossle, *Irish Masonic Records*, p. 95.

23. Blainey, *Rush that Never Ended*, p. 73.

24. See E. McEwan, 'The Newcastle Coalmining District of New South Wales, 1860–1900' (PhD diss., University of Sydney, 1979).

25. Lay, *One and All*, p. 128.

26. Penman, 'Freemasonry in South Africa', p. 284.

27. See Oswald Doughty, *Early Diamond Days:The Opening of the Diamond Fields of South Africa* (London, 1963).

28. See above p. 44.

29. See above p. 42.

30. See E. Rosenthal, *Gold! Gold! Gold! The Johannesburg Gold Rush* (London, 1970).

31. T. Dunbar Moodie, *Going for Gold: Men, Mines, and Migration* (Los Angeles, 1994) and Peter Richardson, *Chinese Mine Labour in the Transvaal* (London, 1982).

32. Elaine Katz, *The White Death: Silicosis on the Witwatersrand Gold Mines 1886–1910* (Witwatersrand, 1994) pp. 2, 63.

33. At the end of 1886 there were around 7,000 Europeans on the Witwatersrand. C.W. Biccard Jeppe, *Gold Mining in South Africa* (London, 1948) pp. 30, 34.

34. Brian Kennedy, *A Tale of Two Mining Cities, Johannesburg and Broken Hill 1885–1925* (Melbourne, 1984) p. 1.

35. UGLE Gold Fields Lodge No. 2478 returns. Correspondence, 28 October 1893.

36. Cosmopolitan Lodge had been established by the Grand Lodge of Scotland in Johannesburg in 1896, and the Grand Lodge of Ireland also issued warrants for Johannesburg Lodge and Malvern Lodge by 1900. See Draffen, *Scottish Masonic Records* and Crossle, *Irish Masonic Records. FM*, 28 October 1899, p. 526.

37. *FM*, 1 May 1898, p. 248.

38. See Geoffrey Wheatcroft, *The Randlords* (London, 1993) p. 140. Hammond was given as a joining member from Oriental Lodge, No. 687, established under the English constitution, in Constantinople, Turkey. UGLE Gold Fields Lodge membership returns, 1902.

39. UGLE Gold Fields Lodge returns. Letter, 28 October 1893. This was not the same man as Sir Edward Letchworth who was appointed as Grand Secretary of the United Grand Lodge of England. See Roeinton B.F. Khambatta, *The Grand Secretaries of the United Grand Lodge of England 1813–1980* (Prestonian Lecture, 2007) pp. 46–51.

40. Richard D. Dawe, *Cornish Pioneers*, pp. 271, 277.

Chapter 8   The influence of Freemasonry: Members and their Communities

1. See *FMQR*, June 1852, p. 131.

2. Andrew C. Isenberg, *Mining California:An Ecological History* (New York, 2005) p. 65.

3. See Clifford MacCulla, 'The Public Masonic Charities of the United States of America' *Masonic Magazine* (April 1875) p. 293.

4. See George W. Speth, 'Freemasonry in Wartime'. Chronicle Report on South Africa *AQC* 13 (1900) pp. 189–91.

5. *FM*, 20 January 1900, p. 31.

6. For a personal account of the flight of Cornish miners from the gold fields, see Hannan, *Travels and Heartaches*, Chapter 9.

7. *FM*, 28 October 1899, p. 526.

8. *MI*, February 1901, p. 102.

9. *FM*, 26 May 1900, p. 323.

10. *FM*, 7 April 1900, p. 210.

11. *FMC*, 11 November 1899, p. 217. *FM*, 27 January 1900, reported a large meeting of Masons in Portsmouth, with representatives from Winchester, Chichester, Southampton and elsewhere.

12. *MI*, November 1901, p. 34.

13. *FMC*, 3 November 1900, p. 206.

14. *FMC*, 4 November 1899, p. 205, reported that numerous lodges and Royal Arch Chapters had donated £144 to the *Daily Telegraph* Fund in the previous week alone.

15. *FM*, 9 December 1899, p. 617. In 1858, for example, Freemasons had made generous contributions to the Indian Relief Fund.

16. See Dawe, *Cornish Pioneers*, p. 275 and Dickason, *Cornish Immigrants*, p. 68.

17. *MI*, December 1901 p. 50. See also Speth, 'Freemasonry in Wartime', p. 189. Notice was taken of a meeting of Rising Star Lodge in Bloemfontein on the 23 April that was attended by a number of distinguished generals, including Kitchener.

18. *Biographical Record of Houghton, Baraga and Marquette Counties, Michigan* (Chicago, 1903).

19. Lynn R. Bailey and Don Chaput, *Cochise County Stalwarts* 2 vols (Tucson, Ariz., 2000).

20. Dorothy Wickham, *Freemasonry on the Goldfields. Ballarat and District 1853–2013* (Ballarat, 2013).

21. Wade (ed.), *Craft Freemasonry in Sheffield*, p. 30. St George's Lodge records.

22. Robert M. Senkewicz, *Vigilantes in Gold Rush San Francisco* (Stanford, 1985).

23. John S. Hittell, *The Resources of California* (San Francisco, 1869) p. 374.

24. Frederick Allen, *A Decent and Orderly Lynching: The Montana Vigilantes* (Norman, Okla., 2004) and Roger Burt, '"Order without Law": Masons and Vigilantism in Virginia City, Montana, and Tombstone, Arizona' *Heredom* 25 (2017) pp. 581–619.

25. Others members of the party, including General H.D. Washburn, Truman Everts, M.F. Truett, Warren Gillette, Benjamin Stickney and Walter Trumbull may also have been Masons but their membership has not been established. It is likely that Jacob Smith, a much-criticised member of the support team, was a Mason.

26. Some of the principal records of the expedition are the accounts of Hedges and Langford. See Cornelius Hedges, 'Journal of Judge Cornelius Hedges, Member

of the Washburn Expedition of 1870' *Contributions to the Historical Society of Montana* V: pp. 370–94 and N.P. Langford, *The Discovery of Yellowstone Park. Journal of the Washburn Expedition to the Yellowstone and Firehole Rivers in the Year 1870* (1905, reprinted Lincoln, Nebr., 1972).

27. See W. Turrentine Jackson, 'The Washburn–Doane Expedition into the Upper Yellowstone, 1870' *Pacific Historical Review* 10/2 (June 1941) pp. 189–208.

28. Penman, 'Freemasonry in South Africa', p. 285.

29. Barrett, *Civic Frontier* and Wickham, *Freemasonry on the Goldfields*.

30. Barrett, *Civic Frontier*, pp. 44–46.

31. Ibid., pp. 156, 284–85.

32. Collins, *Independent Order of Oddfellows (Manchester Unity) Friendly Society, for 1892–3*, p. 222.

33. Wickham, *Freemasonry on the Goldfields*, p. 51.

34. Barrett, *Civic Frontier*, p. 302.

35. Andrew Prescott, 'Freemasonry in the Victorian City' *TMAMR* XCIX (2009) pp. 101–09.

36. Pamela M. Davies, 'An Ancient and Honourable Institution: An Examination of the Development of Freemasonry in Merthyr Tydfil 1810–1914' (Ph.D. diss., Sheffield University, 2010).

37. James W.P. Campbell, 'Studying Masonic Halls' *AQC* 129 (2016) pp. 13–39.

38. Gerald Reilly, 'Freemasonry and the Urbanisation of Harwich' *AQC* 130 (2017) pp. 43–76.

39. Regimental lodges had established a precedent for the formation of such lodges, which were unusual outside of those established under the UGLE. See *FM*, 22 September 1894. Cornish Lodge in London was one such special interest lodge.

40. See also John Hamill and Andrew Prescott, '"The Masons' Candidate": New Welcome Lodge No. 5139 and the Parliamentary Labour Party' *Labour History Review* 71/1 (April 2006) pp. 9–41.

41. See Andrew Prescott, 'Freemasonry in Suburban London 1860–1930: A Case Study' *TMAMR* XCII (2002) pp. 41–82.

42. See Douglas Knoop, *University Masonic Lodge* (Sheffield, 1945).

43. See *FM*, 12 November 1932, p. 275.

44. William J. Smyth, *Toronto, The Belfast of Canada* (Toronto, 2015).

45. In 1914 there were only just over 100,000 Masons in Canada, compared to more than one and a half million in the USA. See Osborne Sheppard, *Freemasonry in Canada* (Washington, 2013) pp. 153, 165.

46. See W.P. Malcomson, 'The Forgotten History of the Orange Order: The Institution's Historic Struggle Against the Royal Arch Purple and the Black Degree (1798–1925)' <https://www.academia.edu/38186136/THE_FORGOTTEN_HISTORY_OF_THE_ORANGE_ORDER> [accessed 3 October 2019].

47. Smyth, *Toronto*, p. 8.

48. Ibid., pp. 124, 171.

49. But see Augustus Casely-Hayford and Richard Rathbone, 'Politics, Families and Freemasonry in the Colonial Gold Coast' in J.F. Ade Ajayi and J.D.Y. Peel (eds) *Peoples and Empires in African History: Essays in Memory of Michael Crowder* (London, 1992) pp. 143–60.

50. See William M. McPhee, *The Trail of the Leprechaun: Early History of a Utah Mining Camp* (New York, 1977) p. 87.

51. See Zhu, *Chinaman's Chance*, p. 52; Rudolph M. Lapp, *Blacks in Gold Rush California* (New Haven, 1977) p. 92. There were only a few hundred 'coloured' labourers in the Californian diggings in the first years of the gold rush and only a few thousand by 1860.

52. *Clark's History of Freemasonry in Iowa 1775–1945* (Cedar Rapids, 2011 edn) p. 8.

53. *New Age*, July 1914.

54. Lapp, *Blacks in Gold Rush California*, p. 255.

55. These included seven in Colorado, two in Wyoming, four in Montana, four in New Mexico, four in Arizona and one each in Idaho and Utah respectively. See William H. Grimshaw, *Official History of Freemasonry among the Coloured People in North America* (New York, 1903) p. 267.

56. P. Rachleff, *Black Labor In Richmond, 1865–1890* (Urbana, 1989) p. 25. See also P.L. Dunbar, 'Hidden in Plain Sight: African American Secret Societies and Black Freemasonry' *Journal of African American Studies* 16/4 (2012) pp. 622–37.

57. Gist, *Secret Societies*, p. 163.

58. It should be noted, however, that while this enthusiasm may have been true of Masons' wives, Zanjani's study of women actively involved in the mining industry concluded that they generally preferred solitude and showed, 'little evidence of sisterhood or networking'. See Zanjani, *A Mine of Her Own*, p. 116.

59. See Kayoko Yoshida and Reiko Miyauchi, 'Invisible Labor: A Comparative Oral History of Women in Coal Mining Communities of Hokkaido, Japan and Montana, USA, 1890–1940' in Jaclyn Gier and Laurie Mercier (eds) *Mining Women: Gender in the Development of a Global Industry, 1670 to 2005* (New York, 2006) p. 147.

60. See Christopher J. Kauffman, *Faith and Fraternalism: The History of the Knights of Columbus 1882–1982* (New York, 1982); and Douglas Brinkley and Julie M. Fenster, *Parish Priest: Father Michael McGivney and American Catholicism* (New York, 2006).

61. See J.S.M. Ward and W.G. Stirling, *The Hung Society: or the Society of Heaven and Earth* vol. 1 (London, 1925) pp. 6–8; Kok Hu Jin, *Chinese Lodges in Australia* (Bendigo, 2005) p. 10. Sun Yet-Sen, the first President of post-Imperial China, was a member of the Hung Society. A Christian, he also showed reverence to ancient traditions.

62. *FMC*, October 1888, p. 211; June 1890, p. 357; March 1891, p. 194.

63. See Wickham, *Freemasonry on the Goldfields*, pp. 36–40.

64. See J.G. Naismith, 'Chinese Freemasonry' (privately printed, 1946). Naismith estimated the international membership of these societies at between 32 and 37 million in the mid-twentieth century, at that time larger than most of the

Western benevolent societies put together. See also Zhu, *Chinaman's Chance*, pp. 89–90.

65. See James, *They Call Each Other Brother*, pp. 148–51 and Bob James, 'Secret Societies and the Labour Movement: Part 2 The Knights of Labour' *Australian Society for the Study of Labour History* 6th Biennial Conference October 1999 <http://www.takver.com/history//secsoc02.htm> [accessed 3 October 2019].

66. M. Murphy, *Mining Cultures: Men, Women and Leisure in Butte, 1914–41* (Urbana, 1997) p. 138.

67. Roger Burt, 'The Role of Fraternal Organisations in Migration and Informal Labour Organisations in Mining Communities: Cornwall, the Keweenaw, and California Compared' (Houghton, 2014) <https://digitalcommons.mtu.edu/cgi/viewcontent.cgi?article=1000&context=copperstrikesymposium> [accessed 3 October 2019].

68. Roy Rosenzweig, 'Boston Masons, 1900–1935: The Lower Middle Class in a Divided Society' *Journal of Voluntary Action Research* 6 (1977) pp. 119–26.

69. Kaufman, *For the Common Good?*, p. 197.

70. Dudley Wright, *Roman Catholicism and Freemasonry* (London, 1922) p. 180.

71. *New Age Magazine*, January 1920, p. 9; July 1920, pp. 326–28; August 1920, pp. 369–70.

72. Prominent Masons such as Robert Crucifix, founder of the influential *FMQR*, helped campaign for the change.

73. UGLE Friendly Lodge No. 239, Jamaica returns. Letter, 26 February 1839. At that time a candidate for initiation had to declare that 'He was born a free man.' Today it is simply that he 'is a free man'.

74. Simon Deschamps, 'Freemasonry and the Indian Parsi Community: A Late Meeting on the Level' *JRFF* 3/1 (2012) pp. 60–71.

75. See Fraser B. Musa, 'The First Indian Freemason' *AQC* 91 (1968) pp. 318–20 and Harland-Jacobs, *Builders of Empire*, p. 222.

76. See UGLE Lodge Returns.

77. *FM*, 3 November 1917, p. 224.

78. UGLE Yokohama Lodge No. 1092 returns. Letter, 27 August 1872. The Secretary was Charles Dallas, employed by the Imperial School for Foreign Languages in Yonesawa, Japan.

79. Yoshio Washizu, 'Anti-Masonry in Japan—Past and Present' *AQC* 107 (1994) pp. 85–116. A very small number of Japanese were initiated in lodges in Holland and Britain from the 1860s but it is not clear whether they were able to be active in Japan.

80. See Casely-Hayford and Rathbone, 'Colonial Gold Coast', for exceptions.

81. D.J. Gillett, 'A Glimpse of Freemasonry in Nigeria' *TLRL* (1970–71) p. 90.

82. J.H. Heykamp, 'Freemasonry in South Africa and Rhodesia' *Philalethes* (February 1948) p. 3.

83.   W.H. McNeill, *Keeping Together in Time: Dance and Drill in Human History* (Cambridge, Mass., 1995).

84.   Dumenil, *Freemasonry and American Culture*, p. 54. In 1891, for example, the Freemasons of New York State included clergy from the Universalist, Episcopalian, Methodist, Congregational, Presbyterian, Lutheran and Baptist churches—every denomination except the Catholics, who excluded themselves. See also Carnes, *Secret Ritual*, p. 61.

85.   See Samuel Smiles, *Self-Help* (1859), *Character* (1871), *Thrift* (1875), *Duty* (1880). Smiles strongly advocated associations for mutual assurance as a means of thrift.

86.   It has been argued that Freemasonry was a major force in promoting the general cause of educational development in the West. See D. Egel, 'Did Freemasonry Help Solve the Common Good Problem? An Examination of the Historical Expansion of Education in the Western United States' (2009) Google Scholar PDF 66.223.50.234.

87.   See R.D. McGrath, *Gunfighters, Highwaymen and Vigilantes: Violence on the Frontier* (Berkeley, 1984) p. 247.

88.   See R. Jones, 'Sociability, Solidarity, and Social Exclusion: Women's Activism in the South Wales Coalfield, ca. 1830 to 1939' in Gier and Mercier (eds) *Mining Women*, pp. 96–118. Mercier also draws attention to the importance that fraternities played in social interaction in her *Anaconda: Labor, Community, and Culture in Montana's Smelter City* (Urbana, 2001) pp. 118–19.

89.   See E. Eklund, 'Company and Labour Loyalties in a Central Queensland Gold Mining Town' *Journal of Australasian Mining History* 11 (October 2013) pp. 24–42.

90.   See Louis B. Wright, *Culture on the Moving Frontier* (Bloomington, Ind., 1955).

91.   The Knights' password became 'diligence, devotion and defense'. See Kauffman, *Faith and Fraternalism*, p. xi. See also Brinkley and Fenster, *Parish Priest*, Chapter 8.

92.   Fabio Braggion, 'Managers and (Secret) Social Networks: The Influence of Freemasonry on Firms' Performance' *Journal of the European Economic Association* 9/6 (December 2011) pp. 1053–81. See also Fabio Braggion and Lyndon Moore, 'The Economic Benefits of Political Connections in Late Victorian Britain' *JEcH* 73/1 (2013) pp. 142–76, in which the recruitment of politicians (most of whom would have been Freemasons) as the directors of firms is shown to have had a beneficial effect on some share prices.

Chapter 9   Conclusion

1.   These returns are now available on a name basis online at Ancestry.com.

2.   Harland-Jacobs has referred to the particular role of Freemasonry in channelling information about imperial affairs and fostering the concept of a citizen of the Empire. Harland-Jacobs, *Builders of Empire*, pp. 240–52.

3. See George H. Nash, *The Life of Herbert Hoover: The Engineer 1874–1914* (New York, 1981) p. 252.

4. Biographical studies of Masons and members of friendly societies commonly reveal close personal links between different orders and the churches. See, for example, Oronhyatekha, *Independent Order of Foresters*, p. 745 following.

5. *FM*, 28 December 1878, p. 599.

6. In this sense, Freemasonry played a role in the 'self-selection' of migrants, which has recently been a subject of interest in academic literature. See Edward Kosack and Zachary Ward, 'Who Crossed the Border? Self Selection of Mexican Migrants in the early Twentieth Century' *JEcH* 74/4 (December 2014) pp. 1015–44 and Francisco J. Beltrán Tapia and Santiago de Miguel Salanova, 'Migrant Self-Selection in the Early Stages of Modern Economic Growth, Spain 1880–1930' *EcHR* 70/1 (February 2017) pp. 101–21.

7. *FMMM*, 2 March 1867.

8. See Peter Ackers and Alastair J. Reid, *Alternatives to State Socialism in Britain* (London, 2017).

9. See Robert A. Gilbert, 'Whither or Wither—A Personal View of the Future of English Freemasonry' *AQC* 118 (2005) pp. 233–42, for a perceptive overview of recent changes and possible future directions.

Appendix 5   Managerial Positions in Cornish Mines Held by Members of Masonic Lodges in West Cornwall in 1883

1. Management details from *Kelly's Directory of Cornwall* (1883) pp. 1159–61. See also R. Symons, *A Geographical Dictionary or Gazetteer of the County of Cornwall* (Penzance, 1884).

2. It should be noted that many of the pursers also described themselves as accountants.

Appendix 11   Maritime Members of the Lodge of Love & Honour No. 75, Falmouth 1801–1900

1. It is notable that none of the men joining Love & Honour or Union Lodge were from France and none appear in *Dictionnaire Des Marins Francs-Maçons, Gens De Mer et Professions Connexes aux XVIIIe, XIXe et XXe siècles* (Nantes, 2011).

2. Where a place is not given, it is not known.

3. *Christian Mathias Sauerland* was initiated in Lodge Carl zum Felsem in Altona-Marter, the Prince of Holsteinbeck, not under the English Constitution. This is Altona, Denmark. Passed and Raised in Love and Honour. The Secretary of Love and Honour has difficulty in obtaining his Certificate from the Grand Lodges. He finally receives one but has difficulty sending it on. In 1839 the certificate is returned and it is now to be found in the UGLE Love and Honour Lodge returns.

4. The Secretary of Love and Honour writes to Grand Lodge asking for *Feliciano's* certificate, saying that Feliciano 'has been initiated into the first degree of Freemasonry and expects to sail from here to his native place in Portugal in the course of a few days'. It is possible that he was initiated the previous year.

5. *Robert Ede* was from Mariners Lodge, Chatham.

6. *Bartholomew Karsten* was born in Elbing, Prussia. He was initiated and passed Rhode Island, USA in 1818. He was raised in Love and Honour and needed his Certificate urgently because he was leaving Falmouth in a week.

7. *Frederick Adolph Begemann Sietzes* was the Commander of the Dutch East Indiaman, 'Queen of the Netherlands'. He was initiated in Love and Honour on 7 April, passed 5 May and raised 1 June. This appears to have been a long stay in port, possibly for repairs.

8. *Thomas Hiscock* needs his Certificate urgently because he 'is about to sail to the Mediterranean'.

9. *George Penny* joined from a lodge in the Cape of Good Hope.

10. *John Pickering* joined from Silurian No. 693, Newport, Monmouth.

11. *Henry Whitehead* joined from Zetland No. 756, Valletta, Malta.

12. *Joseph Manning* had been initiated, passed and raised in a Scottish lodge in Marseilles.

13. *Richard Pincher* later joined a London lodge.

14. A British ship involved in the Africa trade.

15. *Michael Vowells* was initiated Falmouth, passed Woolwich, and raised Sunderland. Three stages of initiation that were conducted in three different places.

16. *Timothy Laing* joined from Union Lodge No. 588, Valletta, Malta.

17. *Henrick Hoenke* joined from Silurian No. 693, Newport.

18. *James Adie* joined from Zetland No. 756, Valletta, Malta.

19. *John Lenty* joined from Tasmanian Union, Hobart.

20. *Ambrose Gibson* was passed and raised in Atlantic Phoenix Lodge No. 271, Bermuda.

21. *Jurgen Kroll* joined from St Johannes, Sweden.

22. *Christian L. Kohn* joined from Ancient Union No. 245, Liverpool.

23. Later joins Lodge of Industry No. 48, Gateshead.

24. *William H.Valler* was from Sussex No. 447, Kingston, Jamaica.

25. *Diedrich H. Siefkes* from a lodge in Rio de Janeiro.

26. *? Hjorth* had an address via the Swedish and Norwegian consulate.

27. From the town of Brahestad.

28. From the town of Sundsvall.

29. *Eugimo Gambaro* joined from Caffrare Lodge, Genoa, Grand Orient of Italy.

30. Leaving for East India.

31. From Dalhousie No. 860, London.

32. From Merchants No. 242, Liverpool and Unanimity No. 89, Duckinfield.

33. From Prince of Wales No. 671, Llanelli.

34. From the town of Mandall.

Appendix 12   Occupations of the Masters of the Lodge of Love and Honour No. 75, Falmouth 1850–1900

1.   Hall, *Love and Honour*. It is notable that the list of the Past officers of Old Dundee Lodge also shows no maritime members. See Heiron, *Old Dundee Lodge*, pp. 259–64.

Appendix 13   Mariners Initiated and Joining Union Lodge No. 588, Floriana, Malta 1860–1869

1.   A number of regimental lodges with travelling warrants met in Malta from the early eighteenth century as they 'passed through'. See Brian W. Price, 'Malta, GC: A Military and Masonic Crossroads' *AQC* 130 (2017) pp. 13–42. The four regular 'civilian' lodges meeting on the island during this period were: Zetland Lodge No. 515, St John and St Paul Lodge No. 349, and Wayfarers Lodge No. 1926, all meeting in Valletta; and Union Lodge No. 588, meeting in Floriana.

BIBLIOGRAPHY

Ackers, Peter and Alastair J. Reid, *Alternatives to State Socialism in Britain* (London: Palgrave Macmillan, 2017).

Allen, Frederick, *A Decent and Orderly Lynching: The Montana Vigilantes* (Norman: University of Oklahoma Press, 2004).

Amherst, Lord and Hamon Le Strange, *History of Union Lodge, Norwich, No. 52* (privately printed, 1898).

Anon, *History of Freemasonry in the City of Galena, Illinois* (Galena: 1874).

Armstrong, W.A., *Stability and Change in an English County Town: A Social Study of York 1801–1851* (Cambridge: Cambridge University Press, 1974).

Armstrong, W.A., 'The Use of Information about Occupation' in E.A. Wrigley (ed.) *Nineteenth-Century Society: Essays in the Use of Quantitative Methods for the Study of Social Data* (Cambridge: Cambridge University Press, 1972).

Ashby, John F., 'Freemasonry and Entertainment' *Transactions of the Manchester Association for Masonic Research* LXXXIX (1999) pp. 39–63.

Ashton, Elwyn T., *The Welsh in the United States* (Hove, Sussex: Caldra House, 1984).

Aston, Jennifer and Paolo di Martino, 'Risk, Success, and Failure: Female Entrepreneurship in Late Victorian and Edwardian England' *Economic History Review* 70/3 (2017) pp. 837–58.

Auhl, Ian, *The Story of the 'Monster Mine': The Burra Burra Mine and its Townships 1845–1877* (Burra Burra, Australia: Investigator Press, 1986).

Bailey, Lynn R. and Don Chaput, *Cochise County Stalwarts* 2 vols (Tucson, Ariz.: Westernlore Press, 2000).

Barrett, Bernard, *The Civic Frontier: The Origin of Local Communities and Local Government in Victoria* (Melbourne: Melbourne University Press, 1979).

Bate, Weston, *Victorian Gold Rushes* (Melbourne: Penguin Books, 1988).

Belton, John and Robert Cooper, 'Scotland's Masons: Membership and Occupations of Freemasons 1800–2000' in Andreas Onnerfors and Robert Peter (eds) *Researching British Freemasonry 1717–2017* (Sheffield: Sheffield Lectures on the History of Freemasonry and Fraternalism, 3, 2010) pp. 99–126.

Beltrán Tapia, Francisco J. and Santiago de Miguel Salanova, 'Migrant Self-Selection in the Early Stages of Modern Economic Growth, Spain 1880–1930' *Economic History Review* 70/1 (February 2017) pp. 101–21.

Best, Geoffrey, *Mid-Victorian Britain 1851–75* (London: Fontana, 1971).

Blainey, Geoffrey, *The Rush that Never Ended: A History of Australian Mining* (Melbourne: Melbourne University Press, 1969).

Blake, W.T.C and J.M. Moore, *Friendly Societies* (Cambridge: Cambridge University Press, 1951).

Braggion, Fabio, 'Managers and (Secret) Social Networks: The Influence of Freemasonry on Firms' Performance' *Journal of the European Economic Association* 9/6 (December 2011) pp. 1053–81.

Braggion, Fabio and Lyndon Moore, 'The Economic Benefits of Political Connections in Late Victorian Britain' *Journal of Economic History* 73/1 (2013) pp. 142–76.

Brinkley, Douglas and Julie M. Fenster, *Parish Priest: Father Michael McGivney and American Catholicism* (New York: HarperCollins, 2006).

Bronson, Orval, 'Freemasonry and Some Luminaries of Nevada Lodge No. 13 F&AM' *Nevada County Historical Society Bulletin* 57/2 (April 2003) pp. 1–4.

Burn, J., *An Historical Sketch of the Independent Order of Oddfellows, Manchester Unity* (Manchester: 1845).

Burt, Roger, *Cornish Mining* (Newton Abbot: David and Charles, 1969).

Burt, Roger, *The British Lead Mining Industry* (Redruth: Truran, 1984).

Burt, Roger, Peter Waite and Raymond Burnley, *The Mines of Cardiganshire: Metalliferous and Associated Minerals 1845–1913* (Exeter: University of Exeter, 1985).

Burt, Roger, 'Industrial Relations in the British Non-Ferrous Mining Industry in the Nineteenth Century' *Labour History Review* 71/1 (April 2006) pp. 57–79.

Burt, Roger, 'Segmented Capital Markets and Patterns of Investment in Late Victorian Britain: Evidence from the Non-Ferrous Mining Industry' *Economic History Review* 51/4 (November 1998) pp. 709–33.

Burt, Roger, 'Freemasonry and business networking during the Victorian period' *Economic History Review* 56/4 (November 2003) pp. 657–88.

Burt, Roger, 'Who were the Mark Masons? A Look at Some Lodges in West Cornwall during the Victorian Period' in Andrew Prescott (ed.) *Marking Well* (London: Lewis Masonic, 2006) pp. 171–80.

Burt, Roger, 'Masonic Networking by Migrating Cornish Miners' in David Beagley (ed.) *Gold and Blue: Freemasonry and Community in Bendigo 1854–2004* (Bendigo, Victoria: Holland House, 2004) pp. 13–18.

Burt, Roger, 'The Membership of West Cornwall Masonic Lodges during the Victorian Period or Why did Men become Masons?' *Transactions of the Lodge of Research, Leicester* 98 (2008) pp. 30–35.

Burt, Roger, 'The Role of Fraternal Organisations in Migration and Informal Labour Organisations in Mining Communities: Cornwall, the Keweenaw, and California

Compared' (Houghton: Michigan Technological University, 2014) <https://digitalcommons.mtu.edu/cgi/viewcontent.cgi?article=1000&context=copperstrikesymposium> [accessed 3 October 2019]. A short version of the article appeared in *Ars Quatuor Coronatorum* 130 (2017) pp. 205–22.

Burt, Roger, '"Order without Law": Masons and Vigilantism in Virginia City, Montana, and Tombstone, Arizona' *Heredom* 25 (2017) pp. 581–619.

Burt, Roger with Raymond Burnley, Michael Gill and Alasdair Neill, *Mining in Cornwall and Devon: Mines and Men* (Exeter: University of Exeter Press, 2014).

Bush, J., 'The right sort of woman: female emigrators and emigration to the British Empire 1890–1910' *Journal of South African Studies* 3/3 (1994) pp. 385–409.

Butcher, M., 'Anti-Semitism in the Early Bendigo Lodges' in David Beagley (ed.) *Gold and Blue: Freemasonry and Community in Bendigo 1854–2004* (Bendigo, Victoria: Holland House, 2004) pp. 39–46.

Campbell, James W.P., 'Studying Masonic Halls' *Ars Quatuor Coronatorum* 129 (2016) pp. 13–39.

Cannadine, David, *Class in Britain* (New Haven: Yale University Press, 1998).

Carnes, Mark C., *Secret Ritual and Manhood in Victorian America* (New Haven: Yale University Press, 1989).

Casely-Hayford, Augustus and Richard Rathbone, 'Politics, Families and Freemasonry in the Colonial Gold Coast' in J.F. Ade Ajayi and J.D.Y. Peel (eds) *Peoples and Empires in African History: Essays in Memory of Michael Crowder* (London: Longman, 1992) pp. 143–60.

Chase, Malcolm, *Early Trade Unionism: Fraternity, Skill and the Politics of Labour* (Farnham: Ashgate, 2000).

Clark, Peter, *British Clubs and Societies 1580–1800: The Origins of an Associational World* (Oxford: Oxford University Press, 2000).

Clark's History of Freemasonry in Iowa 1775–1945 (Cedar Rapids: Grand Lodge of Iowa, 2011 edn).

Clawson, Mary Ann, *Constructing Brotherhood: Class, Gender and Fraternalism* (Princeton: Princeton University Press, 1989).

Clay, Karen and Randall Jones, 'Migrating to Riches? Evidence from the California Gold Rush' *Journal of Economic History* 68/4 (2008) pp. 997–1027.

Cochrane, K. (ed.), *A Collection of Histories of Lodges with a Nautical Connection, Together with Summaries of the Various Grand Lodge Histories* (n.l.: privately printed, 1989).

Collins, Thomas, *List of the Lodges Composing the Independent Order of Oddfellows (Manchester Unity) Friendly Society, for 1892–3* (Manchester: n.p., 1892).

Conway, Alan (ed.), *The Welsh in America: Letters from Immigrants* (Cardiff: University of Wales Press, 1961).

Cordery, Simon, 'Friendly Societies and the Discourse of Respectability in Britain 1825–1875' *Journal of British Studies* 34 (January 1995) pp. 35–58.

Cordery, Simon, *British Friendly Societies 1750–1914* (London: Palgrave Macmillan, 2003).

Crossle, Philip, *Irish Masonic Records* (Dublin: Grand Lodge of Ireland, 1973).

Crossley, Herbert, *History of the Lodge of Probity No. 61* (Halifax: n.p., 1888).

Croteau, Jeffrey, 'Brotherly Deception' *Cabinet* 33 (Spring 2009).

Cummings, D.C., *An Historical Survey of the Boiler Makers' and Iron and Steel Ship Builders' Society* (Newcastle-upon-Tyne: R. Robinson, 1905).

Cusack, E.F., *Bendigo: A History* (Melbourne: Lerk & McClure, 2002 edn).

Davie, Gordon W.S., 'Loyal Order of Moose and Freemasonry' *Ars Quatuor Coronatorum* 119 (October, 2006) pp. 106–28.

Davies, Pamela M., 'An Ancient and Honourable Institution: An Examination of the Development of Freemasonry in Merthyr Tydfil 1810–1914' (Ph.D. diss., Sheffield University, 2010).

Davis, Peter, 'How Freemasonry Evolved in South Wales' *Ars Quatuor Coronatorum* 129 (2016) pp. 41–92.

Dawe, Richard D., *Cornish Pioneers in South Africa* (St Austell: Cornish Hillside Publications, 1998).

Deschamps, Simon, 'Freemasonry and the Indian Parsi Community: A Late Meeting on the Level' *Journal for Research into Freemasonry and Fraternity* 3/1 (2012) pp. 60–71.

Dickason, Graham B., *Cornish Immigrants to South Africa* (Cape Town: A.A. Balkema, 1978).

Dictionnaire Des Marins Francs-Maçons: Gens de Mer et Professions Connexes aux XVIIIe, XIXe et XXe siècles (Nantes: Association Ponantaise D'Histoire Maritime Sous Le Direction de Jean-Marc Van Hille, 2011).

Dodman, R.W., *The Social Aspect of the Manchester Unity of Oddfellows* (Stamford: 1894).

Doran, Nob, 'Risky Business: Codifying Embodied Experience in the Manchester Unity of Oddfellows' *Journal of Historical Sociology* 7/2 (1994) pp. 131–54.

Doughty, Oswald, *Early Diamond Days: The Opening of the Diamond Fields of South Africa* (London: Longmans, 1963).

Downs, Carolyn, 'Networks, Trust, and Risk Mitigation During the American Revolutionary War: A Case Study' *Economic History Review* 70/2 (2017) pp. 509–28.

Draffen, George S., *Scottish Masonic Records 1736–1950* (Edinburgh: Grand Lodge of Scotland, 1951).

Dumenil, Lynn, *Freemasonry and American Culture, 1880–1939* (Princeton, Princeton University Press, 1984).

Dunbar, P.L., 'Hidden in Plain Sight: African American Secret Societies and Black Freemasonry' *Journal of African American Studies* 16/4 (2012) pp. 622–37.

Durr, Andy, 'Rituals of Association and the Organisation of the Common People' *Ars Quatuor Coronatorum* 100 (1987) pp. 88–108.

Durr, Andy, 'From Fraternal Groups to Trade Unions' *Freemasonry Today* 24 (2003).

Durr, Andy, 'Chicken and Egg—the Emblem Book and Freemasonry: The Visual and Material Culture of Associated Life' *Ars Quatuor Coronatorum* 118 (2005) pp. 20–35.

Eakin, Marshall C., *British Enterprise in Brazil:The St John d'el Rey Mining Company and the Morro Velho Gold Mine, 1830–1960* (Durham: University of North Carolina, 1989).

Eklund, E., 'Company and Labour Loyalties in a Central Queensland Gold Mining Town' *Journal of Australasian Mining History* 11 (October 2013) pp. 24–42.

Egel, D., 'Did Freemasonry Help Solve the Common Good Problem? An Examination of the Historical Expansion of Education in the Western United States' (2009) Google Scholar PDF 66.223.50.234.

Erickson, C., *British Industry: Steel and Hosiery* (Cambridge: Cambridge University Press, 1986).

Fahey, Charles, 'Peopling the Victorian Gold Fields: From Boom to Bust, 1851–1901' in Keir Reeves, Lionel Frost and Charles Fahey (eds) *A World in Search of Gold* Australian Economic History Review, Special Edition, 50/2 (July 2010) pp. 148–61.

Faull, Jim, *The Cornish in Australia* (Melbourne: Australasian Educa Press, 1983).

Frisbie, Granville K., *Gold Dust and Trowels: Nuggets of Freemasonry in the Gold Rush Days of California* (San Francisco: Grand Lodge of California, 1977).

Fisk, Audrey, *The Ancient Order of Foresters in Cornwall* (n.p., n.d.).

Fisk, Audrey, *Mutual Self-help in Southern England 1850–1912* (Southampton: Foresters' Heritage Trust, 2006).

Fuller, Anthony C., 'Anglo-Catholic Clergy and the Golden Dawn: The Ritual Revival and the Modern Magical Order 1887–1940' (Ph.D. diss., University of Exeter, 2009).

Gan, Richard, 'Frederick Binckes: The Rise and Fall of an Outstanding Victorian Freemason' *Ars Quatuor Coronatorum* 128 (2015) pp. 155–96.

Gan, Richard, Susan Snell and David Peabody, 'Robert Wentworth Little: A Duplicitous Freemason, Wordsmith and Mystic' *Ars Quatuor Coronatorum* 130 (2017) pp. 107–44.

Gilbert, Robert A., *The Golden Dawn Companion* (Wellingborough: Aquarian Press, 1986).

Gilbert, Robert A., *The Golden Dawn Scrap Book:The Rise and Fall of a Magical Order* (York Beach, Maine: Weiser Books, 1997).

Gilbert, Robert A., 'Whither or Wither—A Personal View of the Future of English Freemasonry' *Ars Quatuor Coronatorum* 118 (2005) pp. 233–42.

Gillett, D.J., 'A Glimpse of Freemasonry in Nigeria' *Transactions of the Lodge of Research, Leicester* (1970–71) pp. 89–93.

Gist, Noel P., *Secret Societies: A Cultural Study of Fraternalism in the United States*. University of Missouri Studies: A Quarterly of Research XV, 4 (October 1940).

Goodchild, John, 'The Freemasons and the Friendly Societies: An Historical Study' *Transactions of the Manchester Association for Masonic Research* LXXXVI (1996) pp. 50–65.

Gorsky, Martin, *Patterns of Philanthropy: Charity and Society in Nineteenth Century Bristol* (Woodbridge: Boydell Press, 1999).

Gosden, P.H.J.H., *Friendly Societies in England 1815–1875* (Manchester: Manchester University Press, 1961).

Greever, William S., *Bonanza West: The Story of the Western Mining Rushes 1848–1900* (Moscow: University of Idaho Press, 1963).

Grimshaw, William H., *Official History of Freemasonry among the Coloured People in North America* (New York: Broadway, 1903).

Gunn, Simon, *The Public Culture of the Victorian Middle Class: Ritual and Authority in the English Industrial City 1840–1914* (Manchester: Manchester University Press, 2007).

Hall, R.J., *Lodge of Love and Honour No. 75, Falmouth: A History from 1751 to 2001* (Falmouth: privately printed, 2001).

Hamill, John, 'And the Greatest of these is Charity: The Development of Masonic Charity' *Ars Quatuor Coronatorum* 108 (1995) pp. 162–74.

Hamill, John and Andrew Prescott, '"The Masons' Candidate": New Welcome Lodge No. 5139 and the Parliamentary Labour Party' *Labour History Review* 71/1 (April 2006) pp. 9–41.

Hamilton Jenkin, A.K., *Cornwall and its People* (London: J.M. Dent, 1945).

Hamilton Jenkin, A.K., *The Cornish Miner* (London: Allen and Unwin, 1948).

Hannan, Norman, *Travels and Heartaches of a Mining Family* (privately printed, 1984).

Hanson, Thomas W., *The Lodge of Probity No. 61 1738–1938* (Halifax: privately printed, 1939).

Harland-Jacobs, Jessica L., *Builders of Empire: Freemasonry and British Imperialism* (Chapel Hill: University of North Carolina Press, 2007).

Harrison, David and John Belton, 'Society in Flux: The Emergence and Rise of Middle-class Civil Society in Nineteenth Century Industrial North West England' in Andreas Onnerfors and Robert Peter (eds) *Researching British Freemasonry 1717–2017* (Sheffield: Sheffield Lectures on the History of Freemasonry and Fraternalism, 3, 2010) pp. 71–98.

Harrison, David and Frederick Lomax, *Freemasonry and Fraternal Societies* (Addlestone: Lewis Masonic, 2015).

Harvey, George, *Henry Clay Frick: The Man* (privately printed, 1936).

Harwood, W.S., 'Secret Societies in America' *North American Review* 164 (May 1897) pp. 617–24.

Heald, Tim, *Networks: Who we Know and How we Use Them* (London: Hodder and Stoughton, 1983).

Hedges, Cornelius, 'Journal of Judge Cornelius Hedges, Member of the Washburn Expedition of 1870' *Contributions to the Historical Society of Montana* V pp. 370–94.

Heiron, Arthur, *Ancient Freemasonry and the Old Dundee Lodge, No. 18* (London: Kenning, 1921).

Hennock, E.P., *The Origins of the Welfare State in England and Germany, 1850–1914* (Cambridge: Cambridge University Press, 2007).

Heykamp, J.H., 'Freemasonry in South Africa and Rhodesia' *Philalethes* (February 1948).

Highet, Robert, *Rechabite History* (Manchester: The Board of Directors of the Independent Order of Rechabites, 1936).

Hittell, John S., *The Resources of California* (San Francisco: A. Roman, 1869).

Hodge, Arthur C., *The Odyssey of a Mason* UGLE Library *Masonic Pamphlets 1872–1932* 10/26 (no date) B10MAS.

Hobsbawm, Eric J., 'The Tramping Artisan' *Economic History Review* New Series 3/3 (1951) pp. 299–320.

Hobsbawm, Eric J., *Labouring Men: Studies in the History of Labour* (London: Weidenfeld and Nicolson, 1964).

Hobsbawm, Eric J., *Bandits* (London: Weidenfeld and Nicolson, 1969).

Hosgood, C.P., 'The Knights of the Road: Commercial Travellers and the Culture of the Commercial Room in late-Victorian and Edwardian England' *Victorian Studies* 37/4 (1994) pp. 519–47.

Howe, Ellic, 'Fringe Masonry in England 1870–85' *Ars Quatuor Coronatorum* 85 (1972) pp. 242–95.

Howe, Ellic, *The Magicians of the Golden Dawn: A Documentary History of a Magical Order 1887–1923* (London: Routledge and Kegan Paul, 1972).

Hughan, W.J., *By-Laws and Regulations of the Lodge of Love and Honour No. 75* (Falmouth: 1877).

Hughan, W.J., *Directory of the Provincial Grand Lodge of Cornwall* (1870–).

Hughan, W.J., *Autobiography* (Manuscript, Library and Museum of Freemasonry) (n.p., n.d.).

Hughan, W.J., 'A History of Freemasonry in Cornwall' *FMMM* in parts 29 September 1866 to 31 August 1867.

Isenberg, Andrew C., *Mining California: An Ecological History* (New York: Hill and Wang, 2005).

Jackson, A.C.F., 'Rosicrucianism and its effect on Craft Masonry' *Ars Quatuor Coronatorum* 97 (1984) pp. 115–50.

Jackson, K.B., *Beyond the Craft* (Hersham: Lewis Masonic, 1994).

Jackson, W. Turrentine, 'The Washburn–Doane Expedition into the Upper Yellowstone, 1870' *Pacific Historical Review* 10/2 (June 1941) pp. 189–208.

Jacobs, Margaret C., *The Origins of Freemasonry: Facts and Fictions* (Philadelphia: University of Pennsylvania Press, 2006).

Jacobs, Margaret, *The First Knowledge Economy: Human Capital and the European Economy 1750–1850* (Cambridge: Cambridge University Press, 2014).

James, Bob, *They Call Each Other Brother: Secret Societies and the Strange Slow Death of Mateship In Australia 1788–2010* (New South Wales: privately printed, 2010).

James, Bob, 'British Freemasonry—Fact or Fiction?' *Transactions of the Manchester Association for Masonic Research* 99 (2009) pp. 87–98.

James, Bob, 'Secret Societies and the Labour Movement: Part 2 The Knights of Labour' *Australian Society for the Study of Labour History* 6th Biennial Conference October 1999 <http://www.takver.com/history//secsoc02.htm> [accessed 3 October 2019].

James, Ronald M., *The Roar and the Silence: A History of Virginia City and the Comstock Lode* (Reno: University of Nevada Press, 1998).

James, Ronald M., 'Defining the Group: Nineteenth Century Cornish on the North American Mining Frontier' in Philip Payton (ed.) *Cornish Studies* 2nd ser. No. 2 (1994) pp. 32–47.

James, Ronald M., 'Home Away from Home: Cornish Immigrants in Nineteenth Century Nevada' in Philip Payton (ed.) *Cornish Studies* 2nd ser. No. 15 (2008) pp. 1–28.

Jameson, Elizabeth, *All that Glitters: Class, Conflict and Community in Cripple Creek* (Urbana: University of Illinois Press, 1998).

Jeppe, C.W. Biccard, *Gold Mining in South Africa* (London: Todd Publishing, 1948).

Jin, Kok Hu, *Chinese Lodges in Australia* (Bendigo: Golden Dragon Museum, 2005).

Jones, Dot, 'Did Friendly Societies Matter? A Study of Friendly Society Membership in Glamorgan, 1794–1910' *Welsh History Review* 12/3 (June 1985) pp. 324–49.

Jones, R., 'Sociability, Solidarity, and Social Exclusion: Women's Activism in the South Wales Coalfield, ca. 1830 to 1939' in Jaclyn J. Gier and Laurie Mercier (eds) *Mining Women: Gender in the Development of a Global Industry, 1670–2005* (New York: Palgrave, 2006) pp. 96–118.

Katz, Elaine, *The White Death: Silicosis on the Witwatersrand Gold Mines 1886–1910* (Witwatersrand: University of Witwatersrand Press, 1994).

Kauffman, Christopher J., *Faith and Fraternalism: The History of the Knights of Columbus 1882–1982* (New York: Harper and Row, 1982).

Kaufman, Jason, *For the Common Good? American Civil Life and the Golden Age of Fraternity* (Oxford: Oxford University Press, 2002).

Kelly's Directory of Cornwall (1883).

Kennedy, Brian, *A Tale of Two Mining Cities, Johannesburg and Broken Hill 1885–1925* (Melbourne: Donker, 1984).

Kenny, J. Scott, *Brought to Light: Contemporary Freemasonry, Meaning and Society* (Waterloo, Ontario: Wilfred Laurier University Press, 2016).

Khambatta, Roeinton B.F., *The Grand Secretaries of the United Grand Lodge of England 1813–1980* (London: Prestonian Lecture, privately printed, 2007).

Killick, John, 'Transatlantic steerage fares, British and Irish migration, and return migration' *Economic History Review* 67/1 (February 2014) pp. 214–30.

Klages, Gregory, 'Freemasons and Orange Order Membership in Rural Ontario during the Nineteenth Century' *Ontario History* C III/2 (Fall 2011) pp. 67–88.

Knight, Stephen, *The Brotherhood: The Secret World of the Freemasons* (London: Book Club, 1984).

Knoop, Douglas, *University Masonic Lodge* (Sheffield: Northend, 1945).

Knoop, Douglas and G.P. Jones, *The Medieval Mason: An Economic History of English Stone Building in the Later Middle Ages and Early Modern Times* (Manchester: Manchester University Press, 1933).

Kosack, Edward and Zachary Ward, 'Who Crossed the Border? Self Selection of Mexican Migrants in the early Twentieth Century' *Journal of Economic History* 74/4 (December 2014) pp. 1015–44.

Lane, John, *Masonic Records 1717–1894* (London: UGLE, 1895).

Langford, N.P., *The Discovery of Yellowstone Park: Journal of the Washburn Expedition to the Yellowstone and Firehole Rivers in the Year 1870* (1905; reprinted Lincoln: University of Nebraska Press, 1972).

Lapp, Rudolph M., *Blacks in Gold Rush California* (New Haven: Yale University Press, 1977).

Lay, Patricia, *One and All: The Cornish in New South Wales* (Queanbeyan, New South Wales: Heritage 2000 Plus, 1998).

Leeuwen, M.H.D. van, 'Guilds and middle-class welfare, 1500–1800: provisions for burial, sickness, old age, and widowhood' *Economic History Review* 65/1 (2012) pp. 61–90.

Limbaugh, Ronald H. and W.P. Fuller, *Calaveras Gold: The Impact of Mining on a Mother Lode County* (Reno: University of Nevada Press, 2004).

Lingenfelter, Richard E., *The Mining West: A Bibliography and Guide to the History and Literature of Mining in the American and Canadian West* 2 vols (Lanham, Md.: Scarecrow Press, 2003).

Lipson, Dorothy Ann, *Freemasonry in Federalist Connecticut 1789–1835* (Princeton: Princeton University Press, 1977).

Logan, Roger, 'The Role of Friendly Society Orders in British Society 1793–1911, with Special reference to the Ancient Order of Foresters Friendly Society' (Ph.D. diss., Kingston University, 2003).

López Villarejo, Francisco, *Masonería y Sociedad en Linares, 1882–1894* (Zaragoza: Centro de Estudios Históricos de la Masonería Española, 1989).

MacAlpine, J. Mark, 'Nineteenth Century Masonic Processions in Shanghai' *Ars Quatuor Coronatorum* 128 (2015) pp. 197–212.

Macbride, Harriet W., 'The Golden Age of Fraternity' *Heredom* 13 (2005) pp. 117–49.

MacCulla, Clifford, 'The Public Masonic Charities of the United States of America' *Masonic Magazine* (April 1875).

Malcomson, W.P., 'The Forgotten History of the Orange Order: The Institution's Historic Struggle Against the Royal Arch Purple and the Black Degree (1798–1925)' <https://www.academia.edu/38186136/

THE_FORGOTTEN_HISTORY_OF_THE_ORANGE_ORDER> [accessed 3 October 2019].

Mandleberg, C. John and L.W. Davies, *Royal Arch Masons and Knights Templar at Redruth, Cornwall, 1791–1828* (London: QCCC, 2005).

Mandleberg, C. John, 'Past Grand Rank' *Ars Quatuor Coronatorum* 126 (2013) pp. 71–94.

Mann, Ralph, *After the Gold Rush: Society in Grass Valley and Nevada City, California 1849–1870* (Stanford: Stanford University Press, 1982).

McEwan E., 'The Newcastle Coalmining District of New South Wales, 1860–1900' (Ph.D. diss., University of Sydney, 1979).

McGrath, R.D., *Gunfighters, Highwaymen and Vigilantes: Violence on the Frontier* (Berkeley: University of California Press, 1984).

McNeill, W.H., *Keeping Together in Time: Dance and Drill in Human History* (Cambridge, Mass.: Harvard University Press, 1995).

McPhee, William M., *The Trail of the Leprechaun: Early History of a Utah Mining Camp* (New York: Exposition Press, 1977).

Meier, G., *Gold Camp Foolery: E Clampus Vitus.*

Mercier, Laurie, *Anaconda: Labor, Community, and Culture in Montana's Smelter City* (Urbana: University of Illinois Press, 2001).

Mills, D.R. and J. Mills, 'Occupation and Social Stratification Revisited: The Census Enumerators' Books of Victorian Britain' *Urban History Yearbook 1989* (May 1989) pp. 63–77.

Mills, J., *Tregullow Lodge No. 1006 1864–1990* (St Day: privately printed, 1990).

Moodie, T. Dunbar, *Going for Gold: Men, Mines, and Migration* (Los Angeles: University of California Press, 1994).

Moore, Charles, *New Masonic Trestle Board* (Boston: various editions from the 1840s).

Morrell, W.P., *The Gold Rushes* (London: A. & C. Black, 1940).

Morris, S. Brent, *The Complete Idiot's Guide to Freemasonry* (New York: Alpha, 2006).

Morris, S. Brent, 'Itinerant American Masonic Lecturers' *Ars Quatuor Coronatorum* 121 (2008) pp. 1–19.

Murphy, Mary, *Mining Cultures: Men, Women and Leisure in Butte, 1914–41* (Urbana: University of Illinois Press, 1997).

Musa, Fraser B., 'The First Indian Freemason' *Ars Quatuor Coronatorum* 91 (1968) pp. 318–20.

Musson, A.E., *The Typographical Association, Origins and History up to 1949* (Oxford: Oxford University Press, 1972).

Naismith, J.G., *Chinese Freemasonry* (privately printed, 1946).

Nash, George H., *The Life of Herbert Hoover: The Engineer 1874–1914* (New York: Norton, 1981).

Newman, Aubrey N., 'The Contribution of the Provinces to the Development of English Freemasonry' *Transactions of the Lodge of Research No. 2429, Leicester* (2002) pp. 14–30.

Oronhyatekha, *History of the Independent Order of Foresters* (Toronto: Hunter, Rose and Co., 1894).

Osborn, Joseph G., *History of Freemasonry in West Cornwall, from 1765 to 1828* (Penzance: F. Rodda, 1901).

Owen, Alex, *The Place of Enchantment: British Occultism and the Culture of the Modern* (Chicago: University of Chicago Press, 2004).

Paul, Rodman W., *Mining Frontiers of the Far West 1848–1880* (Albuquerque: University of New Mexico, 2001).

Payton, Philip, *The Cornish Miner in Australia* (Redruth: Truran, 1984).

Payton, Philip, *The Cornish Overseas* (Fowey: Alexander Associates, 1999).

Peck, Gunther, 'Manly Gambles: The Politics of Risk on the Comstock Lode, 1860–1880' *Journal of Social History* 26/4 (Summer 1993) pp. 701–23.

Penman, A.T., 'Freemasonry in South Africa' *Ars Quatuor Coronatorum* 80 (1967) pp. 280–86.

Perkin, Harold, *The Rise of Professional Society in England Since 1880* (London: Routledge, 2002).

Piatigorsky, Alexander, *Who's Afraid of Freemasons?* (London: Harvill Press, 1997).

Plazak, Dan, *A Hole in the Ground with a Liar at the Top: Fraud and Deceit in the Golden Age of American Mining* (Salt Lake City: University of Utah Press, 2006).

Pooley, C.G. and S. D'Cruze, 'Migration and urbanisation in North West England circa 1760–1830' *Social History* 19/3 (1994) pp. 339–58.

Potter, Warren and Robert Oliver, *Fraternally Yours: A History of the Independent Order of Foresters* (London: Queen Anne Press, 1967).

Pownall, James William, *List of Names of Masonic Impostors and other undeserving persons, who make a practice of habitually seeking assistance from the Almoners' Funds in different parts of the country* (Ashton-under-Lyne: 1902).

Prescott, Andrew, 'Freemasonry in Suburban London 1860–1930: A Case Study' *Transactions of the Manchester Association for Masonic Research* XCII (2002) pp. 41–82.

Prescott, Andrew, 'The Causes of Humanity: Charles Bradlaugh and Freemasonry' *Ars Quatuor Coronatorum* 116 (2003) pp. 60–63.

Prescott, Andrew, 'Freemasonry in the Victorian City' *Transactions of the Manchester Association for Masonic Research* XCIX (2009) pp. 101–09.

Prescott, Andrew, 'Relations between the Grand Lodges of England and Sweden during the Long Eighteenth Century' *Journal for Research into Freemasonry and Fraternity* 3/2 (2012) pp. 185–222.

Prescott, Andrew, 'The Cross-Currents of the Union' *Transactions of the Lodge of Research No. 2429, Leicester* (2013–14) pp. 158–68.

Prescott, Andrew and Susan M. Sommers, 'Searching for the Apple Tree: Revisiting the Earliest Years of English Organised Freemasonry' *Heredom* 25 (2017) pp. 109–36.

Preston, William, *Illustrations of Freemasonry* (ed. G. Oliver) (London: 1867 edn).

Price, Brian. W., 'Malta, GC: A Military and Masonic Crossroads' *Ars Quatuor Coronatorum* 130 (2017) pp. 13–42.

Price, Lawrence L., *'West Barbary': Or Notes on the System of Work and Wages in the Cornish Mines* (1891) reprinted in Roger Burt (ed.) *Cornish Mining: Essays on the Organisation of Cornish Mines and the Cornish Mining Economy* (Newton Abbot: David and Charles, 1969) pp. 111–206.

Price, Richard, *British Society 1680–1880: Dynamism, Containment and Change* (Cambridge: Cambridge University Press, 1999).

Putnam, Robert D., *Bowling Alone: The Collapse and Revival of American Community* (New York: Simon & Schuster, 2000).

Rachleff, P., *Black Labor in Richmond, 1865–1890* (Urbana: University of Illinois Press, 1989).

Ramsay, Alicia, 'The Roots/Routes of the Ancient Order of Foresters in the Anglophone Caribbean' *History in Action* 2/1 (2011) pp. 1–13.

Randall, Robert W., *Real del Monte: A British Mining Venture in Mexico* (Austin: University of Texas Press, 1972).

Ranston, Jackie, *Masonic Jamaica and the Cayman Islands* 2 vols (Addlestone: Lewis Masonic, 2017).

Reeves, Aaron, Sam Friedman and Charles Rahal, 'The Decline and the Persistence of the Old Boy: Private Schools and Elite Recruitment 1897 to 2016' *American Sociological Review* 82/6 (2017) pp. 1139–66.

Reilly, Gerald, 'Freemasonry and the Urbanisation of Harwich' *Ars Quatuor Coronatorum* 130 (2017) pp. 43–76.

Révauger, Cécile and Éric Saunier (eds), *La Franc-maçonnerie dans les ports* (Bordeaux: Presses Universitaires de Bordeaux, 2012).

Rice, George G., *My Adventures with Your Money* (Las Vegas: Nevada Publications, 1986).

Rich, Paul J., *Elixir of Empire: English Public Schools, Ritualism, Freemasonry and Imperialism* (London: Regency Press, 1989).

Rich, Paul J., *Chains of Empire: English Public Schools, Masonic Cabalism, Historical Causality, and Imperial Clubdom* (London: Regency Press, 1991).

Richardson, Peter, *Chinese Mine Labour in the Transvaal* (London: Macmillan, 1982).

Rohrbough, Malcolm J., *Days of Gold: The California Gold Rush and the American Nation* (Berkeley: University of California Press, 1997).

Rosenthal, E., *Gold! Gold! Gold! The Johannesburg Gold Rush* (London: Macmillan, 1970).

Rosenzweig, Roy, 'Boston Masons, 1900–1935: The Lower Middle Class in a Divided Society' *Journal of Voluntary Action Research* 6 (1977) pp. 119–26.

Ross, Theo. A., *Odd Fellowship: Its History and Manual* (New York: M.W. Haven, 1888).

Rowe, John, *The Hard Rock Men: Cornish Immigration and the North American Mining Frontier* (Liverpool: Liverpool University Press, 1974).

Rowe, John, *Cornwall in the Age of the Industrial Revolution* 2nd edn (St Austell: Cornish Hillside, 1993).

Rutterford, Janette, Dimitris Sotiropoulos and Carry van Lieshout, 'Individual investors and local bias in the UK, 1870–1935' *Economic History Review* 70/4 (November 2017) pp. 1291–320.

Sarmiento, Louie B., *The Odd Fellows* (n.l.: n.p., 2019).

Schwartz, Sharron, *The Cornish in Latin America: 'Cousin Jack' and the New World* (privately published, 2016).

Senkewicz, Robert M., *Vigilantes in Gold Rush San Francisco* (Stanford: Stanford University Press, 1985).

Shackleton, Ernest, *South!: The Story of Shackleton's 1914–1917 Expedition* (London: Heinemann, 1922).

Shepherd, F. W., *An Account of the History of Royal Arch Masonry in Cornwall from the Earliest Times to 1977* (Truro: Provincial Grand Chapter of Cornwall, 1977).

Sheppard, Osborne, *Freemasonry in Canada* ed. Paul Rich (Washington: Westphalia Press, 2013 edn).

Short, Martin, *Inside the Brotherhood* (London: Grafton, 1989).

Smiles, Samuel, *Self-Help* (1859); *Character* (1871); *Thrift* (1875); *Duty* (1880).

Smyth, William J., *Toronto, The Belfast of Canada* (Toronto: University of Toronto Press, 2015).

Snell, K.D.M., 'Belonging and Community: understandings of "home" and "friends" among the English poor, 1750–1850' *Economic History Review* 65/1 (2012) pp. 1–25.

Sommers, Susan, '"Hidden in Plain Sight". The Order of the Eastern Star in the Historiography of American Women's Associations' *Journal for Research into Freemasonry and Fraternalism* 4/1–2 (2013) pp. 160–79.

Speth, George W., 'Freemasonry in Wartime' Chronicle Report on South Africa *Ars Quatuor Coronatorum* 13 (1900) pp. 189–91.

Statham, Michael, 'Miners—A Mobile Workforce' *Welsh Mines Society Newsletter* 79 (Autumn 2018) pp. 12–24.

Stevens, Albert C. (ed.), *Cyclopedia of Fraternities* (New York: E.B. Treat, 1907).

Stevenson, David, *The Origins of Freemasonry* (Cambridge: Cambridge University Press, 1990).

Stewart, Trevor, 'Aspects of Freemasonry in the Western Hermetic Tradition' in *The Stewart Papers: New Perspectives* (Hamburg: privately printed, 2017).

Stobie, Geoffrey, *Boscawen Lodge No. 699: A History 1857 to 1994* (privately published, 1995).

Symons, R., *A Geographical Dictionary or Gazetteer of the County of Cornwall* (Penzance: n.p., 1884).

Tabbert, Mark A., *American Freemasons: Three Centuries of Building Communities* (Lexington, Mass.: New York University Press, 2005).

Thompson, F.M.L., *The Rise of Respectable Society: A Social History of Victorian Britain 1830–1900* (Cambridge, Mass.: Harvard University Press, 1990).

Timbs, John, *Clubs and Club Life in London from the Seventeenth Century Until the Present Day* (London: Chatto & Windus, 1872).

Timson, D., 'Freemasonry in Malta' *Transactions of the Lodge of Research No. 2429, Leicester* (1967–68) pp. 81–90.

Todd, A.C., *The Search for Silver: Cornish Miners in Mexico 1824–1947* (Padstow: Lodenek Press, 1977).

Turpie, Graeme, 'Freemasons in the Community' in David Beagley (ed.) *Gold and Blue: Freemasonry and Community in Bendigo 1854–2004* (Bendigo, Victoria: Holland House, 2004) pp. 53–59.

Venzi, Fabio, *Freemasonry: The Esoteric Tradition* (Addlestone: Lewis Masonic, 2016).

Vincent, E.S., *A Record of Freemasonry in the Province of Cornwall* (Truro: privately printed, 1959).

Wade, John S., '"Go and do thou likewise": English Masonic Processions from the 18th to the 20th centuries' *Ars Quatuor Coronatorum* 22 (2009) pp. 75–120.

Wade, John S. (ed.), *A History of Craft Freemasonry in Sheffield 1761–2017* (Sheffield: Sheffield Masonic Press, 2017).

Ward, J.S.M. and W.G. Stirling, *The Hung Society: or the Society of Heaven and Earth* vol. 1 (London: Baskerville Press, 1925).

Washizu, Yoshio, 'Anti-Masonry in Japan—Past and Present' *Ars Quatuor Coronatorum* 107 (1994) pp. 85–116.

Washizu, Yoshio, 'English Freemasonry—A Product of Club Movement?' *Ars Quatuor Coronatorum* 130 (2017) pp. 163–90.

Webb, James, *The Flight from Reason: The Age of the Irrational* (London: Macdonald, 1971).

Webster, N.H., *Secret Societies and Subversive Movements* (London: Britons, 1955).

Weinbren, Daniel, *The Oddfellows 1810–2010* (Lancaster: Carnegie, 2010).

Weinbren, D., 'Beneath the All-Seeing Eye: Fraternal Order and Friendly Society Banners in Nineteenth and Twentieth Century Britain' *Cultural and Social History* 3/2 (April 2006) pp. 167–91.

Weinbren, Daniel, 'Freemasonry and Friendly Societies' in Henrick Bogdan and Jan Snoek (eds) *Handbook of Freemasonry* (Leiden: Brill, 2014) pp. 387–406.

Wheatcroft, Geoffrey, *The Randlords* (London: Weidenfeld, 1993).

Wickham, Dorothy, *Freemasonry on the Goldfields. Ballarat and District 1853–2013* (Ballarat: Ballarat Heritage Services, 2013).

Williams, Douglas (ed.), *Thread of Gold 1752–2002* (Truro: Provincial Grand Lodge of Cornwall, 2001).

Wilson, J., 'Voluntary Associations and Civil religion: The Case of Freemasonry' *Review of Religious Research* 22/2 (December 1980) pp. 125–36.

Worts, F.R., *The History of the Lodge of Peace No. 149* (n.p., n.d.).

Wright, Dudley, *Roman Catholicism and Freemasonry* (London: William Rider, 1922).

Wright, Louis B., *Culture on the Moving Frontier* (Bloomington, Ind.: Indiana University Press, 1955).

Yoshida, Kayoko and Reiko Miyauchi, 'Invisible Labor: A Comparative Oral History of Women in Coal Mining Communities of Hokkaido, Japan and Montana, USA, 1890–1940' in Jaclyn J. Gier and Laurie Mercier (eds) *Mining Women: Gender in the Development of a Global Industry, 1670 to 2005* (New York: Palgrave, 2006) pp. 136–52.

Zanjani, Sally, *A Mine of Her Own: Women Prospectors in the American West 1850–1950* (Lincoln: University of Nebraska Press, 1997).

Zhu, Liping, *A Chinaman's Chance: The Chinese on the Rocky Mountain Mining Frontier* (Niwot, Colo.: University Press of Colorado, 1997).

Primary Material and Archives

Annual returns of Lodge members made by Lodge Secretaries to Grand Lodge. Now held in the Library and Museum of the UGLE, Queen Street, London.

Annual Report, Regulations, and List of the Governors and Subscribers of the Royal Masonic Benevolent Institution for Aged Freemasons and Widows of Freemasons 1900.

Biographical Record of Houghton, Baraga and Marquette Counties, Michigan (Chicago, 1903).

Boscawen Lodge Minutes Books, 11 Volumes, 1857–1990, Cornwall Record Office, Truro, AD 1576.

By-Laws of Tregullow Lodge, St Day, Cornwall (Redruth, 1879).

By-Laws of Cornubian Lodge 450, Hayle (Truro, 1869).

By-Laws of Druids Lodge of Love and Liberality 589, Redruth (Redruth, 1852).

Calendar for Masonic Meetings in East Lancashire 1899–1900.

Census of Great Britain, 1851. Religious Worship in England and Wales.

Complete Manual of Oddfellowship: Being a Practical Guide to its History, Principles, Ceremonies and Symbolism (privately printed, 1879).

Cornubian and Redruth Times.

Devon Masonic Directory for 1899.

Directory and List of the Lodges composing the Independent Order of Oddfellows (Manchester Unity) Friendly Society 1899–1900.

Emulation Ritual (London: Lewis Masonic, 1991).

Exeter Pocket Journal 1857.

Fifty Years of Odd Fellowship in California (California: Independent Order of Oddfellows, 1899).

Foresters' Miscellany and Quarterly Review, October 1862.

Freemasons Calendar and Directory for the Province of Somerset 1899–1900.

Freemasons Calendar for the Province of Warwickshire 1900–1.

Freemasons Calendar and Directory for the Provinces of Leicestershire and Rutland 1899.

Freemasons Calendar and Directory for the Province of Durham 1899.

Freemasons Calendar and Directory for the Province of Essex 1900.

Guild Gazette: A Journal of the Merchant Service Guild (Liverpool).

General Laws of the Ancient Order of Foresters Friendly Society (1875).

Grand Lodge of the Independent Order of Odd Fellows, State of Nevada, *Manual of Instructions* (undated).

Independent Order of Rechabites. Directory and General Reference Book for 1887–8 (Manchester, 1887).

Lectures Used by the Manchester Unity of the Independent Order of Oddfellows (June 1846).

Masonic Calendar and Directory for the Province of Middlesex 1901.

Masonic Calendar and Directory for Northamptonshire and Huntingdonshire 1899–1900.

Masonic Calendar for the Province of Northumberland 1893.

Masonic Calendar and Directory for the Province of Surrey 1900.

Masonic Calendar for the Province of Hampshire and the Isle of Wight 1901–2.

Masonic Imposter Broadside, D.K. Osbourne & Co., Baltimore, MD, 1877. Scottish Rite Masonic Museum and Library, Van Gorden-Williams Library and Archives, Lexington, Mass., A2002/118/1.

Masonic Year Book: Historical Supplement (UGLE 1964).

Michigan Technological University Archives and Copper Country Historical Collection, Houghton, Michigan.

Minutes of the Board of the Lodge of Benevolence. Held in the Library and Museum of UGLE.

Monthly Magazine of the Independent Order of Oddfellows, Manchester Unity Friendly Society XVII (New Series Nos. 25–36, January to December 1886) ed. James Curtis.

Neison, Francis G.P., *Ancient Order of Foresters, Report upon The Additional Statistics Deduced from the Original Records of the Sickness Experience (1871–1875) of the Order: New Tables of Contributions and Benefit* (Leeds, 1886).

New Age Magazine.

Proceedings of the Grand Lodge of Arizona.

Proceedings of the Grand Lodge of California.

Proceedings of the Grand Lodge of Montana.

Proceedings of the Grand Lodge of Nevada.

Proceedings of the Grand Lodge of New York.

Proceedings of the Grand Lodge of I.O.O.F. of Montana.

Proceedings of the Provincial Grand Lodge of Cornwall.

Proceedings of the United Grand Lodge of England, Minutes of the Board of General Purposes, 1 June 1859.

Provincial Grand Lodge of Cornwall. Minutes of meetings.

Records of Golden Star Lodge No. 9, Deadwood Golden Star Lodge, Homestake Adams Research and Cultural Center, Deadwood, South Dakota.

Records of Oustomah Lodge, Independent Order of Oddfellows. Held in the Doris Foley Library, Nevada City, California.

Return of Rates of Wages in the Mines and Quarries *Parliamentary Papers* 1890–91 [c6455].

Roll of the Members of Escurial Lodge No. 7 F &AM,Virginia City, Storey County, Nevada: also a Short History of the Lodge to December 1st 1867 available in the Bancroft Library.

Royal Clarence Lodge, Subscription and Account Book 1813–1850, East Sussex Record Office M.S. MAS 9/3/1.

Rules of Court 'Tower' No. 5349 Branch of the St Austell United District of the Ancient Order of Foresters Friendly Society. Held at Newquay, Cornwall 1907.

Rules for the Independent Order of Oddfellows Manchester Unity Friendly Society 1887 (Manchester, 1887).

Statistics of Fraternal Societies 1904.

West Lancashire Masonic Calendar 1899–1900.

SUBJECT INDEX

PLACE INDEX

LODGE INDEX

Lightning Source UK Ltd.
Milton Keynes UK
UKHW012259070223
416610UK00001B/264

9 781905 816248